# THE ORIGINS OF ZIONISM

# THE ORIGINS OF
# ZIONISM

DAVID VITAL

OXFORD
AT THE CLARENDON PRESS

Oxford University Press, Walton Street, Oxford OX2 6DP

OXFORD LONDON GLASGOW
NEW YORK TORONTO MELBOURNE WELLINGTON
KUALA LUMPUR SINGAPORE HONG KONG TOKYO
DELHI BOMBAY CALCUTTA MADRAS KARACHI
NAIROBI DAR ES SALAAM CAPE TOWN

© *Oxford University Press, 1975*

*First published as paperback 1980*

**British Library Cataloguing in Publication Data**
Vital, David
    The origin of Zionism.
    1. Zionism - History
    I. Title
    956.94'001          DS149          79-41325
    ISBN 0-19-827439-4

*Printed in Great Britain
at the University Press, Oxford
by Eric Buckley
Printer to the University*

*For Alisa*

# *Preface*

---

THE history of the Jewish people is long and complex and does not lend itself easily to discussion in the terms in which the histories of other nations, however ancient, are, by convention, conceived. With the onset of the great Exilic period close to two millennia ago Jewish political history—if the term is applicable at all—becomes shadowy and, for long periods, dormant. Diplomatic history in the formal sense and military history are entirely absent from about the middle of the second century until the end of the nineteenth —although, of course, Jewish diplomats and Jewish soldiers serving non-Jewish interests are common enough. At first glance the social and economic history of the Jews is easier to deal with, yet it too is of a peculiar kind. For there immediately arise such questions as how useful it can be to look at the various Jewish communities (even for analytical purposes) in isolation from the larger societies in which they had come to be embedded; and whether, on balance, it is the characteristics common to all or most communities, as opposed to those specific to each one, that deserve the greater emphasis. In these circumstances, some think it not unreasonable to conceive of the history of the Jews in their Exile as, primarily, a history of culture, or of a set of kindred cultures, or of one of ideas, but not, in the accepted sense, of a nation, even a nation of highly distinctive, if not unique, characteristics.

For the recent and contemporary history of the Jews these problems and ambiguities have dwindled, although, certainly, they have not vanished. For it is not the least of the intended (and successful) consequences of the Zionist revolution that it re-created a Jewish polity and led to a substantial fraction of the Jewish people assuming an aspect and social and institutional structures which are akin to those of other nations.

It is with the origins of this great change—the 'normalization' of the Jews, as the Zionists have often termed it—that this book is concerned. Of course, the whole vast scene of Jewish life at the end of the nineteenth century was one of tumult and change and the rise of Zionism was only a particular aspect of it. Accordingly, without some regard for the total scene's complexity, variety, and many paradoxes the roots of Zionism are difficult to lay bare and the inner significance of the movement in the recent history of the Jews remains obscure. This consideration will explain and, I hope, justify the structure of the book itself in which a comparatively extended introductory section is followed by an account of the Zionist movement itself in which the focus on the central themes is made to sharpen steadily. It will also explain why much that is of interest and importance within the context of the general scene (the state of religious orthodoxy and the condition of the great Jewish communities in the Islamic lands, for example) has been referred to very briefly or left out of the account entirely—for, clearly, this is not a general history of the Jews, but, at best, a contribution to it.

This still leaves the question which it is proper to ask and necessary to answer: who were the Jews in this intermediate period—in the sense of what was the nature of the Jewish people and of what might be termed Jewish peoplehood. For, evidently, without a view on or of the matter, however rough it may be, it is impossible to come to grips with the subject at all.

My own response to this question is that I have thought it profitless (and hopeless) to try to define my view on the nature of Jewry and Judaism in rigorous terms—except to say this, that it is a pragmatic one and that it has seemed to me that so far as concerns a time when the vast majority of Jews did see themselves as members of a single, if scattered people, bound by common descent, a common faith and ritual, common languages, and, to a very significant extent, a common history, they may properly be judged to have been one. This view is implicit throughout the present study: I have tried to construct my account of the origins of modern Jewish nationalism on the basis of the contemporary evidence and what has been decisive for the terms in which the account as a whole has been cast is how the men and women involved in these events saw themselves, rather than how we, in retrospect or *a priori*, may choose to see them.

It is in the nature of a project of this kind on so complex and ramified a subject that many debts are incurred. I am happy to have an opportunity to acknowledge them.

My greatest debt, personal no less than scholarly, and the one which I have least hope of discharging, is to Sir Isaiah Berlin. I can only record that he gave me help and warm encouragement in every way and at every stage and that I am profoundly grateful to him.

I must thank Dr. Michael Heymann, Director of the Central Zionist Archives in Jerusalem, and his staff for their great courtesy and assistance over a long period of time; and also the staffs of the YIVO Institute in New York, the Jewish Division of the New York Public Library, the National and University Library in Jerusalem, the Public Record Office in London, and the Reading Room of the British Museum for friendly assistance and for permission to quote from documents in their possession.

The late Dr. Binyamin Eliav, Professor Shemu'el Ettinger, and Mr. R. A. May were kind enough to read large parts of this book in draft and save me from many errors.

I had the benefit of the valuable and unflagging assistance of Miss Eva-Noemi Simon for some two years, as of the help, for varying periods, of Miss Shifra Don-Yihye, Mrs. Ayala Levav, Mrs. Herzlia Levin, Mrs. Ruth Rotem, and Mr. Avraham Rosenbaum. It is a particular pleasure to express gratitude to Mrs. Malka Rome for typing and retyping the entire work more times than either of us can remember.

Responsibility for the book, faults and all, is of course mine.

*September 1974.*

# *Contents*

# List of Illustrations

## PLATES

Plates appear between pages 208-9

*Illustrations 1–3 and 6–8 by courtesy of the Central Zionist Archives, Jerusalem*

## MAPS

# A note on transliteration and translation

IT is extremely difficult to render Hebrew in Latin characters with accuracy, but without pedantry. But I have thought it sufficient to give such rough phonetic equivalents as will be plain to the English reader and only in a few cases to indicate those sounds for which no readily understood equivalent is available. Thus I have not distinguished between the two *t*s in Hebrew, *tav* and *tet*; and I have rendered the *pe degusha* as *p* and the *pe refuya* as *f*. But the guttural *'ayin* has been indicated (by ʿ); the two gutturals *ḥet* and *khaf* (both roughly equivalent to *ch* in 'loch') have been written as *ḥ* and *kh* respectively; and the *ẓadi* (equivalent to the *ts* in 'cots') has been written as a single letter *ẓ*.

I have not always thought it necessary to be consistent where the English of a term is very familiar and written in a manner tolerably close to what accurate transliteration would require. So, for example, Israel rather than Yisrael; *Ẓion* rather than *Ẓiyyon*. Where the English is specifically called for, however, I have written Zion, Zionist, Zionism, for example (but *Ẓioni*, *Ẓionut*, if it is the Hebrew that is intended).

In the case of place-names, I have used the familiar English ones where appropriate (not Yerushalayim and Moskva, but Jerusalem and Moscow) and where local usage has changed over the years I have generally preferred the practice of the time, namely the late nineteenth century (St. Petersburg not Leningrad, Kattowitz not Katowice, Lemberg not Lvov).

Names of persons are more difficult. The common Jewish surname Rabinovitch can be spelt in at least two dozen different ways. I have used the spelling preferred and used by the person in question where known to me. Otherwise, I have followed the new *Encyclopaedia Judaica*.

Dates have generally been given according to Western (Gregorian calendar) usage. Julian calendar dates have been indicated by the addition of (O[ld]. S[tyle].). The full Jewish year, which runs from September/October to September/October, has in most cases, and where absolute precision is not important, been given as the Gregorian year parallel to the last nine months of the Jewish year. Thus 5735 would be given as 1975, although, strictly, it runs from 17 September 1974 to 5 September 1975.

Responsibility for the translation of source material in the various languages into English is mine. Where translations into English already exist (as in the case of Herzl's diary, for example) they have been checked against the original and amended where necessary.

There remained the question of the name of the Holy Land itself. 'Palestine' was a Roman invention which fell into local disuse until the arrival of the British. To most Jews it meant nothing. They knew the country as the Land of Israel, *Erez-Israel*. This is a book about Jews and this is the term I have used.

# PART ONE

---

## *The Context*

# 1

## *Exile, Return, and Redemption*

Five things befell our fathers . . . on the ninth of Av
. . . On the ninth of Av it was decreed [to Moses]
against our fathers that they should not enter the
Land, and the Temple was destroyed the first and
the second time, and Beitar was captured, and the City
[of Jerusalem] was ploughed up. When Av comes in,
gladness must be diminished.

The Mishna, Taʿanit, iv. 6

i

THE distinguishing characteristic of the Jews has been their Exile.
From one, obvious angle of vision they could see their Exile as the
part-forcible, part-voluntary removal of the Jews from Ereẓ-
Israel—the Land of Israel—and the loss of all political rights over
their country in the wake of the failure of the last, bloody revolt
against Rome. Thus conceived, its ending, the Return, would
entail no more than an essentially uncomplicated restoration of the
political and demographic *status quo ante*. But the destruction of
the Jewish polity and the resulting Exile were also seen—and, as
the centuries went by, increasingly seen—in symbolic and theological terms as well, as manifestations and consequences of the
will and wrath of God. And thus conceived, the restoration of the
Jews to Ereẓ-Israel implied, above all else, Redemption.

This latter view never entirely supplanted the simple historical
vision, but it very greatly complicated the attitude of rabbis and
laymen alike both to the Land itself and to the notion of the Return
to it. The idea of the Return and the idea of Redemption came to
be dissolved into each other. The restoration of the Jews to their
ancestral Land, when it occurred, would be a matter of extraordinary and universal significance auguring or even instituting
a millennial situation in which something like the harmony between

man and his Creator that had obtained before the Fall would be
restored. Naturally enough, the more one was attracted to this, the
transcendent conception of the Jews' relation to their Land, the
less one was disposed to interest oneself genuinely in the mundane
questions raised by thought of an actual, physical transfer of population to it—even in some remote but still seriously foreseeable future.
For to the immense difficulties such an enterprise would have
incurred centuries before the invention of the modern techniques
of transportation and social organization and control there was
added its impossibility in philosophical and theological terms by
those who believed the affairs of the world to be governed, in the
last resort, by divine will.

God had granted every nation its proper place, said the celebrated
Maharal of Prague (Rabbi Yehuda Liwa—or Loew—ben Bezalel,
1512–1609). To the Jews he gave the Land of Israel. Equally, he
had ordained, as a matter of the natural order of things, that no
nation should be subservient to any other and that each nation
should cohere, rather than be scattered. The condition of the Jews
in Exile was therefore clearly unnatural and anomalous and the Jews
had every right to anticipate a messianic Redemption, which is to
say, an ending of their Exile. Yet that did not entitle them to press,
even to pray excessively, for their Return, let alone set themselves
to bring it about. Their exceptional condition was no less a consequence of divine intention than the natural order. They must therefore be patient. They must not venture to hasten the end.

This austere and clear-cut position was not one which a man of
any degree of piety or learning would have explicitly denied until
quite recent times. Yet in practice the attitude of most Jews to the
Land and to the Exile from it and to the Return to it tended to be
somewhat equivocal. The real Erez-Israel did concern them. The
real Return, while perhaps almost unbearably distant, was never
entirely relegated to that impossibly distant, chiliastic point in time
when the divinely ordained Redemption–Return might be expected
to occur. And, indeed, Jewish tradition, belief, and observance all
allow, if not entail, a high degree of ambivalence on just this issue.
In the first place, the rhythm of exile and return is one that persists
throughout the traditional history of the Hebrews and the Jews. It
may be said to begin with the Patriarchal wanderings in search of
the Promised Land, continuing through the Exodus from Egypt,
the reconquest of the Land of Israel, the typically delayed establish-

Exile, Return, and Redemption

ment of the capital in Jerusalem until three centuries after Joshua's crossing of the Jordan had passed, the Babylonian captivity (an Exile that was not entirely ended until 1950), and the Return under Ezra and Nehemiah. There followed the constant struggle with hostile great powers, the brief re-establishment of political autonomy by the Maccabees, the Roman conquest, the new Diaspora, the revolts against Rome, and the last and greatest of the Dispersions. The seemingly acceptable, 'non-Exilic' exiles—such as that of Moorish and even Christian Spain where for long periods the Jews were a virtually integral part of civil society—all ended too in calamity and fresh dispersion. In brief, the Jews were habituated to looking back at a repeating pattern of promise, fulfilment, transgression, punishment, and pardon, a cyclical granting and withdrawal of the gifts of territory and sovereignty, and of concomitant lament and thanksgiving.

Secondly, the very high degree of ritualization and formalization of religious observance which had been instituted bit by bit in Exilic times served, through the forms and content adopted, to preserve, almost to absurdity, the sense of a vital tie to an actual living land: the prayers for rain delivered regularly even in the wettest parts of Europe; the annual harvest festival (*Shavuʿot*); the close study of the body of land law and of the law governing the practice of agriculture which are integral parts of the Talmud; and, more generally, the repetition, in a great variety of verbal forms in every service of prayer, of the fundamental belief that the people of Israel had been granted a land and that the present (Exilic) condition was temporary and would come to its appointed end.

Thirdly, this very tendency to hold the present to be, in this special sense, a temporary and unfortunate (although not untypical) phase of Jewish history kept in being, and perhaps even strengthened, the continuing belief in the exceptional nature of the bond uniting the people of Israel to its Land and a highly charged vision of the qualities and attributes that might be ascribed to it: a country of quasi-magical qualities where all is intensified, where, above all, one is in a relationship with the Eternal such as can be achieved nowhere else; the country in which one—or one's descendants—would finally attain security and dignity, possibly glory; finally, a country where, alone, it is possible for a Jew to be fully and unambiguously what he is; in sum a country never to be forgotten and always to be cherished for its promise not only of something very close to supranatural Redemption, but redemption too from the all-too-concrete slavery and pain of the Exile actually experienced.

It is to this religious and mystical conception of linked Return and Redemption that are due the facts that at no time from the onset of the great Dispersion was Erez-Israel entirely without a Jewish population and that the Jewish community within it, the *yishuv*, was periodically replenished by the drawing power of the Holy Land. It was beyond question for a religious Jew that the more profoundly and whole-heartedly one strove to serve God the more powerfully was one moved to do so in the Holy Land itself. 'We must surely know', wrote an anonymous pupil of Naḥmanides who travelled to Erez-Israel at the beginning of the fourteenth century, 'that of all the seventy lands which God had created, it was the Land of Israel that he chose . . . Nor did he set a guardian angel over it, as he did for the other lands, but the Holy One Blessed be He himself rules over it.'[1] And therefore, in the phrasing of his near contemporary, Rabbi Asher, a Spanish Jew who had vowed to emigrate to the Holy Land, 'There is the place for fulfilling the commandments and receiving upon oneself the Kingdom of Heaven. Our worship there is acceptable, for there is the House of our God and the Gate of Heaven.'[2] From here the path to the powerful idea of the Return as a mystical experience before all else was a short one. Mystics and millenarians—the cabbalists of Safed, the followers of Shabbetai Ẓevi, and later the adepts of ḥasidism—formed a major part of the *yishuv* in the sixteenth, seventeenth, and eighteenth centuries or exerted an important influence within it.

Still, in the last resort, the concern of the mystic was not with the resettlement of the country but with his own relationship with the Divine. Rabbi Naḥman of Bratzlav (1772–1810), among the most venerated of the rabbi-saints of East European ḥasidism, attested that he had been irresistibly drawn to make his famous journey to the Holy Land and that it was an event of immense importance to him. All that he had known before making it, he told his disciples, had turned out to be 'insignificant' (*ke-lo mamash*). The learning and understanding to be acquired in Erez-Israel was as far removed

---

[1] Avraham Yaʿari (ed.), *Masʿot Erez-Israel*, Tel Aviv, 1946, p. 94.

[2] Solomon Schechter, 'Safed in the Sixteenth Century: A City of Legists and Mystics', *Studies in Judaism*, second series, Philadelphia, Pa., 1908, p. 205. At the beginning of the seventeenth century, the town of Safed contained eighteen Talmudic colleges and twenty-one synagogues.

from the learning of other countries as east from west. While all had been confusion in his mind before his journey, thereafter he held the Law whole. Yet the concrete object of his voyage, simple *contact* with the Land, he had achieved as soon as he stepped off his ship at Haifa. 'It is impossible to begin to understand the immensity of his happiness at that moment when he stood on the holy soil', relates his disciple in the classic account of the journey; 'for he said, that as soon as he had walked four ells in Erez-Israel he had fully accomplished what he had wished to achieve.'[3] Indeed, Rabbi Naḥman then proposed to turn around and begin the voyage home immediately and only with difficulty was he persuaded to remain. Eventually, he visited Tiberias. He went nowhere else, not even to Jerusalem.

In contrast, among Jews whose practice was less overwhelmingly mystical in orientation, interest in the real Erez-Israel, where it obtained, tended to be to greater practical effect. It could be argued that the real beginnings of the modern resettlement of Erez-Israel by Ashkenazi Jews from Eastern and Central Europe was the doing of the pupils of Rabbi Eliahu, the Gaon of Vilna. They were systematic and deliberate. They came to the country in three large, organized parties in the years 1808 and 1809 and established their first community in Safed. They intended to remain and went about their affairs with energy. Hardly had they arrived than they dispatched one of their leaders as an emissary back to the communities from which they had come with a written call to others to join them. They made no bones about the poverty of the country they had found. But there was none like it, they said. 'Even in its ruins none can compare with it.' They pictured the reawakening Land in highly coloured, quasi-anthropomorphic terms. They extolled the simple virtues of the mountain air, the water, and the climate of Safed, contrasting it with those of north-eastern Europe. They clearly saw themselves as representatives of the whole people and had no doubt that they had every right to demand of other Jews both material aid and reinforcement in numbers. And they did well: within seven years their numbers had risen from two to six hundred.[4]

Some orthodox Jews left Europe for Erez-Israel because they believed it would serve them as a refuge from the disastrous and

[3] Text in Avraham Ya'ari (ed.), *Mas'ot Erez-Israel*, Tel Aviv, 1946, pp. 480, 487.
[4] Avraham Ya'ari (ed.), *Igrot Erez-Israel*, Tel Aviv, 1950, pp. 329-31.

ineluctable effects of the Emancipation on the traditional patterns of Jewish life. By the middle of the nineteenth century the inroads of religious reform and of secularism, agnosticism, and apostasy were considerable even in Central Europe. The anti-Semitic movement was not yet of the dimensions it was to reach in Germany and Austria-Hungary in the last two decades of the century and all seemed set fair for the continued integration and assimilation of the Jews. The orthodox therefore had good reason to be troubled. Among the most coherent and pessimistic of the orthodox observers was Rabbi ʿAkiva Schlesinger (1832–1922) of Pressburg who argued that Judaism was now fated to decay in the Exile because it was truly impossible, in practice, to reconcile an ancient culture oriented towards the holy with the new, bright, immensely attractive, general culture oriented towards the satisfaction of day-to-day, material needs. For example, it was disastrous for Jews to learn foreign languages; each such language was yet another opening on to an undesirable landscape. On the other hand, it could not be denied that the impulse to learn the languages of the surrounding peoples was not an idle one, but founded, on the contrary, on genuine economic and social needs. Such needs could not be controlled; the dangers of remaining in the Exile were therefore clear. What had to be sought was an escape, a refuge from modernism and secularism; and where better, thought Schlesinger, than in the Land of the Fathers, the cradle of Judaism itself, where the culture of corruption had not penetrated, nor seemed likely to.[5] He himself went out to Ereẓ-Israel in 1870.

The feature common to the approach of all the orthodox was that their concern with the country was governed—and limited—by their preoccupation with the fundamental and dramatic circumstance of their inhabiting it. How they were to organize themselves, what social, let alone political, role they were to play there, in what relation they would be with the other inhabitants of the country— these were all questions to which they gave little thought, or none at all. The fact of their return was an overwhelming one, but the pattern of Jewish life founded on study and prayer, to the exclusion, so far as possible, of all else, that had evolved in the Exile, was one which they had every intention of preserving and which in their new life only required intensifying. In a word, they were

---

[5] See A. I. Shaḥrai, *Rabbi ʿAkiva Yosef Schlesinger*, Jerusalem, 1942, p. 10 and *passim*.

out to preserve tradition (if, indeed, in heightened circumstances) not to upset it. They added to the size of the Jewish population of the country; they did nothing of significance to alter its character, nor did they intend to. Certainly it would not have occurred to them to think of the Land as the focus and site of a great change in the material, let alone the cultural and religious, life of the Jews. The idea of Erez̧-Israel as the scene and, in a sense, the instrument of social change was one which only Jews infected by secularism, if only minutely or even unconsciously, were likely to dwell upon.

It is true, of course, that the place of Erez̧-Israel in Jewish belief and in what might be termed the Jewish outlook in its most representative and characteristic forms was precisely of that element of Judaism which all those who strove to secularize Judaism and to departicularize the Jews were most anxious to be rid of. For the more powerfully and consistently one wished to emphasize the universal qualities of Judaism as a preliminary to its establishment and general recognition as a 'world' religion or ethical system, the more conscious one became of the fact that the attachment to Erez̧-Israel epitomized all that was particularistic and non-assimilable in it, and non-reducible to universal categories—or, as its enemies might say, tribal. So to the extent that the Emancipation in Western Europe seemed to offer Jews an opportunity to escape from the particular—the tribal—and sail across the broader waters of humanity at large, it entailed and encouraged a move away from the ancient tie to Erez̧-Israel, certainly away from its central place in Jewish belief and practice. At the same time, the impact of the Emancipation as a *secularizing* force in itself did also facilitate a revised view of Erez̧-Israel as a Land shorn of its chiliastic attributes and therefore as a candidate—among others, as will be seen—for a role in the secular redemption of Jewry. And with this less theological and rather more mundane view of the Land came, under the other influences of the age, a tendency to look back, essentially, on the secular history of the Jews in their Land as an age of glory and civil and intellectual accomplishment, a golden age, the romantic age of the Jews. It is therefore not surprising that where Jews were very far removed from strict tradition, or were, in the technical sense of religious practice not Jews at all, it was above all the historical, geological, geographical, and mythological rather than mystical Erez̧-Israel that attracted them, if anything.

The broad moon lingers on the summit of Mount Olivet, but its beam has long left the garden of Gethsemane and the tomb of Absalom, the waters of Kedron and the dark abyss of Jehoshafat. Full falls its splendour, however, on the opposite city, vivid and defined in its silvery blaze. A lofty wall, with turrets and towers and frequent gates, undulates with the unequal ground which it covers, as it encircles the lost capital of Jehovah. It is a city of hills, far more famous than those of Rome; for all Europe has heard of Zion and of Calvary, while the Arab and the Assyrian, and the tribes and nations beyond are as ignorant of the Capitolian and the Aventine Mounts as they are of the Malvern and Chiltern Hills.[6]

From this vision of ancient glory to the idea of actually reconstituting the Jewish Kingdom was not far, especially if, as a non-believer, or as a non-Jew, one were uninhibited by theological objections to the enterprise. For the further removed one was from the direct influence of traditional Jewish society, the starker appeared the contrast between the ancient glories and the contemporary degradation and between the social and political conditions that obtained for other peoples on the one hand and the depoliticized, broken-backed framework of Jewish national life on the other. The greater, therefore, was the attraction of a radical solution.

ii

Within the bulk of Jewry, however, in those communities that retained the traditional forms after, and despite, the Emancipation in the West, and above all in the essentially untouched and un-emancipated heartland of Jewry in Eastern Europe, no such clear contrasts were apparent and no radical proposals were advanced. The weight of the traditional categories was still very great. What had gained a little ground by the middle of the nineteenth century was the thought that the great stirring of national feeling in Central and Eastern Europe might hold a significance for the Jews which, on the whole, the affairs of other peoples had not held hitherto. When the editors of the Hebrew journal *Ha-Magid*[7] were asked by their readers in Poland in 1863 what course they should adopt—should they join the revolt of the distrusted, violently anti-Semitic Poles against the common oppressor, or should they follow the

---

[6] Benjamin Disraeli, *Tancred*, bk. iii, chap. 1.

[7] Published at this time in the East Prussian border town of Lyck, but with a readership extending into Poland and Russia.

ancient course of prudence and remain obedient to the Russians—
the junior editor, David Gordon (1831-86), unlike his senior,
replied that the quarrel between Russians and Poles was no affair
of theirs. These were certainly great times, times of awakening and
resurgence for nations seeking to regain ancient honours which had
been denied them. But the redemption of the Jewish nation ought
to be an equal, not subordinate part of this movement. There were
now many, said Gordon, who had begun to think along these lines
and rightly ask why the Jews should absent themselves. It was true,
they were in a minority. There were many more who had given up
all hope and claim to a country of their own and who argued that
salvation would have to be gained *here* and that meanwhile the
Jews must remain patiently and quietly in the countries of their
present exile. In time the Jews would cease to be persecuted and
would share in the benefits accruing to all the inhabitants of their
countries. That was to be the nature of their salvation and it would
be idle to expect more. But those who argued in this way, said
Gordon, were telling the world that they had eyes for immediate
and material needs only—private needs. 'A sense of the general
honour of Israel is strange to them.' His own concern was not with
the material welfare of the Jews, nor with the subjection of the
Poles to the Russians, but with the detachment of the spirit of
Israel from the only soil in which it could grow. For he believed
that the moral consequences of the Exile were no less severe than,
and were inseparable from, the material; and that neither could
be remedied without a Return.[8]

What then was to be *done*? Like many men of his class and times,
and in common with the majority of contemporary publicists,
Gordon had inordinate confidence in the power of an enunciated
thesis to lead, by virtue of its truth, to action. So while he was
convinced that the times were propitious and that the essential
thing was to make the Jews realize the fact and seize their chance,
he was vague about how they were to be brought to this realization and what, precisely, they were then to do. The idea of some
sort of mass movement of population that would regain Erez-Israel
by main force he dismissed as frivolous. He was aware, if only in
very general terms, that the material and political obstacles to any

[8] 'Be-shuva va-naḥat tivashe'un', *Ha-Magid*, xiv, 1863; S. L. Zitron, *Toldot Ḥibbat
Zion*, Odessa, 1914, p. 17. (David Gordon should not be confused with his contemporary,
the poet Y. L. Gordon. See Chapter 2 below.)

such enterprise were enormous. Moreover, he was acutely conscious
of the pervading disunity in Jewry and of the total absence of any
group or organization that could mobilize it and represent it. Again,
like many other Jews of his time, he had been struck by the unprecedented rise of the new notables of western Jewry, in particular
by those who had acquired power and influence without at the same
time disowning their people. And like the eminent Talmudic
scholar, Zevi Kalischer (1795–1874), Rabbi of Thorn, who had
earlier reached conclusions analogous to his from the very different
standpoint of strict orthodoxy, he looked to the magnates, among
them the Rothschilds and the Montefiores, to take the lead. For,
indeed, it was not clear where else one could turn. There was Dr.
Lorje's Society for the Colonization of Palestine in Frankfurt an
der Oder; useful, but a small affair, too limited in scope and too
provincial to make any headway in so great an enterprise without
massive assistance and more influential leadership. While, perhaps

if the House of Rothschild and Sir Moses Montefiore stood at its head,
together with the leaders of the Board of Deputies of British Jews and
the Alliance Israélite Universelle, and other notables who have the
strength to stand in the courts of kings and speak for their brothers,
then the Society would, with the help of God, reach its goal; then the
government of Turkey would, at the request of the kings of Europe,
protect those of our brothers who work the land of their fathers.[9]

What Gordon and Kalischer failed to see was that the enterprise
they had in mind, however ill defined, was very far indeed from
the kind of charitable project on behalf of which an appeal might
usefully be made to the philanthropists of the West. It was one thing
to ask them to intercede with their own governments on behalf of
other Jews within their countries, or even on behalf of the Jews of
other countries, where the intercession was exclusively humanitarian in content. It was quite another thing to propose to the major
European governments that they undertake to press the Ottomans
to facilitate large-scale immigration into Erez-Israel on the basis of
a conception of Jewish national identity and unity which few, if
any, of the philanthropists themselves could be expected to be
sympathetic to, even if there were, only a few years after the ending of the Crimean War, the remotest possibility of a sympathetic
hearing in the European ministries for so extraordinary a proposal.

[9] *Ha-Magid*, 18, 1863.

The Dr. Ḥayyim Lorje, whom both Gordon and Kalischer—and a large company of other men in Prussia and Prussian Poland and beyond—had thought might hold the key to limited progress at the lower level of *practical* affairs, was a man of modest standing, the proprietor of a boarding-house for Jewish children attending school at Frankfurt an der Oder. But he was a graduate of a German university (no small thing in his society at the time) and he claimed descent from the celebrated sixteenth-century master of the cabbala, Rabbi Izḥak Luria (the ARI). It is hard to say of which of his claims to distinction he was the prouder. He was orthodox in observance and a dabbler, or more, in the cabbala. But precisely what it was that moved him, in 1860, to announce the establishment of the *Colonisationsverein für Palästina* is not known. He believed that the Revolution of 1848 was an event auguring the millennium (*yemot ha-mashiaḥ*—literally: the days of the Messiah) and it was the events of that year, presumably, that had also aroused his interest in a Jewish national revival. He saw a return to the land of the fathers as a form of purification after the defilement of the Exile. At the same time, he was open to the influences of German life and of Germanic efficiency in particular. Somehow these combined in him to produce his special contribution to the still entirely inchoate movement he was joining: the idea that it was necessary to establish an *organization*.[10]

Lorje did what had never been done before, but has been done on an ever greater scale since. He systematically published articles in both the Jewish and the non-Jewish press to advance his views and regularly responded to those who attacked him. He set out to recruit men of position and reputation to his cause and shortly established a roster that included the Chief Rabbi of Great Britain and notables of almost equal standing in Germany, France, Hungary, and Lithuania. When *Rome and Jerusalem* was published with no mention of his *Colonisationsverein* he characteristically wrote Hess a note of protest which moved the latter as promptly to apologize and to join the Society.[11] He tried to persuade the

[10] Cf. G. Kressel, 'Ha-ḥevra ha-rishona le-yishuv Ereẓ-Israel', *Zion*, vii, 1941/2, pp. 197–205; Israel Klausner (ed.), *Ha-ketavim ha-ẓioniim shel ha-rav Zevi Kalischer*, Jerusalem, 1947, *passim*; Mordechai Eliav, *Ahavat Ẓion ve-anshei HOD*, Tel-Aviv, 1970, pp. 128–32; Theodor Zlocisti (ed.), *Moshe Hess u-venei doro*, Tel Aviv, 1947, pp. 222–5, 240–2.

[11] Moses Hess (1812–75), a native of Germany, was an early and important proponent of socialism in that country, later contemptuously attacked by Marx for sentimentalism. He had been brought up in a religious household, but moved away from Jewry and Jewish

itinerant representatives of the orthodox communities of Erez-Israel to co-operate with him and in part succeeded. He organized the collection of funds and the convening of meetings. He won some opponents to his side by dint of argument and by the impression his patent sincerity and good intentions made. It was not long before he became very widely, if vaguely, known as a man who presided over an enterprise concerned with the Return. His greatest *coup*, the recruitment of Rabbi Zevi Kalischer, was the direct result of his spreading fame. It was Kalischer who heard of Lorje and sent him the manuscript of *Derishat Zion*. Lorje arranged for its publication—an act which some think his lasting gift to posterity.

But having founded his Society and got it started he was unable to decide what to do with it and his conduct as its chief did neither him nor his enterprise much good. Everything suggests that he was an extremely difficult man to get along with. He was devoid of tact, he was secretive, he was suspicious, and he was extraordinarily quarrelsome. Moreover, he was childishly pompous: no sooner had branches been established in other German cities (in Berlin, Breslau, and Leipzig), than he altered his title from the comparatively modest *Geschäftsführer* to the absurd *Generaldirektor*. Nor, for all his striving for efficiency, was he a competent administrator. After nearly three years of stewardship, with a membership of many hundreds, his society's appeal for funds had yielded 1,000 thaler in all, while office expenses had already reached 400 thaler

affairs for many years, except, by his own account, for a flash of interest in 1840 at the time of the Damascus affair. In 1862 he published *Rome and Jerusalem* which can be seen, in retrospect, as an extremely perceptive analysis of the contemporary Jewish predicament and a classic of Zionist literature in that it argued for the re-establishment of a Jewish state. The book's influence was limited, however. It is notorious that Herzl did not begin it until two years after the publication of his own *The Jewish State* and did not finish reading it until three years later. See below, Chapter 2, pp. 27–8.

The Damascus affair arose over the disappearance of a Capuchin friar in Damascus in 1840. His monastic order circulated reports that he had been killed by Jews for ritual purposes. They were supported by the local French Consul who joined the Syrian authorities in the subsequent investigation, played a particularly ignoble part in all that followed, and, in turn, enjoyed the backing of his own government. A large number of Jews, adults as well as children, were arrested. Torture was freely applied, false confessions were extorted, and there were several deaths. As the story leaked out, protests multiplied in Europe and for the first time in the modern era western Jewish notables, among them members of the Rothschild family, Moses Montefiore, and Adolphe Crémieux, came together to press for action on behalf of the victims. The shock to the newly emancipated, relatively self-confident Jews of Western Europe was very great. It helped establish the mood in which the Alliance Israélite Universelle was founded twenty years later.

and other, unspecified obligations amounted to 800 thaler. Above all, not a single settlement was established in Ereẓ-Israel through his efforts, nor is there any evidence that practical steps to do so had been taken or that he had arranged for the travel of a single settler. The one really promising opportunity that came his way—when a group of Romanian Jews applied to him for help to make the journey—was missed. In the end his bad manners and his high-handedness led his colleagues to take the Society out of his hands and transfer its centre—over his violent protests—to Berlin. But they did no better than he. By 1865 it had, to all intents and purposes, died. 'What good has come of their having, in their wisdom, removed Dr. Lorje from the affair and put the Berliners at its head?', complained Gordon to Kalischer. 'He, at least, had done all he could. He awoke sleeping hearts. And they? Clearly, it is essential that men of our nation *in other countries* be found, men of note whose hearts have really and truly been touched by the love of Zion; then, without a doubt, they will succeed in doing God's will.'[12]

### iii

The territory known to the Jews as Ereẓ-Israel and to non-Jews (in ancient times) as Palestine had had no real political or even administrative unity since the fall of the Frankish kingdom of Jerusalem. In the earlier part of the nineteenth century, under the Ottomans, it was divided into two. Judea and Samaria and the northern part of the Negev constituted one *sanjak* (district) and were governed from Damascus, as was the country east of the Jordan. Galilee and the coastal plain down to Gaza were governed at various times from Acre and from Sidon. Later, Judea, the coastal plain from Jaffa to the south, and the northern Negev were reconstituted as the *sanjak* of Jerusalem; Samaria became the *sanjak* of Nablus; and Galilee the *sanjak* of Acre—each with its coastal strip. All three were parts of the *vilayet* (province) of Beirut. The country east of the Jordan continued to be governed from Damascus. Later still (1854) Jerusalem was detached from Beirut and given a semi-autonomous status as a *muta-sarriflik* under a governor responsible directly to Constantinople.

The total population of Ereẓ-Israel at the beginning of the nineteenth century has been variously put at between 150,000 and

---

[12] G. Kressel (ed.), *David Gordon*, Tel Aviv, n.d., p. 11 (emphasis in original).

300,000 Muslims, Jews, and Christians. Of these at most 10,000
were Jews, settled principally in the four towns of Jerusalem,
Hebron, Safed, and Tiberias, towns which held a particular place
in the tradition and were known as the 'four holy lands' (*arba arzot
ha-kodesh*). The largest Jewish community was that of Safed (about
4,000 in number), and there the Jews were in the majority. The
next in size was Jerusalem (some 3,000 in the year 1800 out of a
total population of 9,000–10,000 of whom 4,000 were Muslims
and 2,750 were Christians). But from the 1830s on, the Jewish
population of Jerusalem began to grow more or less steadily. By
1840 the Jewish community was the most numerous of the three
(5,000 Jews, as opposed to 4,500 Muslims and 3,500 Christians).
In 1860 they constituted half the total population of just under
20,000. In 1880 there were 17,000 Jews out of a total of 30,000.[13]
There were about a dozen other minor centres with smaller Jewish
communities, of which the ones worth noting by the middle of the
century were Haifa and Jaffa.

The Jews congregated in the towns partly out of piety and partly,
if not chiefly, because the towns offered somewhat more security
than the under-administered and unpoliced countryside. But
even in the towns their lot was a hard one, as, indeed, was that of
the other *dhimmis*—the Christians. They were subject to certain
humiliating and burdensome legal restrictions, to the extortions
of corrupt and tyrannical local officials and tax-farmers, and to the
ravages of thuggery within the towns and brigandage outside them.
Nor was Erez-Israel a land which promised much in the way of
livelihood. A great deal of what was later to prove the best of its
always meagre reserves of farming land was then swamp. Malaria
was endemic. The local techniques of irrigation were primitive.
There were no natural mineral resources of any significance. The
commercial life of the country was at a very low level, as might be
expected in a minor administrative district of Syria, well away from
the main international trade routes, with few roads, no railways,
no more than open roadsteads for the few ships that called at the

[13] Cf. Izhak Ben-Zvi, *Erez-Israel ve-yishuva b'imei ha-shilton ha-ʿotomani*, Jerusalem,
1955, p. 365; Yehoshua Ben-Arye, 'Hitpathuta shel Yerushalayim', *Keshet*, xii. 4, 1970,
p. 37; Mordechai Eliav, op. cit., Appendix A, and Ben-Zion Gat, *Ha-yishuv ha-yehudi
be-Erez-Israel (1840–1881)*, Jerusalem, 1963. There is considerable conflict between
authorities and few figures in which one can place real confidence. The first year for which
reliable census figures are available is 1922. These gave the following for Jerusalem: 34,000
Jews, 13,500 Muslims, and 14,700 Christians.

country's ports, and only the barest trickle of pilgrims willing to run the risks of travel in the interior unless sufficiently powerful and well organized to protect themselves.

The first changes in the legal and social status of the non-Muslim minorities took place with the ejection of the Ottomans from the country by Mehemet Ali in 1831 and their replacement by an Egyptian administration under Mehemet Ali's son Ibrahim for a period which lasted until the return of the Ottomans in 1841. In an effort to improve their standing with the European powers the Egyptians gave the Christian inhabitants virtually complete equality with Muslims; and while the Jews were not granted the same rights, their situation was nevertheless considerably eased. They were afforded greater protection from petty violence and extortion, equality in the new civil courts, and some representation on the local government councils. They were permitted to repair synagogue buildings (no repairs had been allowed under the Turks) and to pray at the Temple wall without special authorization. Over all, public administration was made stronger and more effective. The Bedouin were curbed, brigandage was largely stopped, pilgrimage from abroad was made easier.

But again, the goodwill of the authorities was only fully effective in the main towns, not in the small towns and villages. And even in the larger towns sporadic killings and pillage were not entirely ended. In Safed the peasant revolt of 1834 hit the Jews particularly hard; in Hebron there was a massacre of Jews *after* the entry of Egyptian soldiers sent to put down the Muslim rebels.

The Turks did not revert to former practice on their return. The liberal trend was generally maintained and the relative status of the Jews improved by bringing it roughly into line with that of the Christians. The new generosity to the *dhimmis* stemmed partly from the political debt the Turks owed the European powers for helping them to push the Egyptians back; and with the appearance of foreign consuls in Jerusalem (British, the first to arrive, in 1839;[14] Prussian in 1842; and French in 1843) it was a debt, the honouring of which could be demanded and supervised. But the change was also, in part, the intended result of the Tanzimat reforms, promulgated in 1839, and beginning to take effect throughout the Ottoman

---

[14] It was wariness of Russian penetration of the region, however, which prompted the British to take this step. See M. Vereté, 'Why was a British Consulate established in Jerusalem?', *English Historical Review*, lxxxv, April 1970, pp. 316-45.

Empire. These reforms promised, among other things, equal treatment of all peoples, Muslim and non-Muslim alike.[15]

The influence of the foreign consuls and their *locus standi* as protectors of certain categories of non-Muslims were enhanced and institutionalized by the terms of the Treaty of Paris (1856) ending the Crimean War which laid down the status of non-Muslims with considerable precision—specifying, for example, the rights and privileges, modes of election, and salaries of rabbis and priests. With these changes came ever growing numbers of Christian pilgrims—particularly Russians—and Jews who wished to settle permanently in the country. The political advantages of extending the circle of their protégés was obvious to the European powers. At one stage the Russians even thought of modifying their hostility to Jewry in general, and to Jews who had left the Empire in particular, with a view to exploiting the small, but now fairly steady stream of Russian Jews into the country for their political purposes.[16] But, in fact, the disfranchised Russian Jews preferred the protection of the British consul, when they could get it. The British were both the most influential of all foreign representatives and, on the whole, the most helpful to the Jews, which meant, in practice, those who had lost the protection of their countries of origin.[17] But while this system of institutionalized intervention of foreign representatives on behalf of Jewish and Christian residents of the country had a profound influence on the general climate of relations between the administration and the inhabitants, only a minority of Jews were directly affected. Until well into the second half of the century most Jews in the country were native-born Ottoman subjects. In Jerusalem it was not until the late 1870s that the community of Ashkenazi (Eastern and Central European) Jews equalled that of the Sephardi (Near-Eastern) Jews; and Ashkenazim did not actually outnumber Sephardim until the end of the 1880s.[18] Furthermore, the Jews of Erez-Israel at this time were without political ambitions and almost totally uninterested in the purposes of the European powers, let alone concerned to help further them except in so far as these were likely to have an immediate local impact. It was private, social, and religious liberty that they were after. The Ottomans therefore

[15] Cf. Moshe Ma'oz, *Ottoman Reform in Syria and Palestine 1840–1861*, Oxford, 1968.

[16] Derek Hopwood, *The Russian Presence in Syria and Palestine 1843–1914*, Oxford, 1969, p. 53.

[17] Ben-Zvi, op. cit., pp. 363–4.

[18] Cf. Eliav, loc. cit.

worried less about them than they did about the Christian inhabitants of the country who were the more natural candidates for the
protection extended by the Europeans and whose significant increase in numbers owed more to European missionary activity—
abhorred, but now generally tolerated, by the Turks—than to the
very moderate influx of Christian immigrants. Thus, by and large,
relations between the Turkish authorities and their Jewish subjects
began to ease steadily from their return in 1841 onwards—a year
marked, incidentally, by the decision to issue a *firman* appointing
the first Ḥakham Bashi, or Chief Rabbi in Jerusalem—and so
continued until the change in the character of Jewish immigration
which occurred in the early 1880s was noted.

The economic condition of the Jews changed less dramatically.
There was some benefit from the influx of immigrants and the
growth of communication between Ereẓ-Israel and the outer world,
and between the Jews of Ereẓ-Israel and those of Europe in particular, and from the effects of the community becoming—at least
in part—an object of philanthropic concern to Jews elsewhere. But
over all, there can be no question of the penury and, only too often,
the squalor in which much of the *yishuv* lived and of the seeming
hopelessness—for those who were not immersed in worship and
the study of the Law and concerned with other matters. A survey
of the occupational structure of the Jewish community of Jerusalem
in 1877 (by heads of families) found that a fifth were paupers and
that almost one-third were rabbis, judges, teachers, and other
communal officials. Thus it is likely that almost one-half of the
Jewish population of Jerusalem had to be supported out of public
funds—in practice, out of funds collected among Jews abroad, the
so-called *haluka*, and distributed by the communal organizations
(*kolelim*) set up largely for that purpose. Since many of the craftsmen, petty traders, and unskilled workmen who made up the rest
were, in fact, grossly underemployed and extremely poor, at least
partial reliance on the *haluka* was probably even more widespread
than these figures would suggest.[19] It is important to note that in
the view of very many of those concerned no shame or indignity
attached to the receipt of *haluka* funds. Those who moved to and
lived in Ereẓ-Israel at this time did so, as we have seen, out of piety
and religious devotion almost exclusively; and therefore for a Jew

[19] Moses Friedländer, 'Die jüdische Bevölkerung Palästinas', in Alfred Nossig (ed.),
*Jüdische Statistik*, Berlin, 1903, pp. 394–9.

who remained behind in the Exile to contribute to their needs was
no more than a matter of his paying decent respect. Nevertheless,
the system bred its own cumulative distortions and petty corruption, considerations of vested interest, minor tyrants among those
who controlled the distribution of the funds, and sycophants,
trimmers, and time-servers among those who received, or hoped to
receive them.

Ultimately, a desire to rebuild their lives on firmer foundations
began to take root among the Jews of the country. The beginnings
of systematic Jewish philanthropy from the West, first in the
person of Sir Moses Montefiore and under the auspices of the
Rothschilds and later largely concentrated and institutionalized
in the Alliance Israélite Universelle founded by French Jews,
generally met with a warm response. Housing was improved and
began to be developed for them beyond the confinement of the city
walls of Jerusalem; crafts were taught and some light industry established; in 1870 an agricultural school was set up by the Alliance
near Jaffa. Still the *haluka* and its multitude of clients dominated
until late in the nineteenth century and tended to confirm the image
of Ereẓ-Israel as a land which, on the one hand, was too worn and
poor to support any but a stark and wretched existence, and, on
the other hand, as a land to which one's sole *concrete* connection
was necessarily generalized and philanthropic, rather than specific,
purposeful, and arising out of its manifest relevance to one's own
future.

MAP I. Area of permitted residence to Jews in Imperial Russia comprising the Pale of Settlement and the ten provinces of Russian-ruled Poland

# 2

# Aspects of European Jewry in the Nineteenth Century

i

THE essential patterns of Jewish communal life and the key internal rules by which Jewish communities were governed in their exile were set in the dark times which followed the crushing of the last great rebellion against Rome in the years 132-5—when the virtual depopulation of Judea began, the country's very name was changed by Roman order to Syria Palaestina, and all reasonable hope of reconstituting a Jewish commonwealth within it was lost. And for all that the Jewish Dispersion was gradually to extend out of the Ancient World of the Mediterranean and the Middle East and into practically all of Northern and Eastern Europe, the basic uniformity and interdependence of Jewish social and intellectual life as set in the first few hundred years of the Common Era were to remain in being down to the times of the rise of modern science and the Industrial Revolution. 'The Jewish communities of seventeenth-century Frankfort and Cracow, of Constantinople and Cairo bore an uncanny resemblance to those of Tiberias [in Palestine] and Nehardea [in Mesopotamia] at the beginning of the third century.'[1] But in the eighteenth century the old, comparatively uniform, pattern of Jewish life began to crumble and in the nineteenth century it disappeared—but at different speeds and with different consequences in different parts of the world. Least affected by change were the communities of the Islamic lands. Most radically affected were those of Western Europe where the rise of absolutist, 'enlightened' regimes pursuing mercantilist policies in the economic sphere and centralistic policies in the political and the administrative sought either to eject the Jews totally or to break

[1] Salo W. Baron, *The Jewish Community*, Philadelphia, Pa., 1942, i. 156.

down their particularities and bring them within an orderly and comprehensive social system in which privileges (as opposed to rights) flowed evenly from the sovereign. The bulk of Jewry, settled in Poland-Lithuania, was sheltered for a while from the pressures to conform and the attractions of an opening into society at large to which the Jews of Germany and Austria notably were subject. But from the end of the eighteenth century, upon the distribution of Polish lands between Austria, Prussia, and Germany, they became subjected to an increasingly violent series of upheavals —the axis on which the history of the Jews may be said to turn until the final horror of 1939–45 changed the structure and, it may be thought, the temperament of Jewry for all time.

The changes that came over Jewish life were, of course, slow at first and always erratic, even in Western Europe, for in the last resort things turned on the degree to which the formal and informal disabilities to which Jews had long been subject throughout the Christian and Muslim world were lifted. Many of these disabilities dated from the Middle Ages, some were of ancient origin, others belonged to quite recent times. The forty-four clauses of Pope Pius VI's *Editto sopra gli ebrei* of 1775 revived and consolidated medieval degradations and restrictions along with such modern improvements as the seventeenth-century prohibition on the erection of tombstones over Jewish graves. Generally, outside a very few enclaves of toleration (notably Holland, and then England from the seventeenth century), and until the very end of the eighteenth century, Jews lived throughout the Christian and Islamic world under some combination of legally institutionalized disabilities and to the threat of violence at the hands of lord and mob alike. Regulated, restricted, or even totally denied were the Jew's right of residence, his occupation, his freedom of movement and public worship, his effective recourse to justice, his right to property, his dress, his right to bear arms, even, in some countries, his right to marry and rear a family. The Jews, in a word, were not properly part of civil society, but set apart from it, and to such effect that universally until the modern era—and in very many parts of the world down to our own times—the history of the Jewish Dispersion has been the history of a continual effort to cope with the pressures directed both at the Jewish community and at the Jewish individual and of the concomitant migration of Jews elsewhere whenever the pressures became too great to sustain. It has thus been dominated by continual fluctuations in the relationship between the Jews and the non-Jews, rather than, as with other peoples, by social change within the nation itself. And the starting-point for the history of *modern* Jewry is therefore the great transformation in that relationship which took place in some parts of Europe, and to a minor extent in the Islamic lands, as a consequence of the Emancipation —the slow and irregular process, often reversed, whereby some, but not all, Jews came to be released from the disabilities under which they had long laboured.

The two salient features of the Emancipation were these: it took place sporadically and unequally in such a manner that some Jewish communities were affected, while others were not; and it took the form, for the most part, of a breaking down of the barriers to the Jew's entry into civil society as an individual, not of the establishment of the Jewish *community* on a basis of equality with other ethnic groups. 'Aux Juifs comme nation nous ne donnons rien; aux Juifs comme individus nous donnons tout', was Stanislas de Clermont-Tonnerre's celebrated formulation of the terms on which the Jews of France were to be emancipated by the Revolution.[2] Similarly, the new opportunities offered, however reluctantly, to the Jews of nineteenth-century Germany, were, at least in principle, opportunities to behave as—and in time to become— Jewish Germans. There was never any question of recognizing them as comprising a constituent nation along with the German nation proper within the German territories and later within the Reich.

As individuals, however, the Jews in the West were freer than before to be drawn into the great expansion of economic activity that took place in Western Europe in the nineteenth century and to begin to participate in the general intellectual and political life of the countries of their domicile. The seepage of Jews into society at large and, more significantly, into positions of some influence in the economy, a process which had gained momentum under the pre-revolutionary regimes, was now legitimized, as it were, at any rate in the minds of many of the West European Jews in question and in the absence of strong opposing forces. But the effect within Jewry internally was to confirm and generalize the phenomenon of a double cleavage—between those Jews who were willing and able

---

[2] In the National Assembly, 24 December 1789. Cf. Arthur Hertzberg, *The French Enlightenment and the Jews*, New York, 1968, pp. 359–61.

to participate successfully in Gentile society and those who were
not, and between the Jews in the West where forms of assimilation
were possible and those in the East where by and large they were
not. Thus in many cases the result of the great liberation was a
profound and, for the most part, irreversible weakening of the
individual Jew's social and cultural dependence on his own community and of the ties between one community and another.
Beyond these divisions and the tensions consequent upon them
were the new and much bitterer tensions between the Jews in
process of emancipation and assimilation and the society around
them. These were the more painful for the often furious reaction
of European society at large to the Jew's legal emancipation being
a fact of his new life which, by the terms of the Emancipation itself,
the individual Jew had to face, essentially, on his own. The process
of assimilation hinged on retaining membership in two, in important respects incompatible and traditionally hostile, cultures—or,
with greater traumatic effects, seeking to pass from one to the other
entirely.

Nevertheless, the effect of the Emancipation from civil and
economic disabilities, where it obtained, was generally intoxicating.
The social and cultural pull of the societies of Western Europe,
notably those of Germany, Austria, France, Hungary, England,
and later Italy, was powerful. After all, Western Europe was the
authentic home of modern ideas and techniques and the source of
the promise of political and social reform, of the principle of distinguishing between the affairs of God and the affairs of man, and,
above all, of the revolutionary notion that change and progress
were both feasible and desirable. Accordingly, once it had become
clear to much greater numbers than ever before that contact with
the sources of contemporary philosophy, art, and politics need no
longer be fleeting and covert—that such contact was in fact possible
on a basis approaching that of regularity and, in some respects,
equality—it was to the centres whence all this emanated that the
Jews began to turn. Where the great majority of the Jews of Eastern
Europe and the (modern) Islamic world remained to the end on
the whole unimpressed and unattracted by the indigenous culture
of surrounding society, those of Western Europe, and of such
highly Westernized parts of Central Europe as Hungary, sensed
from the first that confronting them was a not unthinkable *alternative* to their ancient, assuredly rich, and psychologically powerful,

but inward-looking, essentially static, and scholastically oriented modes of life and thought.

But the countries of the West, as opposed to those of Eastern Europe and the Islamic world, were lands in which, for the most part, a single language and national culture dominated and where differences of language and culture and the very presence of culturally and linguistically distinct ethnic minorities could only appear—and, in a sense, were—anomalous. How far and in what ways, then, ought the Jew to adjust himself, how far could he adjust himself, how far would he be permitted to adjust himself? These were the questions which were to hang over the Jews of Western Europe throughout the nineteenth and twentieth centuries; and their dilemmas and predicament were to a large degree the product of their incapacity to find a solution that was satisfactory both to themselves and to the non-Jews around them.

For some, however, the intrinsic attractions of the new modes were actually enhanced by what they took to be the sheer practical and moral necessity of seeking the highest possible degree of integration into the society around them. Schools and synagogues —the structural heart of Jewish cultural autonomy—ought therefore to be *reformed* and the newly created Jewish citizen had to eschew, or radically adapt, traditional ritual and whatever else might seem an obstacle to social integration.

I am a Prussian citizen [he should be able to say]. I have sworn solemnly to promote and support the weal of my Fatherland. Both duty and gratitude demand that I achieve this with all my might. First of all, I must endeavour to join with my fellow citizens, to approach them in custom and habit, to enter with them into social and personal connections; for the bonds of sociability and love bind more closely and strongly than the law itself. And only through these bonds can I achieve the aim of living with my fellow citizens in harmony, peace, and friendship.[3]

But others thought that such an enterprise led ineluctably to a drive to assimilate totally and made for a wish to bury and deny the past which could not be judged as anything but shameful. 'The Germans have so frequently and thoroughly demonstrated to us that our nationality is an obstacle to our "inner" emancipation, that

---

[3] Formulated by David Friedländer (1750–1834), a follower of Moses Mendelssohn, and proponent of Jewish modernization. Quoted in Jacob Katz, 'The German–Jewish Utopia of Social Emancipation', in Max Kreutzberger (ed.), *Studies of the Leo Baeck Institute*, New York, 1967, pp. 74–5.

we have finally come to believe it ourselves,' wrote Moses Hess, 'and, giving up our Jewish culture and denying our race, have made every effort to be deserving of the "blond" Germanism.' But in any case it was an enterprise that would not succeed.

In spite of the excellent mathematicians among them, our Jewish Teutonmaniacs, who bartered away their Judaism for State positions, grossly miscalculated their chances. It did not avail Meyerbeer that he painstakingly avoided the use of a Jewish theme as the subject of any of his operas; he did not escape, on that account, the hatred of the Germans. The old honest *Augsburger Allgemeine Zeitung* seldom refrained, while mentioning his name, from remarking parenthetically, 'Jacob Meyer Lippman Beer'. The German patriot Boerne, likewise, did not gain much by changing his family name, Baruch, into that of Boerne. He admits it himself. 'Whenever my enemies founder upon the rock of Boerne,' he writes, 'they throw out, as an anchor of safety, the name Baruch.' I have experienced it personally, not only with opponents, but even with my own party members. In personal controversy they always make use of the 'Hep' weapon, and in Germany it is always effective. I have made it easy for them to wield their weapon by adopting my Old Testament name, Moses. I regret exceedingly that my name is not Itzig.[4]

Still this was a minority view. By the end of the century the loss of self-confidence and the inroads upon traditional communal and family life made by the immensely powerful social and cultural attractions of German society at large were to lead the German Jewish community into clear decline. Initially the largest in the West and the wealthiest, the most advanced in modern sciences and techniques, and the most prestigious in Jewry as a whole, its numbers were only kept constant after 1870 (approximately at the half-million mark) by the unending stream of immigrants from the Jewish communities in the East. A high rate of intermarriage, a steadily decreasing number of children in each family, a general move from villages and towns to large towns and cities, and a marked fall in the number and membership of organized communities—these were among the causes and the symptoms of its metamorphosis by 1933 into a tired community in which deaths had for some time been outnumbering births and of whose members 45 per cent were over 45 years of age.[5]

[4] Moses Hess, *Rome and Jerusalem* (translated by Meyer Waxman), New York, 1918, pp. 90–1.

[5] H. S. Halevi, *Hashpaʿat milḥemet ha-ʿolam ha-shenia ʿal ha-tekhunot ha-demografiot shel ʿam Israel*, Jerusalem, 1963, pp. 65–75. In a remarkable statistical study published in 1911,

ii

The question whether the adjustment of Jewish ritual, social practices, and communal organization to conform in style, and, more especially, in content, to the norms of Gentile society would ultimately make it possible for the Jew to live in 'harmony, peace, and friendship' with those around him was to remain open in Germany until 1933. It may be said to be an open question in France and England to this day. But in Eastern Europe it was never a serious proposition at all—even though it did have some proponents. This was partly because, as will be seen, Jewry in the Russian Empire, in Austrian Galicia, and in Romania was so placed *vis-à-vis* the non-Jews and, for long, so structured internally that the inward pull of traditional belief and practice, as well as of traditional communal authority, was vastly more powerful and longer-lasting than in the West and remained preponderant over secularism and assimilatory and universalist forces—intellectual as well as political—until well into the twentieth century. It was partly, too, because the question how and to what degree Jews could and should adjust to the surrounding social and cultural norms was devoid of practical significance for all but a fraction of the Tsar's Jewish subjects (and of the subjects of the King of Romania) by reason of the deliberate and generally consistent policy of repression of which they were the object. The Jews retained a special status under law until the Revolution of 1917. There was no Emancipation and, except for a brief period, there

*Der Untergang der deutschen Juden*, F. A. Theilhaber showed that of every 100 Jewish girls born fifty years before, 2 had been baptized, 22 remained spinsters or childless wives, 3 had had illegitimate children, 18 had married non-Jews, and the 55 who had married Jews had borne only 118 children of *both* sexes. It was therefore already clear then that German Jewry was not reproducing itself biologically. Particularly marked was the declining birth-rate of German Jews in the nineteenth century—consistently lower than that of non-Jews: approximately an eighth lower in the second quarter of the century and falling to two-thirds lower than the corresponding rate for non-Jews by the 1930s. In the years 1875–80 the average number of children born to a married couple was 4·2; by 1920–6 it had fallen to 1·69. The declining birth-rate was still more marked in the case of mixed couples: 1·7 children in 1875–80; and 0·58 children in 1920–6. The over-all effects of cultural assimilation, a high and steadily rising rate of intermarriage (16·9 per hundred exogamous marriages in 1901; 59 per hundred in 1929), the low birth-rate, and accelerating urbanization (in 1871 only 20 per cent of all German Jews lived in large towns and cities; in 1933 71 per cent lived in large towns and cities and 33 per cent lived in Berlin alone) may be measured by the concomitant decline of organized communal life. At the beginning of the twentieth century there were still 2,300 organized Jewish communities; by 1933 only 1,600 remained. The figures for Austria, Czechoslovakia, and Hungary (but not the Austrian territories incorporated into Poland after the First World War) show a similar pattern.

was no pretence of equality. They were a people systematically and ever more rigorously set apart. As a Russian governmental commission once conceded in an uncharacteristically frank analysis of the condition of the Jews (in 1888)—

> Without granting [the Jew] equal rights, we cannot, properly speaking, demand from him equal civic obligations . . . Repression and disfranchisement, discrimination and persecution have never yet tended to improve groups of human beings and make them more devoted to their rulers. It is, therefore, not surprising that the Jews, trained in the spirit of a century-long repressive legislation, have remained in the category of those subjects who are less exact in the discharge of their civic duty, who shirk their obligations towards the State, and do not fully join Russian life. No less than six hundred and fifty restrictive laws directed against the Jews may be enumerated in the Russian Code, and the discriminations and disabilities implied in these laws are such that they have naturally resulted in making until now the life of an enormous majority of the Jews in Russia exceedingly onerous.[6]

In 1880 world Jewry numbered between 7·5 and 8 millions; of these the overwhelming majority (88·4 per cent) were in Europe and at least 75 per cent (5·7 million) in Eastern Europe: in eastern Prussia, Austrian Galicia, Romania and the other Balkan states, and, above all (some four millions) within the Russian-ruled territory known as the Pale of Settlement (*cherta osyedlosti*) established formally in 1794 and consolidated by stages in the course of the nineteenth century until its dissolution in 1917. Briefly put, the Pale resulted from the clash between, on the one hand, the policy of excluding Jews from Holy Russia firmly set by the sixteenth century, and, on the other hand, the westward and southward expansion of the Russian realm into regions which were heavily populated by Jews. Ivan IV ('the Terrible') believed—and so informed King Sigismund II of Poland—that the Jews had 'led our people away from Christianity and brought poisonous herbs into our State'.[7] And he felt free to confront the problem with simple measures. When his conquests brought him into the Polish border town of Polotsk in 1563 he promptly ordered all Jews who refused baptism in the Orthodox faith to be drowned in the River

---

[6] Quoted in S. M. Dubnov, *History of the Jews in Russia and Poland*, Philadelphia, Pa., 1916–20, ii, p. 364.

[7] Shemu'el Ettinger, 'Medinat Moskva be-yaḥasa el ha-yehudim', *Zion*, iii–iv, 1953, p. 137.

Dvina. But the successive partitions of Poland under Catherine II ('the Great') and the incorporation of most of the Grand Duchy of Warsaw into Russia under Alexander I ('the Blessed') brought far too many Jews under Russian rule far too rapidly for the dilemma to be resolved with such facility, even if so vigorous a solution had been judged appropriate in the Age of Enlightenment. Instead, by irregular steps and moved at various times by such contradictory considerations as regard for Russian public opinion and fear of Jewish economic competition on the one hand, and the need to populate the new southern territories and a regard for what was and was not proper in a country intended to be governed by the rule of Law on the other, an elaborate system of restricted residence and occupation was evolved. The centre-piece of the system was the 'Pale'.

The Pale covered a fairly large area stretching roughly from Lithuania in the north to the Black Sea in the south, and from Poland and Bessarabia in the west to White Russia and the Ukrainian Governorates of Chernigov and Poltava in the east. Within it the Jews formed a very high proportion of the total population: 9·4 per cent in the Ukraine and as much as 12·7 per cent in White Russia.[8] But this was not the full measure of the extent to which they (96 per cent of all Russian Jewry)[9] were crowded together. The right of residence *within* the Pale was itself circumscribed again and again by a series of decrees of expulsion from certain cities (Kiev, Nikolaev, Sebastopol, among others), from entire regions (notably those on the western borders of the Empire), and increasingly and most critically from rural areas. The consequent misery and impoverishment apart, the repeated waves of expulsion during this period greatly accelerated the conversion of the Jews of Russia and Poland from a predominantly village and small-town society into an urban one. Whereas at the beginning of the nineteenth century only 10–15 per cent of Russia's total urban population was Jewish and there was not a single Jewish community numbering 10,000 souls, by the end of the century Jews constituted approximately 30 per cent of the total urban population and there were no less than 40 communities of 10,000 souls or more, totalling 1·5 million altogether or almost a third of the entire Jewish population

[8] 1900 figures.
[9] In 1897. Of a total of 5,110,000 Jews in the Empire in that year 4,900,000 lived in the Pale.

of the Empire. By the census year of 1897 fully 82 per cent of
Russian Jewry were listed as inhabiting cities and towns; and since
the number of towns and cities within the Empire which they were
permitted to inhabit was itself restricted by the over-all limits of
the Pale, cases of the Jewish population in certain large towns and
cities reaching 70 or 80 per cent of the total were not unknown.[10]

The economic and social effects of the crowding of the Jews into
the towns of the Pale were the harsher for coinciding with a rapid
rise in their absolute numbers, a trend which they shared with
almost all other peoples of Europe in the nineteenth century, but
was opposite to that of much of western Jewry, as has been noted.

Between 1800 and 1900 the total Jewish population of the world
increased by rather more than four times (from about 3 million to
between 12 and 13 million), or somewhat more rapidly than the
general population. And East European Jewry (some four-fifths of
the total) shared—and more than shared—another marked demographic feature of the times by participating in the vast contemporary migratory movement. The Jews moved partly from Eastern
to Western Europe, but preponderantly overseas to Latin America,
South Africa, and, above all, to North America. Of the some 65
million Europeans who migrated overseas between 1800 and 1950
4 million were Jews—or about 6 per cent. (The entire Jewish
population of Europe was 1·5 per cent of the total at the beginning
of the period and never more than 2 per cent of the total at its
peak.) At the height of the great migratory wave, in the first decade
of the twentieth century, the westward movement of Jews was
running as high as 115,000 annually. In the year 1906 the migration
of Russian Jews alone reached the rate of 24 per thousand. All told,
one-fifth of all European Jews migrated overseas in the first quarter
of the present century (as compared with 11·3 per cent of the
Italians) in a migration that was not only more feverish than that
of any other people except the Irish, but also, again unlike any
other but the Irish, clearly intended from the start to be permanent.[11]

Those who moved to the West became subject to the influences
that were already in operation on the Jews who were native to those

[10] Halevi, op. cit., pp. 34-5.

[11] The proportion of males and of the economically active was lowest among the Jews
and the Irish, as were the figures for those returning from the United States to their country
of origin—8 per cent of the Jews and 7 per cent of the Irish in the years 1908-10, as compared
for example with 64 per cent for the Hungarians and 61 per cent for the North Italians.
Halevi, op. cit., pp. 10-11, 16-17.

parts. But for those who remained behind matters were otherwise. First and foremost the hold of the community over its individual member—possibly the greatest of the forces making for Jewish national survival through centuries of the Dispersion—remained extremely potent for the majority of Jews well into the present century. 'For the Jew the community was his national home and his refuge in the midst of hostile surroundings.'[12]

The profoundly rooted view of the Jewish people as one in respect of which it made no sense to distinguish ethnic attributes from religious still obtained on the whole. Similarly, the community retained a temporal role along with the spiritual. The services of the communal organization and its functionaries were indispensable for the performance of all the major social and religious rites from circumcision to burial, for the supply of acceptable foodstuffs, for the education of children, and for that continual process of instruction in Jewish Law which had traditionally incarnated the Jewish system of values, for the charitable support of widows and the care of orphans and of the poor, for the adjudication of disputes between Jews and many of their other legal needs, and, not least, for the transaction of all major business between Jews collectively and the local sovereign authority. And here, indeed, was the reason for the dislike in which the absolutist and centralizing regimes held it. There was commonly a hierarchy of communities, in the sense that the moral leadership and social prestige of the great centres of Jewish population—in effect the large communities —were generally accepted by the minor centres and by the innumerable small village communities which much of European Jewry comprised. There had been periods when the Jewish communities in certain countries were able to form a country-wide union which for a while assumed powers of adjudication and representation for all. But on the whole, the authoritative determination of the social and religious norms of Jewish life was in local hands and the high degree of uniformity of practice maintained throughout Europe and the Islamic lands for so long was due to the fact that the rabbis—the learned men versed in the case-law of the *halakha* to which all Jews had recourse—predominated over the lay leadership.

The rabbis derived their authority in part from their individual capacity to expound the *halakha* and this, within certain limits,

---

[12] Arthur Ruppin, *The Jews in the Modern World*, London, 1934, p. 343.

was of universal application; and in part from their capacity to achieve consensus among themselves. In the absence of a formal hierarchy of rabbinical authority (on a basis analogous, for example, to the Roman Catholic episcopal system), this last was a function of the rabbis' own generally profound respect for the traditional proprieties of their calling, of the great regard in which they held the learning of their most eminent brethren, and of their own (consequent) conservatism. They operated within the limits set by their conservative regard for the need to maintain the paramountcy of the *halakha*, on the one hand, and of the accepted modifying principles whereby the local community was entitled to order its affairs in the light of its local needs and of its own understanding of what the maintenance of the essentials of tradition required, on the other. In the long run, there was thus little to circumscribe the discrete community as the ultimate and decisive repository of influence, if not power, over the individual Jew provided apostasy and heresy held no attractions for him. Only where the secular, non-Jewish sovereign specifically invested a particular rabbi or union of communal organizations with country-wide, supra-communal authority—as was the case most notably in the Ottoman Empire—was the local community's central role significantly diminished.

The authority of the rabbinate therefore cut across political boundaries and, to the extent that western Jews retained communal membership and loyalties, was in no sense a feature of East European life alone. So too with the second source of authority in Jewry, that of the lay plutocracy. As the prime day-to-day functions of the community were in ritual, philanthropy, and education, and activities in all three fields required funds, it was perhaps inevitable that those members of the community who could afford to support community activities would gravitate to positions of influence and power within it. And since the wealthy members of the community generally had a firm foothold in the general economy they tended to share with the rabbis the role of representatives of the community *vis-à-vis* emperor, king, prince, and lord. This function, in turn, enhanced their purely local and internal influence within the community itself. The growth of central and monopolistic political authority in the modern epoch in almost all of Europe and in much of the Near East greatly strengthened the hold of those Jewish leaders, lay and religious alike, who were fortunate enough—or, in not a few cases, unfortunate enough—to be selected by the ruler to act for him within the community. But as financial (or taxation) considerations came to the fore and, in the eighteenth century, the desire to extend direct governmental authority to the Jewish communities by means of special legislation (such as the Prussian *General-Judenreglement* of 1787) rather than permit continued Jewish communal autonomy in the medieval corporative manner began to take effect, the moral, judicial, and often quasi-political authority of the rabbi came to be increasingly irrelevant to state purposes. The more easily controlled, better understood, and more immediately exploitable economic and social resources of the wealthy began to be preferred and to form the key basis of communication between the Jewish community and the state. One incidental result of this development was the establishment of self-perpetuating, and not infrequently hereditary, oligarchies whose prestige and authority have in some cases survived down to our own times.

The Emancipation of western Jewry, by weakening the community, accelerated and facilitated the process by which wealth came to be the key both to leadership *among* the Jews and to the assumption, by general consent, of a representative function on their *behalf*—rather than, if never entirely supplanting, piety and learning. There were, of course, ample precedents in the past for the great prominence to which certain individuals now rose, as for the shadowy but much publicized political leverage which many of them acquired. Perhaps for this reason the advent of a new generation of quasi-emancipated Jewish financiers who walked with princes led many hundreds of thousands of Jews in both the West and the East to see them as the heaven-sent intermediaries who would in time deliver their less fortunate brethren from oppression and humiliation. In any event, the scope of their capacity for leadership and representation soon extended far beyond their initial base in Western and west-Central Europe. In parallel, the deep-rooted sense of common responsibility which had generally characterized intercommunal relations in the Exile continued to operate to some extent in the new context of the partial Emancipation. And in obedience to it, and out of a powerful sense of *noblesse oblige*, those members of the new plutocracy who did not move out of their communities altogether generally accepted the role of intermediaries with good grace. But, of course, not all in equal degree. Comparing the energy with which James de Rothschild (along with his brothers and such other notables as Sir Moses Montefiore and the non-plutocratic but influential Adolphe Crémieux) had come to the assistance of the Damascus Jews who had been wrongly charged with ritual murder of a Catholic priest in 1840 with the restraint displayed by another French Jewish banker and rival railway entrepreneur Benoît Fould, Heine wrote derisively (and somewhat unjustly):

> We must give the Chief Rabbi of the *Rive Droite* [Rothschild] the credit of having shown a nobler spirit in his sympathies for the House of Israel than his learned rival, the Chief Rabbi of the *Rive Gauche*, M. Benoît Fould, who, while his co-religionists were being tortured in Syria at the instigation of a French Consul, delivered some excellent speeches in the Chamber of Deputies on the subject of the conversion of Rentes and the bank rate, with the imperturbable calm of a Hillel.[13]

The capacity of the new rich to assume leadership of the Jews was nevertheless greater than their capacity to act effectively on their behalf. In matters of purely Jewish concern the influence of even the most eminent and fabulous of all—the Rothschilds—was very restricted. Not even the prospect of a vast and badly needed loan in 1850 could persuade Pope Pius IX to accede to the condition which Charles de Rothschild had attempted to place on it, namely an improvement in the condition of the Jews in the Papal States,[14] which was much the worst in Italy, and distinguished by comprising the most humiliating restrictions practised anywhere in Europe at the time. In Eastern Europe, where there were, in any case, proportionately fewer men of great wealth, the leverage which local bankers and entrepreneurs could exert on behalf of their fellow Jews hardly went beyond the ability to gain an audience with the authorities for purposes of intercession and muted protest. But the minor, local, notables within the Pale did retain their own peculiar role of intermediaries between the Russian provincial authorities and the mass of penurious, often pauperized, Yiddish-speaking Jews. These petty notables were the small merchants and successful tradesmen, estate agents and factors, millers, and the

---

[13] Quoted in Count Egon Corti, *The Reign of the House of Rothschild*, London, 1928, pp. 224-5. The reference to the Rive Droite and the Rive Gauche is to rival railway lines from Paris to Versailles, the former built by Émile Péreire (also a Jew) and sponsored by the Rothschilds, the latter built by Fould.

[14] Bertrand Gille, *Histoire de la maison Rothschild*, Geneva, 1965-7, ii, pp. 70-4.

like, of whom it could not be properly said that they constituted a plutocracy, but who were none the less distinguishable from the mass of Jewry by their having at least an adequate (in some cases substantial) income and were therefore natural and traditional occupants of the principal posts of honour and influence in the local community: the *tovim, parnasim,* and *gabba'im,* elders, wardens, and vestrymen.[15] Here possession of communal offices and influence was not only based upon the usual grounds—the fact that it was upon the comparatively prosperous that the upkeep of the essential community functions and functionaries depended —but also on the grounds that it was they alone who were in a position (and therefore required by immemorial tradition) to pay off whoever wielded local authority when he exacted his levy, tax, forced loan, bribe, or whatever other form the tribute took. Finally, it was to them the authorities turned, increasingly, as the scope and intensity of police control over the Jewish population of the Empire broadened after the accession of Nicholas I not only for fiscal purposes, but for the material execution of governmental decrees which the Russian central and provincial authorities were unwilling or unable to implement through their own regular machinery. The most notorious of these concerned conscription of Jews into the Tsar's armies. They were among the harshest of the overt measures directed against the Jewish population and in many ways reflected the self-contradictory nature of the Russian Government's long-term policy towards its Jewish subjects more clearly than any other. And because the minor Jewish notabilities of the Pale were involved, by design, as the instruments of their execution, they also sowed a degree of intracommunal distrust and incipient class conflict among Jews such as Eastern European Jewry had rarely, if ever, known before.

The provisions of the *ukase* on the recruitment of Jews (26 August 1827) and the brutalities which it inflicted on the Jewish subjects of Nicholas I have been abundantly described both in formal historical accounts and in contemporary literature.[16] Nominally,

---

[15] As a formal, legally recognized structure, the communal organization, the *kahal,* was abolished in Russia by government decree in 1844.

[16] See, for example, Saul M. Ginsburg, *Historishe Verk,* 2 vols., New York, 1937, especially ii, pp. 3–20. On the primitive and cruel treatment of cantonists and on forced conversions, see S. Beilin, 'Iz razskazov o kantonistakh', in S. M. Dubnov (ed.), *Evreiskaya Starina,* ii, St. Petersburg, 1909, pp. 115–20. The most detailed account in English is still that of Dubnov, op. cit. ii, pp. 13–45. See also Louis Greenberg, *The Jews in Russia,* New Haven,

it took the form of a measure to equalize the obligations of all subjects by extending military duty to the Jewish population of the Russian Pale and Poland. In fact, it imposed a greater burden on the Jews, qualitatively and relatively, than on any other ethnic, religious, or social group. Jewish recruits had to be provided at the rate of 10 per 1,000 Jewish inhabitants, instead of the common rate of 7 per 1,000. And the age group from which Jewish recruits were to be conscripted was lowered from the universal eighteen to *twelve*. The child and adolescent conscripts were placed in special preparatory establishments for military training where, from the first, they were subjected to a specific educational and disciplinary regime designed to impel them to accept the Christian faith—by main force, if necessary. Those who refused to conform were almost universally subjected to extremely cruel treatment at the hands of corporals and priests alike, treatment which comparatively few seem to have survived.[17] Those who succumbed were in any case seen as—and to all intents and purposes were—largely lost to Judaism, for the preliminary years spent as 'cantonists' did not count towards the twenty-five years of military service proper. And of that Tolstoy wrote, 'Conscription in those days was like death. A soldier was a severed branch, and to think about him at home was to tear one's heart uselessly.'[18] But in many ways the sharpest cut of all was the provision which laid the responsibility for supplying a full quota of Jewish recruits directly on the Jewish community itself. The Jews of each local community were thus held mutually responsible one for the other in much the same manner as they had been—for tax purposes, for example—under Polish rule and, indeed, in most of Europe during the Middle Ages and in modern times until the Emancipation in the West. Thus, on the one hand,

Conn., 1944, i, pp. 48–52. For a sympathetic account of the guiding ideological principles of Nicholas's rule see N. V. Riasanovsky, *Nicholas I and Official Nationality in Russia, 1825–1855*, Berkeley, Calif., 1967. A melodramatic, but bitter and convincing picture of recruitment figures in the memoirs of Yehuda Leib Levin ('Yehalel'), *Zikhronot ve-hegyonot*, Jerusalem, 1968, pp. 30–5; and another in Pereẓ Smolenskin's Hebrew novel *Ha-toʿe be-darkhei ha-ḥayyim*. Smolenskin's elder brother had been pressed into military service at the age of ten. Alexander Herzen recalls an encounter with such a convoy of Jewish child recruits ('these sick children, uncared for and uncomforted, exposed to the wind which blows straight from the Arctic sea, were marching to their graves') in *Byloe i Dumy*, Leningrad, 1946, p. 124.

[17] The law requiring the sanction of higher church authorities in cases of conversion of juveniles was secretly abrogated to expedite the work of the priests specially detailed for this activity. Greenberg, op. cit., p. 50. [18] *Hadji Murad*, vii.

the powers of the community establishment and the social autonomy and separateness of the community itself were much enhanced by the terms of the conscription *ukase*—in plain contradiction to the over-all policy of Russification and the institution of social and religious uniformity which the Tsar and his Ministers were pursuing with ferocious energy on all other accounts. And, on the other hand, the community and its leadership were forced into the vicious and self-destructive role of executors of a hateful decree—the more vicious and self-destructive by reason of the fact that the sons of many of the community notables were exempt from service under the general provisions of the recruitment law which tended to absolve the prosperous, Gentile and Jew alike, from its workings.[19] The generalized terror which the recruitment law instilled in Jewish parents led to an almost universal effort to evade it. The community administrators, under pain of fines, imprisonment, and, often, of the prospect of their own conscription, responded by hiring press-gangs to catch the recruits for presentation to the military authorities. Moreover, these *khappers* ('catchers' or 'snatchers'), as they came to be known, were all too often unscrupulous. Where the due number of adults was short, the proportion of adolescents in the draft went up, and where adolescents of twelve years and over were lacking, children of ten and even eight were snatched from their parents—usually the poorest and most defenceless members of the community—and herded into the recruiting centres. The fear and loathing of the Russian administration which the system soon inculcated in the minds of the ghetto masses were only surpassed by the resulting distrust of the lay leaders of the communities, as the bitter words of a popular lament of the period make clear:

> Treren gissen zich in di gassen
> In kindershe blut ken men zich washen.
> Kleine oifalach reisst men fun cheder
> Un men tut sei on yevonishe kleider.
> Bei Zussye dem choicher iz sieben bonim
> Un fun sei—nit einer in die yevonim,
> Nor Leah die almonehs einziges kind
> Iz a kapore fir kohlshe zind.[20]

[19] Dubnov, op. cit. ii, p. 29.

[20] Quoted in Eliahu Tcherikower, 'He-hamon ha-yehudi, ha-maskilim ve-ha-memshala b'imei Nikolai I', *Ẓion*, iv, 2, January 1939, p. 155. Literally translated: Tears are flowing in the streets, / One can bathe in children's blood, / Tiny children are torn away from

The popular response of the masses was therefore generally directed in the first instance towards the communal leaders and cases of resistance to their authority and of violent attempts to free the recruits from the press-gangs were not uncommon—although in the case of anything resembling insurrection the penalties visited on all concerned by the Russian authorities were extremely severe. Information about mutinous incidents was therefore generally suppressed by common consent. In the final analysis, the communal leaders—religious and lay alike—had to choose between bearing down pitilessly on their own people and their own martyrdom. This not unfamiliar Jewish dilemma continued to face them even under the relatively liberal rule of Alexander II (who abolished juvenile conscription upon his coronation in 1856). In one such case, when the community authorities in a town in the province of Mogilev failed to produce the requisite number of recruits they were penalized by the number to be conscripted being doubled. Despite a further chase after recruits by the press-gangs it proved impossible to fulfil the quota. The provincial government then bore down on the communal leaders, shackling them and sending them off to prison for a while and the town's rabbi—whom the government had appointed *sdatchik* (literally: deliverer-up), which is to say, communal officer responsible for the collection of taxes and the fulfilment of the conscription quota—was sent to penal military service.[21]

The rationale behind the recruitment of children into the Russian army was the need, as Nicholas I and his ministers saw it, to do all that could be done without offence to the principle that Russia was a *Rechtsstaat* to circumscribe, reduce in numbers, and, finally merge Russian Jewry with the socially and culturally undifferentiated, obedient, and pious mass of subjects which was the autocracy's social ideal. This entailed the separating off of 'useful' from 'useless' Jews, and 'useless' Jews from the good Russian people at large, the periodic constriction of the physical limits of the Pale, the prohibition of Jewish dress and so far as possible of other typical social customs, restrictions on the use of both Hebrew

school / And are dressed up in soldiers' uniforms. / Zussye the leaseholder has seven grown sons / And not one is in the army, / But Leah the widow's only child / Atones for the sins of the whole community.

[21] Recounted by a contemporary in *Evreiskaya Letopis'*, 1926, pp. 57–71. See Tcherikower, op. cit., pp. 158–9.

and of the Yiddish vernacular; and the establishment of a special network of state schools for the 'useful' where the supposedly harmful effects of traditional Talmudic education would be neutralized.

In 1841 Count S. S. Uvarov, Minister of Education (1833–49) and principal ideologist of the regime, conceived the idea of establishing a network of state-sponsored Jewish schools which would gradually wean the Jewish population away from 'the prejudices fostered in them by the study of the Talmud', bring their education as firmly under compulsory central supervision from St. Petersburg as that of the rest of the population, and, ultimately, draw them to Christianity. The project was slow to get under way (the first schools were not set up until 1848) and its population was never more than a small fraction of the population of the traditional *hadarim*—to which Jewish parents universally sent their children, even those who later went on to state schools—and the *yeshivot* (talmudical academies). These Jewish Crown schools were naturally regarded with great suspicion and relied for much of their population on the fact that they were at least an alternative to the barracks. When juvenile conscription was abrogated they lost that advantage too. There was never any question of the literacy of the Jews in Hebrew and Yiddish. But, broadly, those who desired modern secular studies for themselves and for their children preferred to acquire it in the regular network of Russian state schools and universities (which the same Uvarov had done much to put on a sound organizational and scholastic basis), the pressure to enter which steadily rose in the course of the century.

In 1873 the project was wound up and in time it was forgotten. In contrast, the conscription measures burned deep into the social and political consciousness of the otherwise pacific and fatalistic Jews of the Empire and probably did more than anything else to alert them to the fragility of their condition. For more directly than the economic misery to which vast numbers of Russian Jews began to be subjected in this period, and more blatantly than the continual petty persecution which was the common lot of the individual Jew at the hands of the authorities, the military system imposed on the Jews was a deliberate attack on their national, religious, and cultural integrity. The secret position paper on Jewish conscription prepared in the Third (State Security) Department of the Imperial Chancery shortly before the August 1827 *ukase* was issued was plainly entitled: 'Memorandum on turning the Jews to the advantage of the Empire by gradually drawing them to profess the Christian faith, bringing them closer to, and, ultimately, completely fusing them with, the other subjects [of the Emperor].'[22]

In the long term, the reaction of Russian and Polish Jews to the systematized pressures instituted against them under Nicholas I— and kept up, in the main, under his successors—depended, in the first instance, on the degree to which they were content to perpetuate the traditional social and cultural modes. Overwhelmingly, they were; and their hatred of the cantonist system and the resounding lack of response to Uvarov's scheme for a network of Jewish Crown schools fully reflected popular attachment to the ancient, inward-looking, self-contained tradition—to say nothing of the almost universal opposition of religious and lay leaders alike. But for the steadily growing *minority* composed of those who were becoming restless under the old religious and social restraints and the rigorously defined and carefully maintained delimitation of the field of acceptable intellectual activity, the autocracy's attempt to force the Jews into new moulds by means of the stick of military conscription and the carrot of secular education was not wholly unwelcome. Their eyes set on the world of new ideas and new modes of social life which had opened up for their brethren in the West, as opposed to what they judged to be the perverse immobilism and obscurantism that pervaded Jewish life in the East, they tended to be impatient with the traditionalists and to discount warnings of the implied threat to national and, of course, religious integrity. At their most naïve they remained blind to the brutalities for which the reign of Nicholas I was remarkable in the sphere of Jewish affairs, as in so many others, to the extent of arguing that the Tsar's interest, and that of his ministers, in the re-education of the Jews was entirely benevolent. At their most fanatical they were capable of allying themselves with the government in a common campaign to fetter the dissemination of hasidic (and to a lesser extent classic Talmudic) literature by providing information which led to the closing down of illegal printing-presses, for example.[23]

Small wonder, then, that upon the death of Nicholas and the advent of the Tsar 'Liberator' Alexander II the remaining doubts of the modernists were swept away. One minor, but representative literary figure of the Pale was moved to write:

[22] Ginsburg, op. cit. ii, p. 7.    [23] Tcherikower, op. cit., pp. 162–5.

> Awake, Israel, and Judah, arise!
> Shake off the dust, open wide thine eyes!
> Justice sprouteth, righteousness is here,
> Thy sin is forgot, thou hast naught to fear.[24]

Reporting to the Board of Deputies of British Jews in 1872 on 'the improved spiritual and social condition of our co-religionists', even the aged Sir Moses Montefiore, who knew more about the position in Eastern Europe and in the Islamic world than any other western Jewish magnate, was impressed. 'They have now indeed abundant reason to cherish grateful feelings towards the Emperor, to whom their prosperity is in so great a measure attributable; and if there remain some few restrictions, the hope may surely be entertained, that, with the advance of secular education among them, those disabilities may be gradually removed.'[25]

The modernist movement among Jews—the *haskala* (enlightenment) as it is generally known—was almost devoid of men capable of thinking in systematic political and economic categories. It was essentially literary in character and expression and, in the broadest sense of the term, philosophical. It had no comprehensive organization, no central publication or publishing house. It was composed of local groups, for the most part—circles of literati that first appeared more or less openly in the cities on the fringes of the Pale, in Riga, Odessa, Kishinev, then more surreptitiously in the heart of the Jewish world, in Vilna, Minsk, Berdychev. The ideas current among, and promoted by, its adherents were rarely formulated with consistency and were often mutually exclusive. Strictly, it was less a movement than a *tendency*, an attitude broadly characteristic of the emerging Jewish intelligentsia whose one irreducible and common ideological denominator was a compound of dissatisfaction with the condition of their people and a generalized belief in the necessity and the possibility of change through the establishment of a cultural *modus vivendi* between Jewry and the world around it. If an original father figure and path-finder for the *maskilim* is to be named, he must be Moses Mendelssohn. Certainly, it was the dramatic transformation of Jewish life in Western Europe that was taken as proof of what could be achieved and as the guiding paradigm for progress in the East. The initial welcome many *maskilim* gave

---

[24] A. B. Gottlober (1811–99). English translation by Jacob S. Raisin in his *The Haskalah Movement in Russia*, Philadelphia, Pa., 1913, p. 231.

[25] Quoted in Lucien Wolf, *Sir Moses Montefiore*, New York, 1885, p. 218.

Uvarov's project for Jewish Crown schools carried an unmistakable echo of Wessely's greeting the opening of the Austrian state school system to Jews under the terms of the 1782 *Toleranzpatent* as evidence of Joseph II's humanity and desire to bring joy to his people.[26]

For content too it was to the West the *maskilim* looked, and first and foremost to Germany.[27] For in practice modernization meant secularism, and it was therefore to the great Western centres of secular learning and of fresh political, social, and historiosophical ideas that they turned—initially because they were, quite simply, located in the West, notably in Germany, but later because, while the number and level of indigenous universities and other focuses of activity in the arts and sciences in Russia itself rose, they were closed to all but a diminishing fraction of Jews who wished to enter them.

The *haskala* marks the transition of eastern Jewry from a people remarkable for their social and ideological uniformity (for all its occasional ferocity, the conflict between *ḥasidim* and *mitnagdim* never touched on the essentials of religious observance and principle, still less on the unique character of the Jewish people or the primacy of religious over secular affairs) to one comprising a great variety of tendencies, many of which were (and remain) mutually incompatible. For while the *maskilim* were for the most part united, implicitly, in their desire to break with tradition and greatly to reduce, or even totally jettison, the long-accumulating weight of ascriptive (or group) values in Jewish life, they were profoundly divided on the content and proper locus of the new grafts of secularism and liberalism that were to be made on Jewish society.

Thus logically, the *haskala* embodied a demand for a degree of Russification. For some this meant not much more than the adoption of the Russian language for essentially instrumental purposes as a parallel vehicle of communication and expression, an essential bridge to the rest of the Tsar's subjects and beyond them to the world outside. But for others it came to mean a great deal more:

---

[26] N. H. Wessely (1725–1805) was Mendelssohn's disciple and collaborator on the translation of the Pentateuch into German.

[27] And increasingly for social practices, house furnishings, and clothes, no less than for professional and speculative learning. S. M. Ginsburg gives an account of an early adept of the *haskala* in the traditionalist community of Minsk who kept 'German' clothes in a suitcase for his journeys to the much more liberal Riga and Odessa, changing back into acceptable dress upon his return. 'Hundert yohr familien-geshichte', op. cit., p. 37.

total merger with, and assimilation into, the Russian people whose pains and quandaries would thenceforward become theirs, while their own ancient and specifically Jewish agonies were sloughed off in the process. In practice the move to Russify the Jews thus led either to an unspoken alliance with the Russian authorities themselves—for there the *maskilim*'s desire to encourage the acquisition of general, secular culture appeared to meet the authorities' wish to propagate it—or else to active participation in the revolutionary movements of the day. O. V. Aptekman, an early Jewish recruit to the 'going to the people' of the early 1870s, went so far as to resolve on baptism as a preliminary to the plunge because he saw the step, not without relish, both as a striking break with the past and as a measure ensuring that, 'literally renewed', he would thereby be 'drawn near the peasants among whom I was to live'. For him, as for his fellow populists, 'everything has been decided. Everything is as clear as day.'[28]

In the event, the simple Russifiers of the first sort, those who attempted to advance within the existing social and political framework, were to be left exposed and isolated in the wake of the great tide of misery to which the mass of Russian and Polish Jews were subjected by the autocracy in the last quarter of the century.[29] Those of the second kind were never very numerous. Few Jews could feel comfortable in social movements whose specifically *Russian* populist character was greatly stressed—and whose markedly anti-Semitic character soon came to the fore, as will be seen. But with the shift of emphasis among the revolutionaries to political, as opposed to social, action and later to the application to the Russian case of political ideas and revolutionary techniques founded on a general, purportedly universally valid analysis of society in which Russian, Polish, and Jewish problems could all, it seemed, be subsumed, Jews who did wish for a break could at last find a congenial home.

However, a radical break with tradition was, in any case, never a practical proposition for more than that fraction of Russian and

[28] Quoted in Franco Venturi, *Roots of Revolution*, New York, 1966, pp. 503-4.

[29] The prototype expression of the politically passive Russification tendency was the Society for the Diffusion of Enlightenment among the Jews founded in 1867 by a group of privileged Jews resident in St. Petersburg. Their intention was defined by one of their founders as that of eradicating Jewish 'separatism and fanaticism . . . and aloofness from everything Russian' with a view to becoming 'full-fledged citizens of this country'. Quoted in Dubnov, op. cit. ii, p. 214.

Polish Jews who were so placed geographically and economically and so equipped educationally and linguistically that the choice was theirs to make. Unlike the Jews of Western Europe, the great majority of Russo-Polish Jews lived in compact, generally self-contained communities. Moreover, they were fully at home in the Hebrew-Yiddish culture of the Pale and literate in their own languages far beyond the standards obtaining in the non-Jewish population. As late as the end of the nineteenth century Yiddish was the mother-tongue of 98 per cent of the Jews of the Pale and, by one contemporary estimate, there were still six children in the traditional *ḥadarim* for every Jewish child in a Russian-language school.[30] On either count, the notion of pulling free of the embrace of the classic, tightly knit community, and of working both an internal social revolution and a profound change in the relations between Jews and non-Jews by acquisition of the language of the country and reading 'books which explain how people in this land live' (as a character in a contemporary Hebrew novel put it),[31] was therefore little more than a vision. Moreover, it was a vision which many disliked: the orthodox because it implied the negation of all they believed in and stood for, and many of the *maskilim* too because they could not bring themselves to turn their backs upon a cultural past which had been preserved for them by the very instruments which the ultra-secularists were intent on cutting down or doing away with altogether—the Jews' great accumulation of intermingled secular and religious learning, their liturgy and literature, and above all their language. 'The *Tora*, bequeathed to us by our ancestors, is the elixir which quickens our spirit', are the words the *maskil* Pereẓ Smolenskin (1842–85) puts approvingly in the mouth of the traditionalist Gabriel in his novel *Gemul yesharim*.

Only by virtue of the *Tora* are we fully alive, and were we to allow ourselves to be robbed of it, we might just as well be dead. For then our life would perish and our memory would fade; for we would then be responsible for the deaths not merely of ourselves, but of hundreds of generations, of four thousand years of our existence. At one stroke we would erase ourselves from the pages of history, as though we had never been. And it is for that that we fight with our heart's blood and consider

[30] Cf. Yehuda Slutsky, 'Ẓemiḥata shel ha-inteligenẓia ha-yehudit-rusit', *Ẓion*, xxv. 3–4, 1960, pp. 212–13.
[31] Samuel in R. A. Braudes, *Ha-dat ve-ha-ḥayyim*, Lemberg, 1885, p. 43. Cf. David Patterson, *The Hebrew Novel in Czarist Russia*, Edinburgh, 1964, pp. 160–2.

no sacrifice too dear. We are prepared to offer ourselves and our children completely on the altar of that love, the love of our ancestral faith, the *Tora* of our fathers and their memory.[32]

Assimilation was therefore suicidal and unthinkable, a betrayal. There was much to criticize in Jewish life (Smolenskin's novels are packed with Dickensian descriptions of intracommunal intrigue, hypocrisy, and dark doings), but the process of renovation, he believed, must be internal and based on the premiss that the Jews are members of a nation, albeit older than other nations, different from other nations, bound by a common faith and sentiment, rather than by a land, a *spiritual* nation, but none the less fully a nation because it so regards itself and because it has maintained its unity in its special way. Indeed, even when there was a land to bind the Jews one to another it was things of the spirit which took precedence over mundane considerations and calculations of personal, political, and material interest. It was the *Tora* and the Hebrew language which made the Jews the people they were and which still make them a people, if today only a people in the spiritual sense—for in the everyday affairs of life the Jews were like all other men.[33] The *Tora* and the Hebrew languages are the land of the Jews.

Smolenskin's attempt to redefine the Jewish identity in terms that precluded any tendency towards assimilation as a matter, first and foremost, of elemental ethics and decency—namely that assimilation would constitute a betrayal—rather than on the practical grounds that it could not possibly work for more than a fraction of the Jews, if for any, thus encapsulated a programme. Jews could and should be both backward- and forward-looking, both loyal to their past and concerned with the present and the future, both part of a private world of their own and simultaneously, and no less sincerely and effectively, part of the general world of men and affairs around them. It was a conception of the condition of the Jews and of the possibilities open to them which did not differ materially from that of Mendelssohn and his followers. It was mild, liberal, ingenious in its notion of how the dilemmas of Jewish particularism could be resolved, and above all optimistic. Not all *maskilim* shared Smolenskin's attachment to the tradition

<hr />

[32] Translation in Patterson, op. cit., p. 164.

[33] Cf. ''Et lata'at', *Ma'amarim*, Jerusalem, 1925, ii, pp. 8–24. Smolenskin was to alter his conception of Jewish nationality and of the role of Erez-Israel after 1881.

and his tendency to apologize for its institutionalized upholders, but his view that deliberately to assimilate was to submit to a process shot through and through with indignity and intellectual dishonesty was common enough; and all shared his sanguine view of Jewry's evolution in the West and of the prospects for an analogous evolution in the East. The terrible reign of Nicholas I was over. The new reign had begun well, even for the Jews. All was in movement. It only remained for the Jews to seize the opportunity: for if *they* did not desire change there would certainly be none. And since they had not far to look to see that they themselves were a small minority within an increasingly restless but still predominantly conservative mass, the optimism of the *maskilim* was heavily tinged with irritation and a sense of urgency.

'Awake, my people' was the title of a poem by Yehuda Leib Gordon (1830–92), who on purely literary grounds must probably be rated the greatest *maskil* of all. 'This land of Eden is now open to you, / Her sons now call you "brothers" . . . / Why do you keep apart from them? . . .'

Gordon's views derived from an unstable and unhappy mixture of aggressive and straightforward criticism of rabbinic Judaism, strong secularism, an extraordinary capacity for self-delusion in respect of the nature and tendencies of the Russian autocracy, and the highest possible regard for the matter and language of the national culture. He was the finest Hebrew poet of his day and towards the end of his life was beset by overwhelming fears that his was a vanishing craft and a dying cause. 'Awake, my people' (*Hakiza ʿami*), written in 1863, neatly epitomized the fundamental unreality and *naïveté* underlying the hope of reconciling nineteenth-century Russia with a Jewry still possessed of, and loyal to, a great part of its heritage and peculiarity.

# 3

## *1881*

i

IN the panic that followed the assassination of Alexander II
(1 March 1881, O.S.), the late Tsar's Minister of Interior, Loris-
Melikov, was dismissed and his plans to move a little further along
the course of reluctant, cautious, and very gradual liberal reform
that had, on the whole, characterized Alexander II's reign were
entirely abandoned. The character of the new reign was typified
by the informal (but very real) installation of the new Tsar's
former tutor, Konstantin Pobedonostsev, now *Ober-Prokuror* of
the Holy Synod of the Russian Orthodox Church and, in effect,
its controller on behalf of the state, as principal ideologue of the
regime. Tsar and mentor were both men of high principles and of
a bigoted and distinctly brutal cast of mind; and they shared the
view that the state must follow the 'true, straight path' of no concessions to liberalism whatsoever. Within a matter of weeks the
Empire was finally set upon that disastrous path of maximum
resistance to change and the enforced maintenance of Russia's
traditional social and political framework in which it persisted to
the end—all in the parade-ground spirit that had characterized the
reign of Nicholas I, rather than that of the somewhat milder and
marginally more benevolent one that had just ended.

The year 1881 was also a year in which the long-term social
effects of the mismanaged emancipation of the serfs, famine, and
agricultural and industrial unemployment and under-employment
had all combined to swell the growing 'barefoot army' (*bosaya
komanda*) of pauperized peasants and urban *lumpenproletariat*,
particularly in southern Russia. These last were rightly seen by
the regime as a considerable focus of social and political tension,
as a major cause of the rising incidence of crime, and as a reservoir
of misery from which a *jacquerie* might just possibly evolve. But

C

confidence in the police and the other arms of the security system having been undermined by the failure to protect the Tsar from assassination, many of the notables of the regime were of the view that it was of the highest importance to channel the explosive energy latent in the barely controllable mass of restless and impoverished peasantry away from themselves.

At the same time, the view of the peasantry taken in high places —a view greatly strengthened under the influence of Pobedonostsev —did not turn simply on concern for the internal security of the Empire. Fear of the peasantry was increasingly combined with a tendency to view them, the *narod*, the quintessential people, in highly sentimental, Slavophil terms which were similar in many respects to those in which the revolutionary populists too saw them. To Pobedonostsev it was clear that it was among the peasants that the heart and soul of Russia, the real Russia, lay, not in 'unpleasant' Petersburg inhabited by 'people with no activity, with no clear thought or firm decision, occupied with the petty interests of their "I", submerged in intrigues to advance their own petty ambitions, their greed for money, their pleasures and idle chatter'. Accordingly, the autocracy should look elsewhere for its true partner. It was on the mystical, yet at the same time simple and heartfelt tie uniting the autocrat and his peasant subjects of *inner* Russia, of the country, of 'the isolated places' where 'the spring is still salubrious and breathes freshness', where there 'live people with Russian souls, doing good work in faith and in hope', that it ought, ultimately, to rely and place its hope for the future.[1] It followed, in practice, that any political, social, or economic grouping that tended to come between the autocracy and its common subjects, or to harm the latter, or simply to be in a state of conflict with them, was liable to be regarded with hostility, was automatically a candidate for repression, and was exposed not merely to persecution at the hands of the authorities on the material plane, but to moral obloquy and hatred.

Moreover, unless there were good reasons, on other grounds, to protect a social class or category whose interests conflicted—or appeared to conflict—with those of the peasants, there seemed to be obvious advantages in encouraging, or, at the very least, tolerating an onslaught by the peasants on these their real, or supposed, enemies in the hope of it serving as a catharsis. The peasants' basic

---

[1] Quoted in R. F. Byrnes, *Pobedonostsev*, Bloomington, Ind., 1968, pp. 154-5.

antagonist, the landlord, was seen, with justice, as a central pillar of the regime itself. But the case of the Jew was different.

The Jews of Russia were admirably suited to the role of institutionalized object of peasant hostility. They were loathed not only by the peasants, with whom their relations were mostly on the basis of the Jews' function in the economy at large as petty traders, middlemen, innkeepers, estate agents, and money-lenders, but loathed overwhelmingly by the men of position in Russia—the bureaucrats, the military, the men of the Church, the Slavophil intellectuals who supported the regime, and by the Tsar himself. Here again the populists, by and large, were at one with *their* enemies. Ignorance of the realities of Jewish life, of the divisions within Jewish society, and of the precise nature of the religious, cultural, and intellectual tradition of the Jews was no more an obstacle to the formation of judgement by the literate of Russia, than by the illiterate. Thus in an age of striking social change and of revolutionary agitation there were added to the ancient hatred founded on the Christian Gospels and the teaching of the Church two partly contradictory contemporary beliefs.

On the one hand, the Jews, in Bakunin's terms, were 'by force of tradition and instinct . . . a restless, quarrelsome, scheming, exploiting, and bourgeois nation'.[2] On the other hand, they were the primary bearers of revolutionary infection, the source of all that was vicious in modern capitalism, and possessed of incalculable and mysterious social powers into the bargain.

> They have engrossed everything [wrote Pobedonostsev], they have undermined everything, but the spirit of the century supports them. They are at the root of the revolutionary socialist movement and of regicide, they own the periodical press, they have in their hands the financial markets, the people as a whole fall into financial slavery to them; they even control the principles of contemporary science and strive to place it outside Christianity.[3]

ii

The first massive pogrom hit the Jews of Elizavetgrad (now Kirovo) at Eastertime, 15 April 1881 (O.S.). From then, until the early

[2] To Albert Richard, 1 April 1870. Edmund Silberner, *Ha-sozializm ha-ma'aravi u-she'elat ha-yehudim*, Jerusalem, 1955, pp. 291–2.

[3] To Dostoyevsky, 14 August 1879. Byrnes, op. cit., p. 205.

summer of 1884, one by one the major Jewish communities and a host of minor population centres in the Ukraine, in White Russia, in parts of Bessarabia, and in the city of Warsaw[4] were visited by great mobs of peasants and petty criminals who attacked the Jews both in their person and their property on a scale which had had no modern precedent. By the end of 1881 alone, pogroms had been visited upon 215 Jewish communities in southern and south-western Russia, and a contemporary estimate then put the numbers of homeless at 20,000, those ruined economically and without means of livelihood at 100,000, and the value of the property destroyed at $80 million.[5] It is true that by the standards of our own times the casualties were not heavy: rarely more than a few dead even in the worst cases, the number of injured hardly ever greater than two figures—and then, as often as not, as a consequence of the incendiary fires, rather than of direct attack upon the person. Apart from the unfortunates who were physically attacked and the miserable women who were raped, it was, in fact, the vast scale of pillage and the resultant economic ruin which struck both the Jews and outside observers most forcibly. The Jewish quarters in hundreds of towns were simply being put to sack. In Minsk fully a fifth of the city was burned down: 1,600 buildings. In the small town of Korets, in Volhynia, 1,000 buildings were set alight (and the dead numbered 39). Nevertheless, by European standards of the last quarter of the nineteenth century, as reflected in contemporary press accounts, the physical brutality was striking enough.

The pogroms generally unfolded according to a common pattern, well exemplified in the *Le Temps* (Paris) report of the particularly bloody one which took place in the south Russian town of Balta at Passover, April 1882.

On the tenth, at three o'clock in the afternoon, the riot began; the Jewish inhabitants . . . prepared to defend themselves; whereupon the municipal authorities had them dispersed by troops who beat them with rifle-butts. On the eleventh, at eight o'clock in the morning, 600 peasants from the surrounding country recommenced the attack and maintained it without further obstacle. It was a scene of pillage, murder, arson, and

---

[4] No other Jewish community in Poland proper was touched, nor were there real pogroms in Lithuania.

[5] Eliahu Tcherikower (ed.), *Geschichte fun der Yiddishe Arbeter-Bavegung in di Farainikte Shtaten*, New York, 1943–5, i, p. 19.

rape to make one tremble with horror; 700 Jews were injured, 40 seriously, 3 were killed [the figures were later corrected: 211 injured of whom 39 seriously, 9 killed]; girls were raped; all houses inhabited by Jews, with 16 exceptions, were demolished [later corrected: 976 houses, 253 shops, and 34 public houses]; all household furniture was broken or burned; everything destroyed. The Jews are dying of hunger. Only on 12 April did the Governor, Miloradovitch, come from Kamenets to re-establish order; 200 rioters were arrested and punished by court-martial with imprisonment for from seven days to three months.[6]

The reaction of western Christendom, in Austria, in Britain, in Germany, and in the United States, was for once identical with that of western Jewry—which the Alliance Israélite Universelle in Paris expressed with its customary formalism and accuracy when it informed its members that 'for several months Europe has been witnessing a heart-rending spectacle. All the horrors of a time of barbarism that one would have thought gone for ever have been renewed.'[7] What the Victorians, Jews and Gentiles alike, found most shocking, however, was the conjunction of public atrocities and official complicity in varying degrees. The Russians were compared with the Turks and the Jews with the Bulgarians. The Russians, Cardinal Manning told a great public meeting at the Mansion House in London in February 1882, ought to be grateful for the service they were being rendered by the details of the horrors being brought to their attention.

I ask your Lordship, if there were to appear in the newspapers of the continent long and minute narratives of murder, rapine, and other atrocities round about the Egyptian Hall, in Old Jewry, in Houndsditch, in Shoreditch—if it were alleged that the Lord Mayor was looking on, that the Metropolitan police did nothing, that the guards at the Tower were seen to mingle with the mob—I believe you would thank any man who gave you an opportunity of exposing and contradicting such statements.[8]

There was, in fact, no question that at the provincial and local level the pogroms had been facilitated and even encouraged in a multitude of cases, that the intervention of the police and the

---

[6] *Le Temps*, 21 April and 13 May 1882. The Russian telegraph service refused to transmit the dispatch and it was then sent, after delay, from Austrian territory. See also *The Times*, 11 and 13 January 1882.

[7] Alliance Israélite Universelle, *Bulletin Mensuel*, August–September 1881, p. 131.

[8] Anglo-Jewish Association, *Outrages Upon the Jews in Russia, Report of the Public Meeting at the Mansion House*, London [reprinted], April 1933, p. 16.

Cossacks was very often deliberately delayed until the danger of the mob getting totally out of hand had risen too high for tolerance, that punitive action—even arrest and judgement for the common-law offences of murder, rape, arson, and theft—was sporadic and mild in almost every locality, and that where, as was the case in Lithuania, the provincial governor was not prepared to countenance any disruption of the public order, if only on general principle, there none took place or was promptly stamped out.[9] But the question whether the great wave of violence of 1881–4 had been deliberately instigated and orchestrated at the direct behest of the government in St. Petersburg—as opposed to merely being regarded with complaisance and a measure of smug approval—is less easily answered.

At first glance, the popular fury vented on the Jews—in which social and religious hatred was inextricably mixed with an equally, if not more powerful desire for plunder—points elsewhere, as does the plain absence (thus far) of any documentary evidence linking the central government to the *organization* of the pogroms. Further-more, as has been indicated, there was no uniformity of conduct across Russia, even within those towns in the Pale of Settlement which were most heavily populated with Jews. Again, while the punishment of the *pogromshchiki* under the criminal law was generally light as compared with the punishment normally inflicted on peasants (or others) involved in public disorder, let alone mass violence, it remains that some exemplary punishment was inflicted in very nearly every case. In Odessa—the one Russian city in which a pogrom had already taken place in comparatively recent times (1871)—1,385 arrests were made and a tenth of that number of accused was actually made to stand trial. And even in Kiev there were both arrests (about a thousand) and convictions. Many of the convicted were flogged. Many were exiled to Siberia. But contrary to precedent, there were death sentences in only one case, and that was towards the end of the wave when the toleration of the central authorities had waned. In the contemporary view (of both the Russian public and of foreign diplomatic observers) the penalties inflicted were extremely light. But penalties there were. Finally, it is clear from official documents that, while the central authorities (and the Tsar himself) either approved of the pogroms or sympa-

---

[9] In contradistinction, where the provincial governor approved of the pogroms, as in Kiev, the results were particularly hard.

thized with the *pogromshchiki*, their occurrence had been unexpected in the highest places and the need was felt, albeit after the event, to set up committees of investigation to inquire into what had actually transpired.

On the other hand, there were the facts that numerous pogroms had erupted over a very large area of Russia almost simultaneously, that the peasants' belief (attested to by the emissaries of the government itself) that the Tsar had ordered them to strike at the Jews was an extremely stubborn one, and was common throughout the country, that the *pattern* of attack was a well-nigh identical one in almost every case, that certain newspapers—which were, of course, subject to official censorship—had begun to whip up anti-Semitic feeling before the event and assert that responsibility for the bad times and for the assassination of the Tsar[10] should be laid with the Jews, and, lastly, that there were great numbers of handbills and posters in evidence, all calling for an attack on the Jews, mostly primitive and handwritten, but others lithographed, and thus betokening *organization*.[11] So while there is no proof that the government *as such* did instigate and co-ordinate the pogroms and while, on the contrary, there is abundant evidence that the principal officers of the state were divided in their approach and that the government, in so far as it may be considered collectively, was ambivalent and divided in its view and in its policy, there are a great many indicators suggesting that some consciously counter-revolutionary organization, enjoying, at the very least, access to, and the sympathy of, a great many highly placed persons, played a key role in the events of 1881–4.

It is very probable that the body which decided to exploit the peasant unrest and channel it against the Jews at this moment of crisis and fear for the security and future of the autocratic system was the *Sviashchennaya Druzhina*[12] ('Sacred Band of Warriors') founded immediately after the assassination of Alexander II. It was composed mostly of senior officials of the regime and devoted to the proposition that the forces of revolution had to be fought with their own lack of scruple and with comparable methods and instruments of conspiracy and violence. The assassination had convinced them that the overt and official apparatus of repression

---

[10] One of the members of the conspiracy to kill Alexander II was a Jewess, Hesia Helfman.
[11] Eliahu Tcherikower, *Yehudim be-'itot mahpekha*, Tel Aviv, 1957, p. 355.
[12] Cf. ibid., pp. 341–65.

had failed and that it was necessary to embark upon a secret crusade against the enemies of the established order by other means. The employment of 'other means' led them, however, into conflict with the ultimately more powerful school that refused to countenance lawlessness by officials of the State. A period of uncertainty ensued. Ignatiev, the new Minister of Interior, who had been appointed in the place of Loris-Melikov at Pobedonostsev's suggestion, was a member of the 'Band' while Pobedonostsev himself was not, but firmly a man of law and order.

In due course Ignatiev left the group and Ignatiev's own replacement, Count D. Tolstoy, ordered its disbandment (26 November 1882). After a period, it sank out of sight.

In the long term, the question of responsibility for the pogroms was of less weight than that of the attitude of the educated Russian public at the time and of the Russian authorities after the event. Of the former it was plain that, regardless of whether the autocracy was supported or fought, sympathies, such as there were, lay with the perpetrators, rather than the victims, almost without exception. In this respect the surge of simple anti-Semitism that had occurred at the time of the war with Turkey three years previously was maintained. In the case of the populist revolutionaries feelings were joined to calculation. The Jews were a fit object of peasant violence; and once precipitated, violence, they believed, could be channelled into other directions as well if only the peasants were convinced that behind the Jews was the autocracy itself. A handbill issued by *Narodnaya Volya* on 30 August 1881 (well after the first wave of pogroms had passed) congratulated the 'Good people, honest people of the Ukraine' for rising against the Jews—consistently labelled *Zhydy* or 'Yids'—on just those grounds: the alliance between the three forces of oppression, Tsar, landowning nobility, and Jews. But the appeal was mainly to hatred.

Above all, the people of the Ukraine suffer from the Yids. Who seized the lands, the forests, and the public houses? The Yids. Before whom does the *muzhik* supplicate, sometimes in tears, to be allowed to get to his plot of land, the legacy of his fathers? Before the Yids. Wherever you look, wherever you turn—there are the Yids. The Yid insults man, deceives him, drinks his blood. Life in the villages has become impossible because of the Yid.[13]

[13] Ma'or, 'Ha-keruz ha-antishemi shel "Narodnaya Volya"', *Zion*, xv, 1950, pp. 150-5.

There were other currents of thought among opponents of the regime, notably Kropotkin and Lavrov. But they did not suffice to soften the blow to those Jews who had seen the revolutionaries as their natural allies.

So far as the general approach of the Russian government towards the Jews was concerned, it was soon evident that policy, both at the material level of its concrete dealings with them and at what might be termed the abstract or philosophical level of its approach to the Jewish Question as a whole, was now in process of being reformulated in much harsher terms than had ever been conceived and pronounced upon in Russia since the first partition of Poland. And it was perhaps this intensification and consolidation of the overtly anti-Semitic character of Russian policy on the Jews and the particular terms in which it was to be publicly rationalized and proclaimed, rather than the material brutalities inflicted by the Russian mob, that at first bewildered the Jews, and then horrified them, and finally caused vast numbers of them actively to seek a decisive remedy. What might just conceivably have been shrugged off, in time, as yet another instalment in the extended tragedy of the Exile (the *maskilim* characteristically fell into the habit of calling the three-years-long wave of pogroms by the euphemistic tag *sufot ba-negev*—'the southern storms'), with faces set with traditional patience towards a more hopeful future, could not be so easily stomached when the considered reaction of the government in St. Petersburg, in the event, was to make abundantly clear where its real sympathies lay and how it proposed to deal with the Jews in the future. At all events, the question whether the condition of the Jews of the Russian Empire could or could not be stomached, and what practical conclusions ought to be drawn by them if it could not be, was now to become the greatest of all issues on which Jewry —particularly, but not exclusively, that of Eastern Europe—was to be divided.

The first considered reaction of the central government was defined in a circular addressed to the provincial governors of the Pale in August 1881. It restated the long-standing desire and efforts of the government to assimilate the Jews into the rest of the population in view of the fact that 'the consequences of the Jews' economic activity, their national isolation, and their religious fanaticism were harmful to the Christian population'. It claimed that to encourage their assimilation the Jews had 'been accorded very nearly the same rights as the indigenous population'. It argued that, unfortunately, the 'anti-Jewish agitation' in the spring had shown 'irrefutably' that, despite the efforts and goodwill of the government, the 'abnormal relations between the Jewish race and the rest of the population were continuing as before'. So while the government, for its part, had most energetically stamped out 'excesses and arbitrary acts' against the Jews, it saw the central problem for the future as one of how to put an end to the abnormality in the relations between Jew and non-Jew and how to protect the latter from the 'evil' activities of the former. The governors were therefore instructed to set up committees of inquiry to collect data on the functioning of the anti-Jewish laws and the economic activities of the Jews and to submit proposals in the spirit of the instructions themselves.[14]

In May of the following year a series of 'Temporary Edicts' (later known as the May Laws), principally designed to harden and broaden existing special legislation limiting the Jews' right to lease and own land and reside in the country, outside the towns of the Pale, was issued. In the stated interests of reducing the incidence of drunkenness among the Russian lower classes, an additional decree issued in December severely restricted the Jews' right to retail alcoholic liquors—one of their main occupations. These measures were never rigorously implemented. Had they been, the social results would have been disastrous. One contemporary source estimated that some 300,000 families, at least one million persons, would have been reduced to pauperdom[15]—probably an exaggeration, but a fair indicator of the psychological impact of the decrees. In any event, it was clear that conditions were going to be harder both for those Jews who managed to remain in the country villages and for those crowded into the towns of the Pale of Settlement and that, more than ever, they would be at the mercy of every petty and corrupt official in the country. Some of the other regulations issued in 1882 were insulting, rather than damaging. For example: Jews were no longer to be recruited for service in the navy. A year later, with some solemnity and, ostensibly, in a more benevolent frame of mind, a State Commission for the Revision of the Current Laws concerning the Jews (the Pahlen Commission) was set up (February 1883). Five years later it

---

[14] Alliance Israélite Universelle, *Bulletin Mensuel*, August–September 1881, pp. 137–9.
[15] *Frankfurter Zeitung*, 18 March 1882.

issued a massive report in which the majority recommendation was gradually to replace the repressive legislation imposed upon the Jews by measures leading to the equalization of their status with that of other subjects.[16] But it was the minority view which favoured still more severe restrictions which, in the event, was adopted by the government. All in all, there was ample confirmation that the government of Russia was now determined to deal with what Pobedonostsev had termed 'our great ulcer'.

### iii

The lasting consequence of the events of 1881–4 was, as we shall see, to destroy for all except an insignificant minority any real hope that Russia would move, however slowly, towards more liberal rule and towards the legal emancipation of the Jews in particular. The immediate effect of the pogroms was sharply to reduce the Russian Jews' sense of physical security, notably in the Ukraine, and to precipitate the great migration (already referred to)[17] to Central and Western Europe, and overseas to more distant countries, above all to the United States. The idea of leaving Russia was relatively new. It had always been illegal to leave the country without permission. But of much greater inhibitory weight were the deeply ingrained immobilism and fatalism of the Jews of the Pale and their profound belief, fostered both by their leaders and by their folklore, that the land beyond the hills was unlikely to prove greener and that the devil one knew was generally preferable to the devil still unknown. Who now started the wave of migration that so rapidly became a flood is not clear, nor are the precise, local causes behind it. It was not confined to a particular stratum. Jews of all classes were in the first groups to cross the frontier into Brody, the Galician frontier town which became, for a while, the principal staging-post for the migrants. 'Some are rich and some are poor', the committee of the Alliance was informed by Charles Netter, its emissary at Brody. 'When I say rich, I mean people who were so before the events of April. There are some who have managed to keep as much as 2,000 roubles, others who have not the means of clothing their children. There are boys and married people, merchants, students, and workmen.' Netter was particularly struck by the high proportion of middle-class, Russian-speaking, half-assimilated Jews at this early stage of the migration.

---

[16] Cf. above, p. 30.  [17] See above, p. 32.

The men wear neither *pe'ot* (side-locks) nor caftans; they are hand-some, tall, clean, intelligent . . . The women are almost elegant. I saw one the other day who expressed herself decently in French. The usual language of these people is Russian. When they speak German they speak it with a Russian accent. Few of them employ [Yiddish].

Among the young people there are many, perhaps half, who were students expelled from the gymnasiums with the excuse that there was no more room. First, they were reproached with not wanting to assimilate, now it has been found that they are assimilating too well. A quarter of the young are craftsmen sent away from their workshops by their Christian masters, or by the other workmen, or by Jewish masters who were ruined in April. I have porters on my list who were chased away from the port of Odessa by Greek porters . . . Among the refugees are old soldiers decorated several times for heroism . . . One greybeard who came to me, who had won three decorations on the battlefield in his 21 years of service, had been expelled from Kiev for failing to be in the authorized category [of residents] . . .[18]

The crucial feature of the sudden and undoubtedly spontaneous appearance of first some hundreds, and then, quite soon, thousands of Jews, mostly destitute, who wanted to move on past Brody to other places, was the multiplier effect of the rapidly gathering host of refugees itself on those they had left behind. By the summer of 1881 there were at least three to four thousand in the town. The response of western Jewry was then to establish an elaborate organization to care for them and to help them to move on. But as word spread into the Pale that help could be obtained in Brody the numbers of refugees rose more rapidly still. By the following summer 10,000 had passed through and on and another 12,000 were assembled in the town waiting. For as the worthies of western Jewish philanthropy began to try for a lasting solution of the problem even on this unexpected scale—and although they were still thinking, at this time, entirely in terms of those already collected in Brody—word of their good intentions spread further into the Pale and increased the number of candidates for resettlement again, until, in despair, the philanthropists found that they were as much concerned to stem the tide of migrants as to assist those who had already made the move. They stopped short of persuading the Jews to return because it was judged unthinkable to do so.[19] But

[18] Alliance Israélite Universelle, *Bulletin Mensuel*, October 1881, pp. 153-5.

[19] So argued a representative of the Alliance Israélite Universelle at Brody, E. F. Veneziani, and no one of consequence seems to have contradicted him. YIVO Institute, New York, Leah M. Eisenberg–Julius Berenstein Collection, microfilm roll no. 1 (1869–81), pp. 346 ff.

they did what they could both to make clear that they, for their part, were not encouraging the Jews to evacuate Russia and to inhibit those who were hesitating from doing so. They were aware that if the wave grew much higher it would be beyond a scale they were equipped to cope with—or happy to cope with. They felt that the influx of Russian and Polish Jews into Central and Western Europe and into the United States threatened to upset the *modus vivendi*, recently achieved there, in their view, between the newly emancipated Jews and the Gentile world. They do not seem to have sensed the colossal proportions the movement of population was soon to take.

Whether the Jews should begin to evacuate Russia, and to what degree, was one question. The other question, on which there was less debate and anxiety, was the question of where they were to go. For most of those concerned the answer was: to America. It was true that the representative body of American Jews, the Board of Delegates, had attempted to stop the migration to the United States at the end of 1881 (without success). It was also true that, with some exceptions, of whom Baron de Hirsch was the most notable, contemporary Jewish philanthropists thought that no country, not even the United States, could absorb as many as 100,000 migrants[20]—the figure that had begun to appear on their horizon as the ultimate limit of the movement. Then, as had been reported to them, the process of absorption in the United States was a difficult one and accordingly great care had to be taken, they believed, to ensure that only the young and the strong and, if possible, the unattached should make the journey (while, in fact, the Jews were perversely obstinate in their refusal to leave their families behind while they found their feet in the New World). Finally, a great many Jews were moving no further than Austria and Germany, some to France, others to England—partly for fear of the unknown, partly for lack of means for cheap passage across the ocean or because they found that they had been cheated on their tickets and could not continue, and often because, as they moved westward on their way to the Americas, they found they could manage well enough at the intermediate stop. But for all that, America was the goal of most migrants and 'America' soon took on a symbolic quality suggesting a fresh departure, a new life,

[20] Cf. Zoza Szajkowski, 'How the Mass Migration to America Began', *Jewish Social Studies*, iv. 4, October 1942, p. 298.

promise, and unlimited horizons that it was not to lose for seventy years.

Erez̧-Israel, so far as the philanthropists were concerned, was not a serious proposition at all. It was unfortunate, reported the Alliance, that the publicity that had attached to schemes, such as Lawrence Oliphant's to settle Jews in Gilead,[21] along with 'the lure of Palestine on everyone's imagination', had so excited Russian Jews that some were beginning to think of emigrating to Erez̧-Israel and becoming farmers. But in the first place, the fact that Oliphant's scheme would require anything between 25 and 50 million francs was enough to show the impossibility of implementing it. And secondly, and even more to the point, those Jews who had begun to think of going to Erez̧-Israel

have not considered that Palestine is a poor country, where there is no commerce, no industry, and where there are no roads nor [other] means of communication; that the Jews who inhabit it now are destitute and for the most part live on charity which is sent them from elsewhere. The arrival of new immigrants can only add to the misery. Those who want to go there to work the land have above all failed to consider that in order to farm it is necessary to be a farmer and that one does not become one overnight. One must have several years of practical experience and particular knowledge of the country and the climate. Such preparation is indispensable; without it agricultural settlement is condemned to fail in advance.[22]

Their own representative in Erez̧-Israel itself, Samuel Hirsch (who had taken over the direction of the Mikve Israel Agricultural School near Jaffa from Charles Netter), saw matters in the same light. When small groups of Russian Jews began to trickle into the country, on their own, without adequate resources and with no hope of establishing themselves, he took in as many as he could and put them to work at the school. But, he told the committee in Paris, the various committees and communities caring for the refugees from Russia 'would be rendering these poor people a great service if they prevented them from making for Palestine where they will inevitably be doomed to misery and will fail to obtain succour'.[23]

[21] See below, pp. 94 ff.
[22] AIU, *Bulletin Mensuel*, August–September 1881.
[23] *Bulletin de l'Alliance Israélite Universelle*, 2nd series, 5, 2nd semester, 1882.

# PART TWO

---

## *The Love of Zion*

# 4

## The Bridgehead

### i

THE genesis of the Zionist movement occurred in the period immediately subsequent to, and to a large extent as a consequence of, the events of the years 1881-4 in Russia and the simultaneous and analogous pressures exerted on the Jews of Romania (of which more will be said later). By 1884 all the main social elements that were to compose and fuel the movement in its formative years had emerged in recognizable shape and the essential outlines of the narrow limits within which it was to operate for well over a decade were visible. However, the Jewish *Risorgimento* and the loosely organized bodies of like-minded men and women who supported and promoted it and were, in turn, its most notable and lasting expression did not emerge in any tidy, easily explicable manner. It was not the invention—still less the creation—of a single man or a single group of men. Half a generation was to pass before it acquired a preponderant leader and something like a clear formulation of aims. Its adherents, the groups and circles of *Ḥovevei Ẓion* (Lovers of Zion), as they came to call themselves,[1] emerged spontaneously and more or less simultaneously in scores, if not in hundreds, of localities in the Russian Empire and in Romania. The most considerable material achievement of the period—the establishment of the first settlements of farmers in Ereẓ-Israel—was set in motion before the document which can, with hindsight, be reasonably regarded as the first manifesto of the movement was published; and it was the work of individuals who cannot be grouped in less than three quite disparate and disconnected categories, and even then at the cost of some oversimplification. In brief, the movement began as the direct response of a multitude

---

[1] The terms *Zionist* and *Zionism* were coined at a later period. See below, p. 222.

of individuals and local circles to a situation which they regarded as untenable, a response unmediated by some trumpet-call of national leadership and without those individuals and groups being fully aware of each other until positions had already been taken and commitments made. Its subsequent evolution took the form of a cautious amalgamation and coalescence of these local groups and the gradual emergence into prominence of a body of key activists—*leaders* would be too strong a term—by a barely traceable process of, as it were, random mutation and natural selection. It was a slow process. It was never completed. It was only one of a number taking place in the general ferment to which East European Jewry was now subject. And for many years to come it was the affair of a minority, too small and too incoherent to become a major influence on the mass of Jews, let alone represent them in any simple, parliamentary sense.

To understand the confused and conflicting response of Russian and Polish Jewry to the events of 1881 and the years immediately subsequent to it, it must be remembered that they were totally without the means of arriving at one which was coherent. There was no recognized representative institution such as the Board of Deputies of British Jews. There was no chief rabbinate sanctioned, let alone appointed, by the State on the Ottoman model. There was no single unofficial religious leader—or coherent and easily identifiable group of leaders—generally recognized by the majority of Jews. Observant Jews, still in the overwhelming majority, were divided into the conflicting schools of the *ḥasidim* and their traditionalist opponents the *mitnagdim*, and divided within the schools by the allegiance owed to the most visible local ḥasidic 'rebbe' or traditional and established rabbi. Some of these had a reputation which extended beyond their community, but none was of the stature and influence of, say, the Gaon of Vilna of the previous century, a figure of national proportions. Since the organized life of the Jews centred round the local community and there were no regular and effective means of communication and consultation between communities, movements of opinion evolved chaotically and unsteadily without the underpinning of systematic, institutionalized methods of arriving at consensus and formal and reasonably durable commitment. Information spread privately, by word of mouth and by letter, for the most part. Where communal leaders, or men of some prominence, or literary men were concerned, there were elaborate—but still entirely unsystematic and unorganized—networks of correspondence. On great questions messengers (*shelihim*) might be sent at local initiative to other communities to spread the desired word. But the number and variety of communities were so great, the areas so vast, and the funds available for travel on public affairs so small that the radius of this kind of activity rarely extended beyond the limits of the province, at best. Besides, there were the police and the censorship to contend with. Social organization in Russia was subject to official authorization. What was not licensed was prohibited and punished upon discovery. Travel was subject to the possession of a passport and the areas in which Jews could travel freely were restricted. Anything that smacked of an effective intercommunal association of Jews was doubly suspect in the eyes of the authorities, fearful of all national and proto-nationalist associations and movements of opinion and ready to believe that one involving the Jews could not but be intent on purposes profoundly subversive of the Russian state. Accordingly, all consultation on matters judged delicate or dangerous was conducted with great care. Y. L. Gordon, the poet, by no means a cowardly man, refused to have anything to do with a modest plan to collect funds for a philanthropic venture in Erez-Israel on the grounds that there was no proof that the purpose was commensurate with the risks. Letters were written in an elaborate and elliptical style in the hope of confusing and tiring the censors. Personalities were referred to by initials. When really serious business had to be conducted it was conducted abroad— as we shall see.

In these circumstances, and within the limits imposed by the government, the Jewish periodical press played a role of first importance. For through it basic information on events could generally be circulated and something of the range of current views and suggested recipes for salvation be indicated to a fairly wide circle of readers. The editors of the Russian-language weeklies *Razsvyet* and *Voskhod* became *ex officio* national figures with considerable powers of moral censure and commendation, whose support was valued and whose opinion was respected, if not always accepted. Periodicals were, of course, subject to the pressures and vagaries of the censorship and their editors were acutely and continually aware of the fragility of their position and of the risk that the vital focuses of debate on Jewish national affairs which they

68         *The Love of Zion*

controlled might be liquidated by decree. The war with the censorship was the more difficult to cope with by reason of the fact that it
was generally a silent one: censorship was imposed after publication
and it was the editor's duty to see that nothing offensive to the
authorities was published. Since the authorities were extremely
sensitive to any implication of criticism, great care had to be taken;
but for the more courageous of the editors, the exercise of due care
was sooner or later shown to be incompatible with doing their duty
as they understood it. *Voskhod* got into serious—and characteristic
—trouble when it dealt heatedly with what was to be the last of
the great pogroms of the period, that of Nizhni-Novgorod, which
took place in June 1884 and in which nine Jews were killed by the
mob. The cause, argued *Voskhod*, was to be traced to the denial
of equal rights to the Jews, to their consequent pariah status in
society, and to the constant incitement by the Russian press proper
to violence against them: the remedy was for the government to
show that it regarded the Jews as equal citizens and force the anti-
Semitic press to cease to incite. This earned the editors a reprimand
and a warning against 'frequent and impertinent' criticism of the
authorities on the basis of lying interpretations of official acts
calculated to provoke one section of the population to enmity of
another. Some years later, after another warning had failed to have
a lasting effect, the weekly was suspended for six months.[2] Thus
while the Jewish periodical press served the Jews reasonably well
as a means of disseminating information and, within limits, opinion,
it was rigorously deprived by the authorities of the representative
or mediatory function it might have performed. This last could
only be performed—imperfectly, uncertainly, and generally with
the poorest of results—by the Jewish notables whose (limited)
representative capacity derived, to all intents and purposes, from
their being either appointed or tacitly recognized by the authorities
as entitled to mediate—or more strictly, to intervene and petition
on behalf of the commonalty of Jews.

In the past, this ancient function of *shtadlanut* (intercession) had
generally lent the tolerated mediators (or *shtadlanim*) a considerable
measure of influence within the community itself by virtue of the
influence they had, or were thought by other Jews to have, over the
local governor, or police chief, or better still, in the remoter spheres

---

[2] Yehuda Slutsky, *Ha-'itonut ha-yehudit-rusit ba-me'a ha-tesha'-'esre*, Jerusalem, 1970,
pp. 200 ff.

of government, at the capital. But the attributes which gave the Jewish notables access to officialdom—and particularly to the central officialdom—in late nineteenth-century Russia were, at the same time, those which cut them off, in some cases sharply, from the mass of Jews in the Pale of Settlement. They tended to speak Russian well and dress as other Russians of equivalent education and means. They were generally privileged by education and wealth to live where common Jews could not and to engage in occupations from which the latter were barred. The greater their wealth the greater, generally, was the indulgence of the authorities. But the greater too was their personal stake not only in the fast-developing railroad and industrial economy of the time, but a stake in the perpetuation of Jewish settlement in Russian territory. It is undeniable that there were few, if any, who did not dearly wish to improve the condition of the other Jews and did not hope for the eventual emancipation of all through the granting to them of equal rights with other Russian subjects. These hopes, which had accorded with the liberal, progressive belief that had been prevalent among them, the belief that, sooner or later, whatever general social and economic advance was made in Russia would spin off on to the Jews, were now at a low ebb. But they still feared anything likely to retard still further the slow assimilation of Jews into the ranks of the other subjects of the Tsar and anything that would further separate the Jews or re-emphasize their place apart in society.

Although the commonalty of Jews still tended to look to the comparatively privileged to intervene on their behalf—if only because, in effect, there were no others to speak for them—their own attitudes and the degree of their loyalty to the Russian state and to the Jewish people respectively were different, by and large. The underprivileged had little regard for the state and less for its rulers. They had no demonstrable interest in the former and nothing but distrust for the latter—whom they knew only as a fountain of spite and oppression. They had little sense of possessing a stake in the economy. They had no wish to assimilate into the ranks of Russians plain and simple, nor could they comprehend those Jews —many, but still a distinct minority—who toyed with the idea. They were themselves still greatly absorbed and fascinated by the content, intricacies, and antiquity of their own tradition, whereas, as they could see for themselves, only the tiniest segment of Russian and Polish society attained to an equivalent degree of familiarity with *their* religious and philosophical literature. The idea that absorption and assimilation might be thought to constitute, or promise, cultural or intellectual advance astonished them. If anything, Russia and things Russian were thought of as embodying a threat, not a promise. At bottom, their approach to their collective relations with the Russian state hinged on the question whether they would or would not be left alone, at any rate within the bounds of reason. Now that, for the first time since the massacres at the hands of Ukrainians in the seventeenth century, it had begun to appear that they would not be left alone and that conditions would get steadily worse, the idea that took root among them with greatest speed and power was that of a deliberate, self-willed mass transplantation to a more hospitable land. This was an entirely traditional reaction with solid precedent in the history of the Jews. But the Russified and privileged Jews, by the same token, because they feared any suggestion that their status was, in fact, the traditional one of an alien people in temporary settlement in the country, were initially hostile to the idea of evacuating Russia; and large numbers of them retained their objection until the First World War and the Revolution effectively eliminated it as a practical possibility.

This was partly a matter of sentiment and prior commitment too: the Jews would not and could not flee Russia because 'Russia was their motherland, the land of Russia was their land, the skies of Russia their skies'.[3] Moreover, to leave Russia was to accept the verdict of the anti-Semitic enemy himself. To the question put by the editors of *Novoye Vremya*: 'What shall we do with the Jews? Shall we beat them or shall we not?' a common reply was that they had to be exiled to the remotest parts of the Empire or expelled entirely. Such, for example, was the substance of the Elizavetgrad council's petition to the central government. At the trial of a group of *pogromshchiki* in Kiev it was the Jews the public prosecutor had attacked and invited explicitly, to leave the country: 'The western frontier is open to the Jews; why don't they cross it for their own good?' And Count Ignatiev, the Minister of Interior, had repeated these words (in January 1882), adding that the 'Jews have already taken ample advantage of this right and their emigration has in no way been hampered', and authorized a delegation of Jewish petitioners to make the plain message public.

But among members of the Jewish intelligentsia there was, too,

[3] G. B. Lifshitz in *Razsvyet*, xix, 1881, p. 731, quoted in Slutsky, op. cit., p. 122.

a reluctance to accept the judgement that the problem of the Jews was ineradicably specific and a refusal to accept that it was hopeless to seek to integrate one's analysis of it into fashionable thinking on general social and political issues. The idea, for example, that the problem of the Jews was, at least in part, a function of their economic 'marginality' and dispensability and that the first step towards a cure was to restructure Jewry on more productive lines —turning the pedlars and innkeepers and petty traders into farmers and miners and machinists—was not easily abandoned. It attracted support because it suggested a path whereby the problem of the Jews could be subsumed in the general problem of Russia: they would first be made to pass through the ante-room of 'normalization' from which they would emerge less unlike the other peoples of the Empire and fit to participate in the broad movement of renewal. It also attracted by virtue of those of its elements which were undeniably valid: the poverty of the Jews and the fragility of the role in the economy which great numbers of them performed were beyond dispute and merited treatment in their own right. Accordingly, it retained its force for many years.

Yet another factor which affected the perspective in which the wholly and partly assimilated Jews saw matters was the sheer physical gulf separating many of the privileged from the under-privileged. It was one thing to read censored newspaper reports of pogroms in the relative security of St. Petersburg and Moscow; it was quite another to witness them in Kiev and Odessa. In contra-distinction, physical proximity to the beastliness where it existed, brought privileged and unprivileged together. Even when the mob did not actually penetrate into the comfortable quarters of the cities of the Pale where those Jews who had made their way successfully to them lived side by side with non-Jews, the impact of the events was direct and in many cases psychologically shattering. The reaction of those among the privileged, and those who were well placed to enter their ranks—notably the university students—who still lived within the Pale, or still retained close family ties with the residents of the Pale, was thus often the sharpest and bitterest of all. 'We have been sold and betrayed by this miserable country'; the Jews were like sufferers from a malignant disease that must be cured by radical means. There were two solutions: equality of rights or emigration. As there was no hope of acquiring equal rights, but, on the contrary, good reason to expect further restriction of existing rights, the only solution was to emigrate.[4] Thus Dr. Emmanuel Mandelstamm, chief of the eye department at Kiev University medical school (and therefore a notable example of this latter category). It was a conclusion which he was bold enough to pronounce as early as June 1881. And it was an idea that gained stronger support as the full significance of the events of those years sank in—as it became steadily more difficult to believe that the autocracy could be moved to modify its increasingly hostile attitude to the Jews, let alone take positive steps to ameliorate their condition by, for example, extending the boundaries of the Pale or permitted settlement. Nevertheless, on the first occasion on which something approaching a representative body of Russian Jewish notables gathered to discuss the situation—in September 1881, at the home of Baron Horace Guenzburg in St. Petersburg, by express permission of the same Count Ignatiev who was shortly to encourage them to emigrate—the consensus was clearly against migration and the sole result was the drafting of yet another petition to the Minister. And significantly, on this issue the leaders of the rabbinate were, for the most part, at one with the plutocrats and the professionals.[5]

Thus the idea of leaving Russia altogether came to be not only an idea that recommended itself in varying degrees to some Jews of all classes, including certain categories of the privileged, as offering a solution (the classic solution) to the problem of the Jews under the Russian autocracy, but even more plainly came to imply a vote of no confidence in Russian Jewry's traditional and established leaders, such as they were. For the great majority of actual leaders at every level from St. Petersburg down to the meanest *shtetl* (or Jewish hamlet) remained opposed to any attempt at a *radical* reordering of Jewish life—which in the circumstances of the late nineteenth century did appear to entail the evacuation of Russian territories. And they failed to formulate, let alone hold out, real promise of an alternative. They promoted no idea except that of cleaving so far as possible to the *status quo*. But while the pogroms continued and as the anti-Jewish policy of the government was consolidated the notion that life for the Jews in Russia would ultimately be tenable if minor adjustments were made and if the Jews waited in patience for the storm to blow over was much more

    [4] Israel Klausner, *Be-hit'orer 'am*, Jerusalem, 1962, p. 94.
    [5] The notables requested permission to set up a standing committee to co-ordinate philanthropic activities on behalf of Russian Jewry. They were turned down.

difficult to accept than ever before. There was no evidence to support it as a truly practical proposition. And there was nothing in it to satisfy the growing hunger of the braver spirits for an approach to the problem of the Jews which contained something more positive and satisfying than an endless and humiliating dependence on, and accommodation to, the will of others.

The brief display of unity that occurred when a day of fasting and prayers was observed in virtually all the Jewish communities of the Empire on 10 Shevat 5642 (18 January 1882, O.S.) was thus misleading. At best, it provided an opportunity for setting a basis for common action. In the event, the opportunity was missed. The synagogues, with their dual role as houses of prayer and houses of communal assembly, were filled to overflowing. And within them Jews of all classes and all degrees of loyalty and attachment to the national and religious tradition were brought together by the never entirely dormant sense of isolation and helplessness and of being reserved, ineluctably, for a unique moral and social condition— a feeling suddenly reinforced and revitalized by the action of mob and government in collusion. But brought together only initially, and briefly.

Those closely attached to tradition, to say nothing of those who wished to maintain it *in toto*, immutable and unyielding, continued to regard the peculiar condition of the Jews in the profane order of things as, ultimately, a function of the Jews' special role in the divine order. For them, the almost certain prospect that times of relative peace and stability in relations between Jew and Gentile were now to be superseded by a period—perhaps a long period— of pressure, turmoil, and deliberately inflicted pain was, of course, a source of great apprehensiveness, even dread. Nevertheless, it could be accommodated into what was conceived to be the natural (but divinely ordained) order. One might attempt to soften or fend off the blow, actual or prospective; but one did not rail excessively and one did not actively seek deliverance before the appointed time. The Lord's purposes were inscrutable. If fault was to be found it was to be sought first and foremost within Jewry itself. It was not that the malevolence and wickedness of those who held power in the surrounding world were in any doubt. It was rather that the Jew's true business was with his God and not, except very narrowly and for purposes that were trivial for the most part, with his Gentile neighbour. This was the meaning of the Exile and this

was its content. The Jewish predicament was extremely painful.
But it was not *morally* intolerable—at any rate, not to the man who
subscribed whole-heartedly to the ancient corpus of belief and law.

It was the Jew whose attachment to the tradition was loosening
who found the condition of his people intolerable. And, broadly
speaking, the greater his hopes had been for a new dawn for Jews
in a new Russia, the harder had he now been hit. If, moreover,
he was young, relatively unencumbered by, or entirely free of,
dependants and social and economic obligations, and if, like
many of the Jewish university students, but also others of their
generation, he was of an impatient, questioning, and nervous cast
of mind, then the disposition to reject the intolerable and the
perverse aspects of the Jewish condition and to look for a rationally
evolved, radical, and embracing cure to them was very great.
Young men and women of this disposition thus became natural
recruits for any movement which seemed to offer a prospect of
action aimed at a sharp, effective, and lasting change of circumstances and it was in this period, accordingly, that the recruitment
of Jews to those all-Russian revolutionary movements in which the
Slavophil element was absent or muted began to increase very
rapidly. It is also at this point that those who were still sufficiently
attached to their background and origins to be unwilling totally to
abandon them, who were conscious of the very specific nature of
their disappointment and hurt and, in many cases, of a degree of
shame at having been over-eager to abandon the old and the
intrinsic to no purpose, and so of a not wholly insignificant desire
to atone, and those who, above all, were moved by the frustrating
and almost overwhelming sense of the powerlessness and indignity
of the Jewish condition—it was these who were now impelled to
make a break in a different direction.

ii

Three reasonably coherent categories of migrants to Erez-Israel
set out from Romania and Russia in the years 1882–4 with the
explicit intention of remaking the pattern and economic basis of
their own lives and, by so doing, precipitating a very large-scale
reordering of the condition of Jews everywhere. In all three cases,
the drive to put their own feet on solid ground in a more agreeable
and ostensibly more promising social and political climate was

intertwined with, if not inseparable from, a desire to achieve the wider national purpose. But the proportions, as it were, in which personal and national (or social) purposes were mixed in the minds of the migrants and served as sources of their behaviour in practice varied from case to case—as they were to vary in the case of every wave of Jewish migration (or ʿ*aliya*) into Erez̧-Israel down to our own times. The group in whose thinking the national and social —indeed, the abstract and the theoretical—elements were strongest and most explicit was, as it happened, the smallest, the least well-equipped for the job in hand, the one with the least support out-side its own circle, the one most deeply riven by conflicts of opinion and personality, and, beyond any doubt, the one whose legacy in terms of material achievement was to be the slightest. Nor did it leave much of a legacy in the form of a continuing organization. Nevertheless, it was the first group which was possessed of sufficient boldness and originality to think explicitly in terms of a thorough reshaping of the forms of Jewish life—social, economic, and, ultimately, political. It is thus the first group to which, with hind-sight, the term 'Zionist' may properly be applied.

At the end of 1881 and the beginning of 1882 groups of Jewish students began to form in many of the principal cities of the Empire. Impatience and irritation at the timidity of the notables, loathing for the regime and for the indignities which were the lot of the Jews, and a fervent desire to cut clear and re-establish national self-respect were the dominant notes struck. A young gymnasium student who managed to gain admittance to the founding meeting of the Moscow students' society later described the atmosphere.

The meeting, which was in secret, of course, because of the police, was held in a fairly large hall on Karetnyi Row. It was very crowded. The throats of the speakers were sore from excess of talk and excess of smoke. The discussion was very stormy and went on for four to five hours. Students of several schools of higher education participated, among them a few women. All the discussions were in Russian, of course. We two, as mere gymnasium students, had no right to join in. We stood near the doorway and listened. The meeting was presided over by a medical student called Rappaport who later served as a doctor in Nikolaev for many years. Those participating in the discussion were solely concerned with the choice of the country of migration; there was no debate on whether or not Russia should be left for some other country in which an independent state would be established; it was not an issue. The meeting did not vote on a clear-cut resolution. But by the time we left the hall we ourselves were already enthusiastic *Ḥovevei Ẓion* and had already formed the simple and absolute decision to found a society of young people who would go to Ereẓ-Israel and settle there.[6]

A similar society, called *Ahavat Ẓion* (Love of Zion), was founded by some eighty students in St. Petersburg. They believed that the rehabilitation of Jewry was conditional on the revival of Jewish political autonomy, but, like the Moscow students, disagreed about whether the revival could best be precipitated in America or in Ereẓ-Israel. They seem to have been aware that they knew very little about the facts of the subject and held lectures and divided into small discussion groups for serious study of the contemporary Jewish condition. They held parties at which songs of Zion were sung and at which Yiddish was spoken in deliberate and self-conscious contradistinction to Russian. And they devised a badge in the form of a six-petalled rose representing the Star of David on which the word 'Zion' was embroidered.

Everywhere, those students who had taken the significant step of joining a *Jewish* society were united on the one cardinal issue of migration: the Jews must evacuate Russia *en masse*. But they had no idea how it was to be done. They too looked, at first, to the notables. In St. Petersburg they went in a body to Baron Guenzburg to press him to form a public committee which would take the matter in hand. After Ignatiev's statement on the western borders of Russia being open there was no question, they argued, but that the Jews were being told that they were not wanted and that they must leave. Nor was there any question but that the pogroms had been organized from above. Nor would the pressure be relaxed. It was therefore futile and wicked to delay. They solemnly warned Guenzburg and the other notables 'in the name of the young generation that has not yet lost its self-respect, which loves its people, weeps for the injury done to it, and fears for its future, and in the name of all the House of Israel now given over to plunder and spoliation, abuse and shame' that they (the notables) would be damned for all time if they failed to act. But nothing came of the move. Guenzburg merely put them off by disclaiming the ability to judge so grave an issue and promising to consult with appropriate representatives of other communities.[7]

---

[6] Menaḥem Ussishkin, 'Ha-ẓeʿadim ha-rishonim', in Sh. Eizenstadt (ed.), *Yeḥiel Tchlenov*, Tel Aviv, 1937, p. 10. Ussishkin's companion was Yeḥiel Tchlenov. Both were to be among the foremost leaders of the Zionist movement in Russia.          [7] Klausner, op. cit., pp. 133-4.

The response of the established leaders of the communities to the novel appearance of the young in this context of general communal affairs was mostly hostile. There was some cheering from journalists and literary figures. The editors of *Razsvyet* took them up for a while. David Gordon had warm words for them. But otherwise they found little support; and on the whole, they were not taken very seriously even by those who applauded them. Soured and apprehensive communal leaders neither shared their youthful exaltation nor enjoyed their persistent sniping. Besides, the more carefully they themselves looked into what was involved in a massive resettlement of Jews the more daunting the prospect became. This was particularly true of those who considered the Erez-Israel solution—the 'Palestinians'. That it would be splendid to have a government of one's own in Erez-Israel was not in doubt, wrote Hayyim Hisin, then a secondary-school student in Moscow, in his diary (March 1882). But there was no sound reason to believe that the Sultan would agree to one being established; and even if he did, where would the enormous sums required for the venture be found? Could the requisite help be expected from western Jews or from the local magnates? *They* were rarely generous in public causes. And, lastly, while it was true that Erez-Israel had once been one of the most fruitful countries in the world, it was now all 'naked hills and sandy ravines'. It seemed to follow that there was therefore no serious alternative to America—with its vast, fertile lands freely available to settlers and its promise of a free and prosperous life—as the arena in which the Jewish liberation was to materialize.[8]

At its most explicit the idea of an 'American' solution took the form of a plan to gather a sufficient number of Jews in one of the empty sectors of the western territories of the United States to entitle them to petition Congress to incorporate the territory as one of the constituent states of the Union—a Jewish state. But nothing came of it. The movement of migrants to the United States did grow mightily, but it remained overwhelmingly a movement of individuals with virtually identical intentions, but with no common plan. The few groups that did leave Russia for America in the early 1880s with joint purposes rapidly faded. Several communal settlements were established in the western United States.

---

[8] A. Druyanov (ed.), *Ketavim le-toldot Ḥibbat Ẓion ve-yishuv Erez-Israel* (3 vols.), Odessa, 1919, and Tel Aviv, 1928, 1932 (henceforth Druyanov), i, no. 27, cols. 53–6.

(One, in Oregon, lasted until 1887). There were no resources for a great common venture. The idea itself was insufficiently powerful to kindle the imagination of more than a handful. And it had an intrinsic flaw. When Tchlenov showed Hisin a newspaper report on the steps being taken to restrict the immigration of Chinese into the United States it was evident to him that the same steps might be applied eventually against the Jews. Whereupon Hisin changed his mind—without his sense of the difficulties of the proposed enterprise in Erez-Israel being in any way affected then or later.

So far as Erez-Israel was concerned, the decisive move from academic debate and sporadic attempts to exert mild public pressure was initiated by the students of Kharkov. They had been brought together on the occasion of the day of fasting and prayer proclaimed for all Jews on 10 Shevat and with emotions running high had answered a call to a meeting by one of their own number, Israel Belkind, twenty years old, son of a Hebrew teacher in Mogilev, who had been brought up by his father in the dual culture promoted by the men of the *haskala*. Between twenty and thirty attended. By some accounts the session went on almost continuously for several days.

The discussion of the Kharkov students turned first on the question whether the problem of the Jews was of a special nature which required specific treatment, or one which could be dealt with practicably within the context of action on behalf of all inhabitants of the Empire. The majority were agreed that the Jews did indeed constitute a special case and that their problem required special treatment, namely that they must be concentrated in a single country in which they would no longer be alien. This could not be in Russia and Poland and it therefore followed that the Jews must leave. But it was not clear that they would do so spontaneously. Their national sentiment must therefore be fired to encourage them.

On the question whether national safety and the national revival could be achieved anywhere but in the ancestral Land of Israel agreement was not immediate, but the 'Palestinian' faction soon came to dominate. The third point on which the students agreed was that the national renaissance could not be effected without a profound and comprehensive restructuring of Jewish society; and first and foremost, the Jews must revert to being an agricultural people.

Having agreed on the pre-eminent importance of their three

basic ideas—national renaissance, migration to Erez-Israel, and return to the land—the students formed a society to propagate them. They took as their motto the Biblical injunction *Daber el benei Israel ve-yisaʿu* (Exodus 14: 15: '[And the Lord said unto Moses] speak unto the children of Israel, that they will go forward'). And they attempted to make common cause with a group of older people in Kharkov who too were beginning to think of migration to Erez-Israel, if on the basis of a less systematic framework of ideas. But they soon grew impatient with their elders and impatient, too, with their own initial notion that it was their primary function to *propagate* these ideas. The active spirits argued that it was not enough to advise and help others to act. They themselves must leave for Erez-Israel. They themselves must be the pioneers and form the vanguard of the national movement. They must be both bridgehead and example. If they did not set the movement going, who would?

There can be no doubt that the Kharkov students were imbued with an extraordinarily—and in the opinion of their elders, excessively—powerful sense of the urgency of the national predicament and of the uselessness of all other formulas but theirs. Their outlook, like that of the Russian populists, combined views of extreme pessimism and optimism. And, indeed, the mark of the teachings of the moderate populists, Chernyshevsky, notably, and through them of Fourier, for example, among the pre-Marxian Western socialists, was apparent in other ways—in their notion of the crucial, exemplary role they were themselves to perform, their belief in the primacy of social and economic (as opposed to political) organization, and in the commune as its essential component—as will be seen.

The progress and culture of Europe, they argued, were not to be relied upon. If the Jews stayed in Europe they faced two dire and ineluctable alternatives: to suffer the endless burden of persecution, or else to 'vanish and descend from the stage of life'—whereas the wish of the people was to live, and by its own powers. So it must leave and it must acquire a territorial base. That base could only be in Erez-Israel, for only in that deserted land could the Jews hope to be in the majority. Certainly all this would demand much effort and sacrifice. For some it would mean the abandonment of a good and promising life—at any rate, at the level of material things. For this at least they themselves must be prepared. Were they then prepared to drop everything and turn themselves into farmers—now, without delay? And were they prepared to be that vanguard which was the necessary condition of all that would follow? The question was put to the members of the circle. There was no formal vote. Fourteen signed up. The rest dropped out.

With the activists now firmly in the lead, the little group was reformed and the new departure confirmed by a change of name. The society now called itself *Beit Ya'akov lekhu ve-nelkha* (Isaiah 2: 5: 'O house of Jacob, come ye and let us walk [in the light of the Lord]'). It was soon known by its acronym BILU; and its members as Biluim—the men (and women) of BILU.

Initially, the Biluim had high hopes. They proposed to recruit 3,000 members for their first model farming village and believed that the move to Erez-Israel could be made within six months. And for all their impatience with the well-established they seem to have had little doubt, at first, that massive financial support could be wrung from them. As soon as the spring thaw had come and the winter university term had ended they set out to preach their message, recruit new members, and raise the indispensable funds. In the event, they did reasonably well so far as recruits were concerned: several hundred young people had joined them nominally by the end of April. (One estimate puts the number as high as 500.) But their failure to collect funds was just short of total: no more than a few hundred roubles here and there. They argued with the wealthy; and they threatened. When Belkind was told by the wealthy men of his home town of Mogilev that the community was not interested in migration to Erez-Israel and that the entire programme was therefore baseless, he went out and collected the signatures of a thousand heads of families and three hundred youths within three days. But this led to no change of mind among the comfortable. His comrades met with much the same reception elsewhere.

The Biluim were young, unknown, and extremely aggressive in manner. It would have been surprising if more than a handful of the generally fearful and unimaginative merchants who formed the bulk of the small class of the affluent among the Jews of Russia and Poland had been prepared to help. In any event, the failure to find funds soon killed their plan to spearhead a great movement of migrants and left them a tiny group of earnest, but impoverished, unskilled, and inexperienced would-be farm labourers whose purposes were out of all proportion to their means, destined to continue to be entirely dependent on the charity of the very philanthropists whom, in their hearts, they despised. The hardier spirits were none the less determined not to lose momentum. The key to Palestine was in Constantinople and they believed, vaguely and incorrectly, that much could be done there. So two of their number set off for Turkey, to be followed promptly by a third when it turned out that neither of the first two knew French and could therefore get nowhere with the authorities—or with anyone else. But at least the voyage across the Black Sea represented progress of a kind. Soon there were sixteen in Constantinople— with no money, no friends, at the mercy of rapacious lodging-house keepers, sinking into debt, totally ignorant of, if not oblivious to, the intricacies of the government with which they were solemnly intent upon negotiating for a grant of land and persuading to adopt a generally benevolent attitude to their plans for Erez-Israel. Again, they had to recognize their failure. Meanwhile, nobody awaited them in Erez-Israel, nor did they have the slightest idea of what they would do when they got there, apart from seeking to work and settle the land.

Odessa was near. For four roubles everyone of us could steal back in thirty-six hours, turn again to his work, and wait for better times. But it did not occur to any one of us to do so.

We were all agreed on going to Erez-Israel. It was not clear to us what we would do there. There was talk of working as stevedores in the port of Jaffa and similar occupations . . . The main thing was to be in Erez-Israel, to live there, to work, and to play a role.

We sent letters to all the comrades in Russia. We explained the true situation and we suggested that they do as their consciences dictated. Those who came would be admitted as members; while those who were fearful and faint-hearted could stay at home, as the Bible says.[9]

The decision was taken to delay no longer. They felt that public confidence in them (the extent of which they greatly exaggerated) had to be justified, that it was imperative to push on and show by example that it was possible to settle the land, that the Turkish objection to the coming of Jews could be ignored, and, above all, that the movement was alive. Two 'delegates', it was decided, would remain in Constantinople and continue to press for a firman

---

[9] Israel Belkind, *Di Erste Shritt fun Yishuv Erez-Israel*, New York, 1917–18, i, p. 149. The reference is to Deuteronomy 20: 8.

D

of authorization and support for their project. The rest of the group, thirteen men and one young woman, left for Ereẓ-Israel on 30 June 1882. On their way, in Cyprus, they learned that they would probably be refused permission to land. But they ignored the warning, as so many Jewish migrants to the country were to do in later years. After some minor difficulties they landed in Jaffa a week after their departure from Constantinople.

For the next two and a half years the Biluim lived a hand-to-mouth existence, starvation staved off by what they could earn as unskilled agricultural labourers working for the Mikve Israel agricultural school whose director paid them at market rates (one franc a day) and by an occasional trickle of funds from supporters in Russia doled out to them from time to time by the representative of the charitable foundation set up by Sir Moses Montefiore some years before. It was an extremely hard life. The work in the fields, particularly in the summer, took a long time to get used to. The representatives of Western and Eastern philanthropy alike regarded them as foolhardy and hot-headed and were not amused by their radical ideas on social organization and their nonconformism in the realm of religion. The other settlers from Russia (of whom more will be said), who were now beginning to arrive and in more organized a fashion, were divided in their attitude to them: the young welcomed them, the middle-aged feared their irreligiousness. The Biluim themselves debated and divided and divided again on almost every issue that arose. Some were prepared to join the other settlers and did; others insisted on waiting for an opportunity to establish their own 'model' community. Some yielded to an offer to place them with craftsmen in Jerusalem to learn metalwork and other useful trades on the grounds that these would be needed in their future community. Others rejected any move away from the land. The hard life and seeming hopelessness of the enterprise took their own toll. The group was thus subject to continual withdrawals and defections and these were barely compensated for by the small groups of fresh recruits that arrived from Russia from time to time. So although, all told, between fifty and sixty Biluim reached Ereẓ-Israel between the middle of 1882 and the end of 1884, the consequence of the withdrawals was that there were less than twenty members left in the country when, at the end of 1884, when all seemed beyond saving, substantial help finally came from supporters in Minsk who provided funds for the purchase of a tract of land at Katra, about 25 kilometres south of Jaffa. The land was devoid of any building, there were no implements, no farm animals, and it was too late in the season to sow a crop. But the offer was accepted and the little band moved into a shed that had been hastily set up to provide them, at least, with shelter. They now had their land and they had their 'model' community, which they called Gedera. They duly made a valiant effort to put their principle into practice. But Gedera never prospered greatly and it remained the sole, small, concrete achievement of a movement which was to expire totally within a few years.

BILU never overcame the rapid decline that followed so soon after its sudden and promising beginning. Ironically for a movement which was obsessed and motivated by a sense of urgency and by the supreme need to act, its lasting contribution to the national renaissance was essentially in the realm of the moral and the ideological.

The distinguishing characteristic of the Biluim was their consistent belief in the pre-eminent importance of ideas and organization— a belief, in effect, in the need to form a *party* and to formulate an explicit *ideology*. Their subsidiary conviction was in the value of example and of the dramatic and significant *act*. And while it would be impossible to establish which belief derived from which, it can be said that each reinforced the other. Whereas all those participating in the general movement of migrants to Erez-Israel were profoundly conscious of the national significance of their acts and were often almost as devoted to the idea of a return of the Jews to the soil as were the Biluim, and, further, were impelled, if only by their circumstances, to operate in concert on all matters of importance, the approach of most, at heart, was pragmatic, cautious, matter-of-fact. They did not schematize and did not theorize. They knew the world to be hostile and they did not think it likely that it could be suddenly transformed. They had no doubt that they were good, loyal sons of their people and saw no need to pass through the fires of debate, conviction, and conversion as a preliminary to reconstituting themselves selfless, dedicated servants of the nation. Above all, they feared the haste and the heat which were characteristic of everything the Biluim did. And they feared, as did many figures in Europe who warmed to the Biluim because of the latter's manifestly high principles and willingness to make a sacrifice, that somewhere, somehow, by their imprudence, the Biluim would compromise the common purpose. If they had their way, complained David Gordon, they would endanger the entire enterprise. Instead of the resettlement of the Land proceeding step by step, those with means going over first and setting up villages, farms, and factories into which the impoverished could then be absorbed, the Biluim wished great numbers of entirely unprepared people to sell their belongings for the price of passage and make the move even in the knowledge that there were none to receive them, none to support them. This might be adequate and workable for the migrants to America, said Gordon, but the resettlement of Erez-Israel and the flight of the persecuted to America were, in fact, two quite different and separate affairs. The latter, at the present time, was unavoidably urgent and rushed. But the former was 'a great and exalted matter upon which the future welfare of the people would depend; and for it to be put into effect time, wisdom, knowledge, and money would all be needed'.[10]

This was not at all the style of the Biluim. But it was not thoughtlessness they could properly be accused of. The Biluim's ideas on social and political organization went through a number of systematic, written formulations and reformulations in the period between their confident beginnings in Kharkov and the final settlement in somewhat chastened, but still brave mood in Gedera. Several of these documents have survived in whole or in part. The first were fairly simple, highly charged calls to patriotic youth to join them. But these were soon replaced by ever more elaborate and carefully phrased sets of the rules by which BILU was to be governed and by which it was to be guided. The most complete and elaborate—with 78 clauses—was prepared in 1884, not long before their organizational and proselytizing *élan* was for all intents and purposes finally diverted into the prosaic business of running a collective farming hamlet. From first to last they are basically consistent. The later versions may properly be seen as attempts to amplify and make explicit the readily identifiable, but none the less somewhat nebulous, ideas which cemented the active members of the group together in Kharkov and elsewhere in Russia. Read along with the diaries and private correspondence of the more articulate Biluim there thus emerge a number of clear, interconnected ideas, no single one of which was of particular originality,

[10] *Ha-Magid*, xviii, 10 May 1882, pp. 145-6.

but all of which, taken together, formed a unique social programme which was to run like a red thread through the entire history of the Jewish resettlement of Erez-Israel down to 1948, and beyond.

The ideas of the Biluim may be grouped under three heads: national, individual, and socio-economic. Of these the national were, perhaps, the least original and were marked off from those of their contemporaries by little more than the fervour and high colour that charged their vision. This comes across best in private correspondence.

My final purpose, as is that of many others, is great, comprehensive, immense, but it cannot be said that it is unrealizable. The final purposes or *pia desideria* are to take possession in due course of Palestine and to restore to the Jews the political independence of which they have now been deprived for 2,000 years. Don't laugh, it is not a mirage. The means to achieve this purpose could be the establishment of colonies of farmers in Palestine, the establishment of various kinds of workshops and industry and their gradual expansion—in a word, to seek to put all the land, all the industry, in the hands of the Jews. Furthermore, it will be necessary to teach the young people and the future young generations the use of arms (in free and wild Turkey everything can be done) and then . . . Here I lose my head in speculations. Then, there will come that splendid day whose advent was prophesied by Isaiah in his fiery and poetic words of consolation. Then the Jews, if necessary with arms in their hands, will publicly proclaim themselves masters of their own, ancient father-land. It does not matter if that splendid day will only come in fifty years' time or more. A period of fifty years is no more than a moment of time for such an undertaking.[11]

Individually, the members of the fully formed BILU were conceived as belonging to three distinct categories of members divided according to degree of involvement in the affairs of society and submission to its requirements. The demands on the inner group, which was clearly intended to lead the movement as a whole and to exemplify in their personal conduct the high standards of sacrifice, single-mindedness, and dedication which BILU stood for as a whole, were correspondingly severe. These, 'the standard-bearers', were defined as those who had undertaken to 'devote all their powers, for all time,, to the good of society and to abstain from all former pleasures'. They were to be drawn from the young

---

[11] Ze'ev Dubnov to his brother Shim'on (the historian), 20 October/1 November 1882. Druyanov, iii, no. 1163, cols. 495-6.

(no older than twenty-five years of age), the free, and the sufficiently wise and knowledgeable 'to understand what was demanded of [them] by the times in which [they] lived and the exalted and sacred idea' on which the movement was founded. They were to give up all private property and to dedicate all their 'strength, powers, and courage to the good of the society'. They were not to marry for a period of time (unspecified). They were to be subject to the strict discipline of obedience to those of their own number whom they had elected to govern them. The daily life of the commune formed by this inner élite of the society was to be agricultural and strict rural life was binding on all members.

The communes of the Biluim were not intended as units of a secluded and monastic order, but rather of a militant order of teachers, guides, and leaders for the rest of the Jewish population whose welfare and whose progress towards freedom and autonomy were the justification for the entire enterprise. Their general socio-economic ideas emerge clearly from the discussion of the relationship between the Biluim and the other Jewish inhabitants of the country. They conceived of the future Jewish society as one founded on social justice, the absence of economic exploitation, *Jewish* labour, *Jewish* agriculture, the overriding right of the Jewish people as a whole in respect of all land that Jews had acquired in the country, even land acquired privately, and a powerful sense of national purpose cementing all the population together and which the Biluim themselves were systematically to propagate. They envisaged themselves on periodic detachment from their communes, serving as instructors among the other settlers. They thought it might be necessary for them to establish some sort of commercial organization to protect the Jewish farmer from the rapacity of the common run of rural traders. They were sure they would have to see to it that the newcomers had adequate medical, veterinary, and technical services, as well as schools. They recognized the importance of acquiring facility in the use of the Hebrew language as the future vernacular of the country. Their plans were thus, in many ways, remarkably comprehensive and perceptive. Yet apart from some recognition of the general desirability of instructing young men in the use of weapons ('very necessary for those inhabiting countries of the East'), there is no hint of the political in their programme. Nor, except for the naïve and futile effort to cajole the Ottoman authorities into granting a firman in their favour, was

there any aspect of their activities that could be called political.
For all the immense energy they evidently devoted to the elabora-
tion of social and economic principles on which their organization
was to be based, and for all that they conceived BILU itself as
absolutely central and indispensable to the larger purpose of the
re-establishment of Jewish political autonomy in Erez-Israel, such
material as has survived is devoid of any suggestion that they gave
serious thought to the political, constitutional, and administrative
structure of the country, or even to the precise character of the
relationship between the commonalty of Jews and themselves.

The question of the future relations between the Jews of Erez-
Israel on the one hand and the Arabs and the members of other
ethnic and religious communities in the country on the other did
not register in their minds either. All in all, it is difficult not to
conclude that they assumed that the manifest legitimacy of their
ideas and the sheer force of their personal example would suffice
to ensure their moral supremacy in the evolving society around
them and the acceptance of their leadership and guidance by all
concerned.[12]

This extraordinary confidence in their capacity to pursue a quasi-
prophetic role amongst their people probably derived, in part, from
the example of the Russian populists ('going to the people') of
which they were all aware, for all that the social and cultural attitudes, along with the capacity to articulate them, of even the
meanest of Russian and Polish Jews were worlds away from those
of the peasantry around them. But perhaps of greater weight was
the long, almost total divorce of Jews from the world of politics
and power and their profoundly rooted habit of thinking about
their own affairs exclusively in terms of influence, self-discipline,
and consensus, rather than in terms of rules sanctioned by force.
The Jewish communities of Europe (those of the Ottoman Empire
were in a somewhat different case) were, indeed, an object of force;
but they wielded none themselves. Their internal affairs were
ordered, if at all, on a basis of voluntarism and acquiescence
moderately and partially backed up by economic pressures. It was
therefore natural enough for the Biluim to continue to think in
terms of moral leadership and of a voluntaristic society bound

[12] See, in particular, 'Megilat takanot shel BILU' in Shemu'el Yavne'eli, *Sefer ha-zionut;*
*tekufat Hibbat Zion*, Jerusalem, 1961, ii, pp. 93-8; also Hayyim Hisin, *Mi-yoman ahad
ha-Biluim*, Petah Tikva, 1967.

together by tradition, belief, and the *external* pressures upon it,
rather than by the framework and instruments of the State.

What the Biluim formulated, believed in, and did their best to
establish and propagate was, in effect, the mystique of the *pioneer*
—selfless, determined, well equipped physically and mentally—as
both spearhead and paradigm of the Jew in rebellion against his
condition. It was a mystique which was to grow in power as years
went by (despite the decline of BILU itself), which profoundly
influenced the character and quality of life of the *yishuv*, and which
added enormously to the growing sense that the enterprise as a
whole had a significance and content which went some way beyond
even the great central aim of national revival.

### iii

The only country in Europe besides Russia in which moral, social,
and economic pressure on the Jews was exerted in the latter half
of the nineteenth century as a matter of declared public policy was
Romania. As in Russia, the effect was to impel large numbers of
the country's Jews to migrate—predominantly to the United
States, but partly to Erez-Israel. The movement out of Romania
was roughly contemporaneous with the ultimately much larger,
and in the long run more significant and decisive, wave of migrants
from Russia. And the coincidence, which was fortuitous, had the
effect of giving the Jewish settlers into Erez-Israel—later known
as the First ʿ*Aliya*—something of an ecumenical character in the
eyes of both those who participated in it or supported it and those
whom it disturbed and who opposed it: notably the leaders of
western Jewish philanthropy and the Turkish government.

Barely noted at the time, but of significance for the future, was
the arrival in the winter of 1881/2 of a group of several hundred
Jews from the Yemen as well. Yemeni Jews had been trickling into
Erez-Israel since the end of the fifteenth century at least. Greater
numbers, driven by famine and a burden of oppression that was
to grow in the course of years and drawn to the country by profound religious sentiment, were now to follow from time to time.
However, unlike the Russians and the Romanians, most Yemenis
were content, at first, to settle in Jerusalem; and they were Ottoman
subjects. They were thus not accounted a particular problem by
the Turkish administration, the more so as a considerable period

of time passed before they moved out of the ambit of the old *yishuv* and into that of the new.

The Romanian Jewish community was the fourth largest in Europe, numbering approximately 250,000 in the last quarter of the century.[13] They constituted between 5 and 7 per cent of the population. In the city of Jassy, at the turn of the century, Jews accounted for no less than 57·7 per cent (45,000 out of a total of 78,000).[14] Their social and economic circumstances were not strikingly different from those of the Jews in the rest of Eastern Europe: few professionals, a small class of well-to-do merchants, and for the rest craftsmen (often dominating certain fields), draymen, innkeepers, petty traders, and paupers living chiefly in small towns and villages. Although poverty was endemic there was some migration of Polish and Russian Jews into the Romanian principalities in the middle decades of the century. Culturally and intellectually the Jews were subject to much the same movements of modernization and secularization as elsewhere, somewhat strengthened by the absence of countervailing traditional influences such as those exerted by the great centres of piety and learning in Lithuania, for example. Though a large community, the Jews of Romania were firmly on the periphery of the true heartland of European Jewry to the north.

With the detachment of the Principalities from the Ottoman Empire by agreement among the Powers and by stages, leading to the final, formal grant of full political autonomy in 1878, the condition of the Jews greatly worsened. The new Romania, now coming under the full control of a landowning and commercial oligarchy nourished by economic privilege and a limited franchise, lost no time in defining its attitude to the Jews. In some respects the regime's hostility to the Jews was even greater than that of the Russians, for it refused to admit the Jews even nominally into the class of citizens or subjects of the monarchy. Jews *as such* were denied citizenship even where their families had lived in the Principalities for centuries; and their consequent statelessness was

---

[13] The 1890 Romanian census figure is 269,015. Other sources give other figures, but all are of the same order of magnitude. The natural rate of increase in this period was high (20·8 per thousand per year), but began to fall in the twentieth century. In part, this reflected the somewhat different (more Westernized) character of the Jewish component of the new population; but equally it reflected the depressed moral and material condition of the Jews generally.

[14] *Jüdische Statistik*, p. 443.

made the central peg on which almost all anti-Jewish legislation was hung. They were not to be part of civil society at all. Moreover, it was characteristic of the atmosphere in which this policy of extreme xenophobia was made and executed, and which the Jews were forced to breathe, that, essentially, their statelessness and special status were enforced as a matter of principle and doctrine, rather than of putative facts of residence, for example. Jews *as Jews* were stateless, not because they, or their ancestors, had inhabited Romania for less than a given period of time. Indeed, the Romanian authorities, with unusual consistency, applied their restrictive principles to Jews of all nationalities, even when the governments concerned fully recognized and attempted to protect their subjects. In a famous decision in 1877, a Romanian court confirmed that a Jew of Austrian nationality was no more entitled to acquire legal possession of a building than any other (e.g. Romanian) Jew, stating as its grounds that 'the Jews do not have a country of their own and therefore do not belong to any state'.[15] So long as the Romanian government was in partial tutelage there was hope that the pressure of foreign powers, combined with persistent intercession by leading members of the community, might in due course impel it to soften its policy. The leading local *shtadlanim* therefore preferred to continue the fight for equal rights—indeed, for any rights at all—without drawing radical conclusions. However, in the event, and contrary to the provisions of the final grant of independence at Berlin in 1878, the release of the government from the last forms of external supervision only led to an intensification of its anti-Jewish policy and to an even less inhibited anti-Semitic campaign in the press and in the streets. New laws harmful to the Jews were promulgated and old ones revived, large-scale expulsions of Jews from the villages and the prohibition on their owning and leasing land were continued. Jewish-owned inns were confiscated, the entry of Jews into the whole of the civil service and the professions was forbidden, and the basic physical security of the Jews was subjected to constant threat from mobs. At this point, when it appeared that there was little to be hoped for from the Powers, the mood of the Jews changed and the movement of migrants, predominantly to the United States and partly to other countries including Erez-Israel, began.

Between 1881 and 1910 67,000 Romanian Jews (a number

---

[15] Alliance Israélite Universelle, *Bulletin Mensuel*, 1878, p. 71.

roughly equivalent to one-fifth of the total Jewish population of the country in the period) migrated to the United States.[16] And as in Russia, once the idea of escape through emigration took hold and the movement began in earnest, some minds began to turn towards Ereẓ-Israel, with people coming together in loosely organized groups that are best described as circles of the like-minded, usually under the stimulus and influence of one or two particularly energetic and strong-minded members of the local community. These circles, of which there were over thirty by the end of 1881, had at first no very clear idea how to proceed and few of their members had sufficient funds to cover the costs of transport, land purchase, and initial capitalization. For a while they did little more than put it about that they were intent upon a *Return*, assuming, with simplicity, that other Jews, better placed, would assist them as a matter of pious duty. Indeed, simplicity—and enthusiasm—were the common characteristics of those Romanian Jews who were attracted to the idea of the Return. Some informed *Ha-Magid* and sat back to wait. Others applied to the Alliance Israélite Universelle in Paris and the Board of Deputies of British Jews in London for loans to supplement what small sums they, as would-be settlers, could raise themselves. However, the Alliance was unable to help, for, as the prospective settlers of Botoşani (in north-eastern Romania) were informed, Ereẓ-Israel 'is poor and hungry and its inhabitants suffer hunger and thirst. New-comers would increase the scarcity. The land can only be worked by those who have farmed from youth and it is our view that there are none such among you, for if there were they would be able to earn a living in their own country.'[17] More commonly, there was no response at all. When it became clear that there was nothing to be hoped for from the West, the local 'emigration societies' decided to come together.

On 30 December 1881 representatives of thirty-two such local groups met in Focşani in southern Moldavia for three days of discussions. It was the first gathering of its kind in living memory, probably the first in modern times. About one hundred people

---

[16] So far as is known, the movement of emigrants from Romania was exclusively Jewish at this time (*Jüdische Statistik*, p. 348), whereas Jews appear to have accounted for 80 per cent of the immigrants registered in the New York port of entry at the turn of the century as of Russian origin and 5 per cent of those registered as of German origin (Halevi, op. cit., p. 11).

[17] Arye Samsonov, *Zikhron Yaʿakov*, Zikhron Yaʿakov, 1942, p. 13.

attended: fifty-one were delegates, the rest local Jewish notables
and journalists. The speeches and discussions were reported at
length in the Jewish press locally and abroad and everything known
about the meeting suggests that those present were imbued with
a strong sense of occasion. The general tone was set in the opening
speech in which the objects of the conference were defined as
seeking to help impoverished brethren by giving them work 'in
field and vineyard', to remove the stain of the Gentile accusation
that Jews will not work, and to 'regain national honour' and
reawaken in the hearts of the Jews those 'holy feelings which the
sheer weight of pain, want, and poverty had put to sleep for thousands of years'.[18] But sentimental overtones and occasional bursts
of national feeling notwithstanding, the matter in hand was migration and resettlement and the discussions were practical and down-
to-earth, not theoretical or ideological, still less political in any
conscious way.

The questions to which the delegates addressed themselves were
chiefly questions of method and procedure. Who should go first,
the rich or the poor? Some argued that unless the rich went first
there would be no livelihood for the poor, others that the immediate purpose of the operation was to succour the poor and that,
in any case, the rich would not move unless and until some demonstrable success had been achieved. Reports were delivered on what
sums of money had been collected and debates were held and
decisions made on details of organization: how further funds were
to be solicited, where the new central committee for all the groups
represented was to be located, how many members it was to have,
by what rules the central committee and the society at large were
to be governed, what each prospective settlement would require
(at the very least a synagogue, a school, a bath-house, a hospital),
members of which professions would have to accompany each
party (a doctor, a midwife, a schoolmaster, a ritual slaughterer, an
agricultural expert, it was decided), and lastly how the settlers
were to be accommodated before all was ready for them on the site
(a hostel was to be built in Jaffa or Haifa). The principal resolution
was clear cut: the first one hundred families would begin their
voyage in the spring; and there was further detailed discussion
on the selection procedure, the moral standards that were to be
required of them, the appropriate age span and family status, the

[18] *Ha-Magid*, 8 February 1882, p. 45.

trades and crafts that would be given priority, the personal resources that would be required of the volunteers over and above what could be granted them out of the new general funds being collected. And finally, two delegates were to set off within one month to choose land for purchase.

In the sense of urgency with which the delegates were infused and the speed with which they proposed to operate may be seen the measure of the harsh condition of Romanian Jewry. Progress after the conference was equally rapid. Quite large sums of money were donated by the local affluent (60,000 francs had been collected in Jassy alone by the beginning of May), land was purchased at Zamarin (renamed Samarin, then Zikhron Ya'akov) about 25 kilometres south of Haifa, and the first large party of emigrants numbering 228 souls set out for Erez-Israel in August. But the enthusiasm, high hopes, and great confidence with which the new country-wide Palestine Emigration Society had embarked on the enterprise owed something too to the activities of two outsiders.

Eliezer Rokeah (1854-1914) was a native of Jerusalem who had settled in Safed in his youth. Unusually for a member of the old *yishuv*, he was powerfully attracted to the ideas of the *haskala* and believed that the reordering and modernization of Jewish life and culture which the *haskala* implied should be pressed in Erez-Israel no less than in the Diaspora. He fostered a settlement of a group of like-minded people from Safed on a stretch of land purchased nearby. But he was opposed by the established leadership of the local Jewish communities; and when he tried to save the hamlet from collapse by mobilizing support for it in the Diaspora, the conflict between the maverick and the local notables became direct and violent. For to their opposition on principle was added the communal leaders' fear that funds might be diverted away from the *haluka*.[19] Rokeah then left the country to look actively for help. After a series of picaresque adventures he arrived in Romania (in 1880) to press the Jewish community of Bucharest, and later those of other towns, to action.[20] He spoke publicly, he wrote for the local Jewish press, and he founded a journal of his own, the first of several periodicals he was to establish and edit. And he made a considerable impression on his audiences—probably by his

---

[19] See above, pp. 19-20.

[20] Rokeah's activities are exhaustively chronicled in Israel Klausner, *Ḥibbat Ẓion be-Romania*, Jerusalem, 1958, chapters 3-5 and *passim*.

ability to take the Land out of the realm of legend and historical imagination by telling them what it was really like and what they would require in practice if they moved there. He was also much involved in the convening of the Focşani conference and the speed with which it got under way clearly owed something to his drive and to the stimulus of his presence. That this stranger to Europe could play any role at all in the affairs of Romanian Jewry and that many were prepared to accept his lead says much about both their ingrained timidity and the depth of the chord which this restless, but essentially mediocre man had struck.

The same was demonstrated, if anything more strikingly, with the appearance of Laurence Oliphant, an adventurer of a different and superior order, a man of intellect and imagination, and altogether a remarkable example of the Victorian who travelled, wrote, dabbled in politics, and adopted social causes, always with system, seemingly unlimited self-confidence, and a consistently high degree of moral fervour.[21] Oliphant's involvement in Jewish affairs came by way of a concern for the survival of the Ottoman Empire along lines which were in keeping with the Beaconsfield–Salisbury policy of support for Turkey against Russian pressure. He believed that the Congress of Berlin of 1878 had 'amounted to a European coalition against Russian aggression on Turkey in Europe, which must put an end henceforth and for ever to any designs on her part on Constantinople'.[22] The pressure could therefore be expected to be exerted in future against Turkey in Asia, particularly through Armenia and Kurdistan, but ultimately in the direction of Palestine, whose religious and strategic attractions would sooner or later prove irresistible to the Russians. Turkish administration in these parts had therefore to be cleaned up and improved in good time and Palestine itself 'regenerated'. Oliphant believed that this could best be done by the encouragement of Jewish settlement, particularly in the parts of Palestine which lay east of the Jordan and which were sparsely settled and under- and badly administered. The immediate benefit to the region was plain, as was the benefit to the Jews themselves. As the plan provided for the Jewish settlers to become subjects of the

---

[21] He was greatly drawn to his contemporary General Gordon and the passages in which he writes of Gordon are particularly moving and revealing. Cf. *Haifa, or Life in Modern Palestine*, Edinburgh, 1887, pp. 274–80.

[22] *The Land of Gilead*, Edinburgh, 1880, p. 516.

Sultan it would in time lead to a strong alliance based on mutual
interest between Turkey and the Jewish people. This, thought
Oliphant, should make his project doubly attractive to the Porte,
for 'owing to the financial, political, and commercial importance
to which the Jews have now attained, there is probably no one
Power in Europe that would prove so valuable an ally to a nation
likely to be engaged in a European war, as this wealthy, powerful,
and cosmopolitan race'.[23] As for his own country, Britain ought
certainly to be interested in any plan to strengthen the Ottoman
Empire internally against external pressures; and besides, it would
have reason to welcome the commercial advantages stemming from
an influx of Jews and Jewish enterprise into the stagnant economy
of Palestine and southern Syria. Finally, there were the imponder-
able and incalculable aspects of the venture: those pertaining to
the revival of Jewish settlement in Palestine which those Englishmen 'who see in the relations which our country now occupies
towards the Holy Land the hand of Providence' could not lightly
ignore.

These ideas came to be fully formulated in the course of a
journey through the country in 1879, at the end of which Oliphant,
armed with letters of introduction from the English Prime Minister
and the English and French Foreign Secretaries, began to negotiate
with the Porte. The lands in question were fertile and almost unoccupied. What was needed was an *irade* authorizing the formation
of a company to colonize them and, more generally, some assurance
of the Turkish government's benevolent view of the scheme in its
entirety. Almost a year of systematic lobbying passed before the
Turkish ministers could be induced to express themselves favourably, while making it clear, at the same time, that all depended
ultimately upon the Sultan. However, when Oliphant was at last
received by ʿAbd al-Hamid he was told that, on the contrary, while
he, the Sultan, favoured the project, his ministers were unanimously
and unalterably opposed to it. Convinced that he had been toyed
with and deceived, Oliphant left Constantinople in a fury, returned
to London, and, feeling he now had nothing to lose, made his plan
and his views on the treatment he had been accorded by the Turks
fully public.[24]

---

[23] Ibid., p. 503.
[24] Yaʿakov Rozenfeld, 'Min ha-Bosforos' (from *Razsvyet*, 11/23 July 1882), in Yavne'eli,
op. cit. i, pp. 209–17.

The fact was that such support for his plans as he had gained in Turkey was too mild to make so much as a dent in the wall of Ottoman suspicion. Despite the essentially pro-Turkish policy of the British government of the day, the question whether it was not all an ingenious European trick clearly hovered over his discussions. When the less friendly Liberals returned to power in 1880 the chances of chipping effectively at the wall were further reduced. And when the British occupied Egypt in the summer of 1882 any lingering hope of gaining Turkish support that Oliphant might have retained was in fact dissolved. The only material result of his efforts was, unwittingly, to help cast the incipient migration of Jews from Russia and Romania in the least favourable light in Constantinople by virtue of his own association with it—for it was to the Jews of Russia and Romania, of course, that he looked for recruits for the 'land of Gilead'.

However, the sudden appearance in Constantinople and London, and then in Galicia and Romania, of a Gentile of considerable distinction, sufficiently well equipped socially and politically to move and operate in quite exalted circles, and intent upon promoting the return of the Jews to Erez-Israel, had a galvanizing effect on the movement itself everywhere. When he returned to Eastern Europe in the wake of the events of 1881 in Russia news of 'the Lord' (*ha-sar*) Oliphant spread rapidly through the Pale and elsewhere. He appeared at Brody and made it clear that he was all for the refugees being channelled to Erez-Israel, rather than to the United States. And this was soon known. He corresponded in friendly fashion with Smolenskin. He travelled to Romania where he encouraged the Jews to emigrate to Erez-Israel 'in preference to America, where Judaism, scattered and dispersed in all parts, threatens to disappear' and promised the Emigration Committee 'to treat on their behalf at Constantinople'.[25] It was he whom the Biluim went to see in the first place when they arrived in Turkey and from whom they expected help. 'Lord!', wrote one hundred and five *Hovevei Zion* from Nikolaev (in southern Russia) to Oliphant, 'Providence itself has delivered the wand of our nation's leadership into your hands and with your possession of it a new era in the history of the Jews with all its suffering begins.'[26] He was spoken of as a 'Redeemer', and a 'second Cyrus'. He raised extravagant and infinitely naïve hopes which he himself had later

[25] *Jewish Chronicle*, 12 May 1882.     [26] Druyanov, i, no. 10, col. 24.

to damp down. Above all, he encouraged the Jews who wished for a Return to think it a feasible venture—less, however, by what he could promise, let alone accomplish, than by his own appearance *ex machina* and the conclusions from it which they drew, namely that they were not entirely alone and that they had friends in court (which was false) and that it was both necessary and possible to raise the enterprise from the level of philanthropy to that of public affairs (which was correct). Momentarily, for the multitude of semi-isolated communities in Eastern and South-Eastern Europe, Oliphant was the focal point of national sentiment and purpose. Had he been a Jew himself, instead of a Victorian gentleman from England, and had he fully understood, and been fired by, the magnitude of the function which was waiting to be filled, he might have chosen to seize the 'wand' which the innocents of Nikolaev wished to place in his hands. Instead, he retired shortly to a house on Mount Carmel, whence he continued to explore the surrounding country and take a kindly and condescending interest in the new Jewish settlers.

iv

The third category of migrants to Erez-Israel in the early 1880s emerged, like the Biluim, from Russia. But in many other respects, they were more akin to the emigrants from Romania. Their purposes were simpler than those of the Biluim, their ideological position, such as it was, stemmed from national–religious sentiment uncomplicated by broader social aims and principles, and, being predominantly family men and women, their immediate need for adequate food, shelter, and livelihood necessarily overshadowed all other considerations. However, unlike the emigrants from Romania who had moved according to a pre-arranged plan and as an organized body (the first party of settlers in Zikhron Yaʿakov had even carried their own building materials with them), the great majority of the Russian Jews arrived in the country much as other Russian and Polish Jews had streamed into Brody: in small family groups or individually, in haste, ill prepared, prey to rumour, mostly penniless, fearful, suspicious, and more or less consciously seeking support from others—from local communities, from western Jewish philanthropy, from the few of their own number who had the means of survival for a time, at least. Thus, apart from those who had contacts and kinsmen among the members of the 'old' *yishuv*, and whom they joined in Safed and Tiberias, primarily, the majority of the new arrivals did not differ materially in circumstances, and only marginally in motivation, from the much greater stream of refugees moving out of Russia towards Western Europe and the Americas; and they were no more capable than the Biluim of establishing themselves in farming villages, or even in urban trades and crafts. Had it not been for a handful of men of action in whom were combined both something of the daring and clear purpose of the Biluim *and* the resources to put them to good effect it is doubtful if this small, initial wave of migrants from Russia would have left any mark at all.

The most notable of these was Zalman David Levontin (1856–1940). Levontin was in every respect typical of the middle range of Russian-Jewish *maskilim* possessed of a firm foot in both cultures —'a man out of doors, but a Jew within his home', in Y. L. Gordon's phrase—and he was therefore, like many others of his class, both peculiarly vulnerable to the disappointment and humiliation which Russian policy towards the Jews now imposed upon them and, at the same time, drawn to a cure for the Jewish condition that could be founded squarely on the national tradition, rather than on final escape from it. 'Even as a boy,' he wrote in his autobiography, 'when I studied geography and learnt that the Republic of Liberia had been founded by Negroes in Africa, I asked myself: if the Negroes could found a free republic for themselves, why should we not go and found a state for ourselves too in the land of our ancestors?'[27] He was also a man of energy and impatience. 'You were quite right, and I agree with your view that your work on the theory of the question of the settlement of Erez-Israel is very valuable', he wrote to a friend of similar principles but different temperament, '. . . but, as for me, I have found it *necessary* to leave our country and go to the Holy Land, or in other words, to move from words to deeds.'[28]

Levontin set out from Russia at the end of January 1882, armed with a kind of power of attorney from two groups of families, the one in his home town of Kremenchug, the other in Kharkov, whom, after much labour, he himself had persuaded to allow him to act on their behalf in Erez-Israel. Like the Biluim, his plan was to set up a farming village as rapidly as possible. Unlike them, he

[27] *Le-erez avoteinu*, second edition, i, Tel Aviv, 1924, pp. 7–8.
[28] Levontin to Mordekai Ben-Hillel Ha-Kohen, 30 January 1882 (O.S.). Druyanov, iii, no. 1122, col. 347 (emphasis in original).

had no interest in socialism or other ideas of general social application and was a man of system and deliberation (he had been a bank
official). He found, on arrival, that, apart from the representatives
sent out by the Romanian Emigration Society, with whom he
promptly made common cause, and the Biluim, he was alone in
coming to Jaffa equipped with a concrete plan of action. He spent
the months of February and March in systematic travel through
the country, carefully accumulating information on such land as
was available for purchase, on the estimated costs of settlement,
on the probable immediate needs of the settlers, on learning to
discriminate between those members of the old *yishuv* who were
out to rook the immigrants and those who were prepared to help
them, and on taking the measure of the new Turkish regulations
forbidding the sale of land to Jews intending to settle in 'large'
numbers (without it being immediately clear, either to the Turkish
officials or to anyone else, how many people constituted a 'large'
community). But in any case, few of the candidates for immediate settlement milling about in Jaffa could muster the price of
farmland, and Levontin's own resources were too small to suffice for more than some assistance to them while they waited.
Meanwhile, ever the man of good order, he formed a committee
'whose task it is to establish the colonization of our brethren in the
Holy Land on a rational basis' and sent out a call through the
Jewish press for the 'one thing—funds—we are not adequately
provided with, and which we hope our brethren in all parts of the
world will provide'.[29] But funds only trickled in until an elderly,
childless uncle of Levontin's agreed to come to his rescue. A stretch
of uncultivated land on the edge of the coastal dunes south of Jaffa
was then found. The prohibition on purchase by foreign Jews was
circumvented by the land being registered in the name of Hayyim
Amzalak, a local Jew and a warm sympathizer and who, as British
Vice-Consul in Jaffa, was privileged to make the transaction without interference from the Turkish authorities. In August 1882
Levontin and thirteen other heads of families set out to strike root
in their new home which they called Rishon le-Zion. Thereafter,
the great question was whether, as Levontin and his friends
expected, others would follow, and in what numbers.

By the end of 1884 Levontin's settlement at Rishon le-Zion and
the Romanians' settlements at Samaria and Rosh Pina had been

[29] *Jewish Chronicle*, 5 May 1882.

followed by four others, among them the Biluim's Gedera. Together
with Petaḥ Tikva, which had been started by a group of orthodox
Jews from Jerusalem in 1878, then abandoned, and was now
started up again, there were thus eight entirely Jewish villages in
the country. To that extent, the bridgehead and beacon which the
Russian Jews explicitly, and the Romanian Jews somewhat less
deliberately, had wished to set up was now in evidence. Yet no
more settlements were to be established before the end of the
decade, nor was progress to be really substantial for a long while
after. The total population of the eight villages reached only 2,415
in 1890/1.[30] The total figure for the entire period of the First *Aliya*
(1882–1903) was between twenty and thirty thousand (an annual
average of about a thousand, or just under 3 per cent of the full
migration of Jews out of Europe to other continents.[31] Despite the
growing unwillingness of Russo-Polish and Romanian Jewry to
submit to moral injury and material oppression with the docility
and philosophic resignation which Jews and non-Jews alike had
come to regard as traditional, if not proper in the past, the movement to Ereẓ-Israel failed to gain momentum and the participating
settlers and their supporters in Eastern and Southern Europe were
unable to exploit the initial effort and expand it as they had hoped.
Neither by direct action nor by example were they able to divert
more than a fraction of the mighty stream of Jews moving westwards, let alone precipitate a mass move out of Europe whose
conscious *raison d'être* was a Return to the Land.

Why was this so? The causes seem to have been in part external
to the Jews of Eastern Europe and in part internal, and can be
further divided into those relating to conditions and the climate of
opinion in Europe and those relating to conditions in Ereẓ-Israel
itself. No single element can be judged decisive, nor were they all,
even in combination, entirely fatal to the movement. But taken
together they go a long way to explain the sharp discrepancy
between thoughts and action and between hopes and achievement.

The material and moral backing offered migrants by the communal and philanthropic organizations of western Jewry depended
overwhelmingly on their destination. For those wishing to leave
for the Americas, or, having left Russia and Romania, to return,

[30] D. Gurevich and A. Gerz, *Ha-hityashvut ha-ḥakla'it ha-'ivrit be-Erez-Israel*, Jerusalem,
1938, p. *34.
[31] R. Bachi, 'Ha-okhlosia: demografia', *Ha-enẓiklopedia ha-'ivrit*, vi, p. 671.

help was not infrequently available. For example, the representative of the Alliance Israélite Universelle proposed in 1882 that Brody be cleared of the refugees at an estimated cost of 4 million francs; and this was agreed to at a conference of representatives of the charitable organizations, the Alliance alone being prepared to put up a quarter of the sum. There was the large sum of money collected in Britain expressly for the refugees from Russia, the 'Mansion House Fund', and there were lesser contributions from Jewish organizations elsewhere, including the United States. There were the direct services performed by the philanthropic organizations: help to the travellers, some guidance to regions where work might be available, and the not inconsiderable moral backing they provided as living evidence for the refugees that they were not totally abandoned in a hostile world. All this was extremely limited, and in quantitative terms far below what was required. But little or none of it was available for Jews coming to Erez-Israel, neither the material support, nor the moral backing—except, *in extremis* and selectively, in the form of help to return to Russia or to continue on to the Americas or elsewhere.

The overt arguments advanced against *'aliya* were all of a practical order: settlement in Erez-Israel meant settlement on the land, the land available for purchase and cultivation was either infertile or in unhealthy districts, men from northern countries would have difficulty working 'under a hot sun', the Arab farmers sold their produce at prices too low for Europeans to compete with, public security was poor, the tax system was iniquitous, and the 'cultivator' was either 'a prize for the farmer of tithes' or, worse, 'at the mercy of corrupt officials'. As for northern Palestine and the 'trans-Jordanic country' where, it was true, there was much excellent and unoccupied land, there 'Turkish rule is weak and . . . there is no system of police and very little safety for life and property' and settlers would be subject to the depredations of the Bedouin. Besides, there were no roads and no railways, no outlet to the sea. And, 'lastly, what is the state of civilization by which emigrants would be surrounded?' It followed, wrote a prominent English Jew in protest against the London *Jewish Chronicle*'s editorial support for 'the new Exodus',

that Palestine, however dear to us from its glories in the past and its hopes in the future, was not at this present time a region to which we could conscientiously encourage emigration . . .

It is quite true that whether we like it or no, there will be a large emigration of Jews from Russia, Poland, and Roumania to Palestine, the expenses of which will be covered either by the resources of the emigrants themselves, or by the contributions of those Jews in various countries who have for generations past furnished the 'Haluka' to Jerusalem and kept up the unhappy state of things in that city, which is the source of so much deep-seated misery and of so great a moral and physical depression.

We can unfortunately exercise no influence on these emigrants. All we can do is to advise them as strongly as possible to choose another direction; but if merely because they persist in going to Palestine we were to afford them some sort of assistance, and thus act against our own judgement, we should be rendering ourselves responsible for the ruin which, most of us think, must inevitably follow.[32]

The bases of the argument were provided by the men of the Alliance who undoubtedly did know more about the practical problems involved in the settlement of Jews in Erez-Israel than anyone else. While they tended to exaggerate the difficulties and, oddly, implicitly to discount their own success at the agricultural school at Mikve Israel, they were aware that in the absence of industry, commercial opportunities, and effective communications with other Near-Eastern countries, settlement meant settlement on the land—if the immigrants were not to be rapidly reduced, that is, to a mass of paupers, permanently and disastrously dependent on the charity of their brethren abroad. Since the philanthropists of the day thought well-nigh exclusively in terms of temporary aid and of assisting migrants *en route* to their ultimate destination, rather than of long-term assistance to them upon arrival, their opposition to the movement towards Erez-Israel rested on a logic that was not easy to refute. And, accordingly, the practical prospects for settlement—and therefore for a continuation of immigration beyond the first spontaneous wave—depended, in the first instance, on what resources the immigrants themselves could provide or, alternatively, what their communities could and would contribute. But the fact was that the overwhelming majority of immigrants from Russia and Poland had, as has been said, no resources of their own and were therefore, in this respect, no better placed than the Biluim. Nor could there be, at this stage, any public gathering

---

[32] F. D. Mocatta, one of the leading figures in the Anglo-Jewish Association, in the *Jewish Chronicle*, 19 May 1882. See also *Jewish Chronicle*, 24 March, 31 March, 21 April, 2 June 1882, for part of the extended correspondence on the subject in which Charles Netter of the Alliance and David Gordon for the opposing side both participated.

within the Russian Empire remotely like that which had taken place in Romania at Focşani at which the issues could be thrashed out and the funnelling of communal resources for so vast an enterprise proclaimed and organized. For one thing, such a conference would have had to have been held in secret, which apart from making it to some extent a self-defeating exercise, would have been a step far too radical for the timid notables of the community to envisage.[33] For another, as we have seen, few of those who had either the private means to help or the social prestige within the communities to induce others to do so were so inclined. The anti-Jewish policies of the Russian government operated at this time primarily against the poor, and the well-to-do were under correspondingly less pressure to emigrate and greater inducement to bend with the wind.

Against this background an ineradicable uncertainty attached itself to the 'Palestinian' option—as opposed to the 'American' or to that of immobility—from the first. After all, it was for a distant country of which little was known and of which much that was reported was clearly fable and hearsay. For those interested, there was no lack of advice; but it was contradictory. The leading figures in Jewry were bitterly opposed to it; on the other hand, they were remote from the immediate needs of the Jews of the Pale. Arguments offered in its favour by lesser figures *ipso facto* carried less conviction. It was extremely hard for an ordinary man to judge the value of anything he was told. Who, then, was to be believed; who was to be followed? The Jews, Levontin's brother wrote to him from Moscow,

have always relied on authority, and so they do today, relying on some 'great man', so that if a notable personality . . . advises against the settlement of Ereẓ-Israel they drop the idea; while if . . . [he] argues in its

[33] At a second conference of notables held under the auspices of Baron Guenzberg in April 1882, again with the express permission of the Minister of Interior, and at which it was resolved to 'reject completely the thought of organizing emigration, as being subversive of the dignity of the Russian body politic and of the historic rights of the Jews to their present fatherland', the participants thought it necessary to refute current allegations concerning the existence of a secret, separatist, inter-communal organization: 'We, the undersigned, the representatives of various centers of Jewish settlement in Russia, rabbis, members of religious organizations and synagogue boards, consider it our sacred duty, calling to witness God Omniscient, to declare publicly, in the presence of the whole of Russia, that there exists neither an open nor a secret Kahal administration among the Russian Jews; that Jewish life is entirely foreign to any organization of this kind and to any of the attributes ascribed to such an organization by evil-minded persons' (Dubnov, op. cit. ii, p. 307).

favour, they believe him. So too with this matter: a great deal was expected of Oliphant and [the Jews] believed in him because all the journals said that he was, indeed, a great man, a wise and sensible man, an 'authority'. But if now someone else comes along and points out his failings, their spirits fall and they are at a loss.[34]

Moreover, the easily aroused scepticism soon had facts to feed on. It was not long before Oliphant's failure to gain Turkish support was understood to be only the first sign of the wholly unanticipated and rapidly crystallizing *active* opposition of the Ottoman authorities. It is not clear at precisely what point the Turks had begun to watch the movement of Jews from Eastern Europe, nor what it was that had triggered off their interest, but there is no doubt whatever that as early as the middle of 1881 the Porte was fully alert to the phenomenon and that although a clear policy on the subject may not have been finally formulated, attitudes had hardened into hostility by the end of the year.[35] For a while, the issue was confused by uncertainty on both sides which was fed by the reluctance of the Turks to call a spade a spade and by the consequent encouragement of the Jews to hope for the best. Rumours that the migration of Jews into Palestine was about to be prohibited had reached Romania before the Focşani conference (December 1881). But when the Turkish envoy in Bucharest was asked point-blank whether there was any truth in the story his answer, after referring the query to Constantinople, was a categorical denial.[36] The conference then proceeded in good heart. Six months later, a new inquiry in the wake of fresh rumours led to a response in modified form. Romanian Jews were still free to settle in Palestine, but only provided they adopted (or readopted) Ottoman nationality, undertook not to return to Romania, and did not settle in 'large' communities, but in groups of between one hundred and two hundred families at most.[37] But meanwhile a harsher formulation of policy had already been made public in Odessa (outside the Ottoman Consulate-General, 28 April 1882): Jews were not permitted to settle in Palestine at all, but could immigrate to other provinces of the Empire if they wished and on condition that they became Ottoman subjects. After that the confusion of multiplying, over-

[34] Y. Y. Levontin to Z. D. Levontin, 29 May 1882 (O.S.). Druyanov, iii, no. 1144, cols. 409–10.
[35] N. J. Mandel, 'Turks, Arabs and Jewish Immigration into Palestine: 1882–1914', unpublished Oxford doctoral thesis, 1965, p. 488 and n., and pp. 3–5.
[36] *Ha-Magid*, 25 January 1882, p. 31.          [37] Ibid., 21 June 1882, p. 196.

lapping, partly conflicting public statements, directives, administrative and police actions in Constantinople, in Jerusalem, in Jaffa, in Haifa, and elsewhere is too great to disentangle. Varying categorizations of prohibited immigrants were listed from time to time, but some lumped the Jews from Russia and from Romania together, while others did not, some included Bulgarians, some did not, some were directed at all Jews, including those from the Western countries, some only at Jews arriving with the intention of settling, some included bona fide pilgrims as well. To the regulations restricting the entry of Jews and forbidding their settlement were added parallel regulations forbidding the sale and lease of land to Jews and even the construction of houses. All these regulations grew in number and complexity compounded by the fact that they were applied with unequal rigour from place to place and over time. This confusion and lack of system were in part functions of the general poverty of Ottoman administration and the inequality of devotion and integrity which characterized Ottoman officials from regional and district governors all the way down to the lowest land-office clerk and the policemen on duty at the port of Jaffa. But it was no less a product of sporadic pressure by the European powers who, whatever they may have thought of the migration of Jews into the country *per se*, were consistently opposed to any erosion of the system of capitulations whereby foreign nationals retained very considerable immunities from legal, fiscal, and police pressure or interference on the part of the Turks. The perpetual reformulation and amendment of the regulations were largely responses to the intervention of the powers—often to be followed, relatively quickly, by fresh attempts to bring about the desired result with diminished diplomatic costs.

The refusal of the Ottomans to deviate from their policy of limiting Jewish settlement to the absolute minimum—if it was not possible entirely to prevent it—reflected the relative clarity with which the Sultan and the Porte perceived their aims in this connection. These were, in the first place, to avoid providing the powers which were beneficiaries of the capitulatory system with a vastly increased field of concern and of opportunities for action. From which it followed that the intervention of the powers on behalf of their Jewish subjects was to some extent counter-productive, for it confirmed and reconfirmed Ottoman suspicions and fears. In the second place, as Ottoman officials told representatives of the

Alliance Israélite Universelle in so many words, they did not wish to have yet another, potentially troublesome nationality problem on their hands 'après la question bulgare, roumeliste et autres'.[38] The succession of envoys of greater and lesser distinction who had arrived in Constantinople to attempt to negotiate with the Porte in these early years and the reports from Turkish consular officials in Russia and Romania on the climate of opinion amongst Jews all tended to confirm and reinforce the diagnosis of the movement that had been arrived at so quickly at the Porte. So much so, in fact, that evidence of the effect of these reports soon filtered back to Europe and the word began to go out that it would be wise to exercise discretion.[39] But even if this had been possible, it was too late for results, for by then policy in Constantinople had set.

The material effects of Turkish policy on the movement to settle in Erez-Israel were of two kinds. One was to pit the hardier and less flexible spirits against the Turkish authorities in an almost perpetual game of cat and mouse, of prevarication and counter-prevarication, of intervention and counter-intervention, whereby every method of evading the restrictive regulations and of eluding exposure and punishment was tried by the Jews and ever-recurring waves of pressure and constraint against them flowed back in response from Constantinople and Jerusalem. And since the consequence of this conflict was both to impel the Jews to bring whatever slender political resources they could mobilize into play and greatly to strengthen their own internal, national consciousness and cohesion, the result of the collision was to intensify and accelerate those developments which it was the fundamental object of Turkish policy to inhibit—at any rate, so far as those Jews who had managed to get a toe-hold in the country were concerned.

The second effect of Turkish policy was substantially—but never entirely—to inhibit immigration both immediately and physically by refusing Jews permission to land and, in the longer term, by casting doubt in the minds of potential migrants on the practicability of the entire enterprise. If the Turks were unalterably opposed to the idea of a Jewish return, even on the most modest of bases, and if the predominant picture was one of migrants being turned away and of drifting from port of entry to port of entry and, at best, gaining admittance to the land of their fathers through the humiliat-

---

[38] Mandel, op. cit., pp. 12–13.
[39] See, for example, *Ha-Magid*, 19 July 1882, p. 230.

ing and disreputable expedients of false testimony and bribery, what future did it have now and how seriously could it be recommended as a more honourable and secure alternative than the 'American' option?

Nor was this all, for to this source of doubt and scepticism was added the plain fact that for all their high hopes and despite their calculations, the settlers themselves were very soon in another kind of trouble. Both those at Rishon le-Zion and those at Samarin and Rosh Pina had grossly overestimated their capacity to make the villages economically viable within a measurable—let alone a short—period. The hard-headed and sharp-eyed representatives of western Jewish philanthropy who visited them were touched, in spite of themselves, by the novel spectacle of Jews, lately come from the towns of South-Eastern Europe, working devotedly in conditions of great hardship, without adequate resources, and with pitifully little experience. But they could see well enough the miserable conditions of the wives and children left behind in the towns, some starving, while the men painfully cleared the land and built the houses; and they could calculate the capital investment the settlements would require if they were ever to succeed and compare their sums with what they knew of the settlers' resources. No doubt the existing settlements could be saved, they thought, and the novice farmers duly taught how to manipulate a plough properly and plant their vines. But the half-built villages would first have to be put under proper and skilled management and there must certainly be no *further* nonsense of this kind: for in combination the political and economic obstacles to substantial Jewish settlement were insuperable.

The Samarin experiment is decisive [Veneziani reported to the Central Committee of the Alliance Israélite in June 1883] . . . Every impulse to emigrate to Palestine and every attempt, at colonization, however timid it might be, must be absolutely and expressly checked for the present by all the means in our power. There are a thousand reasons, some of which I have already mentioned, which require us to act in this manner: the clumsy committees, the emigrants' absolute lack of agricultural experience and of resources, the enormous sums swallowed up in the attempts made thus far with no result. Whenever I have had occasion to take ship in these parts I have met numbers of miserable Jews who have come here I know not how, who are not permitted to land, who have no resources to go further. It is a lamentable spectacle and, moreover, it is disgraceful and scandalous to see those poor people subjected to systematic exploitation both by the police and by an organized society of jobbers posted in all the ports along the coast who by shameless commission-taking extort what these unfortunates still possess and lead them from Alexandria to Beirut and back again in the illusory hope of arranging for them to be secretly disembarked. It is time this tragedy ended; and apart from the support which we must render these unfortunates who have settled in Palestine thus far and have been fatally engulfed in disastrous attempts at colonization, it is the one result we should seek to attain—and that by means of all the weight of our authority and all the pressure of our influence.[40]

[40] Alliance Israélite Universelle, *Bulletin Mensuel*, July 1883, p. 98.

# 5

## *Auto-emancipation*

i

THE pogroms of 1881-4 and the sea-change which came over Russian policy towards the Jews of the Empire precipitated what can now be recognized as the first stage of the extended, tragic, and still incomplete evacuation of the Jews from Eastern Europe. The stream to the West, vastly greater, as we have seen, than that to Erez-Israel, was a mass national migration which rapidly changed the demographic map of world Jewry out of all recognition. In the main, it was directly motivated by fear, pain, and hunger, which is to say, by pressures, the sources of which were external to Jewry. The corresponding promise which it held out was betterment of the condition of the individual Jew by his immediate emancipation from oppression by the state and the grant of real hope of an adequate livelihood. The most conservative of Eastern European Jews feared, and with good reason, that the removal of Jews from lands in which they formed large and dense communities to others where they would necessarily be diffused relatively widely, would lead, in time, to laxity in religious observance and, ultimately, to an irreversible process of assimilation. The assimilationists and integrationists were equally opposed to emigration on other grounds (that have been noted). But so long as the external pressures were maintained and the barriers to migration were not replaced—or raised, where there had been none—the movement could have remained in being, a national movement which engulfed ever wider and more differentiated circles of what was then the bulk of Jewry. It *required* no leaders, no institutions, and no ideology.

In contrast, the movement to Erez-Israel was one of individuals and tiny groups, too few and ill cohering to have an appreciable effect on the over-all structure and distribution of Jewry for decades to come. It offered little (and in some respects no) relief

from external stress, no rapid improvement in the material conditions of life, and only a very marginal improvement, if any, in the
relations between the individual Jew and the state authorities.
For the assured individual emancipation available in the West,
it substituted an ill-defined promise of collective, national transformation. It functioned as a fusion of the simple response to the
external pressures with much more complex, active, internal
ideological, and sentimental drives. But for these to have had a
really marked and large-scale effect, even remotely comparable to
that of the movement to the West, the objective conditions of
settlement in Erez-Israel would have had to have been a great deal
easier. In brief, the return to Erez-Israel only made sense to the
extent that it was taken to imply a revolutionary change in the
condition of the Jewish people as a whole, leading only in time, and
as its consequence, to a change in the condition of individual Jews.
Principle was therefore of the essence. It raised questions which
differed in character from, and were much more numerous and
varied than, those prompted by the move out of the Russo-Polish
Pale to the Americas. And given the climate of opinion and the
facts of the environment, neither the desirability of the ends which
it implied, nor the feasibility and availability of the means to those
ends, were beyond debate, let alone self-evident.

The rapid development of the movement of Return thus depended
in the first instance and at a minimum upon the emergence of a new
body of national leaders and a wholly new concept of national
organization and mobilization. Unlike the classic categories of
communal leaders, the rabbis and notables, whose now failing
authority rested upon personal status and putative indispensability,
the new candidates for leadership had to rely on the conviction
their interpretation of events and their plan for action would carry
—in other words, on their ability to formulate a programme and
show evidence of some capacity to implement it. Men, programme,
and institutions did all appear in due course, but slowly, and for
long without reaching that degree of integration of organization
and ideology at which imagination is kindled and confidence flares
outward beyond the circle of the initiated. In great part this was
because the *systematic* answers to the questions What had happened?
and What was to be done? were not evolved by those who found
the courage, themselves, to break sharply out of Eastern Europe,
but by others who were still embedded in the mass of ghetto Jewry

that remained behind, and subject to the overwhelming influence of the world immediately around them.

The first serious, persuasive, and indigenous formulations of answers to these questions were by M. L. Lilienblum and Y. L. Pinsker. It was therefore around them, initially, that what was later to be called the Zionist movement began to form.

ii

In Moshe Leib Lilienblum (1843-1910) life and letters combined to produce what is beyond doubt the most vivid and instructive epitome of the social and moral crisis of Russo-Polish Jewry in the latter half of the nineteenth century. Lilienblum was born in Kaidan (Kedainiai), near Kovno (Kaunas), Lithuania. His father, a cooper, but, like many Jewish craftsmen, a man of some learning, was entirely the creature of his place and times. He saw to it that his only son began his studies before he was five, wished him to begin the Talmud at seven, and, above all else, that he become that most prestigious of figures, a man noted for his rabbinic learning. Equally in the tradition, his father had him betrothed by the time he was thirteen and married off less than three years later. From the first, study was intended to be the centre and framework of his son's life. This was all well within the classic system: but it was none the less a system which carried within it the seed of its own disintegration. In Lilienblum's bitter recollection of his childhood and adolescence (in *Ḥaṭ'ot ne'urim*):

> I was four years and three months old, before my little powers had developed, when I was given over to the burden of *Tora* and the burden of teachers, and from then on I was to be imprisoned all through the day in my school-room. I was not allowed to derive any enjoyment from the pleasant years of childhood; I was not allowed to grow in strength [physically] through freedom and children's games . . . I was deprived of all knowledge and all matters that did not fall within the ambit of the study of the Talmud . . .[1]

In his sixteenth year he moved to his father-in-law's town, Vilkomir (Ukmergē), where he remained until 1869 and there, initially, he realized many of his father's hopes. He became extraordinarily well versed in the traditional learning, even by the rigorous standards

[1] *Ketavim otobiografiim* (edited by S. Breiman), i, Jerusalem, 1970, p. 88.

of Lithuanian Jewry, and gained a small reputation for himself as a scholar. But equally, he got to know and acquire an appetite for secular literature from which even Vilkomir could not be totally sealed off. By the time he was in his early twenties the total and exclusive immersion in Talmudic studies to which he had been subjected, coupled to the early marriage and the family with which he was soon saddled, had begun to oppress him. The fascination which the Talmud had held for him began to pall and the immense labour which the effort to master it entailed wearied him. More seriously still, he began to question its *utility*. He now found himself at odds with his fellow scholars and with the community at large; and it was at this point, out of the elements of his own predicament, and almost entirely alone with his thoughts, that Lilienblum evolved his exceptionally trenchant critique of the role of religious practice and teachings in Jewish life. Its initial formulation was in an article entitled 'Orḥot ha-Talmud' ('The Ways of the Talmud') published in 1868.

The heart of Lilienblum's thesis was the sharp distinction he drew between that part of the Law which was immutable and that part which was not, between the truly God-given Law (*Tora she-min ha-shamayim*) and man-made Talmudic Law (*Tora she-beʿal peh*—literally, the 'verbal Law'). That the God-given, Mosaic Law must be read in the light of the great body of accretions to it embodied in the Talmud and that the latter partook of the sanctity and authority of the former—these were clear and hallowed principles, absolutely central to the rabbinic system. To question them, as did Lilienblum, was grossly heretical. But Lilienblum argued, with some justice, that historically, the Talmudic (man-made, if divinely inspired) Law had been evolved by the sages in the early stages of the Dispersion as a means of helping the Jews to adjust to the new social needs and conditions of the times. And if it later lost this function and became, on the contrary, the principal means whereby Jews were kept out of the mainstream of life around them, then, given the condition of the Jews in the Middle Ages, even this was not without some social justification. But now the old practices and the old forms of intellectual and social constriction were just so many obstacles to changes that were, at long last, both badly needed and possible. It followed that the Talmudically ordained rules of religious observance must be reformed and that the reform must be in the direction of facilitating the entry—or re-entry—of Jews into society at large and into the economy around them. Life and Law must, once again, be 'joined up'. Certainly the essentials of the teachings of Moses and the Prophets must be retained, but all that was peripheral to them and anachronistic had now to be shorn away. The opportunity for change was there and the rabbis must come together and institute the changes in the organized and orderly manner that Lilienblum saw as the *sine qua non* of the entire operation. But time was short. If they did not act, the fabric of religious norms that bound the Jews to one another and upon which national survival depended would be dissipated, irreversibly, by the centrifugal pull of change around them and in the wake of the general loss of faith and the common whoring after cosmopolitan ideas.

Lilienblum's views developed almost wholly from the inside, from within Jewry, and without too much thought for, and barely under the influence of, the world outside it. They derived directly from his profound sense that the modes of Jewish life were dark and oppressive and that the worn, rabbinic path led to a dead end. And they rested on the simple assumption that the outside world —of which he knew very little at this stage—would indeed accept, or was already accepting, a reborn and reformed Jew. His views were thus optimistic and forward-looking and profoundly critical of the tradition as a whole. He did not doubt now (or later) that the desire of the Jews to maintain their national identity and existence was in itself a valid and proper purpose, or that deliberate assimilation was to all intents and purposes unworkable in practice and perverse (like suicide) in principle.

As his ideas became known, his situation in the small town of Vilkomir became more difficult, then impossible. In 1869, assisted by new allies among the *maskilim* of Kovno, he left his firmly orthodox wife and his children and moved to Odessa. Odessa was technically within the Pale of Settlement and had a large Jewish population (approximately 50,000 at this time). But its community was without parallel in Russia for the laxity of religious observance, the relative pervasiveness of free thought, and the degree to which the processes of cultural assimilation into the fairly hetero-geneous local population were at work.[2] Thus, here in this new and

---

[2] For example: the proportion of Jewish pupils in the Odessa district gymnasiums at this time was three times the average for the cities of the Pale. Y. Slutsky, 'Ẓemiḥata shel ha-inteligenẓia ha-yehudit-rusit', *Ẓion*, xxv. 3–4, 1960, pp. 227–8.

E

comparatively open society, Lilienblum was for the first time brought face to face with the problem of the *secular* integration of the Jews into non-Jewish society. It was sharpened and deepened for him by his personal circumstances, for he found himself, after a while, without a reading public for his writings and, for long periods, without employment, miserably poor, and from time to time on the verge of starvation. By the same token, the questions that had obsessed him in Vilkomir were remote from the concerns of the Jews of Odessa. And in his poverty and misery as a *melamed* (a teacher of Hebrew, Scripture, and elementary rabbinics), his solitude, his struggle later on to learn sufficient Greek, mathematics, and other subjects required for entry into the university, they began to recede from his own horizon as well. He turned to other aspects of the condition of the Jews.

In the course of his years in Odessa Lilienblum moved away from the fairly simple optimism which had underlain the views he had held and propagated while at Vilkomir. It was ever less evident to him that the drastic internal reform of Jewry which he favoured would in itself suffice to put right the Jewish–Gentile disjunction. But it was not his view of orthodoxy as an intolerable burden that changed significantly, or his concomitant belief in the intrinsic value of the study of living languages and the exact sciences, as opposed to the dream world of rabbinic intellectualism. It was rather that he became aware, as he had not been before, that for the mass of Jewry the question of education was secondary and that the influx of a small, if growing, élite into the Russian schools and universities was having, and would have, no effect on the vast numbers for whom the 'most important of all questions is the question of livelihood',[3] for whom it must be made possible to earn a decent living with reasonable ease and by their own efforts, and who must not be perpetually forced to rely on debilitating charity and corrupting illegality. But this, the easing of the endemic poverty of Russo-Polish Jewry—to say nothing of its elimination—was clearly and absolutely conditional on their being granted equal treatment and equal opportunity by the Russian state. Nothing was to be gained by denying that much in Jewish life was unsatisfactory and distasteful and in need of rapid and profound reform. But nor was anything to be gained by failing to see to what extent the degradation was due to the systematic and pitiless constriction

---

[3] Lilienblum, *Kol kitvei*, ii, p. 47.

of Jewry by the autocracy. Fortunately, there was now (in the 1870s, under Alexander II) some hope for change both in Jewry *and* without.

Fortunately? In his increasingly pessimistic mood, and having learnt a great deal more about the non-Jewish world both at first hand and, thanks to his growing command of Russian, through his wide reading of contemporary literature and of the press, doubts were growing. He no longer saw the extra-Jewish world as a sunny expanse into which the prisoners of the ghetto must be allowed to escape. He was horrified by its brutalities and depressed by its politics. He lost his early enthusiasm for many of the major literary figures of his times, in particular for those, like Chernyshevsky, who believed in the direct social utility of intellectual pursuits. Pisarev's heroic ideal of men able to organize their lives purposefully, cutting, if necessary, against the grain of society, he dismissed as fantasy: even if it were applicable to writers (like Pisarev), not everyone could write and, not every writer could achieve what he wished for even within the narrow confines of his craft,[4] nor were writers necessarily to be trusted to put social purposes above their own. In any case, those who wrote tended to exaggerate the social value of their work. 'If you think the emancipation of the serfs was the work of writers, you are in error; it was ordained as an act of state and there were other reasons than literary argumentation for its being adopted. And had there been no edict, one word of which carried more weight than a thousand journals, the serfs would not have been emancipated to this day.'[5] He was depressed as never before by the immensity of the problems of society and the feebleness of its members. And all this applied with added force to the problem of the Jews and sapped away at his confidence both in the feasibility of an accommodation and in its utility.

Generally, don't set your heart too strongly on the education of our brethren. Will our people really cease going astray in a few score years? The reform of the military conscription laws and the grant of equal rights that may now follow it will wipe out all foolishness and all error among them, but these will then be replaced by European civilization and all its abominations and I no longer know which I prefer: the errors of Israel or the civilization of Europe.[6]

[4] Letter to Yehuda Leib Levin, 8 January 1874, *Ketavim otobiografiim*, iii, p. 143.
[5] Ibid. iii, p. 142.
[6] Letter to Moshe Kamyonsky, 3 July 1874. Ibid. ii, p. 148.

iii

'The condition of our people is terrible', Lilienblum wrote in his diary in February 1881. 'All the Jewish periodicals are full of reports from everywhere in the Pale of our Settlement that because of the terrible famine stores have been set up in many towns to sell all sorts of foodstuffs cheaply to the poor, and to distribute them freely to the needier still.' 'The local newspaper', he noted on 20 March, 'reports the rumour that the populace will attack the Jews this coming Easter. It seems that the famine that oppresses the Jews all through the Pale of Settlement is not enough for the persecutors, and they must now incite the populace to loot and plunder. But why should they strive so, to no purpose, to bring back the Middle Ages?' On 10 April: 'Upsetting reports of attacks on the Jews are multiplying.' On 17 April: 'Alarming reports from Elizavetgrad. Confusion, brutality, the blood freezes, the heart stops, what is it all?' On 28 April: 'Alarming reports like those from Elizavetgrad are coming from Kiev too and other places.' On 5 May: 'The situation [here in Odessa] is terrible, terrible and very frightening. It is as if we were besieged, the courtyard is bolted shut, . . . we sleep in our clothes . . . for fear that robbers will fall upon us and so that we can then quickly take the little children . . . and flee wherever the wind will carry us. But will they let us escape? . . . And will they pity the infants who do not yet know they are Jews, that they are unfortunate . . . Terrible, terrible! Till when, O God of Israel?' On 7 May: 'I am glad I have suffered torment . . . For once in my life I have felt what my forefathers felt all through their lives. They lived continually in fear and terror; why should I not feel something of the dread which they felt throughout their days?' On 11 May, when the Odessa pogrom had ended: 'Fear has passed. The attacks have ended and city life has returned to normal. But what is the fate of our brethren elsewhere?'[7] A drunken Russian woman had danced in the street during the pogrom shouting, 'It's our country!', he noted in his diary on 24 September. 'Can *we* say that?', he added.[8]

Once again, confrontation with the unanticipated impelled him to rethink his views, to pull what he knew and what he felt together. The slowly growing sense that Russo-Polish Jewry was in hopeless crisis and that the structure of their relations with society

---

[7] *Ketavim otobiografiim*, ii, pp. 187-9.     [8] Ibid. p. 196.

at large, and with the state in particular, was one of irresoluble conflict became fully explicit in the course of the summer of that year. But what was the nature of the conflict and what was its source? By the autumn his ideas for an answer were sufficiently sharp for him to set them down, first in his diary and in letters, then in a series of powerful articles, the first of which appeared in *Razsvyet* in October. It was markedly simple in style and argument and appealed to common sense and common experience, rather than to authority. It proposed to place the events of the year within the full historical experience of the Jews and to explain them in terms of the intolerable but immutable structure of the Exile. Its didactic purpose was, first and foremost, to remove the illusion that the troubles of the Jews were fortuitous and adventitious and would or could be swept away by an act of will or by the passage of time.

We tend to think that the troubles Israel suffered in the Middle Ages have passed away, that German anti-Semitism is only an ape created by Bismarck the German[9] for his political purposes, that the storms that have blown over us in our country are due to the Jews' lack of rights, and so forth; and that therefore, when Bismarck achieves his set purpose, and the Jews obtain civil rights like other inhabitants, these hardships will come to an end, the nineteenth century will be set firmly on its course, there will be peace and quiet, and the blessing of God will not be absent. But if we remember the well-known rule that anything that comes into the world by a historical process has profound roots in the society in which it has emerged, and in that society's history, we may come to a different conclusion, albeit a very sad one. If, as our fore-fathers of blessed memory said, not all the peoples of the earth have the power to create so much as a single gnat, then certainly no one man, such as Bismarck, has the power to create so great an ape as anti-Semitism; and since we see that the ape has been created and does now stand before us, it is a sign that the earth is well able to bear such evil beasts . . . The question is, What is the force that gives the earth this fertility?[10]

The answer, Lilienblum thought, lay in the universal attitude to the stranger. A stranger can be received into a family, but only as a guest. A guest who bothers, or competes with, or displaces an authentic member of the household is promptly and angrily reminded of his status by the others, acting out of a sense of self-protection. The same sense of self-protection operates within a

---

[9] *Nemets obez'yanu vydumal* ('The ape was invented by a German')—a Russian saying.
[10] 'Obshcheyevreiski vopros i Palestina', *Razsvyet*, xli, 9 October 1881 (O.S.), pp. 1597 ff.

nation, which is for these purposes much like a large family. It operates against competition between the stranger and the native for anything both need or desire. It operates with particular force in all that pertains to livelihood. The practical question is how stranger and native are to be distinguished. In the dark and ignorant Middle Ages the criterion was religion: the Christian was the son of the household, the non-Christian was the stranger. But since the unfortunate stranger, the Jew, had to eat and drink, just like the others, the sons, conflict was inescapable. Generally, the Jew was therefore forced into those trades and occupations which the 'sons' had no interest in or were forbidden to engage in. If the Jew succeeded and the 'sons'' interest or appetite was aroused, the Jew was forced to abandon the field or was expelled totally. The effect of the great, liberating French Revolution was to induce a temporary relaxation of this pattern, a brief wave of generosity and goodwill, as when a man who has suddenly acquired wealth exudes unusual charity and warmth for a while. Then the excitement subsides and matters return to normal. So it was in Western Europe. So it is here in the East. Russia never passed through a stage equivalent to the Middle Ages of Western Europe, nor has a proper emancipation been instituted to this day. There had been something of an atmosphere of liberation at the beginning of the reign of the late emperor and a corresponding, momentary period of goodwill. But it lasted no longer in Russia than elsewhere. The 'Middle Ages' are once again upon us, with the sole difference that it is no longer religion that is the criterion for distinguishing the native from the stranger, but nationality and race. It is these that are now the household gods of Europe in both the West and the East. The Jew is not a Teuton of the German nation, or a Magyar of the Hungarian nation, or a Slav, but a son of Shem and therefore, whether he wills it or not, a 'stranger'. Thus, in the final analysis, nothing has changed. The spectacle of a Jew who has eaten remains intolerable to the non-Jew who is hungry. We, the Jews, may not think of ourselves as strangers; but others do. There is therefore nothing that we ourselves can do to avoid the conflict: no simple change of place or trade or profession would remove its causes. If more Jews turned to farming, direct competition with the native masses would simply increase and the common hatred the latter bear the former would rise. There is only one way out of the predicament: the Jews must cease to be strangers. But how?

The petty-minded and the small of heart propose final and absolute assimilation—a despicable and unjustifiable solution in principle, an unworkable one in practice. There was no evidence to suggest that the surrounding people wished to accept the Jews and, in any case, there was no reason to believe that it was a matter subject to deliberate decision. 'I do not speak of the flight of individuals; there have always been blackguards in mind and deed. They have never done anything to improve the condition of the Jews, on the contrary: . . . they have reduced the ranks of the beaten and increased the ranks of the beaters.' But assimilation *in toto* was another matter: assimilation was national death; a nation could not commit suicide. If it occurred, it would be as a consequence of history, which is to say of processes and events over which we ourselves have no control. No, the solution to the troubles of the Jews and to the fears and resentment of the Gentiles was to find a place where the Jews 'would no longer be strangers but citizens and masters of the land themselves'. In brief, the condition of the Jews was incurable except by surgery. So far as the Jews were concerned, the liberal age was in the nature of a false dawn and a brief respite. Of this the events of the year in Russia and the rise of anti-Semitism outside it were sufficient evidence and were very probably an augury of worse to come. 'None of us knows how many pages inscribed in blood the present chapter holds, nor what other chapters will follow this one.' It might take a century for the Jews to evacuate Europe, but a beginning must be made. Where to? *Not* to America, where, once again, they would be strangers, but to Erez-Israel 'to which we have a historic right which was not lost along with our [lost] rule of the country, any more than the peoples of the Balkans lost their rights to their lands when they lost their rule over them'. The alternative entailed being subject eternally to 'all kinds of storms and not even being safe from a great slaughter'. It required continual self-deception and suppression of dignity and self-respect, humiliation before, and slavish imitation of, those who persecute us. 'For more than six hundred years we have been proving to Europe in vain that we neither eat human flesh nor drink Christian blood . . . and we still think ourselves fortunate if some learned Christian attests that, truly, we do not make Passover dishes from human blood. What disgrace, what shame!'[11]

---

[11] 'Obshcheyevreiski vopros i Palestina', *Razsvyet*, xli, 9 October 1881 (O.S.), pp. 1597 ff.

The idea of a Return would encounter mockery, but the Jews had been mocked before. It would, however, require unity. It was a national purpose to which all other questions would have to be subordinated, and set aside, including the question or issue of religion. Religion was not at the heart of the problem of the Jews, as he had once thought. 'For all its intrinsic importance,' Lilienblum now argued, 'I cannot agree that upon its solution depends the question of the resettlement of Erez-Israel or, otherwise stated, the question whether Israel will return to life or no?—[and therefore one] before which all other questions dwindle into insignificance.' The differences between orthodox and non-believers can and must be bridged. The former must understand that all Jews share a common fate; the latter must learn to leave orthodoxy to the erosion of time. The coming national political renaissance will repair all.[12] The priorities in Jewish life were thus restated by Lilienblum and pessimism made to give way to a measure of hopefulness—a trifle forced, perhaps, but none the less genuine. He had no plan: there is nothing in his writings at this stage to suggest what should be done in practice to generate the Return beyond the very general belief, which he shared with other Hovevei Zion, in the value of agricultural settlements and the still vaguer notion that when there was a sufficient number of them, the Return would have been largely achieved. He thought that a claim for help could be made on the European Powers. If Europe was right not to tolerate strangers, then, surely, the Jews had the right to put

---

[12] 'Ein me'arvin she'ela bi-she'ela', *Ha-Meliz*, xiv, 25 April 1882, and *Kol kitvei M. L. Lilienblum*, iv, p. 13. The article was written in response to Y. L. Gordon's insistence on the pre-eminence of the religious question. Gordon's belief in the possibility of maintaining a dual existence in Russia and his originally rather innocent view of the autocracy had faded, much as had Lilienblum's, and the events of 1881 had swept the last of his hopes away. But on orthodoxy and the Talmud which epitomized it and kept it alive he was unyielding, and the bitterness of his criticism of the Jewish condition and of the unchanging incapacity of the Jews to rectify it only intensified:

> Who are we, you will ask, what is our life,
> Are we a nation like the nations round about us
> Or just a community of men of one religion?
> Let me tell you the secret . . .
> We are not a nation, not a community, only—a herd.

> The herd of God, the holy cattle are we,
> The earth is an altar set before us . . .
> To be a sacrifice we were created. . . .

Thus in his poem '*Eder Adonai* ('The Herd of God') written in October 1882 and dedicated to the author of *Autoemancipation!* (Y. L. Pinsker).

before it certain demands. The Jews had not come freely to Europe. 'We would have preferred to remain in the land of our fathers, rather than become acquainted with the delights of the Middle Ages and anti-Semitism . . . We are human beings and we have the right to live like others; and moreover we have the right to demand some special consideration, for we are the oldest of all civilized nations still in being and have contributed not a little to the general treasury of civilization.' But he clearly had little confidence that help would be forthcoming. The Jews would have to act on their own; but how, it was not clear.

Lilienblum's strength was in a kind of pictorial analysis of the state of Jewry—simple, even somewhat crude, cast in blacks and whites with little grey. His appeal was directed to the head, but it was even more powerfully and effectively aimed at the heart. The condition of the Jews was untenable and dangerous. It was also shameful. And salvation would be achieved only by an adequate response to both needs and a healing of both injuries: the moral no less than the physical. But Lilienblum, at this stage of his life, was a man without an organization and with few associates. In his personal life nothing was, or could be, changed (except that he now gave up his long struggle to master sufficient Latin, Greek, and mathematics to pass the matriculation examinations for admission to the university). He was, after all, a miserably poor *melamed* in a large, but none the less provincial city. He had no contacts outside the narrow circle of the *maskilim*. He therefore had no social standing to speak of within Jewry and none at all outside it. He had already earned himself an unpopular reputation for radicalism on both religious and social issues. His strength lay in the fact that he wrote, and wrote well, with passion and a simple conviction in the compelling power of valid arguments. In this last respect he was typical of his generation of *maskilim*. In most others, and, in particular, in his lasting impulse to consider his own experience as a paradigm for the common lot of his contemporaries, he was unique. His views owed hardly anything to those of others. And it was, perhaps, for this reason alone that his analyses were invariably trenchant and his theoretical conclusions crystal clear. What some half-perceived, and others denied, he stated without any ambiguity whatsoever: the Jews of Eastern Europe—and, so far as he knew, the Jews of all Europe—had reached a dead end. But while all this was in striking contrast to the general run of writing in the periodical press, it was well in keeping with the mood and the imperfectly formulated opinions of a great many members of his own class and education. Accordingly, his articles attracted a great deal of attention within the limits of that class—in effect, the reading public of the Russian-Jewish press (as he himself noted, with pardonable satisfaction, in his autobiographical account of the period).[13] There is evidence that among his readers was Z. D. Levontin and that another was Y. L. Pinsker.

iv

Unlike Lilienblum, who had slowly and painfully dug his way through to the modernizing party of Russian Jewry, Yehuda Leib Pinsker (1821–91) was one of its first natural-born members. His father was a man of considerable secular as well as traditional learning, with a minor reputation as a scholar interested in Hebrew grammar and the Karaite wing of Jewry, and a large circle of correspondents and friends among Jewish literati in Central Europe. Having failed as a merchant in Galicia he had moved to the promising New Russian town of Odessa where conditions in the 1820s were easier for Jews and where his early version of *haskala* Judaism could be practised and propagated without constraint. There he helped found one of the first modern Jewish schools in Russia and remained to teach in it for the greater part of his working life. As a consequence, his son Yehuda (Leon) knew Russian and German (which was spoken at home) almost from birth, but little Hebrew. His primary schooling was almost exclusively secular and, as he went on to the gymnasium and then to university (he was one of the first Jews to do so in Russia), the rest of his education was entirely so. He took a degree in law in 1844, but as Jews were still barred from pleading in court and from entry into the state legal service the practice of law as a profession was impossible. After an unhappy year as a schoolmaster in Kishinev he entered the University of Moscow to study medicine, then free to Jews without restriction. He duly qualified, travelled to Germany for further study, and then returned to Odessa, where he received a hospital appointment and made steady progress in his career thereafter. By the middle 1850s he was accounted a notably successful physician.

Pinsker's professional and intellectual prime thus coincided with

[13] *Derekh laʿavor golim*, Warsaw, 1899.

the first, liberal period of Alexander II's reign and he, himself, was in every way a striking exemplar of all that the Russifying wing of *haskala* Judaism wished for at a time when its ambitions for the Jews were greatest and its hopes highest and seemingly most reasonable. He was a Jew who had moved as smoothly and as permanently into the mainstream of Russian upper-middle-class life as the laws of the day and the norms of Russian society proper permitted, officially and explicitly commended from time to time by the bureaucracy, moreover, and thus implicitly adjudged 'useful' to society by its own standards. But he was not an apostate or in any sense a renegade to the Jews themselves. On the contrary, his interest in Jewish affairs and his concern for the condition of the great mass that remained on the other side of the divide grew with time and intensified with the deterioration of the social climate.

Initially Pinsker believed that the gates of the castle could be slowly and softly prised open and the passage of other Jews into Russian society eased. The state was not fundamentally evil in intent and it was amenable to argument. The Jews had much to offer, but equally stood greatly to benefit—if a decent place for them within the Russian system could be found. Fortunately, things were moving, painfully, but nevertheless visibly in the right direction. Both Russia and Jewry were in process of change, their paths were converging, the gaps were narrowing, and the barriers between them were about to dissolve in a climate of dignity and growing mutual respect. What was needed, before all else, was for the Jews to acquire the Russian language in much the same way and to the same end that other European languages had been acquired by western Jewry—as the crucial means both to internal modernization and to the integration of the Jews into society around them. Pinsker helped found the first Russian-language Jewish journal to be published in the Empire and for many years he contributed regularly to subsequent and similar ventures. He took part in the activities of the St. Petersburg-based Society for the Promotion of Culture among the Jews—the prime institutional expression of the integrationist leadership of the day.

It is of some interest that Pinsker's and his friends' choice of Russian as the key instrument of modernization was not automatic. The possibilities inherent in a revival of Hebrew for secular use were not apparent to semi-assimilated Jews like Pinsker. And Yiddish was hastily and somewhat contemptuously dismissed as no more than a primitive dialect of German, a 'jargon' (for all that it was the native tongue of the overwhelming majority of Russo-Polish Jews). German itself, the language of much that was most impressive in the sciences and arts of Europe at that time, was a different matter, yet they were against it too. The entry of the Jews into the modern age, they believed, was indissoluble from their integration into the society around them. Russian was the language of the country, at any rate the language of the state and of the 'indigenous population' (*korennoe naselenie*). Moreover, it was the vehicle of the great literary flowering of the day. Social needs, interest, and secular culture all pulled in the same direction. The Russian-Jewish press was established with all this in mind: to help the Jews to play a role of their own in the literary and scholarly arena; to promote the use of the language for internal consumption; and to serve as a platform for the exposition and ventilation of Jewish problems and needs before the wider audience. Hebrew would retain its special role in ritual and theology, but Russian, it was hoped, would increasingly become the Jews' primary language of expression, like Greek and Arabic in earlier times and like German since Moses Mendelssohn, a major vehicle for literary and scholarly work which Jews would employ both when they addressed themselves to the study of nature and to problems of a universal character and when they studied their own past and their own, specific culture. And the more the use of Russian by Jews spread and the more rapidly first-hand acquaintance with Hebrew and traditional learning receded, the greater would be the need to employ Russian for specifically Jewish purposes. Thus, by a paradox of which Pinsker and those of like mind do not seem to have been more than dimly aware, the propagation of Russian was justified both as a means of helping to free the Jews from the constrictions of their past and as a means of perpetuating their ties to it.

But Pinsker himself, at any rate, was not a doctrinaire. He distinguished carefully between what might be laid down by theoreticians and what would be done in practice by the commonalty. He did favour (in the 1860s) the abandonment of virtually all that was typical of and specific to Russian Jewry—except their religion (construed in the narrow sense)—but saw no reason to *require* the Jews to do so merely because others found their speech, their dress, their social practices, or any other of their attributes displeasing. Nor did he believe that Russification, whether in the broad and profound terms in which the autocracy conceived the process, or in the milder and narrower terms in which the Society for the Promotion of Culture among the Jews conceived it, was (or ought to be) a necessary precondition of emancipation.

Although the imprint of Odessa was apparent in his professional and social status and in his public activities, there was nothing in Pinsker's personality to suggest a city noted typically for its sun and gaiety, a sort of Russian Marseilles. He was taciturn and introverted, slow and careful in thought, generally inflexible once his mind had been made up, slow of movement, especially in the last third of his life when he was in poor health, sensible rather than brilliant, thoughtful rather than passionate, a rock of a man who aroused respect in others, rather than love, a source of moral authority, rather than a leader. He lived a secluded life. He never married. While he wrote a great deal at one period, he never put his full name to his articles and thus not all that he wrote can be identified. His most famous piece, the one on which his reputation still rests, was signed 'by a Russian Jew'. He is known for and by what he did and by the few pieces of his writing which can be positively traced to him, not by what he said to intimates (he had none), still less for what he may be supposed to have thought. What is certain is that his silences and shyness concealed a man profoundly sensitive to outrage and indignity and, good physician that he was, one unwilling to dismiss or override phenomena which did not accord with the established diagnosis. The impact of the pogroms of 1881 was to revitalize and vastly to intensify the pain and disappointment caused him by those which had taken place in his own Odessa ten years before—but which could then, not wholly without reason, be regarded as a local aberration. (Even then seven years were to pass before he re-emerged from his shell to join the new, invigorated Odessa branch of the Society for the Promotion of Culture among Jews, to begin again.) In 1881, however, the facts were plainly otherwise and their effect on Pinsker was shattering. He broke with all that he had stood for before— abruptly, finally, and in a manner that was uncharacteristically dramatic. Several months after the pogrom in Odessa, at a meeting of the local committee of the Society for the Promotion of Culture which was largely devoted to methodical discussion of aid to Jewish students, he suddenly stood up and in a voice trembling with fury denounced those present for 'amusing yourselves with the propagation of culture'. The condition of the Jews had never been as bad, he cried; tens of thousands were in flight to the borders in fear and abject poverty. It was not the education of this or that individual that was at issue, but the fate of the entire nation. He then walked out.[14]

It is probable that Pinsker had not seriously expected the Society to change its modest ways because, as he later wrote, he had by then ceased to believe that anything of value and on the great scale which events required could be done *in* Russia and by the Jews within it. The Russian Jews were nice and upright people. But there were none among them who could lead others, nor, in the nature of things, could there be, he thought. Their condition did not allow it. But things were different in the West. There there were outstanding men, devoted to Jewish affairs, gifted, experienced, capable of organization. There were even statesmen among them. Perhaps no single one of them was a second Moses, but there were certainly some among them capable of leading a second Exodus.[15]

Pinsker went abroad early in the following year (1882), initially for his health, then to seek out the notables of western Jewry and to urge his ideas upon them. He met resistance to what he had to say everywhere except in London where Arthur Cohen, president of the Board of Deputies of British Jews and a Member of Parliament, was sympathetic and advised him to put his argument down in writing in systematic form. This he did in Berlin, on his way back to Russia. His pamphlet *Autoemancipation! Mahnruf an seine Stammesgenossen von einem russischen Juden* ('Auto-emancipation! a warning to his kinsfolk by a Russian Jew') was published there in September 1882. He wrote in German because it was to western Jewry he addressed himself—and, possibly, because he was aware that there was no question of getting his essay past the Russian censorship.

v

*Autoemancipation!* is a manifesto, the work of a man trying hard to control his rage and put his arguments across in cool language— and in the clinical tradition of his profession. The fury, the shame, and the anguish are curbed, but unmistakable.

[14] *Kol kitvei M. L. Lilienblum*, iv, p. 182.
[15] Cf. letter to Lev Osipovich (Yehuda Leib) Levanda, 26 October 1883 (O.S.). Druyanov, iii, no. 1182, cols. 568–74.

When we are ill-used, robbed, plundered and dishonoured, we dare not defend ourselves, and, worse still, we take it almost as a matter of course. When our face is slapped, we soothe our burning cheek with cold water; and when a bloody wound has been inflicted, we apply a bandage. When we are turned out of the house which we ourselves built, we beg humbly for mercy, and when we fail to reach the heart of our oppressor we move on in search of another exile . . . We have sunk so low that we become almost jubilant when, as in the West, a small fraction of our people is put on an equal footing with non-Jews. But he who is *put* on a footing stands but weakly . . . Though you prove yourselves patriots a thousand times . . . some fine morning you find yourselves crossing the border and you are reminded by the mob that you are, after all, nothing but vagrants and parasites, without the protection of the law.[16]

The condition of the Jews is physically harsh beyond all reason. Morally, it is intolerable. Why? What *is* the Jewish problem? What is its nature? What are its sources? Answer that last question, Pinsker tells us, and you have some hope of dealing with the problem. But to do that you have to look at the condition of the Jews unblinkingly, taking note of all its horrors, and drive right across the grain of sentiment and *a priori* assumptions, straight to whatever conclusions the facts of the case will lead you.

Like most such documents, the pamphlet is part social analysis and part prescription for action. Although many of Pinsker's observations are acute, the analysis itself is sketchy, and scientific in intent, rather than content. The prescriptive sections too are clear only in intent: as a programme they are barely better than perfunctory. Altogether, the essay shows clear signs of having been written in haste and in a hot temper. It is not well constructed. It is repetitive. Its focus shifts too often and too erratically from aspect to aspect of the immensely old and complex *Judenfrage*. It is entirely, if pardonably, Europocentric. Its historical references are rarely inaccurate, but they are superficial. Certainly, its strength is not in the force of its logic, or in the depth and breadth of its imaginative vision, nor in its eloquence—of none of which it is devoid, but all of which it has only in limited measure. Its power and its importance and its rightful place in the small company of classics of the Zionist movement all derive from its totality, as it

---

[16] The quotations (with minor changes) are from the English translation by D. S. Blondheim in B. Netanyahu (ed.), *Road to Freedom*, New York, 1944.

were, from its boldness in offering a total and clear-cut solution to
the entire problem, and from the urgency and clarity of its central
message repeated or echoed on every one of its thirty-six pages—
that 'a people without a territory is like a man without a shadow:
something unnatural, spectral'; and that there is no individual
salvation for the Jews, only a collective one. They must therefore
stop running away.

*Autoemancipation!* is, above all else, a slashing attack on Jewish
feebleness, timidity, and apologetics and on the Jews' deeply
ingrained habit of seeking not only the sources of their pain outside Jewry but the cure to it as well. It pivots on Pinsker's central
thesis that the Emancipation of the Jews, as understood by Jewish
optimists and non-Jewish progressives alike, is, and cannot but be,
a failure. The hope that the Jews will be carried to freedom and
dignity on the crest of an admittedly slow-moving but assuredly
irresistible wave of universal liberalism and humanism is groundless and founded on a fallacious view both of the social process in
general and of the determining characteristics of the Jewish people
in particular. The Jews must therefore look to and at themselves.
They must look inward and, to some extent, backwards. They
must recognize that their predicament is unique, and that because
it is unique, it can be resolved only by particular, specially devised
means, as opposed to those that are of universal application. In
effect, the Jews are told to take on the management of their own
affairs directly, to cease being, as it were, the eternal passengers in
the baggage train of other nations, to strike out on their own.

The heart of the problem, says Pinsker, is that the Jews comprise
a distinctive element in every one of the nations in which they are
found, an element that cannot be entirely absorbed and therefore
cannot be readily and comfortably tolerated, but is, on the contrary,
feared and hated and denied equality of status and treatment. This
fear and hatred of the Jews, this Judaeophobia, derives from their
unnatural and anomalous state. By the standards of others, once
they had lost their country the Jewish people should have fallen
into decay long ago. But instead, uniquely, they continued to
maintain themselves as a nation and, by so doing, became in the
eyes of others an uncanny and frightening people, the ghostlike
apparition of a living corpse, of a people without unity or organization, without land or other unifying bonds, no longer alive, and yet
walking among the living—a spectral form without precedent in

history. As such the Jews aroused superstitious fear; fear led to hatred; hatred to a psychosis which has now, after almost twenty centuries, become a malady passed down from father to son, ineradicable, to all intents and purposes, except over a very extended period of time. This Judaeophobia evokes, and is in turn maintained by, a 'Platonic hatred, thanks to which the whole Jewish nation is wont to be held responsible for the real or supposed misdeeds of its individual members'. And thus, 'Judaism and anti-Semitism have passed through history as inseparable companions.' The antipathy to Jews 'exists in all places and at all times, whether in the form of deeds of violence, as envious jealousy, or under the guise of tolerance and protection. To be robbed as a Jew or to be protected as a Jew is equally humiliating, equally destructive to the Jews' self-respect.'

Against this pathological hatred of Jews, so profound, so regular and universal in its manifestation, as to appear 'an inherited aberration of the human mind', polemics are useless. 'Against superstition even the gods contend in vain. Prejudice or instinctive ill-will is not moved by rational argument, however forceful and clear. These sinister powers must either be kept within bounds by force, like every other blind natural force, or simply evaded.'

There is, generally, little love for strangers. But not all strangers are alike. All have a home somewhere—except the Jew. All can therefore requite or deny hospitality—except the Jew. And as he cannot requite it, he cannot demand it. He is neither friend nor foe, but an alien, the stranger *par excellence*. At best, he is granted privileges; and these can be taken from him.

The Jews are aliens who can have no representatives, because they have no country. Because they have none, because their home has no boundaries within which they can be entrenched, their misery too is boundless. The general law does not apply to Jews . . . there are everywhere laws for the Jews, and if the general law is intended to apply to them a special and explicit by-law is required to confirm it. Like the Negroes, like women, and unlike free peoples, they must be emancipated.

It cannot be denied that the emancipation of the Jews, where instituted, is a great achievement. But it is only legal emancipation, not social. Its basis is in reason, not in natural and unencumbered feeling. At best, 'it remains a rich gift . . . willingly or unwillingly flung to the poor, humble beggars'. Ages will pass before it enters fully into the psychological make-up of men. Meanwhile, 'to the living the Jew is a corpse, to the native a foreigner, to the settled he is a vagrant, to the rich a beggar, to the poor a rich exploiter, to the patriot a man without a country, for all—a hated rival'.

The Jews can neither live nor die. They are not a real people at all, not now, not a nation, merely Jews—a herd of individuals whose energies, great in aggregate, are dissipated for lack of union, never fully vanquished, in constant struggle but only to maintain themselves on the margin, pitifully, disgracefully. From a people without a country, they have become a people who have forgotten what it ever was to have had one. In the faithful among them, religion and the hope of redemption by divine power have induced patience and have inhibited almost all thought of national liberation, unity, and independence. The modernists, for their part, have been tempted by the flesh-pots to try to persuade themselves and others that they are full-blooded citizens; but to no avail. Things must be seen for what they are.

With unbiased eyes and without prejudice we must see in the mirror of the nations the tragicomic figure of our people which, with distorted countenance and maimed limbs, helps to make universal history without managing properly its own little history. We must reconcile ourselves once and for all to the idea that the other nations, by reason of their inherent natural antagonism, will for ever reject us. We must not shut our eyes to this natural force which works like every other elemental force; we must take it into account. We must not complain of it; on the contrary, we are duty-bound to take courage, to rise, and to see to it that we do not remain for ever the foundling of the nations and their butt.

The Jews can neither change the world nor wait for it to change. Still less do they have a Providential mission to fulfil in their Dispersion. Instead, it is they who must undergo a change, a change such as will make it possible for them collectively to enter into the family of nations. For although the prospect of a total dissolution of national barriers is impossibly distant, the fact is that the other nations do already live in a state of relative peace. Their *modus vivendi* is supported by treaty and by international law, but more especially by the fact that, for the most part, they deal with one another on a basis of equality and mutual respect. In their dealings with the Jews there is no such basis of equality and no mutual respect. But if equality can be achieved the Jewish Question will have been resolved. Equality can be attained only by the re-creation of full Jewish nationality, by the collective return of the

Jews to the ranks of the nations as a people living in their own homeland. This will not be achieved by the efforts of others, but by self-help. The Jews must not look to others to emancipate them; they must strive for *auto*-emancipation.

Pinsker's solution is a territorial solution. He does not propose a Return. At one point he says plainly that it is not the Holy Land the Jews need but *a* land. At another point he makes clear that he does not object to Erez-Israel; but nor does he believe it a suitable country for settlement. At yet another point he speaks vaguely of a 'sovereign pashalik' in Asiatic Turkey as a possibility to be looked into, although he tends to think the territory should rather be sought in the immensity of North America. It is the fact of territory that is crucial: a *single* refuge as opposed to a multiplicity of refuges which will only perpetuate the Dispersion. Again, he is vague about the status of the Jewish homeland. It must be 'politically assured', it must be neutral, it must be certainly one to which the Jews have unlimited right of entry; but it is not conceived of as housing all of Jewry, only those who are 'surplus'—in effect, those who cannot maintain themselves materially and morally in the land of the Exile. It must be a territory in which the Jews can live and in which they can make a living; it must therefore be fertile and well situated and sufficiently extensive for several million people at least. But how they will order their affairs within it is not spelt out. A period would elapse between the beginning and the completion of the enterprise. What would occur at its end is not clear. The term 'state' is not employed.

The notion that only the 'surplus' Jews must and will flow into the territory derives from the form in which Pinsker himself qualifies his harsh and absolute criticism of emancipated Jewry which forms the first part of the essay. Some Jews can continue to live in the Diaspora—the rich, for example. More generally, experience shows that a relatively small community of Jews will tend to be tolerated by non-Jewish society. It is when the number rises beyond a critical point that friction and conflict ensue. The stream of Jews flowing out of Russia and Romania shows this: by implication, they are contrasted with the stable Jewish population in the West. How far this qualification was intended to account for the difference in the destinies between eastern and western Jews and how far to soften the attack on the complacency and servility of western Jewry is not clear.

Pinsker made no secret of his conviction that the co-operation of western Jewry was essential to the scheme: they had the institutions, the people, the experience, and the freedom to act. If anything was to be accomplished, planning and care and expertise were all essential. These could only come out of the West. It was the westerners therefore who should launch the project by calling for a national congress—in which all of Jewry, presumably, would be represented. Out of this congress, and sanctioned by it, would emerge a directorate. The directorate would take the matter in hand and it would survey available territories, collect funds to purchase land, channel the migrants to their destination in a decent and orderly manner, set them up when they got there. It is clear that Pinsker was not convinced that the institutions and leaders of western Jewry (like all East European Jews he had the Alliance Israélite Universelle principally in mind) would rise to the challenge. But he hoped that they would and as his essay draws to its end and the argument evolves increasingly as a function of its own internal logic, he plainly finds it hard to see how else the enterprise can be carried to its completion.

Where Pinsker is, once again, absolutely clear-minded is in respect of the indispensable, underlying condition of the enterprise: a national resolution or decision (*nationale Entschluss*). The times were propitious: other nations, whose claims were no greater than the Jews', had gained independence. The flow of migrants to Erez-Israel and westwards was a clear sign of rising national self-consciousness among the Jews themselves. Nothing was to be gained by delay. Nor was there anything to be lost by action. At worst, Jews would 'continue to be in the future what [they] have been in the past'.

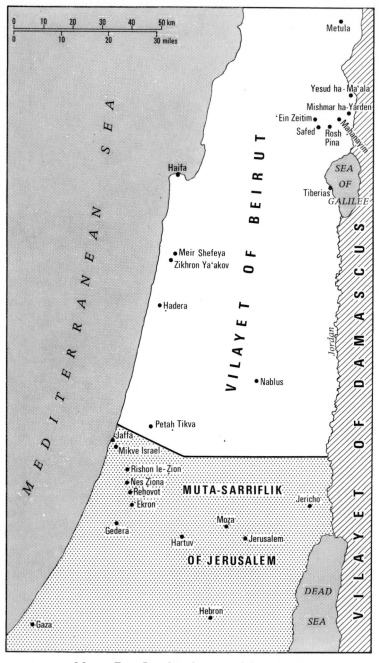

MAP 2. Ereẓ-Israel at the turn of the century

# 6

# Ḥovevei Ẕion

i

THE ideas which Pinsker had tried to press upon leading figures
in western Jewry in the course of his journey among them in 1882
were both irritating and unfashionable. 'If I were to agree with
you,' he was told by Adolf Jellinek, the most eminent rabbi of the
day in Vienna, 'I would have to deny my past and all I had ever
preached and published in the course of over thirty years.' Did
Pinsker seriously expect all that had been achieved since the days
of Moses Mendelssohn and all that had been invested morally and
intellectually in the fight for emancipation to be thrown away?
Were western Jews now, almost a century after the Great French
Revolution, to agree with their enemies 'that, indeed, they were
strangers with neither home nor motherland, no more than nomads,
as you [Pinsker] would have it, fit only to set out to look for a new
country of their own?' Ought they to admit to the charge that they
were without any patriotic feeling for the countries of their domicile?
No. 'We are at home in Europe', said Jellinek, 'and we feel that we
are sons of the country in which we were born and brought up . . .
We are Germans, Frenchmen, Englishmen, Magyars, Italians, and
so on, down to the marrow of our bones . . . We have lost the sense
of Hebrew nationality.'[1] The rabbi's advice to Pinsker was to
proceed to Italy for rest and recuperation from the shock of the
Russian pogroms. Its charms would soothe him; and besides, every
antique ruin could serve to remind him that the Jews had survived
despite all Vespasian and Titus had done to them and that they
would continue to survive despite Ignatiev.

The reaction to his pamphlet when it appeared in print was in
much the same vein: some patronizing sympathy for Pinsker

[1] Quoted in A. Druyanov, 'Pinsker u-zemano', *Ha-Tekufa*, xvi, 1923, p. 323.

personally; expressions of compassion for Russian Jewry—mingled with half-spoken recognition of the fact that little enough had been, and was being, done for them; but, above all, and with rare exceptions, firm rejection of his dangerous and improper ideas. In Mainz his attempt to arouse Jewish national self-consciousness was welcomed by *Der Israelit* as reinforcement in the battle against assimilation, but simultaneously criticized for what the editors regarded as the narrowness of his vision and for Pinsker's underlying failure to appreciate the special nature of Jewry and its universal–historical task (*das Wesen und die Weltgeschichtliche Aufgabe des Judentums*). In Bonn, *Die Allgemeine Zeitung des Judentums* took him to task for trying to set aside the 'product' of eighteen centuries of history (viz. the Jewish religion) and scoffed at him for attempting to set up a non-existent 'national consciousness' in its place—as if the condition of the Jews were really identical with that of the Romanians, the Serbs, the Bulgars, and the rest. He had better apply himself, he was told, to closer study of the history of the Jews and Judaism before he pronounced upon it. For now that a great part of Jewry had been fully integrated into civil society (*völlig eingebürgert*) and duly shared the national consciousness of the nations among which they lived, it was absurd to expect them to give up the corresponding achievement and promote a national, instead of religious, conception of Judaism in its place. The trouble with the author, argued the editors, was plainly that he was infected with Russian nihilism—an outlook on things which emphasized a belief in sickness and death, rather than in higher purposes. His talk of eternal and ineradicable Judaeophobia showed this very clearly. It may be, they conceded, that the Jews had expected too much too quickly and were now disappointed: certainly, the process of emancipation was not proceeding with equal speed in all countries. But it was a profound error to disregard the onward march of history and the continual progress of humanity—even in Russia, whose time would come.

Over all, however, such interest as Pinsker had aroused was neither deep nor lasting. A group of students in Vienna, much influenced by Smolenskin, expressed their support. But from among the leading personalities of Austro-German Jewry, of whom most had been expected and whose support was crucial to his scheme, the sole recruit was the Chief Rabbi of Memel, Isaac Rülf. Pinsker promptly welcomed him with high hopes and a plain invitation to play the central role.[2] But Memel was peripheral to the world of western Jewry; and for all his goodwill Rülf's support could not be more than marginal to the central effort. That was all, for the time being.[3]

Pinsker's doubts about the ability of Russo-Polish Jewry to act for itself, alone, and to some purpose, stemmed in part from his knowledge of the external constraints to which the Jews were subject: the pressures and probable reaction of a profoundly hostile and suspicious government to anything that smacked of national, supra-communal, and collective action by the Jews of the Empire. But equally, and perhaps more fundamentally, there was his profound lack of confidence in the eastern Jews' talents and capabilities for public affairs, the counterpart of his overwhelming sense of the humiliation and indignity inherent in the Jewish condition. He had lived in Russia for decades, he wrote to one of his allies among the eastern Jews, and had met countless nice, moral people. But he had met no leaders; and whence, indeed, could they come? That was why he had originally turned to the West; that was why it was 'our western brothers' who must take the initiative. Among them were outstanding men who had given ample evidence of devotion to the Jewish interest. There were men with real experience of public affairs. There were even statesmen. So if none of them, as had to be admitted, was a second Moses, at least many were highly competent organizers; and it was organization that was needed above all. That, finally, was why he had visited them and, as he put it, put his soul into the effort and played on all the heartstrings.[4]

In the East the reception meted out to *Autoemancipation!* was vastly more favourable. Despite sizeable pockets of hostility— notably among the circles which centred around the Jewish magnates in the capital—support and approval, even enthusiasm were dominant, at any rate in the camp of the modernists. To those who had been stunned by the events of 1881 and 1882 (and it must be remembered that the wave of outright violence against Jews did not end until 1884, while the anti-Jewish policy of the government was in process of fairly steady clarification and intensification throughout the 1880s) and to those whose minds were now being made up, if only on the fundamental issues of national reconstruction and

---

[2] Pinsker to Rülf, 25 September 1882. M. Yo'eli, *Y. L. Pinsker*, Tel Aviv, 1960, p. 139.

[3] For the later evolution of Ḥibbat Ẓion in the West, see Chapter 8.

[4] Pinsker to Levanda, 26(?) October 1883. Druyanov, iii, no. 1182, cols. 568–74.

and resettlement, Pinsker became something of a hero, almost overnight. This was less, perhaps, because of the novelty of what he was saying—little of it, as we have seen, was strikingly different from what others had been writing and, above all, thinking at the time—than because no one before him, certainly no one in the East, had put the case for a revolution in the structure and ethos of Jewry in such sharp and unambiguous terms; and put it, moreover, in a western language, before a western public, with relatively little inhibition and without fear of censorship. Nor had anyone before Pinsker gained so wide an audience, friendly or otherwise, so rapidly, for such ideas. And this despite the fact that the pamphlet could not immediately be published in Russian, but only be reported on in the Russian-Jewish press, and that it does not appear that a Hebrew version of the essay was in circulation much before the beginning of 1884—at which time there was still no text in Yiddish, much the most important language of all.

On the one hand, as a distinguished convert from a modified form of assimilation, Pinsker appealed to, and was seen as a notable ally by those nationalists, like Lilienblum and the less complacent rabbis, who could themselves operate only within the Jewish world. On the other hand, his exclusively *secular* approach to the Jewish problem and his almost outrageous, if only half-explicit, dismissal of the idea of the Return to Erez-Israel as a practical and necessary proposition, served to encourage those who continued to link the salvation of the Jews to some kind of radical disconnection from their religion and their rabbis. It was to the anonymous author of *Autoemancipation!* that Y. L. Gordon dedicated his bitter poem on the incapacity of the Jews, 'The Herd of God', to rid themselves of their sacrificial role.[5] So too another secularist, Yehuda Leib Levin, a Hebrew poet much influenced by Russian radical writers and a confirmed socialist ('The Jewish question is not one of faith but of the stomach') until the events of 1881 and the subsequent years caused him to revise his views: when the idea of the resettlement of Erez-Israel began to be bruited more seriously and energetically 'it was not the material possibilities [of effecting it] that I doubted that worried me, so much as the spiritual', he wrote in retrospect. 'My fear was fear of the orthodox Jews, of the rabbis, fear of the atmosphere of Erez-Israel, permeated with ancient prejudices in which the *maskilim* would be unable to bring their influence to bear.'[6]

---

[5] ''Eder Adonai.' Cf. above, p. 120, footnote.     [6] *Zikhronot ve-hegyonot*, p. 67.

But above all, the more sensitive and thoughtful and, therefore, the more perplexed members of the Jewish intelligentsia were drawn to Pinsker because he had outlined the predicament and set down a solution in simpler and more straightforward and, in an almost indefinable but extremely vivid sense, more contemporary terms than had anyone before him. Lev Osipovich Levanda, for example, novelist, journalist, official expert on Jewish affairs (*uchony evrei*) to the governor-general of Vilna, and a leading figure of the *haskala*, had believed, as had Pinsker, in the compatibility of Jews and Russians on the basis of a limited cultural differentiation, was, like Y. L. Levin, intensely critical of the internal and social structure of Russo-Polish Jewry, and finally, like both Pinsker and Levin, had been drawn away from faith in universal and cosmopolitan prescriptions by the steady rise of anti-Semitism and its great outbreak in 1881. In his case it was, more than anything else, the fact that so many members of the Russian (non-Jewish) intelligentsia had sided with, or, at best, refrained from criticizing, the *pogromshchiki* that had shaken him. 'I was in mourning', Levanda said later; and was not comforted when told of some exceptions—Saltykov-Shchedrin among them. Nor did his temperament allow him to take the easy advice offered him, namely to sit back quietly while the Jews' few allies fought the battle for them. Nor, again, could he bring himself to tolerate the behaviour of the Jewish magnates who opposed migration from Russia or, at best, took it upon themselves, as did Samuel Poliakov the railroad entrepreneur, to recommend they move to the newly conquered Russian territories in Asia. To his mind all this was slavish and disgraceful, a kissing of the hand that beat them.[7] So when towards the end of 1882 Levanda received a copy of *Autoemancipation!*, mailed to him from Berlin, he was tremendously impressed. By his own account, he read and reread it; and when he discovered the identity of its author, with whom he had always had much in common, but with whom he had previously quarrelled over Pinsker's earlier, relatively mild, and apologetic approach to Jewish affairs, he rushed to express his support. So too did Lilienblum, whose articles Pinsker had read in *Razsvyet* and whose influence upon him he acknowledged by sending him a copy of the pamphlet upon his return from Germany.

This gesture of courtesy had an important result. Flattered by

[7] S. L. Ẓitron, *Toldot Ḥibbat Ẓion*, Odessa, 1914, p. 175.

Pinsker's attention and encouraged by the large measure of agreement between them, Lilienblum set out to press Pinsker to act and
at the same time to move closer to his own position on the one
significant issue dividing them—the question whether it was to
Erez-Israel or to some other territory that the migrant Jews should
be directed. Here it was Lilienblum, not Pinsker, who was the
representative figure. Few among Pinsker's new friends were at
one with him in his 'territorialism' (as it was later to be called). To
most minds, as will be seen, Lilienblum's thesis that it was in
Erez-Israel alone that the Jews would cease to be foreigners was
an incontrovertible one and one, moreover, that tugged at heartstrings in a way that the cooler prospect which Pinsker held out
did not. But although Pinsker ended by bowing to the general
pressure and allowing himself to be placed at the head of a movement which was clearly oriented to Erez-Israel his own theoretical
appreciation of the problem of the Jews remained unchanged. He
continued to believe that the solution lay in the resettlement of the
Jews in what would become *a* country of their own, any country
that they would be granted or that they could make their own, and
that it would be good if that country were Erez-Israel, but it was
not essential. When pressed later by supporters to amend *Autoemancipation!* to accord with the broad intentions and the specific
activities of the movement, he refused. His views had changed not
at all, he explained. In any case, the issue was not his to decide, but
for the congress of all Jewry's representatives that he had called for
and which had still to be convened. However, it had to be conceded,
he said, that western Jewry had failed to respond and that eastern
Jewry was divided between, on the one hand, those whose response
was identical to that of the westerners and those, on the other hand,
who offered enthusiastic support for his, Pinsker's, general conception, but rejected any but a 'Palestinian' solution. In these circumstances, he believed he was obliged to bow to the plain desire of
those who did at any rate support him in his general outlook;
nor was it a matter of regret that the popular choice was so clearly
for Erez-Israel. But on the principle of the thing he would not
budge.[8]

Lilienblum wanted Pinsker to take the lead. He had seen very
clearly, almost from the first, that no enterprise of anything like

[8] Lilienblum (writing on Pinsker's behalf) to Tchlenov, 23 December 1844 (O.S.).
Druyanov, i, no. 176, col. 373.

the appropriate order of magnitude could be pushed forward without a great pooling of human and material resources and that therefore a cardinal obstacle to the enterprise lay in the fact that those who had the means and might have the will to settle in Erez-Israel were scattered and divided, 'like solitary ears of corn', in different towns, generally unknown to each other. Casting about for a means of reaching them he had published a notice in *Voskhod*, inviting potential settlers who had at least 4,000 roubles to invest in the purchase of land and equipment to contact him. He was in touch with some of the migrants passing through Odessa and evidently hoped to set up a sort of clearing-house for them. He had reckoned that if at least twenty with sufficient means responded, a tract of land large enough for a small settlement could be bought. But only four people answered his call and the lame idea of introducing some system into the enterprise by an appeal through the press was dropped.[9] He then turned to Pinsker.

I showed him that a distinguished and honoured man like him was well placed to put the idea into execution without waiting for the leaders of our western brethren, as his pamphlet had proposed. They would never make a beginning in this matter, while if he [Pinsker] did, even the wealthy [of Odessa] would not oppose him because of the great respect in which he was held. And *their* example would then be followed by the wealthy of other cities. And so, knowing nothing [at the time] of his illness, of his weakness of spirit, of his excessive modesty, and of his invariable shyness, I continued to demand that he act.[10]

Pinsker hesitated; but at the beginning of September 1883 Lilienblum gained two powerful allies in his effort to persuade him to accept the personal challenge, to drop the notion that it was for western Jewry to take the initiative, and to agree to a start being made in the East. Two Russian Jews whose distinction in the world of science and whose position in society at large gave them particular prestige within the Jewish world, and peculiarly fitted them to influence Pinsker himself in particular, had arrived in Odessa to attend a learned gathering. One was the Kiev ophthalmologist, Emmanuel Mandelstamm, who, as we have seen,[11] had already proclaimed his radical and bitter conclusions about the position and future of the Jews in the Russian Empire. The other was Zevi Hirsch (Hermann) Schapira, a gifted product of the Lithuanian

---

[9] M. L. Lilienblum, *Derekh la'avor golim*, Warsaw, 1899, p. 14.
[10] Ibid., p. 11.      [11] See above, pp. 71–2.

Talmudic academies, whose mathematical ability had led him out
of the ghetto to study in Berlin and then, after a period in Odessa
(where he had become friendly with Lilienblum), to Heidelberg.
In Heidelberg he served as a *dozent* and was later to be appointed
to a professorship. The events of 1881–2 had revived his concern
for the Jews of the Pale and moved him to support the resettlement
of Erez̧-Israel. Lilienblum persuaded Schapira to press Pinsker to
action and the two were then joined by Mandelstamm. Finally, the
old man, as they saw him (he was sixty-two at the time), gave in.

In the latter half of September (the precise date is uncertain)
Pinsker, Lilienblum, Mandelstamm, Schapira, a nephew of
Mandelstamm's, and a certain Levinson (described by Lilienblum
as a man who, 'after diverse adventures, had returned to his people
and origins with greater love than might be found in one who had
never left the society of Jews')[12] met and, after lengthy discussion,
agreed on a short, joint statement of aims and duly and solemnly
signed it. It accorded almost fully with Pinsker's views as laid
down in his pamphlet and, to that extent, represented a concession
which Lilienblum and Schapira, notably, felt obliged to make.
Nevertheless, as Lilienblum wrote later, 'I was very glad, for at
least we were beginning to act, which was what mattered, and the
trend of events and needs as they arose would in themselves serve
to show us what road to travel.'[13]

The brief agreement of principle (drawn up in Russian) began
with the simple, almost anodyne, statement that 'It becomes ever
clearer and ever more urgent from day to day that a way be found
to provide our brethren with their needs in security. To this end,
societies have been founded in Jewish communities both abroad
and in this country which are resolved to make common cause and
seek to set up a central organizational committee.' (There were, in
fact, no such committees outside the Russian Empire and Romania,
as Pinsker and his friends well knew. Probably, the phrasing was in
the nature of an oblique concession to Pinsker's belief that the major
initiatives would have to come, sooner or later, from the West.)

The aims of the 'central committee' were then carefully defined
to accord both with the views of the signatories and with what was
thought politic *vis-à-vis* the authorities, for there was no doubt in
anyone's mind that the police would soon learn something of their
plans.

---

[12] Lilienblum, op. cit., p. 15.          [13] Ibid., p. 16.

The prime aim of the committee will be the establishment of a settlement centre, in Erez-Israel if possible, for those of our impoverished brethren in all countries who are capable of work, but cannot find employment in their countries of origin. It goes without saying, that those who wish to leave their country to join those settlements must first fulfil their obligations to the governments of the countries which they will be leaving.

The 'obligations' they had in mind were first and foremost those relating to military service.

Five short operative clauses completed the statement: the central committee would be chosen by a congress of representatives of the local societies to be called by the following summer; the committee must seek to gain official sanction for its existence and activities; a central fund to which all the local societies would contribute must be set up; dues of individual supporters should be at the rate of one thousandth part of their personal income; and money thus collected would be put at the disposal of the central committee as soon as it had been elected by the congress.[14]

Mandelstamm and Schapira left Odessa shortly afterwards, leaving all further initiative to Pinsker and Lilienblum. A few days later, on New Year's Day of the year 5644 (2 October 1883), thirty-four prominent members of the Jewish community in Odessa were called to a meeting at Pinsker's home and the statement put before them. When agreement had been expressed and support promised by all present, it was resolved that a permanent society of local Ḥovevei Ẓion be formed which Pinsker was to lead with the assistance of three others, among them Lilienblum. Lilienblum, the one whose Hebrew could be best relied upon for purposes of correspondence, was also to serve as secretary. The statement, accompanied by a circular letter which he drafted but which Pinsker signed, was then sent to all likely sympathizers. These were asked to bring the contents to the attention of others known to be active in the cause, or to start recruitment if they knew none. Pinsker and Lilienblum called attention, in the manner of the day, to the fact that the matter had the backing of men of distinction, wealth, and science,[15] and gently reminded their correspondents

---

[14] Ibid., pp. 15-16.

[15] A list of those invited to the foundation meeting at Pinsker's home on 2 October has survived (Druyanov, iii, no. 1180, cols. 563–4), and it is at least probable that the majority attended. A breakdown of the list by occupation closely reflects what constituted leading Jewish society in Odessa and, indeed, with some modification, the leadership of society

of the value the sages had always put on amity in, and unity among, the people of Israel.

*Autoemancipation!* had thus led to the launching of Pinsker as a national figure and as a leader—in fact, *the* leader—of the Hibbat Zion movement. By stages and under the pressure, first of those immediately around him in Odessa (notably Lilienblum), and then of the logic of the enterprise itself and of the responsibilities he was to undertake, he became successively leader of the local Odessa society, then one of the principal promoters of a union of all local societies within the Empire, and finally, for five years (1884–9), the union's formally elected chairman. It is entirely clear that he had anticipated none of this when he wrote his pamphlet. It had, after all, been addressed to western Jewry; and although he resigned himself in time, more or less, to the fact that the help forthcoming from the West was to be painfully incommensurate with the needs of eastern Jewry in general and of his own programme for their salvation in particular, his faith in Russo-Polish Jewry's ability to pull themselves out of the mire unaided remained very limited. However, as evidence of the indifference of western Jewry had mounted, so he had softened to the challenge thrown at him in the West from the first: what of Russian Jewry, could it do nothing for itself? On reflection, he wrote to Levanda, he had begun to think the westerners were right. At all events, he had promised himself not to go back to the West with empty hands. The soil had to be prepared here in Russia. The question, of course, was, how? A mass movement could not be mounted within the Empire and, in any case, Pinsker thought, it would be unmanageable if it were. The

---

throughout the Russian Pale: the difference between Odessa and the Jewish centres to the west and north being in the much heavier influence and standing of both the traditional rabbinate and the ḥasidic *rebbes* elsewhere. However, as both branches of orthodoxy were, with some important exceptions, at first indifferent, and then hostile, to the new nationalism, the composition of the Odessa meeting was not unrepresentative of the social categories on which the movement itself depended initially (if not always to its advantage). Thirty-four men were invited, not counting Pinsker and Lilienblum. Three were members of, or related to, the Brodski family of industrialists and philanthropists (who, of all those invited, were the least likely to have attended). Sixteen are described by Druyanov as (or known to have been) merchants or exporters or simply 'wealthy men' (several of whom were men of considerable learning, active in the *haskala* movement). Three were bankers and one a stockbroker. There was one factory owner and one miller. The professionals were an attorney, a notary, four physicians (including an army doctor and Pinsker himself), and a pharmacist (Pinsker's brother). One of those attending has remained unidentified. Finally, Schwabacher, the chief rabbi of Odessa, and Lilienblum completed the list. Many were wardens of their synagogues, or of the burial society.

movement had to be selective. The Jewish notables were un-sympathetic; fortunately, the middle-class Jews were more promising. Unlike the notables, they were dependable in public matters, they had the interests of the people as a whole at heart, they had a sense of national dignity; and out of their numbers a centre or cadre could eventually be formed. And when that had been accomplished the notables and, in time, the westerners too would follow suit. A basis for action could already be discerned in the circles of 'Palestinians' formed in many of the cities of Russia and Poland. These had now to be bound together and brought to act in concert. Meanwhile, the convening of an all-Jewish world congress would have to be postponed, probably for several years; and, in the interim, an 'unofficial' gathering of representatives of the groups favouring a national programme which had been forming within Russia would be held and views concerted and plans drawn up for presentation to the congress when it was held.[16] Such was Pinsker's own picture of what lay ahead, as explained to Levanda a few weeks after the foundation meeting of the Odessa committee in his home.

Pinsker had recognized certain social responsibilities when he yielded to the pressures to accept leadership, much as he did, later, when he withdrew successive, somewhat cantankerous decisions to resign. He had been moved, at bottom, by a profound sense of *noblesse oblige*. It is abundantly evident that he never relished his prominence; nor did he *grow* with his responsibilities, as many a lesser man might have done. Nor again did he ever seem fully to realize the unique opportunity that was his. Certainly, he did not seize and manipulate the authority thrust upon him with the imagination and decisiveness that the role merited. For it is hard not to judge his opportunity as anything but immense. There can be no question that he had struck a vital nerve and that, in one way or another, no doubt as much by word of mouth as in more systematic ways, the name of Dr. Pinsker as some kind of spokesman and representative and, therefore, as a man who might be able to act for the Jews, spread rapidly through the country. And the more rapidly it spread, the more urgently his new supporters wanted him to take the lead and, at the very least, to bring his message to others. 'It is most essential', a correspondent in Rostov-on-Don wrote to him, pressing for the preparation of a Yiddish translation of his pamphlet, 'that the masses should read all about our ideas,

---

[16] Pinsker to Levanda, 26(?) October 1883. Druyanov, iii, no. 1182, cols. 568–74.

F

[that the] simple grey masses should be inculcated with them. Then there should be no grounds for worry about the realization of our cause.'[17]

'Much-respected Lev Semyonovich!', wrote three physicians of Elizavetgrad after the pogrom in Kunavina, Nizhni-Novgorod (the last of the series), in which seven Jews were killed and the customary damage done to Jewish property,

the horrors of the Kunavina catastrophe have deeply shaken all our society, or, to put it more accurately, all of our faith. Old and young, men and women, rich and poor—all walk about with bent heads . . . The state of panic is beyond description. The thought of the blood of our innocent brethren shed in Kunavina gives us cause to fear that the days of 15 and 16 April 1881 will recur—a thought which freezes the blood of every Jew. Moreover, the panic is justified by reason of the amount of explosive material in the form of a sizeable number of trouble-makers ready, at any moment, to rob and ruin Jewish property and even do much more horrible things, as the pogroms in 1881 [here in Elizavet-grad] proved . . .

Worried and harassed, we have completely lost our heads and find ourselves unable to act decisively, lest we commit a fatal error. That is why we appeal to you for advice, much-respected Lev Semyonovich. What shall we do? We do not doubt that you and all our Odessa brethren have been deeply shocked and troubled by the horrible Kunavina catastrophe. We are certain that you too seek the answer to the questions: what is to happen, what is to be done?

If you have, indeed, reached a decision on this question, we most resolutely ask you to inform us of it by the first outgoing post.[18]

But of all this—his emergence as an accepted national figure—Pinsker made very little. He failed—and, indeed, seems never seriously to have tried—to instil in the movement the very drive and urgency that had informed his pamphlet and had gained for it, and for him, their rightful fame.

It may, however, be questioned whether he was capable of doing so. Throughout this period, Pinsker was a sick man and—at any

---

[17] P. Yampolsky to Pinsker, 1 March 1884 (O.S.). Druyanov, i, no. 77, col. 148. Yampolsky thought 600 copies could be sold in Rostov alone. The total Jewish population of the town was then almost certainly well under 10,000.

[18] Dr. Y. Tsetkin *et al.* to Pinsker, 20 June 1884. Druyanov, i, no. 107, cols. 198-9. The three distraught doctors had in mind the dispatch of a written appeal for help to M. N. Katkov, editor of the influential *Moskovskie Vedomosti*. Although an extreme conservative at this time, Katkov was friendly to the Jews and, rare for his class, had gone so far as openly to denounce the pogroms.

rate by the standards of the day—an elderly one. He was, moreover, a lonely and introverted person; and for all his profound sympathy for the Jewish populace and his burning desire to see their condition subjected to dramatic and permanent changes, he was cut off from them to no small degree by his own, very different, background, ethos, and culture. His virtues and abilities were moral and technical as befitted, it might be thought, a decent, intelligent, middle-class professional whose talent was for unblinking confrontation of the existing environment, rather than for formulating and propagating imaginative leaps into the future. In sum, Lev Semyonovich Pinsker was in no sense a political animal. Rather, he was a man of good works. As such he reflected the essential modes of the movement in this period; and, at the same time, he served to confirm them by the stamp he himself set upon it.

ii

There were at least a dozen local pro-Erez-Israel committees and societies functioning in Russia and Poland in the winter of 1883/4, all broadly equivalent in general purpose and social composition to the one established by Pinsker and Lilienblum in Odessa. Counting groups and circles which operated at a somewhat lower level of institutional formality and self-consciousness, there were double that number at the very least. The evidence is scattered and incomplete, but taken together it leaves no doubt that there was some self-sustaining body of Hovevei Zion ('Lovers of Zion'), meeting fairly regularly, intent on propagating their ideas, collecting small sums of money, and reaching out, if only fitfully, for contact with like-minded people within their own community and beyond it in virtually every major centre of population in the Pale —in Bialystok, Brest-Litovsk, Kharkov, Kremenchug, Lublin, Minsk, Nikolaev, Pinsk, Plotsk, Poltava, Vilna, Warsaw, Yekaterinoslav, and elsewhere. Outside the Pale, there were similar societies, as we have seen, in St. Petersburg and in Moscow, and also in Rostov-on-Don and in Riga.

All such groups shared the Lilienblum-Pinsker belief in the regeneration of the Jewish people through the evacuation of Europe and resettlement elsewhere, ultimately in a condition of (still ill-defined and, quite possibly, much-delayed) autonomy. And for virtually all there was no question but that the resettlement must take place, and that the regeneration would occur in Ereẓ-Israel. Where opinion was initially divided—as in Minsk, for example—the 'Palestinians' ultimately had the upper hand. Partly, no doubt, this was because in an age when it was extremely rare for a Jew in Russia and Poland, however much of a secularist in conscious thought, to be without some grounding—and, for the most part, a very solid grounding—in the law, traditions, and history of his people, it was quite impossible for such notions of regeneration not to lead the imagination back to the ancient glories of the Davidic and Hasmonean Kingdoms. And this, indeed, was perfectly in keeping with Jewish theological and philosophical practice, the corner-stone of which had always been reliance on the events and revelation of the past for guidance in respect of the future. Thus Levanda's thinking had originally been much like Pinsker's; but he was soon so moved by the historical and romantic perspectives opened up by the phenomenon of a handful of migrants setting off for the Land that he changed his mind and became a fervid 'Palestinian'. But there were also concrete elements of their condition which impelled the new nationalists to link evacuation from Russia with migration to, and resettlement in, Ereẓ-Israel. In the first place, the business of channelling and assisting migrants to other parts of the world could, to some extent, be left in the hands of others—of the Alliance Israélite Universelle, for example—whereas the migrants to Ereẓ-Israel were at this time in a different case. Secondly, the Jews already were concentrated in a definable geographical area—in the Pale itself in fact. What assurance was there either in reason or in fact that their transfer and reconcentration elsewhere would not lead, in time, to no more than the creation of a new ghetto, with even more catastrophic results? In any event, with the minor exceptions noted,[19] other territories, particularly the Americas, were the goals of migrants intent on *personal* salvation, whereas, whatever the fundamental prompting to move might be, no Jew would fail to see Ereẓ-Israel, at least to some extent, in terms of national, ideological categories. And the stronger the bent to think in such terms the larger Ereẓ-Israel loomed. Years before the official and collective adoption of the name of Ḥibbat Ẓion (literally: 'Love of Zion')[20] the local societies which comprised the movement adopted names which either included the explicit term 'Zion' or else evoked the Land and the Return to it in some other

---

[19] See above, pp. 77–8.        [20] At the Druskieniki conference, 1887.

way—''Ezra', 'Nehemia', or 'Zerubavel' (which is what the Odessa committee called itself), for example.[21] More general and more abstract names—such as 'Kibbuz nidhei Israel' (roughly: 'The Ingathering of the Forlorn of Israel')—failed to take root.[22]

The act of forming such a local society was an exhilarating one for the participants and the very fact of meeting together for such a purpose a source of intense satisfaction for all. In part this may have derived from the mildly conspiratorial character of what they were about. In part it may be traced to their evolution as local centres of cultural and intellectual—and even quite straight-forwardly social—activity in which Jewish affairs and topics in Jewish history and culture were discussed in novel, modernist, and secularist terms, so that they rapidly turned into centres of competition with and, in time, opposition to, the classic centres of orthodoxy and immobilism.

The firm and almost unquestioning orientation towards Erez-Israel was one of Hibbat Zion's great sources of strength: it placed it squarely within Jewry, rather than on its margin. It was none the less a profound source of weakness as well. Beyond a certain amount of study, discussion, spreading of the doctrine, collection of funds, and the like, all really significant activity, all that was likely to have a direct and fully apposite bearing on the goals of the movement, had to be performed elsewhere, not in Russia and Poland at all, but in a distant and barely accessible country— wherein lay one insurmountable and near-fatal obstacle to the smooth evolution of the movement as such. Too much was verbal and preliminary. Too little required immediate, let alone dramatic and forceful action. It was possible to become a loyal and moderately useful member of the movement and yet continue to lead a life that in most respects remained entirely unchanged. Similarly, the few very independent spirits who had gone off to Erez-Israel had found, as we have seen, that given the harsh material and political conditions in the country and the tiny, grossly disproportionate resources available for settlement, a rapid, large-scale, and lasting influx of immigrants was out of the question and that the most that could be hoped for was to maintain the slow seepage of Russian,

[21] Ezra, Nehemiah, and Zerubbabel were principal leaders of the Jews' return from the Babylonian Exile (or Captivity), and the subsequent rebuilding of the Temple and re-fortification of Jerusalem in the sixth and fifth centuries before the Common Era.

[22] Cf. 'A. Shohat, 'Shemot, semalim va-havai be-Hibbat Zion', *Shivat Zion*, ii–iii, Jerusalem, 1953, pp. 232–3.

Polish, and Romanian Jews into the country on a basis of constant
petty warfare with Turkish officialdom, the immediate problem
for the existing settlers being to hold and consolidate the bridgehead established in 1881–3, rather than to expand it. This was
disappointing. What was more important was that as their needs
and possibilities became known (at least in outline) to their friends
in Europe and as it began to appear at this time that help might be
expected from no other quarter than Eastern Europe itself, the
movement came to be preoccupied with the precarious state of the
settlements. In the short term this was beneficial to the consolidation of both the settlements in Erez-Israel and the local societies
in Russia. In the long term it was a very considerable misfortune.
It provided a release for some of the tension and an outlet for the
will to act that underlay the impulse to join Hibbat Zion; but it
did so at the cost of a scattering of energies in penny packets. It
gave the movement a philanthropic, charitable bent that was to
colour it profoundly for many years and which it never entirely
lost. It led to a near-fatal blurring of issues and purposes and to
far too smooth a carry-over into the new Hibbat Zion societies of
the mental and organizational habits of the properly philanthropic
institutions of the community—which often represented everything Hibbat Zion was in rebellion against. It led, too, to quite
astonishingly great attention being paid to the technical and mundane details of institutional activity—how funds were to be handled
and accounted for, for example—all necessary and proper in the
case of ordinary communal charities, but tending powerfully to
divert the attention of the Hovevei Zion from harsher and more
important matters, not least because concern with the former
provided a substitute for concern with the latter.

   Much of this may be seen in the case of the society of Hovevei
Zion in Vilna founded in the winter of 1881/2, which is to say
almost two years before the Pinsker–Lilienblum call reached them.
Privately, its members entitled themselves Ohavei Zion (a variant
of Hovevei Zion). In public, for fear of the police, they gave out
that the name of their society was Tikvat 'aniim ('Hope of the
Poor'), as befitted a putative charitable organization.[23] They carefully drafted an elaborate constitution of twenty clauses which
specified the rules for internal elections, the precise function and
delineation of leadership and authority, the handling of dues, the

---

[23] Shohat, op. cit., p. 245.

uses to which funds were put, the categories, rights, and duties of members, and the frequency and regularity of meetings. The key clause (number two) laid down that

The aims of the Ohavei Zion society are to spread that idea of the settlement of Erez-Israel for purposes of working its land among the sons of the Diaspora and to implant it in their hearts and to render support to those going up unto the Land of Israel to work its earth, to plough its mountains [*sic*] and its valleys, and gradually to put the idea of the resettlement of Erez-Israel into practice, to remove it from the realm of ideas into that of reality.

All of which was to be accomplished (as stated in clause three) by means of the written and spoken word, collection of money, and recruitment of specialists in agriculture and the crafts.[24] But there was no word in the document about the general condition of the Jews, nor was anything said *directly* about possible solutions. There was nothing in it suggesting thought—systematic or otherwise—of revolutionary social change. There was no hint of the political. The underlying ideological drives and notions—all ventilated with feeling at the society's meetings—were only alluded to vaguely in the document, or entirely repressed. A note of ambivalence and a tendency to trim were thus present in the new movement from the start.

It is equally characteristic that what was particularly welcomed in Pinsker was, as all sensed, the impetus that he intended to give towards organization and system and, if possible, the attainment of official toleration, if not sanction, for the movement as a whole. For the general feeling by the end of 1883 and the beginning of 1884 was that it was these—organization and method and the advantages of legality—that were needed to mend the disproportionate gap between the initial high hopes and broad vistas and the meagre results that had been achieved on the ground. Nothing else would reverse the retreat of the 'Palestinians', already in progress, back into the old endemic mood of pessimism and helplessness.

The Council of the Poltava Palestine group, discussing the main problems of its cause—and taking into consideration the existence of similar groups in other towns in Russia—have come to the conclusion that in present conditions, despite the enthusiasm of all those with true Jewish hearts, our cause cannot be advanced sufficiently, nor achieve the necessary results. The main reason for this sad fact is, as we see it, the

---

[24] Druyanov, iii, no. 1324, cols. 911–15.

lack of any communication among existing groups, lack of unity, and lack of a general plan of action. In other words, our Palestine cause needs what it now lacks: centralization.[25]

Thus in very simple terms, from provincial Poltava to Odessa early in 1884. But so too, in somewhat more sophisticated terms, from Warsaw, where much the most effective and energetic society of all had been established in the summer of 1883. There, as Pinsker was informed when they responded (warmly) to his call, elaborate plans for a supra-communal organization had been laid; and there was a positive dislike and fear of the prospect of a host of ill-managed local societies springing up. 'Groups which are not properly organized will not inspire confidence'; besides which, they were liable to come under restrictive police regulation. The successful settlement of Erez-Israel was conditional on 'absolute unity of aspiration and action' and this, in turn, could be brought about only through the establishment of a world union with 'modest philanthropic purposes' and 'no political colouring whatever'.[26]

'Political', in this context, clearly related to involvement in internal Russian affairs. In a broader and, at the same time, more fundamental sense of the term, it is plain that the active spirits of Ḥibbat Zion were groping for means of social action which were nothing if not political in method and—however distantly— purpose: 'The main reason why nothing has been done to further this sacred matter is not indifference or anything like that, but a failure to take the true measure of the force at work within it.'[27]

In sum, the effect of the Pinsker–Lilienblum initiative was not to launch the movement, or to redirect it in any major sense, but to help galvanize it and pull it together. The two men helped to create a fragile, but fairly steady network of communication between the committees, first and foremost between Odessa and the rest. Certain committees—and with them certain personalities— then emerged into view as particularly energetic, or more obviously effective, or more influential than others: Warsaw, Bialystok, Poltava, and, of course, Odessa. (Moscow, a candidate for such

---

[25] Shilyansky to Lilienblum, 11 February 1884 (O.S.). Druyanov, i, no. 75, col. 145.

[26] Yassinovski to Pinsker, 18 November 1883 (O.S.). Druyanov, i, no. 58, cols. 121–5.

[27] From the first explanatory note to the Rules and Programme formulated by the Warsaw Ḥovevei Zion. Druyanov, i, no. 49, cols. 99–103. These rules were quite as elaborate as those of Vilna and were particularly detailed on the arrangements for the collection and, above all, handling of funds, destined to the settlers in Erez-Israel through friendly individuals in Western Europe.

leadership, by virtue of its activists, was seen to be too remote and difficult of access to the unprivileged Jews of the Pale.) The Lovers of Zion began to discover one another, and so to discover themselves and to take each other's measure. The revelation that on almost all the really broad issues their outlook was much the same confirmed and, in a sense, sanctioned it in their minds. The movement became an increasingly orderly and institutionalized country-wide framework of Jewish public activity and, in a short time, a recognized alternative to older forms. And the ideas it propagated, however generalized and indistinct and ostensibly impracticable their explicit content, gained ever wider currency as pointers to a new road for the Jews to travel. Here, indeed, was its lasting impact. Whatever the limitations of Ḥibbat Ẓion the vehicle and Ḥibbat Ẓion the programme for social action, it was a powerful, if admittedly hesitant, educative force. It showed that supra-communal purposes could be pursued. It stood for a view of things that differed from what was most commonly propagated in this period among Jews on the issue of the Jews themselves. It rejected both immobilism and universalism; and it relied neither on the Gentiles nor on the Deity. In contrast to all other formulas and ideological positions, it stood for a solution to the Jewish Question that was dependent upon what the Jews were prepared to do for themselves, collectively, and made the salvation of the individual Jew conditional upon the salvation of the Jewish people. For the members and adepts of Ḥibbat Ẓion these were differences which entailed changes of mind and the opening of new horizons. And accordingly they themselves came to constitute a great reservoir of formed opinion, one on whose goodwill Herzl was to draw so successfully a decade and a half later, and without which the brighter, better-led, and more exciting, but in some ways less popular and less unembarrassedly Jewish movement he created would never have taken off, let alone become, almost overnight, the first clear expression of Jewish political will since the beginning of the Exile.

The period of Ḥibbat Ẓion is thus the crucial, indispensable period and the character and importance of Ḥibbat Ẓion the keys to the understanding of all that followed. Ḥibbat Ẓion was a grey affair, well-meaning but generally unimaginative, honest but at the same time somewhat fearful. All in all—even in retrospect—it was disappointing. The great moment of intellectual and emotional turmoil at the beginning of the decade passed without being fully

and successfully seized. There may, perhaps, be no cause to wonder
at this because it was pre-eminently a movement—and a minority
movement at that—of a non-sovereign people, of a people that had
been virtually washed clean of political habits and political ideas,
let alone political capabilities. In any event, the major failures and
small successes of Ḥibbat Zion, the style of its operations, the issues
which united and divided its members, the numbers of its members,
the methods by which it collected and distributed funds, and the
precise sums involved—all these, and other cognate aspects and
details of its activities, constituted the matter out of which much
of what was to follow had necessarily to grow, for good or ill.


                                    iii

The indirect evidence that support for Ḥibbat Zion spread rapidly
through the Pale in the 1880s is overwhelming. So too is the
evidence that, predominantly, it took the form of local societies
established through local initiative, whose members either saw
themselves, with varying degrees of seriousness, as prospective
settlers in Erez-Israel, or else were anxious to lend a hand or a
voice in aid of those settled there. And finally, it is plain that underlying such 'practical' activities (as they came to be called in time)
was the sentiment, at once vague and powerful, of injured, and yet
hopeful, nationhood. All this can be elicited from memoirs, diaries,
and letters, from the rather scrappy protocols and elliptical resolutions of the many local and the few country-wide meetings that
were held in the period, and from occasional documentation prepared in advance of such meetings, some of which has survived.
But the condition and structure of Ḥibbat Zion was such that
there were no central records and comprehensive documentation, nor
were even the most active and influential leaders of the movement
themselves ever equipped with a clear and reasonably detailed,
let alone accurate, picture of their constituency. Nor, indeed,
could they be. Regular reporting and written and systematically
maintained records were of low priority for an illegal (even if
not subversive) movement operating in a hostile police state. In
any case, the central organization of Ḥibbat Zion established
following the Odessa initiative, but never fully consolidated, comprised (and was directly representative of) only a relatively small
proportion of the very great number of local societies scattered

through Russia and Poland. This central organization, certainly the backbone of the movement as a whole, from 1884 to 1896, was to all intents and purposes a confederation of the larger, reasonably, if amateurishly, institutionalized local societies of the major cities of the Pale. The much greater number of local, truly provincial societies in the smaller towns, to say nothing of the multitude of little circles, devoid of all regularity of feature whatever and which were formed, then lost from sight, and then re-formed again in countless Jewish townlets, remained, for the most part, outside the ambit of Ḥibbat Ẓion's formal structures, even if subject to no small extent to their influence.

This state of affairs, comprising, as it were, umbra and penumbra, was analogous to the old pattern of the informal rabbinical hierarchy in which it was the incumbents in the greater centres, with some exceptions, who were looked to in a general way for informed and authoritative pronouncements by those in the minor ones, but without the relationship of centre to periphery being one of command or even, in the strict sense, instruction. In brief, much as Eastern European Jewry did not constitute a church, Ḥibbat Ẓion did not constitute a party.

For all these reasons, the sources for proper and comprehensive delineation of the concrete aspects of Ḥibbat Ẓion are meagre. Nor are there grounds for judging them equally reliable in every respect. Membership figures, for example, must be taken *cum grano*, but accounts of funds collected and distributed are likely to be accurate. With these reservations, the following picture emerges.

The great expansion of the movement within the Russian Empire occurred immediately subsequent to the Pinsker–Lilienblum initiative, in the years 1884–6. There is firm evidence of twelve societies being in existence by the year 1882/3 (the year 5643 in the Jewish calendar) and thereafter there was rapid growth for a while:

| | | |
|---|---|---|
| 1882/3 | 12 societies | |
| 1883/4 | 17 new societies | |
| 1884/5 | 28 ,, | ,, |
| 1885/6 | 39 ,, | ,, |
| 1886/7 | 17 ,, | ,, |
| 1887/8 | 5 ,, | ,, |
| 1888/9 | 14 ,, | ,, |
| 1889/90 | 6 ,, | ,, |
| TOTAL: | 138 | |

What of the total extent of the movement? The figure of 138 is suggestive, but not conclusive: it is impossible to establish with any accuracy how many societies set up in these years actually survived, and for how long. There is some evidence, much of it indirect, some of it hearsay, which points to the numbers being greater than that implied by those given above. The Warsaw circle believed (and so informed the others) early in 1885 that there were 120 local societies,[28] or slightly more than double the figure for 1885/6 above. But no clear criterion for inclusion in the Warsaw calculation emerges; and it is likely that their reference was to every locality in which a circle of adepts or sympathizers, however informal and ephemeral, was known to exist. It must be compared to Lilienblum's mention, at the end of April 1888, of 'about eighty' societies with which he had to maintain an active and regular correspondence.[29] On the other hand, the end of the decade was a time of slump in the fortunes of the movement and an almost general mood of pessimism among its leaders.

After 1890, when, as we shall see, legal status was granted to the Odessa committee (but to it alone) by the authorities, the basis for computation changed. Two new types of 'settlement societies', one more, one less popular in potential membership, but all linked to Odessa, as the regulations for the new legal committee necessitated, were formed. More clearly differentiated societies of youths and students were organized. And, in contrast to these open organizations, a select and semi-secret society, Benei Moshe, was formed in 1899 under the influence of Aḥad Ha-ʿAm[30] and dedicated to the notion that moral and cultural preparation had to precede the material salvation of the Jews. By the year 1891/2 there were at least 53 new societies of all categories—most of them, of course, in localities in which the older forms of Ḥibbat Ẓion had been in evidence earlier and which do not seem to have been entirely replaced. A few more were set up in each of the years immediately subsequent. All told, then, it may be taken that some form of organized activity occurred, and persisted for some years, often for the full period of a decade and a half, in between one hundred and one hundred and fifty towns of the Russian Pale and in those major cities outside it which had a permitted Jewish population large enough to sustain the movement—in St. Peters-

[28] Druyanov, i, no. 249, col. 469.          [29] Druyanov, ii, no. 783, col. 520.
[30] See below, pp. 187 ff.

burg and Moscow, as already noted, and even in Kazan and Kaluga, cities whose Jewish population at the time barely amounted to one thousand.[31]

The membership of the various societies varied enormously in number from time to time and, of course, from place to place. 'Membership', in any case, is in some respects an inappropriate term: activists, potential settlers in Erez-Israel, contributors (both regular and occasional) of funds, and more passive supporters have all to be distinguished. Nor was the recruitment of large numbers regarded as an end in itself. Almost from the beginning, once it was apparent that no large-scale migration to Erez-Israel was practicable, fear of assuming responsibility—moral as well as material—for a host of enthusiastic, but impoverished migrants inclined the leading figures in the movement to keep it within quite severe qualitative and quantitative bounds.

Generally speaking, the recorded membership (or, alternatively, the record of dues-payers and other contributors) in the larger Jewish centres was in the hundreds: 459 in Vilna, 400 in Mogilev (in 1883/4); 250 in Pinsk, 150 in Lublin, 100 in Lodz, 300 in Libau, 250 in Elizavetgrad, 210 in Kiev (1884/5); 300 in Bialystok, 170 in Bobruisk, 120 in Gomel (1885/6); 130 in Simferopol, 500 in Berdichev (1887/8). Membership of the new, legal Odessa committee itself was very much larger, however, and extended far out of Odessa itself. It was consistently above 4,000 for five of the seven years 1890 to 1896 (4,808 in 1896).

The total strength of Ḥibbat Zion in the years 1881 to 1896 is thus very difficult to assess, even if it were possible to define membership satisfactorily. In November 1885 the Warsaw committee estimated the total at 14,000.[32] As this would correspond, very roughly, to an average membership of 100 in 150 localities, the figure can be accepted as reasonable for the period. A decade later, in the period of Ḥibbat Zion's decline, the semi-official estimate was 8,000–10,000.[33] The two figures are consistent.

[31] But the number may have been much larger—perhaps even double the figure of 100–150, although the direct evidence to that effect is slim. Much depends, once again, on the criterion for reckoning a group or circle as a 'society' or 'organization'. Sympathizers were almost certainly to be found everywhere. B. Dinur's estimate of 80 associations (a figure probably taken from Lilienblum's letter quoted above) in over 50 cities and towns is certainly minimal (*Zion*, xxii. 2–3, 1957, p. 115 and n.). Zitron, quoting Tsederbaum at the end of the decade, gives the figure of 240 (op. cit., p. 375).

[32] Circular letter on state of the movement, Druyanov, i, no. 366, col. 656.

[33] Klausner, op. cit., p. 257.

Counting not only the active and dues-paying members at a particular period in time, but peripheral supporters including those who had lapsed from the category of activists, disappointed would-be migrants, readers of the sympathetic Jewish press, and, not least, the mere well-wishers who might turn out to attend a meeting, but do no more, a larger figure, conceivably one, two, or three times as great, would be in order. This, in turn, would correspond, very roughly, to one or two out of every one hundred adult Jewish males in the Empire.

The third quantitative indicator of Hovevei Zion activity is that of funds collected for purposes of settlement. Here the line between the major centres of Hibbat Zion and the peripheral groups was crystal clear and known to many of those concerned. Slightly over a score generally managed to collect 400 roubles a year or more. The rest—four or five times as many in number—contributed very much less, if anything.[34]

The total income of Hibbat Zion varied, of course. Generally it was 40,000–50,000 roubles per annum.[35] It thus emerges that the majority of members cannot have contributed much more than a few roubles a year and that if some of the middle-class activists —those upon whom Pinsker had originally placed his hopes—did so, very great numbers were unable to give more than a few copecks from time to time. Of support from the rich, who were few in number, but from whom alone really substantial sums could be obtained, there was almost none at all.

Nothing reveals the incurable operational weakness of Hibbat Zion so strongly as these pitiful, hopelessly inadequate sums. Against an annual income of some 50,000 roubles (£5,000) (in a good year) must be set the contemporary estimate of the cost of settling a single family in Erez-Israel—3,000 roubles. From which it follows that, for all its many thousands of adherents, the move-

---

[34] A list drawn up in 1886 rates the societies in order of contribution, as follows: Odessa 6,529 roubles; Moscow 6,195; Kharkov 3,978; Warsaw 3,947; Vilna 3,400; Poltava 3,338; Bialystok 2,924; Riga 2,122; St. Petersburg 1,650; Kiev 1,400; Minsk 1,372; Kovno 1,200; Kremenchug 1,010; Rostov-on-Don 955; Libau 800; Brest-Litovsk 800; Lodz 734; Dvinsk 650; Elizavetgrad 565; Mir 518; Pinsk 500; Nikolayev 460; Yekaterinoslav 404. Druyanov, i, no. 441, col. 774 n. The figures are interesting because they are clearly functions of the energy expended by the activists and of local variations of receptivity to them, not of the absolute Jewish population.

[35] This was the estimate of the Warsaw group at the end of 1885 (Druyanov, i, no. 366, col. 656) and is confirmed, independently, by the figures for the twenty-three societies listed above.

ment could not permit itself to plan for the transfer, accommodation, and employment of even as few as twenty families a year. Instead, it was impelled to distribute its mean resources in sparsely attempting to cover the cost of a few farm animals here, the digging of a well there. It is true that the pennies, 'these miserable resources earned by the sweat of our poor people',[36] were, in their way, heartening proof of popular devotion to the cause. But they were more powerful evidence still of the really salient aspect of Russo-Polish Jewry, its poverty.

Thus, on the one hand, forced, as its leaders concluded, to restrict themselves in practice to the grey business of extending quasi-charitable support for the new Jewish settlements in Erez-Israel and their gradual expansion, Ḥibbat Zion was soon confronted, on the other hand, with the bitter fact that it was without means which were remotely in keeping with even so modest an enterprise. The consequences for the morale of the movement and for the seriousness in which the very idea of migration to the Land was held might easily have been fatal. They were certainly very grave.

Our precarious situation cannot be maintained for long. I am ashamed to recall that in the course of eight months, from the month of Tevet up to and including the month of Tammuz, we have managed to send the settlements in the Holy Land no more than 40,000 francs, which is to say 16,000 roubles or 2,000 roubles a month. And of late, the sluggishness in all that concerns the transmission of money has increased. If only one out of a hundred of our people in this country were to contribute no more than two roubles a year the total sum would reach more than 60,000 roubles a year. So there are no two ways about it: either our generation, sunk as it is in slavery and indifference and other vices, does not yet merit the sacred idea to which we subscribe, or else it disapproves of what the leadership is doing. In the former case, we ought certainly to stop deceiving ourselves like children at play and, once we have finished the task of building three settlements which we had assumed, drop the work entirely, recognizing our people's feebleness of mind, feebleness of self-respect, and feebleness of national feeling, and proclaim that the entire mass of Jews in this country are unable to do what can be done by a single philanthropist abroad.[37] Alternatively, it will be the duty of the leadership to vacate its place in favour of others who are better.[38]

---

[36] Pinsker to Meyerovich, 31 May 1885 (O.S.). Druyanov, i, no. 294, col. 534.

[37] Baron Edmond de Rothschild.

[38] Circular letter from Pinsker to the societies, 19 September 1886. Druyanov, i, no. 491, cols. 843–4.

Grave—but, in the event, not fatal: in part because, for all their evident weaknesses, the new structures of Ḥibbat Ẓion, as already suggested, did rapidly take root as permanent features of the Jewish social scene; and in part because Ḥibbat Ẓion's inability to cope with the problem that it had set itself did not impinge directly and immediately on the central component of its creed, the call for national reconstruction and regeneration. It did teach a great deal more, more than had originally been grasped, about the nature of the problem. It served, if anything, to intensify the Jews' bitter sense of impotence. And it did lead to a much sharper and clearer look being taken by some members of the movement at the balance and relationship between desirable ends and available means and at the question of modes of matching ends and means, but not immediately. For a while the sheer fact of organization and the new, exhilarating experience of formal and representative conference on national affairs tended to dispel unease and to block out some of the harsher thinking.

### iv

There was no doubt in the minds of the leaders of Ḥovevei Ẓion that their first great item of business had to be the convening of a general conference at which they could meet each other face to face and lay down a joint and agreed plan of action. Nevertheless, it was not until 6 November 1884, fully a year after the Odessa initiative, that thirty delegates were finally assembled for five days in the Silesian town of Kattowitz. The reasons for the long delay are obscure and traceable only in part to the tedious process of many-sided consultation by letter-post. More important was the self-doubt and fear of failure that preoccupied the majority of the activists, if not always fully consciously. Some feared that once the word was out that such a conference had been held, masses of the innocent would expect immediate settlement in Ereẓ-Israel. Those who still looked to the West for salvation could see small profit in a gathering to which westerners could not be drawn to participate. Many thought it inherently unlikely that the independent societies would agree on a common policy, or feared, alternatively, that an *agreed* policy would be devoid of meaning.

There were enthusiasts. One activist in Kharkov thought that the proper function of the coming conference was to establish a 'world-wide Palestinian union' which would first counteract and replace the Alliance Israélite Universelle, then duly emancipate the Jewish people from the unfortunate influence of the Jewish plutocrats—and all this by assuming 'not a philanthropic, but a governmental character'.[39] Even Naḥum Sokolov, the popular columnist (later editor) of the Warsaw periodical *Ha-Ẓefira*, who had originally ridiculed Pinsker, now spoke of the great parliament of Jewry that was impending.[40] Probably, without the continual beavering of the Warsaw group of Ḥovevei Ẓion, led by Sha'ul Pinḥas Rabbinowitz (usually referred to by the acronym 'Shefer'), there would have been no meeting and no co-ordinated activities for a great while longer. 'Shefer', a *maskil* of great learning and, like Lilienblum and so many others of the new literati, a product of and, as it were, a defector from, the world of the Lithuanian rabbis, had originally formed cosmopolitan and mildly socialist views. These changed as he came under Smolenskin's influence towards the end of the 1870s; and his revised views on the un-alterable specificity of the character and the needs of Jewry were confirmed in his mind and immensely strengthened by the events of 1881. He then launched himself in public affairs by providing systematic reports on the pogroms for dissemination in the West. Now he put his growing influence and his great resources of single-minded (and sometimes rather simple-minded) energy behind the plan for a conference of Ḥovevei Ẓion. He was undismayed when the police interrogated him—merely arguing that it showed the importance of keeping the affairs of Ḥibbat Ẓion, so far as possible, within the law. He was not worried by the prospect that many of the societies would wish to retain their independence: it was enough if the dozen or so principal societies were agreed among themselves. The essential thing was to end the dissipation of energy. And if plans were unambitious—if, for example, they were laid for no longer than a single year's activities—even the danger of the whole venture's running into the sand was not, he thought, to be feared.[41]

The fact was that the arguments for holding a conference were so much more powerful in both tactical logic and emotive value than the arguments for delay, that once plans for a conference began

[39] Shlaposhikov to Pinsker, 18 September 1884 (O.S.). Druyanov, i, no. 129, cols. 251–3.

[40] *Ha-Ẓefira*, xlii, 11 November 1884. The article was published shortly after, but clearly written before, the Kattowitz conference. Sokolov was not an adept of Ḥibbat Ẓion at this time.

[41] Letter to Smolenskin, n.d., Schwadron Collection, Jerusalem.

seriously to be discussed doubts ceased to be voiced aloud and matters went ahead almost as a matter of course. Nevertheless, the essential sources of doubt, the fragility and weakness of the movement, and the powerful contrary pressures to which it was subject did all have a direct effect on the planning and running of the conference and so, ultimately, on its results. The pressures and counter-pressures can be seen at work even in the selection of the venue, long before the conference got under way.

Kattowitz had been chosen for many reasons. It was both in the 'East' and in the 'West', being in Poland, but in the German-ruled sector of the divided country. It was the one town in all Germany in which a society of Ḥovevei Zion had been formed. But it was in, or very near, the heartland of European Jewry. Being in Prussian territory, it was presumed safe from the eyes and ears—or, at the very least, the intervention—of the Russian police. But being close to the border with Russia (and the border with Austria as well), it was particularly convenient for those delegates from Russia who, in default of proper travel documents, would have to be smuggled abroad. It was true that the fact that some delegates would have to be smuggled across the frontier was in itself an argument against holding the conference in Kattowitz.[42] And, in the event, four quite eminent rabbis, whose sense of dignity and public office inhibited them from undertaking anything so ignominious, drew back after they had travelled most of the way. The choice was also criticized on the grounds that the meeting should not be held in Europe at all, least of all in Central Europe, but in Constantinople, and that its main business should be to show the Turks that the movement was in no sense an instrument of the European Powers, that the suspicions of the Porte were baseless, and that their opposition to Jewish settlement in Erez-Israel was misplaced because the Jews would be a loyal and productive element within the Ottoman Empire. However, this was the view of a small minority. Few of the prospective delegates could have made so long a journey. Most were convinced, by this time, that the Ottoman government had set its face firmly against the enterprise and that there was more to be lost than gained by so radical and spectacular a move under the

---

[42] Cf. letter from Bialystok Ḥovevei Zion to Odessa, 2 October 1884, Druyanov, i, no. 127, col. 250. However, they softened, and shortly after inquired of the Warsaw society whether the latter could indeed undertake to get their leader, Rabbi Mohilever, across the border in safety. If not, they wanted the meeting postponed. Central Zionist Archives (henceforth CZA), A27/12/1, no. 22.

Sultan's nose. Much the commoner view was that, in any case, the crucial arena of conflict at this stage of the Jewish *Risorgimento* was within Jewry itself and that the fight was not to win recognition by forces external to Jewry, let alone their support, but to gain internal legitimacy. Their urgent business was neither in Constantinople, nor in Jaffa, but in Europe.[43]

So all in all, the choice of Kattowitz, pressed for by the Warsaw committee in particular, was not unreasonable in the circumstances, even if, underlying it, there was much of that restraint and modesty, verging on timidity, that characterized almost everything that Ḥibbat Zion did collectively—as opposed to the high ambitions and soaring hopes of many of its members individually. It was the product of a typical three-cornered compromise between a desire for privacy of deliberation, an equally strong, but contradictory desire to make a powerful impact upon the Jewish world at large, and a barely explicit, but quite real, and again contradictory, fear of nailing their true colours to the mast lest a single dramatic act spell the end of all activity in both the Russian and the Ottoman Empires. The very purpose of the conference was camouflaged, lightly, as the foundation meeting of a charitable society for the promotion of Jewish agricultural settlement formed and named in honour of Sir Moses Montefiore on the occasion of his one hundredth birthday. It was hoped that the aged Montefiore could thus be enticed into backing Ḥibbat Zion and that, on the other hand, the setting up of the society (as *Mazkeret Moshe*) would provide adequate cover for further activities in Russia upon the delegates' return home. The camouflage could only be sustained if the conference was held away from a major centre of Jewish population and public life.

The thirty delegates who reached Kattowitz and participated in the conference were all, with one exception, representatives of societies; and much was made of the fact that they were *delegates*, even though some were, inevitably, self-selected and self-appointed. Even Pinsker was provided with a formal letter of authority signed by the Chief Rabbi of Odessa. The exception was David Gordon, the editor of *Ha-Magid*, who was invited in his personal capacity

---

[43] Cf. Efraim Deinard, *Se'u nes Ẕiona*, Pressburg, 1886, pp. 6–17; Joseph Meisl, *Rabbi Sha'ul Pinḥas Rabbinowitz* ('*Shefer*'), Tel Aviv, 1943, pp. 31–48: and Levanda to Hovevei Zion, Odessa, 10 September 1884 (O.S.). Druyanov, i, no. 125, cols. 243–4.

and because he could report on his attempts to gain Montefiore for the movement. Smolenskin, the most eminent figure in the Jewish national movement at large, and to many minds then (and since) one of the intellectual and ideological precursors of Ḥibbat Zion, was not invited. Lilienblum did not attend either.

In composition, the group was a fair reflection of the geographical and social locus of the movement. Only three delegates came from the West: one from Paris and two from London. But all three were East European in origin (two of the three were natives of Lithuania), only one cut any sort of figure in Jewish society (in London), and none had any status, let alone influence, in western society at large. Four more came from the Polish–Russian borderlands and from Prussian Poland proper, including Kattowitz itself. But although these had western contacts, they were slight. Together, the pitifully weak 'western contingent' served as a reminder of Pinsker's purposes, rather than as a proof of Ḥibbat Zion's capabilities. The easterners included one representative from Romania; all the rest were subjects of the Tsar. St. Petersburg, Moscow, and Rostov-on-Don sent one delegate each, Riga sent two. The others came from within the Jewish Pale of Settlement: six from Warsaw, three from Bialystok, two from Kovno, one each from Kharkov, Mezrich (Miedzyrec Podlaski), Odessa, Pinsk, Poltava, and Ruzhany. The delegates were overwhelmingly middle-aged men and established figures in their communities. Each belonged to one of four categories: rabbis, members of the free professions, merchants and manufacturers, literati. There were no students among them, no representatives of BILU, nor of the other settlers in Erez-Israel. They were predominantly ('Shefer' was an exception) rather staid, slow-moving, prudent people, anxious to get on with real affairs, proud of their preference for the practical over the theoretical, and profoundly anxious to avoid anything that smacked of fuss and unnecessary risk. All were aware that they were embarking on a unique venture, but a little distantly. Their sense of the occasion was profound, but it lacked focus. The only overt recognition made of its quintessential nature came with the election of a rabbi (Rabbi Shemu'el Mohilever of Bialystok) as honorary president of the assembly—a very vague and characteristically indirect acknowledgement of the conference's *national* significance and of the hope that it would eventually find its place in the historic continuum of the Jewish people.

The real presiding member of the assembly, both in name and in fact, was Pinsker, who set the tone for all that followed with an opening address that was brief, clear, resolutely low-key, and severely limited in content to matters philanthropic. He told the delegates that while the Jews' enforced abandonment of agriculture and assumption of their now familiar role of commercial middlemen had been to the detriment of their own internal social and cultural balance, it had for long been to the benefit of society at large. But now conditions had changed. In the contemporary age of steam, telegraph, and vast centres of urban population the Jews were no longer needed. On the contrary, a disastrous rise in friction between Jew and non-Jew was in progress with no end or limit to it in sight. The social and economic role of the Jew had therefore to be changed. Specifically, it was urgent that it be made possible, once more, for the Jewish masses, long stunted by petty trade and petty industry, to return to the ancient and honourable occupation of their forefathers. It was the business of the conference to see to it that plans to promote the necessary change were carefully drawn up. The delegates could be encouraged by the fact that the importance of the need had already been grasped by some and that a beginning had been made, as the settlements established in the brief span of the past two years showed. There was a duty to come to the aid of the settlers 'wherever they might be'. And 'by founding a Montefiore Society for the Promotion of Agriculture, especially for the support of settlers in Ereẓ-Israel, we shall be building the jubilarian [Montefiore] a monument more lasting than one of bronze and opening up before our people a new road to well-being and truly human action.'

That was all: a brief speech that was part sociological gloss on *Autoemancipation!*, with none of its resounding fury, and part proposal to limit the serious business of the conference exclusively to the discussion of the ways and means of organizing aid for the settlers, with the special character—and, indeed, location—of the settlements diluted to the limits of permissible ellipsis. Almost all hint of the larger social purposes to which he had alluded in his pamphlet had been carefully drained away—all but one elusive reference to the Jews' need for air to breathe and room to move about in, lest they succumb to the impending suffocation.[44]

---

[44] Text (in the German original) in Druyanov, i, no. 142, VII, cols. 276-8. A Hebrew protocol of the conference was also prepared (ibid. VIII, cols. 297-301) by 'Shefer' who

The idea of a Jewish state is still, of necessity, very far away [he had written to Rülf at the beginning of the year]. Nor would a sensible man so much as make mention of it. If I dealt with it in my pamphlet, I did so because I had no other choice if I wanted to make myself plain. What I emphasized then, and still do, is the awakening of our sense of national self-respect. That is easily said; the question is, how is it to be? The task is beyond the capacity of our generation and is particularly difficult in the civilized countries which set the tone in Europe.[45]

He was still of this view. Before all else, the westerners had to be brought in and anything that might frighten them away had to be systematically excised, the more so as the ultimate ends of the movement were not only subject to debate and question in themselves, but beyond attainment in any foreseeable future. The task of the conference was therefore to limit itself to practical business. And this, under Pinsker's leadership, it did. He was the most considerable figure among those attending, the only one, so it seemed, who was capable of keeping the group together, the only one, they thought, who could lead. Not all were happy about the direction along which he took them, but none proposed anyone, or anything, else.

Lilienblum, who had become somewhat disappointed in Pinsker in the meantime, wrote later that he thought the choice disastrous. But he kept his views to himself, consoling himself, he said, with the thought that, at least, Pinsker was a man of great integrity and complete devotion to the affairs of the nation and that if there was none other but this man of poor health and limited vision to lead them, nothing was to be gained by quarrelling with reality. Asked by Mohilever what he thought of the Kattowitz meeting, he replied, laconically, that he believed it had been convened before the time for it was ripe.[46]

On what actually constituted a practical, non-ideological, uncontroversial approach to the immediate problems of the movement there was no real division of opinion. A substantial list of

put in all the fervour and national feeling and specific reference both to the centrality of the resettlement of Ereẓ-Israel and to the purposes which underlay it which Pinsker had so carefully left out. Pinsker was furious when he discovered what 'Shefer' had done. The very last thing he wanted was to be accused, as he duly was, of bad faith by circulating two versions of the conference for two distinct audiences, one literate in German, the other literate in Hebrew, one western, the other eastern. (See Meisl, op. cit., p. 36.)

[45] Yo'eli, op. cit., p. 152.
[46] Lilienblum, *Derekh la'avor golim*, pp. 21-2.

topics was raised, debated, and disposed of in the best parliamentary manner. It was agreed that the movement's centre should be Berlin, at any rate in principle; but that in practice, until sufficient support had been mobilized in Germany to sustain an active centre, the headquarters would be in Odessa. There would be a secondary centre in Warsaw. Pinsker's over-all leadership was confirmed. Since it was apparent that too little was known about conditions in Erez-Israel, a mission of inquiry would be sent out to report on the settlements and make proposals. Another delegation would be sent to Constantinople to try to persuade the Porte to relax the administrative impediments to immigration into Erez-Israel. It was resolved to apply to the Russian government for formal permission to operate as a charitable society engaged in the promotion of Jewish agricultural settlement. But beyond this, an uneasy sense of the immensity of the task and the contrasting paucity of available means seems to have weighed over the conference. It was agreed that help would be rendered those settlements which were in receipt of no aid from other sources, viz. Petaḥ Tikva, Yesud ha-Maʿala, and Gedera. And much time was spent on discussion of the sums that would be made available and the modes and conditions of transmission. But no further settlement was to be encouraged, let alone undertaken, until the existing farming villages had been properly consolidated and until more was known about local conditions. There seems to have been no debate on the cardinal question whether a policy of slow and cautious advance made sense, which is to say, whether—and if so, to what extent— it was really commensurate with the needs of eastern Jewry. No general guidelines were laid down for the central committees in Odessa and Warsaw. No provision was made for another general conference.

So, all told, the results of the conference, as Levanda promptly wrote to Pinsker, were 'misty and puzzling'.[47] Certainly, on the face of it, there was everything to be said for introducing system into the enterprise and perhaps something to be said, too, for the delegates' major conclusion that the 'strengthening of the enterprise is more urgent than its expansion', as the Warsaw committee later formulated it.[48] The structure of the proposed organization was to be loose, but that was a simple function of the facts of Jewish

[47] 27 November 1884 (O.S.). Druyanov, i, no. 158, col. 338.
[48] Cf. circular letter, March 1885. Druyanov, i, no. 249, cols. 467–77.

communal life: autonomous communities, no national institutions, low-level jealousies and suspicions, much concern all round with formal position and status. It was an achievement to have had the rule of majority decisions being binding on all accepted. The plan to locate the centre in Berlin was open to criticism (and was criticized) on the grounds that it would put the movement in the hands of people who were far in space, time, and character from the people with whom the movement was really concerned and of whom the Berliners thought little and knew less. Yet this was only a plan; and the prospect for implementation was known to be doubtful from the first. On the other hand, if the operation was to be mounted inside Russia, the call for legal status, however it might inhibit the movement, was not unreasonable. The very ambivalence of reaction which the Kattowitz conference aroused stemmed not a little from the circumstance, which none denied, not even those who condemned the entire enterprise, that it was in itself, by virtue of the fact that it had been held at all, an event. Nothing quite like it had occurred in Eastern Europe since the Council of the Four Lands was abolished in 1764. It aroused expectations[49] which the delegates knew in their hearts they were incapable of fulfilling and which, in their honesty, they had been reluctant to arouse. They were therefore driven by their caution and by a kind of fastidiousness to vitiate much of the effect for which they had been striving by gathering at Kattowitz in the first place, an effect which was at least as important for their movement as the setting up of institutions: a simple demonstration of their capacity for joint action in a common purpose. Even in this last respect, the results were mixed.

Pinsker had drawn comfort from the fact that orthodox and non-orthodox had shown their ability to co-operate.[50] This was premature. Differences did appear and were not entirely resolved or even papered over. The orthodox found it hard to suppress their feelings that it was rightfully *they*, the consistent upholders and representatives of the Jewish tradition, not quondam assimilationists like Pinsker and semi-apostates like Lilienblum, who should play the leading role. Beyond this, the more perceptive traditionalists had begun to sense that there was a deeper conflict

---

[49] See, for instance, a letter from the Nikolayev society to Warsaw sent three months after the conference, complaining that nothing had been done to realize the high hopes that had been aroused: legality had not been secured, the Sultan had not removed the ban on immigration, and so forth (CZA, A27/12/3).

[50] Letter to Rülf, 16 November 1884. Yo'eli, op. cit., p. 155.

in the making and that the clearer the purpose of the movement became, the deeper and bitterer it would be. What if the Return were carried to what, on one reading, was its logical conclusion: a fully autonomous Jewish state? The Romanian delegate, Karpel Lippe, was careful to point out, in his response to the invitation to come to Kattowitz, that, for his part, the idea of political autonomy was 'very far from our thoughts' because, amongst other considerations, no state can maintain itself without a postal service, railways, and the telegraph and these had to be operated day and night throughout the week. 'But if the officials of Israel were to rest on the Sabbath, according to the laws of Moses and Israel, other states, both far and near, would protest; while if we were to permit our officials to violate the Sabbath and the festivals, our brethren, both far and near, would rise up and destroy us.'[51] For the time being, however, the restriction of the business of the conference to the severely practical served fuller understanding and articulation of what was involved. The only concrete issue on which opinion was more or less openly divided was the internal, social character of the new settlements; and the orthodox, who suspected the Biluim of free thought and knew of their free practices had to be pressed hard before there was agreement to channel aid to Gedera. In the immediate aftermath of the conference, too, disagreement and friction between the two camps were largely over petty questions, the really divisive issues being slurred over, with Mohilever, a tough-minded and somewhat turbulent man, well aware of the unpopularity of Ḥibbat Zion within the wider camp of orthodoxy, being little disposed to compromise; and Pinsker, as a man of peace, who valued Mohilever's influence, doing what he could to appease him.[52]

Very little came of the effort to make the movement attractive to the westerners. The aged Montefiore died some months after Kattowitz. He left them neither a moral nor a financial legacy, nor did his heirs have his interest in the condition of the community in Erez-Israel. It had availed the Ḥovevei Zion nothing to call their movement after him and the name *Mazkeret Moshe* soon dropped from use.

They were hardly more successful about Berlin. Their one major ally in Germany, the eminent leader of Jewish orthodoxy, Rabbi

[51] Lippe to Warsaw committee, 28 October 1884. Druyanov, iii, no. 1204, cols. 614-19.
[52] Cf. Y. L. Fishman, *Sefer Shemu'el*, Jerusalem, 1923, pp. 4-72.

'Azriel Hildesheimer, would promise no more than discreet support
in the background, pleading age (although he was only one year
older than Pinsker). The truth was that he was troubled by the
prospect of isolation within the orthodox camp and afraid of compromising, or being thought to be compromising, German Jewry
in the eyes of the German authorities by associating with a foreign
national movement. They were initially more successful with
Heinrich Graetz, the greatest Jewish historian of the day. Travelling
to Breslau after the conference, Pinsker had invited him to join
*Mazkeret Moshe* as an honorary member of its committee and
Graetz accepted. But later, in the light of the criticism to which
Pinsker and his friends were subjected[53] when it became clear that
some, at least, of the principal figures in the movement 'had raised
the flag of nationality' and had not limited themselves to planning
for the future of the Jews of Russia alone, he withdrew, albeit with
apologies and with evident embarrassment and spinning out his
excuses in three letters which followed each other in close succession. He pointed out, quite correctly, that the centre of gravity
(*Schwerpunkt*) of 'it all' (i.e. the Jewish Problem and the Jewish
people) was in Russia, while in Germany only the most limited
sympathy could be expected. Russian Jewry could stand on its
own feet, he assured Pinsker. It ought not to look for fellow feeling
in Germany. The Jews of Germany 'are still sunk in Byzantinism'
and fearful lest 'Jupiter' (Bismarck) denounce them.[54]

The one German Jew of any prominence and promise who was
prepared to take part in the proposed Berlin committee was a
certain Sigismund Simmel, a businessman in his middle age,
reputedly a man of energy and goodwill, whom Hildesheimer had
recommended to Pinsker. But the prospect of leaving the leadership, or even the day-to-day running of the movement's affairs,
in his hands alone was more than the majority of the newly elected
central committee could swallow. Nor did the idea that 'Shefer'
join him as part expert adviser on East European affairs and part
language secretary commend itself to many. The more they thought
of it, the less they liked it, and the more impracticable it appeared.
Lilienblum, who had just been appointed secretary of the new

[53] Notably by Jellinek in *Die Neuezeit*. M. Rosenmann, *Dr. Adolf Jellinek, sein Leben und Schaffen*, Vienna, 1931, p. 165.

[54] Graetz to Pinsker, 23, 30 January, and 7 February 1885. Druyanov, i, nos. 191, 199, 207, cols. 394-5, 405-6, 413.

Odessa centre, but who retained an influence extending far beyond his formal function, was particularly critical. Nothing was known of this merchant, he wrote to 'Shefer', beyond the barren fact that Hildesheimer had mentioned his name to Pinsker and Pinsker had mentioned it to us. Consider the two immediate tasks: one was to get the permission of the Russian authorities to operate legally in Russia, the other was to get the permission of the Turkish authorities to settle in Erez-Israel. There was nothing whatever that Simmel could do about the first; nor, thought Lilienblum, was it clear that he could do more than another about the second. The plan to hand things over to him was absurd, and were it not for his personal regard for Pinsker he would say so publicly.[55] Meanwhile, Simmel's own enthusiasm was waning rapidly. His efforts to create a circle of supporters in Western Europe had failed instantly. It was not so much hostility, he complained to Pinsker, as the general indifference that appalled him.[56] And, like Graetz, he was greatly put off by the expressions of national fervour (*diese nationale Schwärmerei*) as he termed it, to which many of the Hovevei Zion had given vent after Kattowitz: it had to cease, or all would be lost.[57] Gradually, by common consent, the idea of directing the movement from the West was dropped.

Kattowitz was neither a triumph nor a failure. The participants had been set on keeping their sights low. They did as best they knew in the light of prior experience and the conventional wisdom of their class and times. It is a fact that there were none among them who could make the necessary leap out of the realms of communal philanthropy, the free professions, the rabbinate, and orderly and respectable commerce and industry to which they were accustomed and where daring and imagination were suspect, into the wholly new world of the political. So while none left Kattowitz with a sense of great accomplishment, most were satisfied that they had made a start. And so, indeed, on the level of the practical matters which had preoccupied them, they had. But for the rest, the very modesty of their intentions was a source of weakness, as were the cautious and circumlocutionary terms in which the purposes of Hibbat Zion were conceived and outlined publicly. As

[55] Lilienblum to 'Shefer', 27 December 1884 (O.S.). Druyanov, iii, no. 1229, cols. 672–3.
[56] Simmel to Pinsker, 17 December 1884. Druyanov, i, no. 1220, cols. 644–7.
[57] Simmel to Pinskèr, 7 February 1885. Druyanov, i, no. 1241, cols. 711–12.

Levanda argued, excessive prudence was not always a wise tactic.
'We shall tie ourselves hand and foot if we choose to hide our true
aims under all sorts of cleverly interwoven purposes.'[58]


V


The ideological divide between traditionalism and modernism
appeared and reappeared at the two subsequent general conferences
held at Druskieniki (near Grodno) in June 1887 and at Vilna in
August 1889. These conferences were attended by Russian and
Polish Jews exclusively and both took place within Russian territory. To that extent, they reflected the social locus of the movement
a trifle more accurately than had Kattowitz and showed a minor
rise in its collective self-confidence. Neither conference had been
wanted, let alone initiated, by the official leadership. Pinsker had
agreed to a conference being convened in 1887 only with great
reluctance and after heavy pressure from the Moscow society of
Hovevei Zion, with the latter's arguments for meeting being equal
and opposite to the former's for not: nothing of note had occurred
since Kattowitz; and some of the drive and urgency that had
informed Hibbat Zion had been lost. The Vilna conference was
convened on much the same basis, with the addition that Pinsker's
imminent retirement required decisions that could be taken by no
other forum.

The formal agenda of both conferences followed the pattern set
at Kattowitz, but were somewhat more carefully and elaborately
prepared. At each, the basic decision to seek, above all else, to
maintain what had been achieved was confirmed and the topics
discussed were, once again, almost exclusively organizational and
administrative: money matters, the movement's status in law, the
establishment of a permanent office in Erez-Israel, questions relating to the purchase of land, the condition of the settlements, the
mounting of a modest propaganda campaign within the Pale, and
the election of officers.[59] Only the idea of systematic propaganda
by the spoken and written word was new. As before, other, more
fundamental issues were in the air, but were treated obliquely.

[58] Levanda to Pinsker, 19 February 1885 (O.S.). Druyanov, i, no. 230, cols. 443–4.
[59] Summary protocols of the two conferences are printed in Druyanov, ii, no. 602, III,
cols. 212–16; and ibid., no. 999, IV, cols. 742–8. They reflect the agreed resolutions, not
the debates (which were often bitter).

Among the questions to which the delegates had to address themselves directly were whether land should be bought whenever and
wherever possible in Erez-Israel or whether, instead, the slim
funds available should be carefully husbanded and spent exclusively on first-rate farming land; whether the settlers should be
obliged to abide by all the ancient rules and injunctions relating to
the practice of agriculture in the Holy Land, not excluding the
injunction to leave the land entirely untilled in the Sabbatical Year;
and who was to have a voice in the endless series of technical
decisions on the precise form and measure of support for settlers
which the organization was increasingly obliged to take. None of
the issues could be debated, as yet, within the framework of an
accepted, over-all view of the problems of Hibbat Zion. No such
view had been formulated. But the principal activists of Hibbat
Zion were now beginning to be faced with issues which raised
questions of the structure of the leadership, its policy, and its
social and ideological complexion, all intertwined; and one consequence of such questions arising was to hasten the process whereby
the modernists on the one hand, and the traditionalists on the other,
found themselves with an ever more distinct sense of their own
separate identity and outlook. This led, in turn, to a partial shift
of attention from matters external to the movement to matters
internal.

It is worth stressing that the process was a gradual one and that
its effects took time to evince themselves. The Druskieniki conference did end with a row between the two camps. (Pinsker,
gathered with his intimates one evening, so far forgot himself in
his irritation as to drink a toast 'to the downfall of Jesuitry'.)[60] But
there was no break. The traditionalists would not openly oppose
the much-respected Pinsker; and the modernists, knowing the
limits of their sway in East European Jewry, were afraid of cutting
themselves off into isolation. Still, the ground for a sharper fight
had been prepared. For while the modernists conceded the traditionalists a larger share in the leadership and agreed to decisions
being taken by a complicated method of multilateral consultation
by letter-post by way of attenuating the central role of their strong-
hold in Odessa, the traditionalists had conceded little beyond
agreeing, indirectly and with reluctance, to Lilienblum retaining
his office of secretary. Mohilever made it very plain that he regarded

[60] Menahem Ussishkin, 'Dr. Pinsker', *Sefer Ussishkin*, Jerusalem, 1934, p. 313.

the compromise, such as it was, as temporary. He pronounced a public and deliberately offensive plea for the direction of the movement to be put into the hands of 'proper' (i.e. observant) Jews and refused to put his signature to the conference minutes along with everyone else's.

Two years later, at Vilna, he returned to the attack. The formidable Pinsker had retired from the scene ill (he died in 1891) and Mohilever's hands were free. There had been no real progress since the previous conference, he argued; the authority of the Odessa committee had weakened both in Russia and in Erez-Israel; the sums collected in the past year had dropped; the cumbersome method of arriving at decisions had not always been observed; even the attendance at the present conference was disappointing and had to be taken as so much evidence of failure. He also claimed, with less justice, but more heat, that the Odessa leadership had gone out of its way to help the free-thinking Biluim, while neglecting the orthodox settlers of Petah Tikva. Lilienblum defended Pinsker's and his own record, but Lilienblum, anathema to the truly orthodox, was ill placed to do so to good effect. Finally, Mohilever made an open bid for the control of the movement. The weakness of Hibbat Zion, he argued, had lain in the fact that all along its leadership had been in the hands of the modernizing *maskilim*, a class of men in whom the masses had no confidence. He himself had seen this from the first and had tried to correct it. He had failed. Now he would make a second attempt, proposing himself and Shelomo Yosef Fuenn for the joint over-all leadership of the movement. 'It is not honour I ask of you, but [the opportunity] to serve.' In the furore that followed, it was, characteristically at this stage of the evolution of the movement, the representative of the younger modernists who argued for mutual toleration and for keeping the factions together. Eventually, a new formula was devised. Pinsker would have three heirs. Mohilever would represent the orthodox, Fuenn (an observant Jew) the moderates among the *maskilim*, and Avraham Greenberg of Odessa 'the merchants and the men of practical affairs'—and, by implication, the tougher-minded modernists.[61] However, the victory for tradition was a small one because the Odessa centre remained in being and, in practice, Greenberg took over Pinsker's organizing and centralizing

---

[61] Cf. minutes taken down by M. B. H. Ha-Kohen, CZA, A5/6/2; M. L. Lilienblum, *Derekh la'avor golim*, pp. 142–5; and I. Klausner, *Mi-Katoviz 'ad Bazel*, i, pp. 380–91.

functions almost in full, albeit without his formal status and his moral authority. And small as the victory was, it was substantially wiped out eight months later with the founding of the new, legal Odessa committee in which the modernists of Odessa itself and their allies elsewhere were once more to the fore and the ailing Pinsker, once more, very briefly, at their head. None the less, a great issue had been raised for all who cared to see it and a line of division which could not be effaced and which was to reappear and be greatly deepened in later years had been drawn.

With the conversion of the vaguely tolerated, rarely molested, but nevertheless illegal network of Hovevei Zion into the officially sanctioned Society for the Support of Jewish Farmers and Artisans in Syria and Palestine in March/April 1890 the policy of extreme caution set at Kattowitz appeared to have been rewarded. Certainly, it was reconfirmed. It seemed there was now more to maintain and to protect: the organizational base in Russia no less than the settlements in Erez-Israel. Legality had been an early and basic target, set at Kattowitz and won by dint of protracted but open struggle with the St. Petersburg bureaucracy. It was hard not to see this as a considerable achievement. It was tempting to see it as the kind of achievement towards which Hibbat Zion should strive. Hopes rose. Self-congratulatory letters flew back and forth. S. L. Zitron, the first historian of Hibbat Zion and its contemporary, generally a chronicler of sober judgement, speaks of 'a period of experiments and trial' having come to an end and 'a period of daring and construction' beginning.[62] In fact, the new period was nothing of the kind. For while the years immediately after Kattowitz had been, by design, years of consolidation, they were equally a stretch of time in which enthusiasms cooled and fresh and unsettling ideas evolved. As we shall see, the achievement of respectability—and legal status signified little more—thus coincided, almost precisely, with the first serious critique of the road the movement was travelling and the first reasoned doubts about its nominal destination.

vi

The thrice repeated confirmation of the Odessa group's responsibility for the day-to-day running of the movement's affairs was

---

[62] Zitron, op. cit., p. 383.

first and foremost an indirect tribute to Pinsker's personal prestige. Otherwise, there was ostensibly little to say for Odessa as a centre of cross-communal activity. Geographically, it was on the periphery of the Pale. Socially it was atypical of Russo-Polish Jewry and a source of discomfort, if not suspicion, to those who were nearer in both their views and their ties to the mainstream of Jewish life. On the other hand, it was the port of emigration to Erez-Israel and arguably the best possible place from which to maintain contact with the settlers. Much of the day-to-day business of the Odessa committee was, in fact, dealing with those of the settlements for which Baron de Rothschild had not, or had not yet, assumed financial responsibility himself, and with the very thin, but never wholly interrupted, stream of emigrants to Erez-Israel and with questions of land purchase. This direct involvement of the Odessa circle of Ḥovevei Zion in the affairs of the *yishuv* did not end until the entire structure of Jewish life both in Europe and in the Land itself was transformed upon the outbreak of war in 1914.

The approach of the officials of the movement to the financial and technical and social problems of the settlers was honest and well-meaning, but also unimaginative and fussy. No doubt, the slender resources available to them and the tiny dimensions of the new *yishuv* itself combined to reinforce their underlying tendency to caution and pedantry.

For a time, two weak local committees functioned in Jerusalem and Jaffa in unconscious caricature of the two committees in Odessa and Warsaw to which they were answerable. The procedure for handling even the smallest question was hopelessly cumbersome.

X applies to the Jerusalem committee for [the purchase-price of] a horse. The Jerusalem committee duly writes to the committee in Warsaw. Warsaw examines the question from all its aspects and informs Jerusalem of its approval. The Jerusalem committee instructs the Jaffa committee to act. The Jaffa committee at long last, informs X of its final decision: no money![63]

Neither of the two committees in Erez-Israel lasted for long. Nor did the special status of the committee in Warsaw: within two years of the Kattowitz conference its privileges were dissolved (in a cloud of recrimination and hostility which the devoted, but tact-

---

[63] Ḥisin to Dubnov, May 1885. A. Druyanov (ed.), *Mi-yamim rishonim*, i, 1935, p. 87 fn. On another, later discussion on horses and analogous details see Mohilever's angry letter to Fuenn, 26 September 1889. Druyanov, *Ketavim*, iii, no. 972, col. 7.

less and unpopular 'Shefer' had raised about him). Matters then improved somewhat, but a distant, fussy paternalism continued to inform the relationship between the people in Ereẓ-Israel and those in Odessa, to say nothing of those in still more distant Russian, Polish, and Lithuanian cities who took an equally kind, but often impractical, if not crankish, interest.

I sympathise with your wish to establish a reading library in your settlement [wrote Levanda to Rishon le-Ẓion]. Nevertheless, I consider the idea somewhat premature and therefore not too desirable. Taking our people's excessive love of reading into consideration, there is the danger that reading might distract you from your daily tasks to the detriment of the continued development and well-being of your settlement.[64]

For information on the state of affairs in Ereẓ-Israel and for their management, the committee relied on the settlers themselves, on long-established Jewish residents in the country who were friendly to their cause, on special emissaries, and on the contingency of private visitors. They thus had to flounder under sporadic showers of bits and pieces of evidence, advice and requests for help, without a clear picture emerging, with no agreed criteria for judgement, and with frequent loss of temper on all sides.

It is in the nature of things [wrote a representative of Ḥibbat Ẓion in Jaffa to Pinsker in Odessa] that a man knows the character of the place where he was born, as well as the character and customs of its rulers and its inhabitants . . . I therefore permit myself to ask you, sir, not to envelop me constantly in a mass of counsel from afar or to put over me superiors who do not know, or do not wish to know, what [really] faces them.[65]

Not until 1891, after the reconstitution of the Odessa committee as a legal society, was a permanent delegation set up in Jaffa and some freedom of manœuvre granted it. But even then, in practice, there was little improvement. Ze'ev Tiomkin, the delegate, was a handsome, even commanding figure of a man, with much energy and boundless goodwill, but hopeless as an administrator and great sums of money were lost by him on fruitless projects.[66]

The cloudy view of affairs in Ereẓ-Israel, the failure to come to

[64] 21 September 1886 (O.S.). Druyanov, ii, no. 495, col. 2.
[65] Avraham Moyal to Pinsker, 26 July 1885. Druyanov, i, no. 307, col. 548.
[66] See Lilienblum on the subject. *Mi-yamim rishonim*, i, pp. 261–2.

grips with the complex problems with which the settlers were
faced, problems of livelihood, of health, of education, of relations
with their immediate Arab neighbours and the slightly more remote
Turkish officials, problems of personal security, and the more
obscure and intractable problems of social alienation which they,
like all migrants from one country to another, encountered, were
part causes and part products of the deeper failure to put the two
wings of the movement, the one in Russia and the other in Erez-
Israel, into a clear and agreed relationship. In Russia there was
profound uncertainty, timidity, and confusion precisely where there
should have been the sharpest definition and drive; and in Erez-
Israel a mounting sense of helplessness and frustration.

Such is the sad fate of many, if not the majority, of our brethren—
fighters for our national cause [wrote one of the Biluim early in 1885].
First in the struggle, drunk with the mere idea of success, they dis-
regarded everything. Nothing frightened them, nothing stopped them,
neither the barrenness of the country, nor the wildness of the Arabs—
who seemed truly wild to the *first* of those who reached this country,
nor ignorance of the local language and customs. Nothing deterred
them . . .

Nobody knows of all the hardships, sickness, and wretchedness they
underwent. No observer from afar can feel what it is like to be without
a drop of water for days, to lie for months in cramped tents visited by all
sorts of reptiles, or understand what our wives, children and mothers
go through when the Arabs attack us and, though we bravely drive them
away, what every shot means to them. No one looking at a complete
building realizes the sacrifice put into it . . .

The heart bleeds when one sees how one after another these first
fighters disappear. How, after having lost all their money, tortured by
physical and moral distress, they, against their will, have to go back,
leave their homes, their lives, and return half-dead—where to? To the
very place they had run away from and into the same hell of persecution
and misery . . .

But if that is how things stand, the first duty of true friends is to see
that those who are already here and working for the cause . . . get the
help [they need]. The task is very hard. But [our friends] must know
that otherwise success cannot be hoped for . . . Half-hearted measures
only prolong the sickness, weaken the organism . . .

Take, for example, the decision at the Kattowitz conference to send
Petah Tikva 10,000 francs. But such a sum is not enough to build homes
even for five families; and if it were divided among ten there would be
nothing for anybody. The reckoning is simple . . . A family with land,

but nothing else, needs a home to live in, a shed for livestock, a chicken-house for poultry, a barn, etc.—all costing a minimum of 2,000 francs; a team of horses and a minimum of implements come to 500 francs; livestock, without which no settler can exist, 1,000 francs; money for the first crop and money to live through the first year—1,000 francs. All told, minimal needs come to 4,500 francs per family. A family receiving 1,000 francs, or even 2,000 francs, say, for a house might build it and then remain with nothing to improve its condition. The result: exhaustion, apathy, and your help [given] in vain, to no purpose.[67]

vii

Meanwhile, the pressures exerted by the Russian state upon the Jews of the Empire had tightened once more. Pogroms were rare after 1884,[68] but, by way of compensation, the constriction of the Jews by administrative and police measures was pursued relentlessly. In particular, the 'May Laws' of 1882 were applied with ever greater savagery and ingenuity. The simple, stated prohibition on Jews taking up *new* residence in rural areas came to serve as the grounds for their being barred from returning home after a journey to town for the High Holidays in one province, from renewing leases on their homes in a second province, from moving from one village to another in a third. In all cases, the consequence was accelerated pauperization and general social misery in the over-crowded towns in which residence was free. Additional measures of restriction and denial were devised from to time. In 1886 the admission of Jews into secondary schools and universities was cut and permanently set at 10 per cent of the student body within the Pale, 5 per cent outside it, and 3 per cent in St. Petersburg and Moscow. In 1889 the admission of Jews to private legal practice, except by special (and rarely granted) permission of the Minister of Justice, was stopped. In 1891, at the beginning of Passover, a massive and particularly brutal expulsion of an estimated 20,000 Jews from Moscow was suddenly ordained, most of those expelled being artisans and ex-servicemen long resident in the city. It took a year to complete and was at its peak in the winter of 1892. Minor harassment was continuous and widespread. There were cases of Jews being threatened with corporal punishment for failing to take

[67] Menashe Meyerovitch to the committee, Warsaw, 4 January 1885. Druyanov, *Ketavim*, i, no. 172, cols. 366–8. Emphasis in original.
[68] They were renewed in 1903, beginning with the great pogrom of Kishinev.

their hats off upon meeting officials. The bureaucracy was instructed to make the inscription of Jewish origin in personal identity documents in red ink. It can be said, in sum, that the spirit in which the Russian state approached its Jewish subjects was, from this time on, one of manifest and virtually undiluted hostility, and that this hostility took the form of a public policy, the special efficacy of which derived, on the one hand, from the power of the vast machinery devoted to its pursuit and, on the other hand, from the self-righteousness and self-satisfaction with which its instigators and the great majority of its executors acted and caused others to act. When a senior official was so bold as to propose a softening of state policy on the Jews, the Tsar noted in the margin of the document: 'But we must not forget that it was the Jews who crucified our Lord and spilled his priceless blood.'[69]

The cumulative consequence of the long series of measures of constriction to which the Jews became subject in the second half of the decade and of the many signs by which the hatred official (and much of unofficial) Russia bore them was a sharp rise in the numbers emigrating. In the middle of the 1880s the movement had fallen to under 10,000 a year; but towards the end of the decade it rose to over 30,000. In 1891 it reached three times that figure. The situation, in a word, was as in 1881–2—if not worse, as there could now be no serious doubt whatever about the essential nature and settled character of Russian policy.

As in the early 1880s, the great majority of migrants made for North America, with little assistance, or with none. Again, as in the early 1880s, the reaction of the established institutions of Jewish philanthropy, headed by the Alliance Israélite Universelle, was close to panic. They saw the problem as beyond treatment with such material means as they could envisage being within their power to mobilize and were terrified of making any move that might encourage Russian and Polish Jewry 'à se précipiter en masse vers la frontière sans souci de ce qu'ils deviendront, et avant qu'on puisse savoir ce qu'on fera d'eux'.[70] And, once more, as in 1881–2, there was much public protest by both Jews and non-Jews outside Russia, notably in England and in the United States, all with the effect of marginally increasing and facilitating Jewish solidarity.

---

[69] Dubnov, ii, p. 379.

[70] AIU circular, 1 June 1891, quoted in Zoza Szajkowski, 'How the Mass Migration to America Began', *Jewish Social Studies*, iv. 4, October 1942, p. 309 fn.

The grandest single gesture was Alphonse de Rothschild's withdrawal of his participation in a major loan which the Russian government wished to float in Western Europe. The most ambitious was that of Baron Maurice de Hirsch, the railroad entrepreneur, who, taking the full measure of the intolerable condition of Russo-Polish Jewry, dropped his old ideas for retraining the Jews in modern arts and crafts inside the Empire, and embarked on a vast plan to transfer and resettle three and a half million souls overseas within a period of twenty-five years. Hirsch set up a 'Jewish Colonization Association', endowed it with £8 million, and set about the purchase of great tracts of land in Argentina. Three-quarters of a million hectares of land were eventually purchased there for Jewish settlement. In the event, no more than 3,500 Jewish families were ever settled on farms. The total Jewish population in the Hirsch colonies in Argentina and in their vicinity was only of about one thousand families in 1894 and never exceeded 40,000 persons.[71] Nevertheless, the planned and solidly backed exodus to Argentina stood in strong contrast to the poor efforts of Ḥibbat Ẓion.

The pressure to migrate to Ereẓ-Israel had revived too, but the earlier patterns were repeated: relative to the movement of population to the Americas the flow to Ereẓ-Israel was small; it was largely spontaneous; it encountered much the same political and economic obstacles as before; and those who joined it received little assistance, or none. The major western philanthropists would not support *new* immigrants to the country; Ḥibbat Ẓion could offer minor help, or none. In some respects, conditions within the Land had hardened and were to continue to worsen. The Ottoman authorities renewed the prohibition on immigration and settlement as soon as they realized what was afoot. Existing regulations were tightened and even exceeded, and for a while the entry of Russian Jews into all parts of the Ottoman Empire was banned. And while the restrictions on entry were never made entirely effective, in part because of the venality of many of the officials involved and in part because the European Powers (including Russia) continued to object, on principle, to any infringement of rights under the capitulation agreements, the effect of the prohibition on the sale of land to Jewish immigrants was severe. Where land could be purchased,

---

[71] Kurt Grunwald, *Türkenhirsch*, Jerusalem, 1966, p. 73; *Jewish Chronicle*, 31 January 1896.

either because it was already in the hands of foreigners, or because a way had been found to circumvent the regulations, prices rocketed[72]—with the primary effect of putting land beyond the reach of immigrants of small means. The secondary effect of the price rise was further to appal and frighten the Turks and Arabs when ready purchasers did materialize even at inflated prices. The Turks then ordained, and sought to enforce, ever more drastic measures. For some time they barred the sale of land to all Jews, regardless of nationality, even Ottoman. A cyclical pattern had been instituted whereby each wave of immigrants found the conditions and demands of settlement (both real and formal) harder than those which had been experienced by the wave which had preceded it.

Back in Russia, potential emigrants were encouraged by the fact that the peak of the renewed pressure to enter and settle in Erez-Israel coincided with the grant of legal status to the Odessa committee. But the leading members of the committee itself knew better and in any case tended to stick to the precise terms of their new charter (which allowed them to support existing settlements in Syria and Palestine, as opposed to promoting new ones) lest they lost it altogether. The appearance of great numbers of indigent people in Odessa, on the committee's doorstep, with the prospect of their being joined by a whole army of migrants if the first arrivals were not warned away, depressed and frightened them. Few of the travellers, it was thought in Odessa, could be settled properly in Erez-Israel. It was entirely pointless to ship them there if they had no resources of their own. What small funds Ḥibbat Zion had would be frittered away on the costs of subsistence and transport to no lasting purpose for most would then end up in Argentina—at best. The damage to the movement's prestige would be directly proportionate to its visible inability to serve those for whom it was created.[73]

Still, as the new wave of migration receded, the *yishuv* was found to have been moderately reinforced: two major, and several minor settlements had been established. In 1890 30,000 dunams (7,500 acres) of land were bought half-way between Haifa and Jaffa, the

---

[72] For example, the purchase-price of a tract of land at 'Atlit, near Haifa, rose eight times over between 1886 and 1892. Mandel, op. cit., p. 49.

[73] Lilienblum to Ussiskin, June 1882. *Mi-yamim rishonim*, ii, pp. 136-7. Also Greenberg to Mohilever, 16 October 1891 (O.S.), CZA, A9/63/1.

biggest single acquisition yet. A further 10,000 dunams were bought the same year just south of Rishon le-Zion. Hadera was built on the first tract, Rehovot on the second. Smaller points of settlement followed: Mishmar ha-Yarden (1890), 'Ein Zeitim (1891), Benei Yehuda (1891), Meir Shefeya (1891), Moza (1894), Hartuv (1895), Be'er Tuvia (1896), Metula (1896), Mahanayim (1899), and the Sejera training farm (1899). Most of these were offshoots of existing settlements, two were backed by Hibbat Zion, two by Baron Edmond de Rothschild, one was established independently by Jews from Bulgaria.

These were very modest gains. The absolute figures were as slight as ever; the progress made in the 1890s was scarcely greater than that made in the previous decade.[74] And this modesty told heavily against the movement, its methods, its programme, such as it was, its leaders, and—in time, and for some—against its broad conception of what could and ought to be done for eastern Jewry.

There was one novelty. The purchase of the two large tracts of land on which Hadera and Rehovot were built had been initiated locally, not by the Odessa committee or by its official representatives, but by a member of Gedera. The enterprise was fruit of the ingenuity and local knowledge of Yehoshua Hankin (1864–1945), the first of a long line of men in whom the mystique of the Land took the form of an insatiable drive to reacquire it literally and legally, piece by piece, for the Jewish people. Hankin's appearance on the scene may be seen as the first, dim augury of a new, more equal relationship between the settlers in Erez-Israel and their supporters in the Diaspora and of a time when the new men, having begun to strike out on their own, would ultimately alter the balance of forces in Jewry out of all recognition.

[74]

| Year | Jewish rural population | Total area in Jewish possession in metric dunams, urban and rural | Jewish rural land utilized | Agricultural settlements | Farms |
|------|------|------|------|------|------|
| 1882 | 480 | 22,530 | n.a. | 6 | n.a. |
| 1890 | 2,960 | 104,630 | 41,522 | 14 | n.a. |
| 1900 | 5,210 | 218,170 | 114,277 | 22 | 705 |

*Source*: D. Gurevich and A. Gerz, *Ha-hityashvut ha-hakla'it ha-'ivrit be-Erez-Israel*, Jerusalem, 1938, p. *31.

viii

The root weakness of Ḥibbat Zion was its incapacity to transform its own standing within Jewry by a striking success—by being plainly seen to have precipitated a change in the condition and prospects of the Jews. Its achievements were worthy and promising, but they were all small. Its over-all view of the Jewish condition had proved correct, its recipe for Jewish survival was not implausible. What it had not shown, at any rate not convincingly, was how it hoped to put its prescription into effect. It had introduced some new and some quite bold ideas and had gained considerable support for them. It had set up a network of local societies capable of common and continuous action and of a fair measure of consensus. Yet it remained a minority group within Jewry at a time when the greater part of Jewry was without any over-arching national institutions and a generally accepted leadership. Unlike a fledgling party seeking power within an orderly parliamentary system, and according to recognized rules, it had to make headway in an ill-defined, virtually unstructured environment. But it failed to devise an appropriate and effective tactic to expand its social base among the Jews of Eastern Europe rapidly and continuously. And in the West its conquest of the minds of Jews was feebler still, although, as we shall see, it did win the qualified, but vital backing of Baron Edmond de Rothschild, head of one of the wealthiest, and easily the most influential, of Jewish families in Western Europe.[75] The major part of the new *yishuv* was thereby saved from almost instant ruin, but it was not the reputation and influence of organized Ḥibbat Zion that was enhanced. The aid from Paris was not channelled through Odessa. Odessa was left to do what it could to bolster those settlements for which the Baron and his servants had been unwilling to accept responsibility. Weakest of all were Ḥibbat Zion's political and diplomatic operations. There had been plans for a major assault on the Porte and some beginnings in that direction; but they were soon dropped because, in the last resort, it had been realized that there was nothing whatever to be done in Constan-

[75] See below, pp. 212 ff. Lilienblum, at his most acid, put the position as follows: 'Hovevei Zion can be divided into three categories: (*a*) Parisian Hovevei Zion; (*b*) Hovevei Zion who had gone to Ereẓ-Israel and have remained there; and (*c*) Hovevei Zion who are abroad. The first, the Parisians, are *very very* few in number and have done more than anyone else; the others, in Ereẓ-Israel, are more numerous and have done less; the third group, abroad, are still more numerous and have done still less.' *Vos Haist Hovevei Zion*, 1890. Druyanov, *Ketavim*, iii, no. 1016, col. 74.

tinople. In Ereẓ-Israel their dealings with the Turkish officials turned on bribery. This the Ḥovevei Ẓion loathed, and could ill afford, and knew that it could alter nothing for long. The sense of impotence grew and became oppressive. The loyalty and morale of the movement's most energetic and devoted members began to crack.

The affairs of the *yishuv* are in a very bad state and depress me terribly. The Turkish government's interdiction, our lack of funds, the great lassitude among our brethren . . . etc., etc., all add up to evidence that the *yishuv* is weakening. Don't think, my friend, that I am in despair; not at all. I still maintain what I said to you at Druskieniki and have written to you two or three times: so long as the matter of the resettlement of Ereẓ-Israel is merely one of *charity*, so long as the business of the leaders of Ḥibbat Ẓion is merely to grant *assistance* to the indigent in the settlements . . . ages will pass and the settlers will [still be saying] give, give—in appeals, in letters, in telegrams; and the leaders of Ḥibbat Ẓion will go on [as they have hitherto] until they have doled out the last penny and until our people end by refusing to contribute any more to the whole doubtful enterprise. Then, the provisional leadership will duly fall and, upon its ruins, a new one will be erected, one which will *really* try to go beyond the support of the poor and the miserable, and instead do everything that the settlement of the country requires: get the Turkish interdiction cancelled, purchase land to resell [to settlers], give proper advice and instruction to potential settlers who have means of their own, give out clear information on the state of commerce and industry in Ereẓ-Israel, popularize the enterprise among Jews with the aid of public speakers and in print, and so on and so forth.

Thus Menaḥem Ussishkin of Moscow to Lilienblum in November 1887.[76]

Lilienblum, in his reply, was characteristically pungent, level-headed, and in command of the depressing facts. But the high hopes of a few years back had gone. The thing now was to hold on, to keep going as best one could, and hope for an eventual change.

I have received your letter. Forgive me if I tell you that I do not know what you want. You are angry about the charity in connection with the *yishuv* and say that the main thing is to settle people and for that you need people and not a permit.

The last thing I want to do is deny your hopes, but what is it you really want? Do you want to leave the people in Gedera as they are? But never

---

[76] Druyanov, ii, no. 719, cols. 409-10. Emphases in original.

mind that. The main thing [you say] is to settle people, to get the Turkish interdiction cancelled, etc. How easy it is to write such things, how difficult to put them into effect. Take the fact that it is now a year and a half since Dr. Pinsker set up a co-operative venture with nine or ten thousand roubles to buy land at Yesud ha-Ma'ala of which, after purchase, fourteen plots would be left for resale. It then turned out that . . . fifty Napoleons or one thousand francs had still to be paid up. Dr. Pinsker promptly . . . sent *eight thousand francs* . . . to pay the seller and to pay baksheesh, and to pay baksheesh upon the baksheesh, and so on *ad infinitum* . . . The settlers were already subjects of Turkey, the land was to be registered in the name . . . of a subject of Turkey . . . there was thus no legal reason not to complete the matter. And yet a year and a half passed and still nothing has been done . . . Now try and deal in land in Erez-Israel if so simple a matter takes so long and we are still so far from knowing how it will end!

That is why I say, what Hibbat Zion does now is no more than the beginning of the real operation . . . that which will be performed when better days have come, days which it is beyond our power to hasten.[77]

---

[77] Druyanov, ii, no. 722, col. 414. Emphasis in original.

# 7

# *Aḥad Ha-ᶜAm and the Critique of Ḥibbat Ẓion*

FOR a social movement success tends to be its own justification; it is failure that evokes questions. But genuinely searching questions are as good a sign as any of life and fundamental good health—provided, that is, that they emerge from within and are put by men whose loyalty is beyond doubt, even when their arguments are difficult to stomach. For the Jews—and for the Jews of Eastern Europe in particular—loyalty has always counted for something more than position. Not heterodoxy, but betrayal has been the inexpiable offence. Accordingly, a certain underlying and forgiving tolerance of criticism has often coexisted with an extreme sensitivity to it, all depending, in the first instance, on where the critic is ultimately placed—within or without—and, to a lesser, yet still significant degree, on the audience to which he addresses himself —the inner, Jewish one, or the outer audience of Gentiles.

These considerations go part of the way towards resolving the paradox that the sharpest critic of Ḥibbat Ẓion, a man given, almost perversely, to uttering the most painful truths about it, came rapidly—and largely on the strength of his criticism—to be held in esteem by an ever widening circle of devotees, the very people who seemed to him to be rejecting his advice and whose every action tended to increase his gloom about the direction the movement had taken. Equally, it is only against this background that a second paradox can be understood, that the arch-critic of Ḥibbat Ẓion—and later of the Zionist movement proper—was at the same time its most perceptive and subtle ideologue, and the only member of his group whose views and writings can be, and are, read three generations after for their own sake, with interest, without embarrassment, certainly with respect.

ii

Asher Zevi Ginsberg (1856–1927) was born in a small, predominantly Jewish townlet near Kiev. When he was twelve his family moved to the isolation of an estate in the vicinity of Berdichev, which his father had leased from a member of the Russian nobility and which he farmed continuously for eighteen years until, in 1886, the operation of the May Laws prevented a further renewal of the lease. But if his father was somewhat exceptional for his times and class in that he was a man of some means and that the Ginsberg family lived in a style and on a scale analogous to that of the Russian gentry, in all other respects Yeshayahu Ginsberg was a thoroughly conventional figure: a Jew of unbending orthodoxy and of considerable learning in his own right, a faithful *hasid* of the Rebbe of Sadagora, a father whose pious wish was to see his gifted son acquire the authority and priceless aura of a great rabbinical scholar and who did all in his power to bring Asher up in the tradition as most strictly interpreted—to the exclusion of all that was mundane and secular—and who capped his labours by foisting upon his son an arranged marriage.

Before long Asher was recognized as an *ʿilui*, which is to say, a young man of very superior intellectual gifts and a master of Talmudic learning. But he refused to remain within the confines of the tradition and by a combination of subterfuge and uncommon diligence managed to teach himself, and ultimately acquire, a command of Russian and the major Western European languages, along with the literature of each, and a solid grounding in the major items of the contemporary philosophical and historical canon. He did this in clear opposition to his father's wishes: early on, in his boyhood, his parents had been horrified to discover that he was teaching himself the Russian alphabet by dint of deciphering the shop-signs on his way home from the *heder*. But there was no break; only a slowly accumulating, silent resistance to the tradition in which his father sought to contain him. He emerged from his provincial prison, as he saw it, briefly in 1884, then finally in 1886, a man of thirty, embittered by the sense of lost years and by the end of any prospect of acquiring the formal secular education he had wanted, lonely, introverted, wholly self-taught, fully conscious of his mental powers, yet still without more than an occasional fleeting thought of applying them to any social or philosophical or literary purpose, a man whose formative years had been stamped by a double ring of alienation—from the Russians by his compelling and unquestioned sense of Jewish identity and from the Jews by his modernist rejection of the religious tradition.

In his solitude in the country he acquired the habit of forming his views unaided and virtually uninfluenced by others and from a vantage-point which was determined first and foremost by his moral and aesthetic bent. He was, by inclination, a moralist and a perfectionist, a man who successfully and explicitly combined respect for sentiment with a contempt for sentimentality, and who insisted upon (and was thought by many to relish) the exposure of muddle-mindedness and self-deception both as a matter of principle and as a necessary preliminary to the charting of any kind of course on matters of public policy. 'I want to reveal a bit of the truth—the bit which is ugliest', he wrote in his first, devastating article on the affairs of the new *yishuv*. Compared with his contemporaries, he was a man of unusual reticence and sobriety. He was retiring and shy; he never imagined himself cut out to lead others in *practice*. On the other hand, he never hesitated to hand down guiding opinions on *principle*. It cannot be denied that he was something of a prig: there are, perhaps, few confirmed and self-conscious intellectuals who are not; and he was nothing if not deliberate and self-conscious in his intellectualism. As the editor of the first, fully (and, again, consciously) modern Hebrew journal which he ran with *La Revue des Deux Mondes* and *The Nineteenth Century* in mind as models, he was merciless and unyielding in his treatment of contributors who failed to cleave to the literary (and stylistic) standards he set them. He was respected, somewhat feared, and widely misunderstood. He was himself a very fine writer, but again, one who, by the dictates of his self-imposed limits, ploughed a narrow furrow. From a certain angle, he might be seen as hardly more than an occasional, if superior, essayist. He generally needed the stimulus of an event or of an idea put forward by someone else to start him writing. His own leading ideas are scattered in several dozen articles and essays, many of which are barely more than marginal modifications of, and elaborations on, each other. There is no comprehensive statement, no *magnum opus*, no systematic treatise. For one who became (and was soon recognized as) the pre-eminent man of Hebrew letters of his day, he wrote little: four small volumes of essays and a number of autobiographical sketches and other fragments, all now collected in one large, but by no means bulky volume. Yet it is possible to argue that his supreme contribution, his lasting legacy, was, after all, literary. He introduced—it might almost be said, invented—a Hebrew style that serves to this day as a model of clear, astringent writing, sparing of ellipsis, and almost devoid of the then customary Scriptural and Talmudic allusions. He had little interest in belles-lettres. He once rejected a poem by one of the most talented, certainly the most deliberately passionate of contemporary Hebrew poets, Sha'ul Tschernichowsky, because it included the lines 'I shall embrace you, love and kiss you / With passion and with fire'.[1] He detested the irrational and distrusted the metaphysical. Typically, among the writers he held in greatest respect were Locke and Hume and other English empiricists. His own sole passion, if it may so be called, was for public affairs and first and foremost, and almost exclusively, the affairs of Jewry. It was to the issues of the day that he applied his great learning, his formidable intellect, and his uncompromising moral and aesthetic standards. The content of his essays was often ferociously critical; the manner was cool, reserved, polite, and vaguely, yet unmistakably, self-deprecating. He signed his first published essay *Aḥad Ha-ʿAm*—literally, 'One of the People', but in the sense of 'a plain man'. He never varied the signature he put to his writing and it is by his pen-name that he was (and is still) best known. There was no posture in this modesty: but it was not without a measure of self-satisfaction.

His transition from semi-recluse to public figure began in April 1884, when

after a new battle with those around me, I left [the father's estate] with my family to live in Odessa. A new life began for me there. On the other hand, new sources for the completion of my education opened up: I no longer lacked books; and I was able to pursue my study of the French and English languages to such good effect that before long I had reached my chief goal: to be able to understand books written in them. On the other hand, I was drawn to public work and found it possible to do something to further that idea which had come to fill my heart in the past few years. For in Odessa in those days there was a considerable

[1] Eisig Silberschlag, *Saul Tschernichowsky*, London, 1968, p. 15.

centre of Ḥibbat Ẓion, in all its ramifications, and upon my arrival among the 'Ḥovevim' I was fortunate in making a mark and [thus] was able to take part in all their affairs . . . When the central committee headed by Dr. Pinsker, of blessed memory, was set up, I too was elected to join and we would meet regularly on Tuesdays at the Doctor's to deal with the affairs of the *yishuv*. These meetings impressed me profoundly, especially at the beginning, for never before had I had an opportunity to pass whole hours at a time each week in the company of such educated men. Of course, at first I was very diffident, drinking in each word that fell from the mouths of my friends, as befitted a country boy. But little by little my fears dropped away and I came to see that I too, in my poverty, had something fresh to say on occasion and that not all that was uttered by the city men was really acceptable; and from then on I was one of the [regular] speakers and not all that I said was rejected.[2]

After a few months in Odessa he was obliged to return to the country where, with a few interruptions, he remained until the lapse of his father's lease in 1886. Then, once more, to Odessa, but now well known and somewhat more assured and furnished with a truer and better-integrated picture of the world into which he had entered. It was not long before he was leading an entirely informal circle of Ḥovevei Ẓion who were dissatisfied with Dr. Pinsker's leadership and politely critical of the way in which matters were being handled. In 1888 he wrote two minor pieces in a quasi-representative capacity as spokesman for the Odessa *maskilim*. Alexander Tsederbaum, the editor of *Ha-Meliẓ*, was impressed and invited him to contribute something weightier. In November of that year he submitted the article which won him instant notoriety as Aḥad Ha-ʿAm.[3] It was a brilliant attempt to review the purposes and practice of Ḥibbat Ẓion. Its language was gentle, but the message was very clear, even in the title: *Lo ze ha-derekh*—'This is not the way'. And more or less simultaneously, there was founded in Odessa, around Aḥad Ha-ʿAm, and on the basis of his teachings, the semi-secret order of dedicated Ḥovevei Ẓion, Benei Moshe. In 1891 he travelled to Ereẓ-Israel for the first time. Aboard ship, on the journey back, he wrote the pained, devastating summary of what he had seen: *Emet me-Ereẓ-Israel*— 'The truth from Ereẓ-Israel'. The furore which each one of these

[2] 'Pirkei zikhronot', *Kol kitvei Aḥad Ha-ʿAm*, Jerusalem, 1947, p. 468.
[3] It was not published until April of the following year because of trouble with the Government censor.

articles raised made it necessary for him to prepare supplementary expositions of his views and findings. A second journey to Erez-Israel in 1893 produced a new piece. With the doctrine and rules of Benei Moshe, an obituary article written on Pinsker's death, and several cautious attempts to tackle the problem of religion in relation to the national revival, these writings of the late 1880s and the early 1890s form the statement of what he had found in Ḥibbat Zion, and of what he wanted altered.

### iii

Aḥad Ha-ʿAm's central thesis was that the men of Ḥibbat Zion had not fully grasped the nature of the undertaking which they had assumed; that they had set about it in the wrong spirit and with the wrong tactical aims in view; that, in consequence, the movement had lost momentum ('If, as one of the Sages said, it pains the heart to see a belief dying of old age . . . how much greater is the pain when an idea full of the vigour of youth stumbles and falls at the very beginning');[4] and, as a corollary in fact and in logic, the little that had been done in Erez-Israel had been done badly and on the basis of a sad, perhaps tragic, misconception of what could and what could not be accomplished there.

Why had the idea of national revival, so powerful in itself and so remarkable in its effects upon other nations, failed to take hold among the Jews? Surely, not because, as some say, we had ceased to be a true nation, and are connected by ties of religion alone. For we *know* that it is not the case; no one can tell us, on the basis of externals, what is within us. Nor can the argument that the enterprise is failing because of the sins of omission and commission of individuals—the Baron, his servants, the rabbis in Erez-Israel, or others—carry weight. No private individuals, whoever they may be, whatever their distinction, have the power to obstruct an entire nation. Indeed, what national movement could this be if a few persons were able effectively to stand in its way? The real answer lies in the fact that the fathers of the idea of the national revival, in their haste to accomplish great things, 'had abandoned the long road of natural evolution and had, by artificial means, brought a young and tender idea down into the world of the practical before it had matured, before its powers were properly developed'.[5]

[4] 'Lo ze ha-derekh', *Kol kitvei*, p. 11.     [5] Ibid., pp. 11–12.

In its original form, the Jewish national concept had centred exclusively on the well-being of the collectivity, of the entire people in its country, without regard for the private happiness and well-being of the individual. With the decline of the Jewish polity and the consequent waning of the collectivity, and with the rising concern for individual or private well-being, the Sages had begun to argue that this world was no more than a 'corridor' leading to the next and that happiness in the next world depended upon one's conduct in this. Thus where the Law of Moses had been explicitly and well-nigh exclusively concerned with society as a whole, the ends of religion were now held to be private in character, rather than collective, and, what is more, it was now on grounds of private interest that collective or national purposes were justified. The pain inflicted on the Jews in their Dispersion naturally intensified each man's concern for his immediate and private welfare. Little thought remained for those of the nation. Today, in an age in which the religious premisses of the Sages have themselves lost their force, the foundations of national sentiment have weakened further. Alas, it was to private interests, to the individual well-being of the Jews, to their need for refuge, to their empty stomachs, that the leaders of Ḥibbat Zion had appealed. And in so doing, they had painted conditions in Erez-Israel in false colours and promised what they could not hope to deliver. This was neither helpful, nor true, nor relevant to the real issue at stake. 'No properly structured society or great collective enterprise can be set up on the basis of the private interest alone.'[6] The first task of Ḥibbat Zion was to labour to revive the Jews' *national* consciousness and rid them of the consequences of the constraints and acquired habits of the Dispersion, however difficult the task might be and however long the process might take. The rest would follow in due course. What could not be done was to reverse the order, the natural order of things. Thus, in the abstract, early in 1889.

What Aḥad Ha-ʿAm actually saw in Erez-Israel itself some two years later deepened his misgivings about the strategy of the movement[7] and confirmed his suspicion that even at the level of practical affairs—the level which, to his mind, was of lesser import

---

[6] Ibid., p. 15.

[7] In 1884, in the discussions preliminary to the Kattowitz conference, Aḥad Ha-ʿAm had been among those who had argued against Pinsker's wish to give the enterprise a general, humanitarian aspect, obscuring the fundamental, national purpose.

than that of belief—the enterprise was vastly more complicated and the obstacles to fulfilment were both greater and more numerous than the people in Odessa, in their innocence, had realized. 'I will tell you just this,' he wrote home a fortnight after his arrival, 'that if I could, I would add a clause to the regulations of the Society, namely that no one might be elected to the committee in Odessa who had not been to the Holy Land and seen matters for himself.'[8]

However, 'the truth from Erez-Israel' was a complex truth. 'Here I am now in Jerusalem', he wrote home to his parents and his immediate family at the end of April 1891.

I am now very far away from all the business and pettiness of ordinary life; I live in a completely different world—in the world of the past. I cannot convey the smallest part of what I have felt and passed through in the few days since arriving here—where every step, every stone, is a piece of blood-soaked history, where one sees nothing but historical sites on every side, and what sites! Mount Zion, the Temple Mount, the Mount of Olives, and one is continually reminded of thousands of years of misery, battles, and world-stirring events. And it is only when you are here that you sense how laughable and odd is the modern Palestinian *materialism* [of Ḥibbat Zion] with its [implied] belief that the Jews can ever give up Jerusalem! Jerusalem is and remains the heart of Erez-Israel, especially for Jews. And I should like to see the true Palestinian [i.e. Ḥovev Zion] who will remain entirely unmoved on seeing Jerusalem for the first time. Yes, in Jerusalem one sees, with despair, how low we have fallen, how all the other nations progress here, have fine buildings, good institutions, fight with all their might for every inch of the holy soil, while we Jews busy ourselves with empty wrangles, forfeiting everything, and what we do have here is for the most part so poor, so squalid—in both the material and the spiritual sense—that it breaks the heart.[9]

After close to three months in the country 'of my dreams, in that wonderful land that draws unto herself tens of thousands of hearts of all nations and from all states', having asked himself, continually, what hope there was for the Jews there, he returned to Russia bitter and depressed. It was evident to him that Erez-Israel could not provide a full-scale solution to the material prob-

---

[8] Letter to Rawnitzki, 15 March 1891. *Igrot Aḥad Ha-ʿAm*, second edition, Tel Aviv, 1956-60, i, p. 4.

[9] 27 April 1891. *Igrot*, vi, pp. 196-7. Emphasis in original, which is in Yiddish. While Aḥad Ha-ʿAm wrote for publication exclusively in Hebrew, much of his private correspondence was in Yiddish, Russian, and, later, in the Western European languages.

lems of the Jews—their poverty, their insecurity. In that respect, America offered vastly more. But it was equally evident—and now better understood, he thought—that America could not provide a solution to the Jews' social and moral needs. To that end, Ereẓ-Israel was vital. The question that had to be posed and the question in the light of which Ḥibbat Ẓion and all its works had to be judged, was therefore whether the Land was in process of being brought to fulfil its true and essential role. And this was not at all an affair of individuals and their private needs, as was the question of the prospects for the Jews in America and elsewhere overseas. It was the concern of the entire people, collectively, and what was done by individual Jews in Ereẓ-Israel was, accordingly, a matter of national, not private interest and had so to be judged.

In principle, the condition on which Ereẓ-Israel could fulfil its function was the establishment within it of 'a permanent, mass settlement of Jews, based upon cultivation of the soil, such that both the Jewish people and its enemies would know that there was one place under the sun where, even if it were too small to contain all the nation, a Jew too could lift up his head as a man among others . . . and order his life in his own way in his own national spirit'.[10] The obstacles to this were of two kinds: external and internal.

The external obstacles to Jewish national purposes were formidable. First was the fact, as Aḥad Ha-ʿAm believed it, that there was very little cultivable land that was not already in use. What was cultivated could not be purchased; what could be purchased was either totally infertile, he thought, or else had first to be cleared at immense cost in labour and money and, even then, was of limited use—suitable, perhaps, for the planting of trees and vines, but not field-crops.

The second and greater obstacle to Jewish settlement was the Arab population itself. The Jews abroad thought little of the Arabs and supposed them incapable of understanding what went on around them. They were in error, wrote Aḥad Ha-ʿAm, in a passage of remarkable perspicacity. The Arabs, like 'all the sons of Shem', are sharp and cunning. They,

particularly the town-dwellers among them, do see and understand what we are about, but they keep their own counsel and pretend to

---

[10] 'Emet me-Ereẓ-Israel', *Kol kitvei*, p. 23.

ignorance because they see no future danger to themselves in anything we do; on the contrary, they exploit us, as best they can, try to extract the greatest possible profit from the new guests, and laugh at us behind our backs. The peasants are glad enough to have Jewish settlements set up among them because they are well paid for their labour and, as experience shows, prosper steadily from year to year. The great land-owners are equally glad to have us because we pay them prices they had never dreamt of for stony and sandy soil. But, if ever there comes a time when we shall have developed our life in Ereẓ-Israel to the point where we shall be encroaching upon them in a greater or lesser degree, [then we should not expect them] to yield their place easily.[11]

Thirdly, there were the Turks. Again, the Jews were in error if they thought that the Porte was so weak and ill ordered that it was unaware and uninterested in what was going on in Ereẓ-Israel and that bribery would smooth all paths, and that the European govern-ments would protect them. 'No doubt *baksheesh* was a great power in Turkey and the greatest men in the country were unable to resist it.' But at least in the narrow context of their religion and concern for the authority of their government they were jealous patriots and the strength of their feelings ought not to be under-estimated. On that count, nothing would move them. They were therefore absolutely opposed to the settlement of the Jews, and the more Jews settled, the greater would be their opposition.

It was clear that if anything was to be accomplished in these circumstances, and if the purely economic problems of the settlers were to be overcome in the bargain, a cautious, systematic, well-planned approach was vital, one aiming at quality, rather than quantity, appealing to the best and highest motives, not the basest, an approach founded on the lessons of experience, on sound eco-nomics, not on preposterous schemes for rapid enrichment and an easy life, as if Ereẓ-Israel were some sort of a California. But in fact, all had been done in haste and unsystematically. The wrong people had been drawn in for the wrong reasons. They were people who were appallingly unsuited to agricultural settlement. They were ill prepared, ill trained, or not trained at all. They were full of mistaken and irrelevant ideas, ill informed, ill directed, and ill behaved. He had met none who lived entirely on their own earnings and who were any good at farming, or liked it. It was therefore idle to expect that much good would come of them. And if there was

[11] 'Emet me-Ereẓ-Israel', *Kol kitvei*, p. 24.

no change, the sole result would be to set up a Jewish problem where there had been none before.

For all these reasons the resettlement of the Jews in Erez-Israel was both harder than their settlement elsewhere and vastly more important. And both the inner difficulty and the gravity of the undertaking stemmed from the desolate condition of the Jews themselves.

> I stood and looked at [the worshippers] and at the [Wailing] Wall and a single thought filled my heart: these stones are witnesses to the ruin of our country and these people—to the ruin of our nation. Which of the two was the greater ruin? Which was the sadder? If a country is destroyed and the nation is still full of life and power . . . its people will rebuild it. But if a nation is destroyed, who will come to its aid?[12]

It followed that the entire enterprise had to be differently ordered. It was the responsibility of the leaders of the movement to attract 'the worthy' and keep away 'the unworthy', distinguishing those who were possessed of 'physical and moral powers' and of a will to labour hard and to be content with little from those who were not. The external obstacles to mass settlement were beyond the power of the Jews to overcome, at any rate in the foreseeable future. But, in any case, the Jews themselves, socially and morally, were in no fit condition as yet for the task in hand. The 'long hard road of natural evolution' had first to be travelled. And in the meantime, the small, painfully inadequate, morally and aesthetically unsatisfactory new *yishuv* had to be reconceived and re-modelled with its symbolic and representative and catalytic role in mind before all else. The enterprise in Zion must be dedicated not to the 'concentration of the people, but to that which must precede it, the concentration of the spirit'. If the country was too small and poor to serve the former purpose, it was not too small to serve the latter. Conceivably, it was too *great*. 'A single properly ordered settlement, one that was capable of arousing the Jews' love for the Land, is better than ten rickety settlements which only [our] love for the Land can excuse.'[13]

In brief, the *yishuv* must become, in the phrase that was to be a source of interminable debate within the movement, a 'spiritual centre', a model workshop in which the regeneration of the Jewish

---

[12] Ibid., p. 30.
[13] Introduction to the first edition (1895) of *ᶜAl parashat derakhim*, ibid., p. 3.

people was to be hammered out, and out of which, by dint of example and teaching, a new and healthy influence would radiate. This was what was needed and this was what could be done. All else had failed and nothing else could be reasonably contemplated. And this was what was closest to the essential nature of Judaism. True, it was modest. To some it would be disheartening. It left the great question of the *material* condition of the Jews—their safety and welfare—in abeyance. But other means would have to be found to solve that problem. For, once more, there was nothing else to offer them and no good would come of the attempt to pretend otherwise. All else entailed deception and, worse, self-deception.

## iv

The bent of Aḥad Ha-ʿAm's mind and the quality of his writing were such that it was the *critical* component of what he had to say that struck with greatest force. On the one hand, he looked at the movement to which he was devoted with the hard, distrustful eyes of a countryman who was easily irritated and rarely convinced by the over-emphatic, hasty, impractical, and verbose city-dwellers who led—or claimed to lead—it. On the other hand, he judged the movement and its child—the new *yishuv*—by the only standards he thought appropriate to so great a matter: the highest standards and the most extreme. The *yishuv* must be frugal and orderly, dignified and self-sufficient, hard-working and socially cohesive, and comprise dedicated, loyal, and, above all, virtuous men and women, virtually to the exclusion of lesser beings. Otherwise, it was not worth having. If it could *not* be made all that he wanted it to be, then, to his mind, it had to be concluded that the Jewish people were beyond cure and it was then better that the pathetic effort to revive the nation were dropped.

It is, of course, possible to see this view of the matter as an independently and moralistically minded intellectual's heroic effort to compensate for what he took to be the failure of Ḥibbat Zion by formulating revised aims for the movement: a radical scaling-down of its activities in the practical arena, where it was weakest and where the external obstacles to success were greatest, and a shift of attention to a plane where much more could be hoped for because the obstacles to progress, such as they were, were least substantial and entirely within Jewry itself. In this, indeed, he was not alone. Y. L. Gordon, as we have seen, had from the first wanted to put the cultural (and religious) reform of Jewry before—and as the condition of—its material reconstruction. Even the term 'spiritual centre' had been coined and used by others before him.[14] The threads of pessimism and scepticism here are not easily disentangled from the threads of realism and pragmatism. Perhaps the attempt to disentangle them only does violence to the specificity and originality of Aḥad Ha-ʿAm's thought. There is also in all he has to say an unmistakably political strain impelling him, from the first, to cast about, simply, for what can be done, however little, in the circumstances. Thus, in one way or another, the immediate and short-term effect of all that Aḥad Ha-ʿAm wrote and, so far as can be made out, of much that he said, was to help brilliantly to confirm the sense of inadequacy, if not failure, that had come to depress the spirits in Ḥibbat Zion by the beginning of the 1890s.

The long-term effect was more serious. He encouraged—in part, unwittingly—a tendency to remove the *nationally* directed evacuation of Eastern Europe that both Lilienblum and Pinsker had wanted out of the discussion of the practicable, even the attainable. He thus contributed to a further lowering of the sense of urgency, the sense of imminent—indeed, actual—catastrophe, that had informed the activists in the early years of Ḥibbat Zion. And this by pointing out with great force and accuracy the immensity of the obstacles to progress and with the same force, but somewhat less accuracy, the extent to which the Jews in general and Ḥibbat Zion in particular were, as yet, poorly placed to realize revolutionary changes in Jewry's status, structure, and *mores*. In a word, he formulated a justification for turning to other things.

Aḥad Ha-ʿAm underpinned his analysis of the state of affairs in the movement and in Erez-Israel with an extremely effective theoretical distinction which he drew again and again and which formed the axis around which most of what he had to say then and in later years revolved. This was the distinction between the afflictions of the Jews (*ẓarat ha-yehudim*) and the afflictions of Judaism (*ẓarat ha-yahadut*), between private and collective pains, sorrows, and ills, between what Pinsker and the great majority of the other

---

[14]  Z. H. Shapira, a contributor to *Ha-Meliẓ* (5 September 1882) wrote: 'We have neither the strength nor the will to gather all of Israel into the land of our fathers. Apart from it being impossible to accomplish it is not desirable for many weighty reasons. What we must do instead is to create for ourselves a spiritual and material centre (*merkaz ruḥani ve-gashmi*) and to build ourselves a home in a secure place . . .'

Hovevei Zion were concerned with and what concerned him. Hibbat Zion, in his view, had failed to do anything of real consequence and on an adequate scale about the former and had virtually failed even to tackle the latter. Erez-Israel was irrelevant to the one, but it was central to the other. He did not reject the view that the need to re-establish a Jewish polity was dictated by the character of the interminable conflict between Jews and non-Jews; but he did think it inadequate, incomplete, and somewhat mean. The national revival had to be founded, explicitly, on greater purposes; it had a positive content as well and its positive content had to be made plain.

The difficulty about Ahad Ha-ʿAm is that, however arduous might be the attainment of a secular Zion, it was a definable aim, in direct response to, and consistent with, the immediate needs of the greater part of the Jewish people. In contrast, the road to the attainment of a spiritual Zion seemed to many a still longer one to travel, certainly one more difficult to map. Moreover, the final aim was not easily definable, even in theory. Nor was it easily understood—except that it implied, in some general way, a special, quasi-prophetic role for Jewry whose heavy demands upon the private individual would be accepted with devotion. Nor, finally, was it directly relevant to what the real Jews, on the ground and in the Pale, needed and wanted. Hence the ambivalence in Ahad Ha-ʿAm's teaching; and hence too, as we shall see, the ambivalence of his position, influence, and subsequent reputation in the movement, as much in its Hibbat Zion stage as later under Herzl and his successors.

# 8

## *The* Malaise *in the* West

i

I CAN 'try to turn away for a moment from the stupidity and degradation and the frightful poverty that are all around me here [in Russia]', wrote Aḥad Ha-ʿAm in 1890,

and seek to comfort myself [with what is] *there*, over the border, where we find brethren who are professors, members of academies, army officers, and public officials. Except that there too, behind all the honour and the grandeur, I see a double spiritual slavery—moral and intellectual. I see this and I ask myself: do I envy them their [civil] rights, these brothers of ours? My answer, in all truth, is, no, no! . . . If I have no rights, at least I have not sold my soul for them.[1]

'There' was the West: most notably Germany, and the German- and Magyar-speaking parts of Austria-Hungary, France, Britain, the United States. The East–West dichotomy rested on the contrast, real if often overstated, between the relative freedom and security enjoyed by western Jewry and the miserable condition of the great majority of Jews in the Russian Empire, in the Islamic lands, in the Balkans, in Austrian Galicia. It was part of the common currency of Jewish thought in the latter half of the nineteenth century. It was also, as we have seen, a continually re-emerging element of all plans for a remedy to the latter's misery, with the fortunate western communities being expected to come to the rescue of the unfortunate eastern ones as their sole and indispensable allies.

Certainly, in the final quarter of the century it was to Western Europe generally, then at the pinnacle of its prestige and power, that virtually all peoples looked either in admiration, or in fear, or in both, as the veritable centre of the world, the source of all the newest social ideas and economic and military technologies,

[1] "Avdut be-tokh ḥerut', *Kol kitvei*, p. 68.

a group of kindred nations who had at least this in common, that they were all flushed with confidence and devoid of visible rivals for political and military and cultural supremacy. For the depressed, unhappy, but alert, and, on the whole, well-informed Jews of the East, the glitter of the 'West' was, if anything, brighter, more stimulating still. As they looked at 'the stupidity and degradation and the frightful poverty' immediately around them, it suggested a standing lesson in what could be achieved in terms of social and civil liberation and intellectual and economic advance by men of all sorts and all conditions when society was differently ordered. For them, moreover, it was Western Europe that was the real, the authentic Europe. It was the surface order, the evident civilization, the calm, and the learning of Western Europe that a Russian Jew had in mind when he paid another the compliment of describing him as 'a European'.[2] Eastern Europe, in contrast, seemed brutal, imitative, inferior. Of course, the contrast between Western Europe and what lay to the east of it was a stark one for all the peoples of Eastern and Southern Europe and of the Near East, as much for 'historic' nations such as the Poles and the Russians and the Turks as for 'submerged' nations such as the Slovaks, the Armenians, and the Arabs. But again, for the Jews its particular force lay in the connected circumstances that their own brethren in the West so plainly shared in the general rise and progress of the western nations and that it was to the 'West' that vast numbers of the strongest and most determined among the eastern Jews themselves were then in process of escaping. It was in the West that the civil emancipation of the Jews had first occurred and then been carried so far as to seem, at the time, irreversible. What only the most perceptive and knowledgeable easterners realized was that along with its blessings the western emancipation had borne certain bitter and unexpected fruit.

For the great mass of Jewry under Russian rule the essential nature of their situation was crystal-clear, defined by law, and reinforced by acts of policy of a highly centralized governmental machine in which the Autocrat's Jewish subjects themselves played no part and over which they had no influence to speak of. More-

---

[2] 'On the whole Aḥad H[a-ʿAm] makes a very pleasant impression as a European', wrote Chaim Weizmann after meeting him for the first time (in Berlin in 1896). *The Letters and Papers of Chaim Weizmann*, Series A, i, London, 1968, no. 22, p. 62. The faintly patronizing undertone was probably unintentional.

over, since the accession of Alexander III, as we have seen, there
were no longer any grounds for hope of a *future* relaxation of state
policy on the Jews. The eastern Jews were therefore overwhelmingly
a dissident class—in the sense that they wanted and badly needed
radical change; and if change within Russia was impossible, very
great numbers were prepared to effect it by extricating themselves
from that country and moving elsewhere.

   But nowhere in the West was there any such clear and comparatively consistent state policy on the Jews. There were varying
measures of resistance to the completion of the process of emancipation; but it was unsystematic, informal, and for all intents and
purposes *ex post facto* rather than anticipatory. There were now
no restrictions on residence; entry into the universities and the
professions was free; there were virtually no limits on participation
in political life; literary, industrial, and commercial activity was
unrestricted. Only the inner sancta of the German and Austrian
states, the higher bureaucracy and the officer corps, were inaccessible and the third great arm of the establishment, the tenured
university professoriate and the schoolmasters, virtually so.[3] In
France even these last barriers had been almost entirely surmounted.
Entry into the diplomatic service was barred, but Jews were to be
found in most other branches of the civil service, among the generals
and senior officers of the army (eight generals and eighteen colonels
and lieutenant-colonels in 1895),[4] and in the universities—as well
as in the professions, banking, and commerce (as in Germany).
Thus, having regard at least for the surface of things, western Jews
had limited cause for complaint and reason to look to the future
with confidence both in themselves and in the society around them.
It seemed that the one great question that remained to be resolved
was whether they were to be accepted and integrated into that
society socially and culturally, as well as politically and economically
—whether, according to the notions and terminology of the day,
they were to be members of the nation, as well as citizens of the
state—and if so, to what degree, and on what terms?

   But however one approached the question of the ultimate social
emancipation and equalization of Jewry and the admittance of the

---

[3] That said, there were minor regional variations: in Bavaria there were *some* Jewish
army officers, public prosecutors, and secondary-school masters; on the other hand, in
Prussia, after 1885, Jews were not admitted even into the corps of reserve officers. Cf.
Ernest Hamburger, 'One Hundred Years of Emancipation', Leo Baeck Institute, *Year
Book XIV*, London, 1969, pp. 17-19.          [4] *Jewish Chronicle*, 18 January 1895.

Jews into society as full and legitimate members, it clearly evoked
another: was the traditional conception of the Jewish collectivity
and peoplehood tenable in the new circumstance of civil liberty for
the individual Jew? Alternatively, were civil liberties for the
individual justified if he retained a separate identity and he and his
fellows constituted a discrete, extra-national, and, as it were,
parallel community which maintained a set of bonds and loyalties,
to say nothing of a religion, which were distinct from, and possibly
inimical to, those of the nation proper? For all concerned, for both
the friends and the opponents of the Jews and for the Jews themselves, the *Judenfrage* thus became predominantly—although never
exclusively—one of principle and theory, debated in the abstract
and in terms of generalities to which the real or supposed facts of
the case were relevant only in so far as they helped to affirm or
deny the validity of the Emancipation. Naturally enough, the closer
to completion the Emancipation appeared and the greater and more
rapid and notable the advance of the Jews in whatever field of
political, professional, intellectual, or economic endeavour they
were active, the sharper and, for the opponents of Emancipation,
the more urgent the issue became. Alternatively, the more urgent
it could be made to appear by those who found it a useful weapon
in political conflict and who contrived to make it a staple of political
debate. However, as the Jews of Western Europe became more
willing to give up all but a shadow, if that, of their separate collective and individual identity, the grounds for rejecting them began
to slip. The root questions, it was now urged, concerned not the
Jews' surface behaviour, but the inherent and specific nature of the
race itself, the inner and unchangeable bent of their culture, and
whether Jewry as a whole did not only constitute a tight and, for
certain purposes, clandestine society, but was an unstanchable
source of social evil which its members propagated in all their doings
and which it was beyond their power, let alone their will, to cure.

The Jew has remained Jew [wrote Proudhon on the left], a parasitical
race, the enemy of labour, given to all the practices of anarchic and lying
barter, of speculation and of usurious banking. All the currency is in the
hands of the Jews; more than the kings and the emperors, it is they who are
the sovereigns of the age, as indifferent to progress and to the liberty of
the peoples they oppress as to the reconstitution of their own nationality.[5]

---

[5] Pierre-Joseph Proudhon, *De la justice dans la revolution et dans l'église*, Paris, 1930–5,
iv, p. 458.

'Judaism—there is the enemy!', wrote Drumont on the right; a tiny, cohesive minority has enslaved an entire people—as the Normans of William the Conqueror enslaved the Saxons. 'Today, thanks to the Jew, money—to which Christendom itself never attached more than secondary importance— . . . has become all powerful.'[6] 'The Jew', wrote Wilhelm Marr, 'does not have an ideal religion, he only has a business agreement (*Geschäftsvertrag*) with Jehovah . . . We [the Germans] have fallen so deep into Judaization that if we are to work our way out again vigorously the existence of the whole of modern society must be called in question.'[7]

These were verbal and, ostensibly, moral onslaughts and therefore in some ways more—if in an obvious way less—disturbing than the traditional content of attack. Moreover, at this, the initial stage of the modern anti-Semitic movement in Western Europe there was still no question of large-scale physical molestation of the Jews. There were only ugly incidents in which from time to time individuals or small groups were mistreated. There were anti-Jewish riots in Hungary, for example, in 1882 and in 1883, provoked by the sensational Tisza Eszlar blood libel case in which a party of Jews were tried on the ancient, absurd, and revolting charge of having bled a Christian to death for ritual purposes. And the fact that the charges were brought, that the subject was debated in parliament, and that a trial was actually held could be seen as reflecting both the increasingly charged atmosphere of the times and the extent to which conventional beliefs and feelings about the Jews remained unaffected by the European Enlightenment.[8] But it was still possible to draw conflicting and even comforting conclusions from the sequel. True, the President of the Court, as the British Ambassador in Vienna reported,

conducted himself more like an unscrupulous advocate for the prosecution than a judge, rejecting all appeals to prevent, and almost encouraging, the intimidation of the witnesses for the defence by the fanatical audience

[6] Edouard Drumont, *La France juive*, Paris, 1886, pp. 2, 6.

[7] Wilhelm Marr, *Der Sieg des Judenthums über das Germanenthum*, fourth edition, Berne, 1879.

[8] There was a similar case in Xanten, in the German Rhineland, in 1892; and another at Polná, on the Bohemian-Moravian border in 1899. In the former case the accused was released, rearrested under public pressure, then released once more. In the latter case the accused, a Jewish cobbler named Leopold Hilsner, was sentenced to death, but his sentence was then commuted to one of life imprisonment. He was set free only in 1916, by the Emperor Charles. Tómaš Masaryk was one of the few Czech intellectuals to take a position in his favour.

in the Court and showing marked favour to witnesses against the accused, so palpably perjured that the Public Prosecutor refused to accept their evidence.[9]

On the other hand, in the face of the overwhelming evidence of perjury, the same presiding judge ended by joining his colleagues in acquitting the accused and at no stage at all did the central and provincial authorities hesitate to suppress violence in the streets when it erupted. For all the anti-Jewish bias of the state machinery in Germany and Austria-Hungary, there was no question of collusion with the mob, let alone its systematic provocation by people in very high places, as in Russia. In the authoritarian *Rechtsstaat* as much in the open society of France, the substance of the *Judenfrage* was still, ultimately, moral and ideological, not material.

It must be remembered that unlike eastern Jewry, which was numerous, concentrated for the most part in well-defined areas, largely rural, unskilled, only marginally affected by the new secular learning, sharply separated by religion, language, and literacy from the surrounding peoples of whom they knew comparatively little and whom, on the whole, they were under no temptation to emulate, the western communities were small in numbers (less than 100,000 Jews in all France in the latter half of the nineteenth century), scattered, overwhelmingly urban, voraciously and happily absorbing the secular learning, the language, the literature, and the social customs of the peoples among whom they lived, and, above all, tending strongly to hold the Germans and the French and the English in respect and their respective cultural and historical traditions in something like awe. Few Jews of Russia or Romania seriously thought of themselves as *Russians* or *Romanians*; none were encouraged to do so by their circumstances; relatively few wanted to. The western Jews—apart from a very small, ever decreasing minority of out-and-out traditionalists—did want to be proper Germans, Frenchmen, and Englishmen and there was much in their condition and in what many undoubted Germans and Frenchmen and Englishmen said to, and about, them to strengthen their belief that they were, or at any rate could be. Doubts were dispelled by arguments of great ingenuity. Some even claimed that religion was no obstacle. On the contrary,

⁹ Elliot to Granville, 14 July 1883. PRO, FO 7/1050. Quoted in Nathaniel Katzburg, *Antishemiut be-Hungaria, 1867–1914*, Tel Aviv, 1969, p. 239. For the general background, see ibid., pp. 106–55 and *passim*.

Judaism, said the eminent German Jewish philosopher Hermann
Cohen (in 1880), was already in process of forming a 'cultural,
historical union with Protestantism'. The Jews had shaken off the
Talmud and the non-Jews, for their part, the traditions of the
Church. Indeed, 'in a much deeper sense, in all spiritual questions
we [German Jews] think and feel in accord with the Protestant
spirit. Thus this common ground in religion is [itself] in truth the
most powerful and effective unifying force for a genuine national
fusion.'[10] Cohen's optimism about the prospects for integration
waned in time; and he changed his mind about the impropriety of
Jewish religious particularism and separatism. But neither then
nor a generation later did he doubt the cultural superiority of the
Germans over all other peoples. And it was difficult for English
and French Jews not to have analogous feelings about England
and France.

A Jew living in Paris (which contained five-eighths of all French
Jews towards the end of the century) lived in a city of which the
very least that could be said was that it was one of particular archi-
tectural grandeur and the locus of an extraordinary outpouring of
intellectual and artistic energy. Even if he was unsure of his status
in the *nation*, he had no doubt that he was an authentic, living part
of the metropolis; and to be part of the greatest of all French cities,
one which, arguably, was the most splendid of all in Europe, was
to partake of something of enormous and subtle attraction. Non-
Jewish society beckoned invitingly. To belong to it, however
tenuously, could easily, and not unreasonably, be accounted a
privilege. To be attacked by the anti-Semites as interlopers and
spoilers was to suffer not only a moral rebuff, but a threat to that
privilege. To agree—in accordance with the ancient Jewish view
of self—that the Jews were and should remain a discrete, im-
miscible social category was to adopt a self-defeating position and
to jeopardize that privilege. Even if one did not want to assimilate
totally, it was far easier, and seemingly more reasonable, to devise
a formula whereby the retention of some part of the tradition could
be squared in the eyes of all concerned, including one's own, with
the socio-cultural claims and pressures of the nation and the state
in which they lived. And habit, inertia, the creature comforts of
middle-class life in Western Europe, and the very real sense of

---

[10] Cited in Ismar Schorsch, *Jewish Reaction to German Anti-Semitism, 1870–1914*, New
York and Philadelphia, Pa., 1972, p. 57.

well-being induced by the Emancipation itself all served to make some form of compromise and reconciliation of the conflict between old and new appear sensible and necessary.

Western Jews thus came naturally and overwhelmingly to be timid, conformist, and conservative in their fundamental approach to society—in the sense that they wished the over-all direction of social life (as they understood it) to be maintained and fortified. They were among the beneficiaries of the Enlightenment and intensely loyal to it. They enjoyed the fruits and atmosphere of rationalism, secularism, and egalitarianism and feared nothing more than regress back to older principles for the management of society. Those among them who belonged to the political left differed from the majority only in that they judged the principles of the Enlightenment insufficiently, or wrongly applied and wished to take those principles further to what they believed to be their proper and logical conclusion.

For the plain, middle-class Jew, the idea of posing the question at this late stage, let alone deciding *against* the integration of the Jews into society at large, was unthinkable; and those who did so and, above all, those (few) who argued for such a decision they regarded as plainly unreasonable, perverse, disturbing, and possibly dangerous men. In any case, what was the alternative? The old, unemancipated, self-contained, inward-looking and other-worldly Jewish society held little attraction for the modern Jewish bourgeois. The classic Jewish tradition neither sought nor offered anything remotely comparable to the visible and tangible grandeurs of the Gentile state and Gentile society. The eastern Jews who still adhered in great numbers to the old patterns might be pitied, or half-heartedly admired, but not emulated. The alternative, then, if there was to be one, and if it was to make good sense in the western environment, had to be invented afresh—the more so as there were at this time no urgent *material* reasons for doubting the validity of the Emancipation. There were no pogroms; there were virtually no racial or religious laws. There was only a *malaise* and intellectual and social discomfort. The question was rather how seriously the discomfort should be taken. And it was whether the Emancipation was *morally* tenable that was at issue, and how the results of the effort to achieve integration should be judged by ethical and aesthetic standards. It was only very dimly, if at all, whether integration, ultimately, was materially workable and would not end in disaster.

1. Moshe Leib Lilienblum

2. Yehuda Leib Pinsker

3. The first conference of Hovevei Zion at Kattowitz, November 1884

David Gordon (front row, third from the left), Rabbi Shemuel Mohilever (front row, fourth from left), Yehuda Leib Pinsker (front row, fifth from left), Alexander Tsederbaum (front row, seventh from left), Sha'ul Pinhas Rabbinowitz ('Shefer') (second row, first from left)

6. Asher Ẓevi Ginsberg (Aḥad Ha-ʿAm)

7. Theodor Herzl
(*Portrait by Hermann Struck*)

8. Max Nordau

But these too were awkward, unpopular, and—having regard to
the circumstances—somewhat unnatural questions and were asked
only by extremely limited categories of Jews of—and in—the West:
those who had been led out of sympathy and by association to
consider the bearing of the fate of eastern Jewry on that of Jewry
as a whole; those who were themselves eastern Jews newly come to
the West and still of a piece with their original environment; and
a tiny class of exceptionally independent, rebellious, and, above all,
sensitive spirits who knew western Jewry best of all and did find
its condition morally intolerable and fraught with danger. It was
this last category that was struck most forcefully by the harsh and
highly visible changes wrought in the condition of Russian and
Romanian Jewry at the beginning of the 1880s and by the great
migratory tide it brought in its wake.

ii

Initially, the westerners had seen the problem of eastern Jewry as
from a distance and in exclusively philanthropic terms; and, indeed,
the philanthropic view was never fully eclipsed by any other and
persisted well into the following century—until West European
Jewry was itself engulfed in other horrors. The perspective changed
with the rapid influx of East European Jews in their tens of thousands into all the major cities of the West. The social composition
and internal balance of many old and well-established communities
was radically altered. The question of the precise relationship
between the Jews of one country and the Jews of any other, under
which lay the question of the nature of Jewry itself, ceased, at a
stroke, to be an academic one. The appearance of great numbers of
impoverished, oddly dressed, uncouth, and, above all, *foreign* Jews,
Jews, moreover, who were generally uninhibited in their religious
and social practices and in their sense of Jewish identity (because
they neither had, nor thought they had, any other), was a profoundly unsettling phenomenon for the great majority of the
indigenous Jews of Western Europe. It was clear to them that they
had ties of some sort with the new-comers, as it was to the new-
comers themselves. And it was clearer still that non-Jews rarely
hesitated to link both groups together, for good or ill. This in itself
was a source of anxiety for all but the most secure and self-assured
—particularly in France, where there were ancient precedents for

H

distinguishing between acceptable and tolerated Jews and unacceptable, potential deportees. For respectable and loyal *Israélites*,
to be linked up once more with the authentic, the cosmopolitan
*Juifs*, those who were not only non-French, but devoid of ties with
any nation, who evidently corresponded to the anti-Semitic image
of money-changers, innkeepers, pawnbrokers, and other scum,
was unbearable. '. . . thanks to these hordes with whom we are
confused, it is forgotten that for almost two thousand years we have
lived in France . . . What I want to insist upon publicly is that we
have nothing whatever in common with these [Jews] who are constantly thrown in our faces, and that we must abandon them.'[11]

    This was extreme. But the grounds for fearing that the influx
would end by slowing down the process of integration and assimilation were real enough. Then there was the question whether pressure by westerners for international intervention on behalf of those
who were demurely termed their 'co-religionists' in Russia was
consistent with the interests and diplomatic policies of their own
countries. It was, for example, *not* consistent with Gladstone's
foreign policy in the early 1880s—which was anti-Turkish and at
least implicitly pro-Russian. A decade later, as France and Russia
began to draw together in fear of Germany, any public protest by
French Jews against Russian internal policy could be easily denounced as an impertinence (which, by the diplomatic standards of
the times, it was), politically inopportune (as, indeed, it was too),
but also intentionally and slyly pro-German (which it was not).
The most generous spirits among the Jewish notables thus found
themselves unwillingly and embarrassingly involved in a form
of Jewish ultramontanism. Accordingly, where the contradiction
between the loyalties seemed particularly plain, most chose to be
prudent. When Alexander III lay dying in 1894 (it was the year in
which he had finally agreed to formalize the new Franco-Russian
Alliance), it was resolved to have prayers said for him in all the
four Paris synagogues. (Asked why, one of the most prominent and
learned of French rabbis of the day gave two reasons. Firstly, while,
indeed, the Tsar had greatly persecuted the Jews, he was 'a true
believer [un convaincu], even a fanatic, and he was acting con-

---

[11] Bernard Lazare, *Entretiens politiques et littéraires*, i, September 1890, pp. 178-9 and
October 1890, pp. 230-2. Cited in M. R. Marrus, *The Politics of Assimilation*, Oxford,
1971, p. 170. Lazare later changed his views on the Jewish condition. He became one of
the great champions of Dreyfus and later, for a period, a Zionist.

sistently with his conscience in attacking us . . .'. Secondly, 'and above all, we must remember that he was a friend of France and that in the interest of our fatherland his life is precious.')[12] Where, on the contrary, sympathy for eastern Jewry spread wider than the Jewish communities and was given public expression, the Jews themselves were correspondingly solaced and encouraged.

There were refugees who got as far as Stuttgart [in 1881]. Weary, ragged, sick, bloated with hunger, loaded with their poor belongings— they were strewn before the community offices. Their plight touched the hearts of the non-Jewish population too and public collections were held on their behalf. Who could then have imagined that the very same fate awaited the Jews of Germany too? Our headmaster, Dielmann, thought it his humane duty to collect charity from the pupils and not one of my school comrades refused. I gave up my pocket-money, the savings of several years. All this was only a drop in the bucket, so far as the needs [of the refugees] were concerned. However, my class-mates' readiness to help gave me great satisfaction and I felt grateful to them.[13]

One way or another, the spectacle of Jewish misery elsewhere and the sense of a measure of involvement in it willy-nilly tugged at the roots of their self-consciousness as Jews. The effect was much as it had been two generations earlier at the time of the Damascus affair when 'it dawned upon me for the first time', as Hess later put it, '. . . that I belong to my unfortunate, slandered, despised, and dispersed people.'[14] In a word, the events in the East constituted a great, concrete issue of the times for all Jewry, one which affected different communities in different ways and on which it was virtually impossible for all except the very ignorant and the entirely apathetic to avoid taking some position, if only a negative one of explicit disinterest. Moreover, as time went on, for those who were in fact incapable of apathy, real or feigned (whether because they wanted to speed as many migrants as possible on their way and hasten the absorption of those who had dropped behind, or because of straightforward concern for their welfare), it became ever more difficult to draw the line between simple philanthropy and more thoroughgoing action. This was partly because the sheer

[12] Israël Lévi, in Alliance Israélite, *Nouvelles diverses*, 25 October 1894, p. 359, quoted in Marrus, op. cit., p. 157. Lévi (1856–1939), a very considerable Biblical and Talmudic scholar, became Grand Rabbi of France in 1919.
[13] Max I. Bodenheimer, *Darki le-Ẓion*, translation Meir Mohar, Jerusalem, 1952, p. 21. On Bodenheimer himself, see below, pp. 228 f.
[14] *Rome and Jerusalem*, New York, 1918, pp. 67–8.

magnitude of the problem tended to turn people's minds to thinking of a radical and permanent cure for the Jewish condition; partly
because the western philanthropists were under constant pressure,
as we have seen, from the activists of Ḥibbat Zion in the East to
bring their wealth and knowledge and influence to bear on the
movement's behalf; and partly too because the actions of some at
least of the easterners, independently of the guidance of their
western benefactors, and often, as has been noted, contrary to the
latter's wishes, had created a new situation to which the western
philanthropists were impelled by the logic of their good intentions
to address themselves.

Hitherto America has seemed to be the goal towards which the Exodus
from Russia would be directed. But now a new and formidable rival
has made its appearance . . . The interest of English Jews in such a
movement is both direct and indirect. If the immigration into Palestine
be on a large scale, any failure in its operation must inevitably affect
English Jewry, as well as those of all the world . . . the Russian and
Roumanian Jews are bent on going to Palestine. Whatever we may think
of the practicability of the New Exodus, it is evidently to take place . . .
To all the objections to Palestine colonization that can be pointed out
the Jews of Russia and Roumania have one all-sufficient reply, 'We
cannot be worse off there than here.'[15]

From here to sympathy, or even qualified support, for Ḥibbat
Zion was a short step. Few took it; but one of the few western
Lovers of Zion was the man of whom Lilienblum had rightly said
that he had done more than anyone for the resettlement of Erez-
Israel; and all these forces can be seen at work in the manner of
his recruitment into the movement and the way in which his own
involvement in its affairs changed in character and expanded in
scope.

Baron Edmond James de Rothschild (1845–1934) was the fourth
and youngest son of James Jacob Rothschild, the original head of
the Paris branch of the family. He was comparatively little inclined
to business; his elder brother Alphonse succeeded their father as
head of the family's banking house and railway interests. He was
a sensitive and—for his class—a retiring man, fully conscious of
his status both within and outside Jewry as a member of, as it were,
a princely family, suspicious, like many rich men, of attempts to
play upon his vanity and drain his purse, and throughout his life

---

[15] *Jewish Chronicle* (leading article), 31 March 1882.

willing to indulge both his aesthetic and his humanitarian leanings. He was the first and most important of the tiny band of affluent western Jews who felt a profound moral obligation to assist in the venture in Erez-Israel long before there were reasonable grounds for belief in its success. His family had a long-standing, benevolent (if distant) interest in the affairs of the old *yishuv* for whom they had established a school and hospital in Jerusalem in earlier years. But Edmond de Rothschild's involvement in the new *yishuv* and, indirectly, in Hibbat Zion was strikingly different in character— more serious and, having regard to the moral and material obligations undertaken, bold to the point of eccentricity.

Like many others of his generation, Rothschild had been stunned by the onset of the pogroms and he had been among the first of his class to give time, money, and thought to the problem of Russian Jewry. He soon learned of the first trickle of migrants to Erez-Israel and took some interest in their fortunes. But he strongly disapproved of large-scale migration—on the conventional grounds that it was impolitic. Nor did he think it would prosper. At one stage he seriously feared that the migrants would end by falling into the hands of English (Christian) missionaries and even suspected 'the English', which is to say, the British government, of being behind the movement and for that purpose.[16] Then, in September and October 1882, he was approached in rapid succession by Rabbi Mohilever, who wanted him to help send a group of families from Poland, and by Yosef Feinberg, who had been delegated by the settlers in Rishon le-Zion to seek aid in Europe. Neither seems to have known of the other's intercession. Both were helped to reach Rothschild by men whom the latter greatly trusted and who were themselves cautiously sympathetic to Hibbat Zion: the Grand Rabbi of France, Zadoc Kahn, and Michel Erlanger, one of the leading figures in the Alliance Israélite Universelle.

Rothschild was extremely reserved. He received Mohilever somewhat coldly and would promise no more aid than for a dozen families. Feinberg was given no binding response at all to begin with as the Baron first wanted a report on Rishon le-Zion and advice from the director of the Alliance's agricultural school at

---

[16] Letter to Samuel Hirsch (director of the Mikve Israel agricultural school near Jaffa), 6 April 1883. S. Yavne'eli, *Sefer ha-zionut: tekufat Hibbat Zion*, Jerusalem, 1961, ii, p. 81. It is not clear what led him to perceive an English plot in the confusion of embryonic Hibbat Zion. It may have been Oliphant's early involvement.

Mikve Israel as to whether there was any practical point in helping them. Fortunately for Feinberg and his friends, the director's guarded reply was that, indeed, the settlement would probably fail, that it was unlikely that the settlers would know what to do with a grant-in-aid if they got one, but that, on the other hand, they seemed to be good people and evidently meant well.[17] At that Rothschild sent him 25,000 francs for them, explaining that he did not intend to encourage the immigration of Jews into Erez-Israel and stipulating that his name not be mentioned and that the money only be used for housing, the digging of wells, and other such proper purposes.[18] But what he had conceived of as a single moderate donation was repeated and repeated again and as his interest in the specific use made of his resources grew and as his own ideas for the management of some of the settlements developed, the aid he rendered began to take on massive proportions and semi-institutional forms, all to an extent far beyond his own family's traditionally high standards of direct involvement in, and financial backing of, Jewish communal and charitable institutions. Rothschild's material contribution to the new *yishuv* between 1883 and 1899 has been estimated at £1,600,000, an enormous sum for the times and one which must be set alongside the mere £87,000 which was what all the Hibbat Zion societies together, in the East as well as in the West, had managed to contribute to settlement in the same period. His total contribution to the *yishuv* in the course of his lifetime has been put as high as £5,600,000.[19] In this respect he was a towering figure among Jewish philanthropists generally, comparable to Baron Maurice de Hirsch[20] whom he resembled in one other way: he took his philanthropy extremely seriously. Indeed philanthropy soon came to play a central, rather than peripheral role in the lives of both men and the degree of their personal and emotional involvement is attested to not only by the magnitude of the sums which they devoted to their respective causes, but by the consistent and direct part which they took in the expenditure of the money and in determining the allocation of the resources which it purchased. In other ways they differed. Hirsch was, if not a self-made, at least a self-improved man, a great and

17  Hirsch to the Alliance secretariat, 18 October 1882. Yavne'eli, op. cit., pp. 57–9.
18  Rothschild to Hirsch, 20 October 1882. Ibid., pp. 68–9.
19  Alex Bein, *Toldot ha-hityashvut ha-zionit*, second edition, Tel Aviv, 1945, p. 10 fn.
20  See above, p. 181.

dynamic entrepreneur in his own right, a man who habitually
thought for himself, and who, struck by the disaster that had over-
taken East European Jewry, evolved his own, boldly conceived
plans for its rescue. He was relatively unsentimental, irreligious,
and, as befitted a spectacularly successful man of affairs, was quick
to dismiss the notion of a large-scale transfer of Russian Jews to
Erez-Israel as impracticable. His heart was set on the vast, un-
populated, promising lands of Argentina. In contrast, Edmond de
Rothschild was a moderately observant Jew, at any rate in his later
years, with a taste for Jewish history and rabbinical scholarship.
He was not a man of affairs and he had no broadly conceived ideas,
let alone plans of his own, for the amelioration of the condition of
the Jews. But he was unusually—it might almost be said (when
comparing him with other members of his class), peculiarly—
receptive to pleas for help and claims on his generosity. And,
crucially and more unusually still, he responded powerfully (in
spite of his initial reservations) to the idea of the Return to Erez-
Israel. It is this, more than anything else, which explains his
steadily expanding and deepening personal and financial involvement in the new *yishuv*, from the first, comparatively petty donation
to the settlers in Rishon le-Zion to the great purchases of land, the
hiring of agricultural experts, the construction of houses and
farm-buildings, and the grant of regular subsidies to a high proportion of the new and inexperienced farmers and their families—
by whom he ultimately came to be called (and thought of) as *Avi
ha-yishuv* (the father of the *yishuv*).[21] It showed in his careful
attention to the details of what became a large-scale development
scheme, in his visits to the country in which he toured the settlements he patronized like royalty (and was so received by the settlers),
in his close interest in every aspect of their life, in the combination
of anxiety and petulance in his reaction when things did not run
sufficiently smoothly, and in a certain underlying humility in his
fundamental approach to the entire enterprise. Altogether, Rothschild dealt with the affairs of the *yishuv* possessively, somewhat as
if it were a great estate which he held in trust. He observed the
settlers paternalistically and faintly *de haut en bas*. When they did

[21] He too had to contend with Turkish opposition, of course, with the rest. It was only
*posle usilennavo khodataystva* (best rendered as 'after persistent approaches hat-in-hand'),
as a Hibbat Zion emissary in Constantinople put it, that the Baron and his agents got limited
permission to build houses for the settlers in 1887. Kalmanovich to Pinsker, undated, but
evidently written in December 1887. Druyanov, ii, no. 723, II, b, col. 418.

well, he approved warmly. When they misbehaved, he scolded them. As he acted through salaried agents whose technical competence was often vitiated by their inability to find a common language with the settlers, petty rebellions were common. And since the receipt of a subsidy, however noble the purpose which it is intended to serve, cannot, of itself, encourage the recipient to seek to dispense with it, there was something of a natural and inevitable tendency to 'live on the Baron's account', as the phrase went. In consequence, scoldings were fairly frequent.

> Listen to what I tell you and always remember [he warned the people of Rishon le-Zion in October 1883]. I wish to encourage men who work and not beggars. If you do not work, as you are supposed to, I will immediately leave whoever fails to work to his own devices. Follow the instructions of my representatives in all things. He who fails to do so will cease to enjoy my aid and will be made to leave the houses I have constructed and make way for another who will be more deserving of my favour.[22]

On his first visit to the country in 1887 he had the schoolmaster in Zikhron Ya'akov dismissed because he thought (wrongly) that the children had not been taught elementary prayers.[23] The Baron's wrath was feared, and feared further afield than Erez-Israel. When the people in Gedera (like the settlers in Rishon le-Zion before them) duly quarrelled with Samuel Hirsch who served for a while as Rothschild's informal and occasional representative, Pinsker was quick to remonstrate with them. 'You must know, dear sirs,' he wrote to them, 'that the keys of the *yishuv* are to be found only in Paris and that if you cross Mr. Hirsch it is not him [alone] you will be angering, but those who love him and greatly value him and within whose power it is to expand the *yishuv*—or terminate it.'[24]

This humiliating dependence on a distant benefactor had horrified Ahad Ha-'Am when he came across it on his first visits to Erez-Israel. He noted sourly at the time that the Baron's chief representative (Elie Scheid) made no secret of the policy of forcing the settlers into subjection to the administration.[25] He particularly disapproved of the effort to compel the 'Ekron farmers to abandon field crops, which he thought a true and healthy form of agriculture,

22 Text (in Hebrew) in Yavne'eli, op. cit. ii, p. 89 fn.
23 Arye Samsonov, *Zikhron Ya'akov*, Zikhron Ya'akov, 1942, p. 144.
24 14 September 1887. Druyanov, ii, no. 654, col. 303.
25 'Pirkei zikhronot', *Kol kitvei*, p. 472.

in favour of viniculture, which he judged speculative and undesirable because it left people in idleness through the winter months. The only lesson to be drawn from all the millions poured in by the Baron, he wrote bitterly and with some exaggeration, was that outside financial support was itself one of the great obstacles to the growth of the *yishuv*. 'The idleness and weakness, craftiness and deception, the squandered money, the loss of self-respect, and the other such qualities that rot the very roots of the *yishuv*—they are all direct results of this system.'[26] But the administrators, backed by Rothschild himself, had no doubt that the little that had been accomplished would crumble away unless they, the professionals, took charge. And, although they chafed at the limitations of their freedom to go their own way, the settlers themselves never doubted that they had little choice. Typically, the agreement concluded between the Baron's agents and the virtually bankrupt villagers of Rosh Pina on 11 January 1884 set out the terms of their rescue without ambiguity. In exchange for their debts being settled, a grant towards the planting of fruit-bearing trees, a promise of a supply of livestock, communal buildings, a regular subsidy for maintenance, animal feed, and other essentials, their land was placed in trust in the hands of the agents and they themselves undertook 'each and every one to work to the best of his ability and obey the instructions of the overseer'.[27]

Aḥad Ha-ʿAm may have been right in principle; it is less certain that he was right in practice. It is as difficult with the advantage of hindsight, as it was difficult for the Ḥovevei Ẓion of Odessa and Ereẓ-Israel at the time, to see an alternative. In any case, it is virtually impossible to conceive of the people directly concerned doing otherwise than they did. They had always looked to the West for the financial resources and technical expertise which they lacked themselves; and if the aid, when it came, was not in the expected form, not integrated into the movement and subject in any significant degree to their influence, but granted *ex machina* and subject to a rich man's whims, none of this, they thought,

---

[26] 'Emet me-Ereẓ-Israel; Maʾamar sheni', *Kol kitvei*, p. 32. In 1902 he published a long and detailed attack on what might not unfairly be termed the baronial system: 'Ha-yishuv ve-apitropsav' ('The Yishuv and its Custodians'), ibid., pp. 211–45. He argued for the dissolution of the guardianship—which had been thoroughly institutionalized in the course of the years—and wanted responsibility for the affairs of the *yishuv* handed over to a local, elected, and representative body.

[27] Text in Yavneʾeli, op. cit. ii, p. 142.

entitled them to reject it. They disliked their weakness being
exposed so cruelly. They were irritated by the distance at which
the Baron kept them and by his habit of acting through intermediaries. His self-restriction to good works and refusal to play
an intercessionary role was a source of continual disappointment.
Some objected to the pressure from Paris to act secretly, so far as
possible, and keep the underlying purposes and character of the
movement away from the light of day. 'Even if we were to hide our
thoughts under seven and seventy seals,' Lilienblum wrote to
David Gordon, 'we would fail to deceive the Turkish government
. . . The important thing is for a respected man like Rothschild
himself to try to talk face to face with the Sultan . . . and convince
him of the benefits his government would derive if the Jews enriched his treasury by their diligence and labour.'[28] Still, the
general feeling was that by bringing Edmond de Rothschild into
the movement they had won a famous victory.[29] And such, in a
somewhat uncertain and unhappy way, it was.

### iii

Rothschild was thus never a member of Ḥibbat Zion in the formal
sense; he was its benefactor. But that alone made Paris a somewhat
friendlier place for the real Ḥovevim to visit than Berlin or London
or Vienna: for at least the Baron's local prestige assured them of
access to, and a sympathetic hearing in, relatively high places in
Jewish society. 'Leaving Russia [after the Druskieniki conference]
I went first to Berlin,' Pinsker reported in the summer of 1887,
'but there I failed to get anything done for the *yishuv* . . . while
here in [Paris], to which all eyes in Ḥibbat Zion turn, it has been
proved to me that our confidence is not misplaced.'[30] Aḥad Ha-ʿAm
was as disappointed in England as Pinsker had been in Germany
and changed his mind about it being the only country in which 'it
is possible to do great things'. The Chief Rabbi (Adler) had refused
to help, he wrote his friends in 1893. The few local Ḥovevei Zion

---

[28] 21 February 1884. Druyanov, iii, no. 1188, col. 589, fn. 4.
[29] Among the few who did not think so was Dr. Karpel Lippe, a founding member of
Ḥibbat Zion in Romania. He complained that the passing of the Romanian settlements of
Samarin (Zikhron Yaʿakov) and Rosh Pina into the Baron's hands had killed the local
emigration committees in Romania by robbing them of responsibility and thus contributed
to the general decline of the movement. Cf. Druyanov, iii, no. 1204, col. 615.
[30] Druyanov, ii, no. 667, cols. 321-4.

had failed to win anyone of real influence to their party. 'As for the English Jews [generally] and my expectations of them on matters of general concern . . . shame covers my face. I cannot speak [of them].' In Paris, in contrast, the French Grand Rabbi (Zadoc Kahn) had been friendly. Even Baron de Hirsch's man had been receptive and sympathetic.[31] Vienna was different again. The Viennese Jews, 'from great to small, are concerned [only] with their own material affairs', Eliezer Ben-Yehuda[32] complained to Tchlenov. 'The students, for all the noise they make . . . I found nothing in them either; all is emptiness and all their doings are deceptive and imitative and superficial . . .'. In Paris, 'on the contrary, I found more than I expected. Rabbi Zadoc Kahn is a real nationalist and M. Erlanger, too, told me in so many words: we know what we want in Erez-Israel, but we must be cautious. The Benefactor [i.e. Rothschild] is also . . . a nationalist of our stripe.'[33]

But Ben-Yehuda misjudged the Parisians. Rothschild did not greatly like Ḥibbat Ẓion the *movement* and did not believe in it. He remained consistent in his rejection of its underlying purposes, as understood by Pinsker and Lilienblum, let alone the subsequent 'political' Zionism of Herzl, until long after the situation of the *yishuv* had been transformed in the course of the First World War.[34] It is likely that for a while he had it in his power, by virtue of his name and of the influence and resources he could command, to lead the movement, or, at the very least, greatly to extend it out of the East and into the West. But there is nothing to suggest that he grasped the fact; and nothing, very probably, was further from his thoughts and inclinations. The benefit the movement *as such* derived from his highly qualified adhesion to it was marginal and indirect to the end.

[31] *Igrot*, i, pp. 52–9; 'Pirkei zikhronot', *Kol kitvei*, pp. 472, 474.

[32] Eliezer Ben-Yehuda (1858–1922) was a notable member of the class of Lithuanian Jews who had been reared in the stringently orthodox tradition and then gradually been pulled away from it under the intellectual and social influence of the secular enlightenment. Unusually, his adoption of a nationalist position preceded the pogroms of the 1880s: by 1878 he was in Paris, studying medicine, preparatory to moving to Erez-Israel. His great idea was to revive Hebrew as the spoken language of the Jews as the condition of their national revival and their unity. This was his major preoccupation as teacher, publicist, and, above all, lexicographer from his arrival in Jerusalem in 1881. He edited and published the first Hebrew periodicals in the country and, in time, produced the first great modern dictionary of the Hebrew language.

[33] Ben-Yehuda to Tchlenov, 13 February 1887. Druyanov, ii, no. 551, cols. 112–13.

[34] But see Isaac Naitditch, *Edmond de Rothschild*, Washington, D.C., 1945, *passim*.

At the heart of the philanthropic approach there was, after all, the distinction between the immediate and material needs of the Jews in Eastern Europe and the theoretical and ideological issue of the needs of Jewry as a whole—the Jews conceived, that is, as a social category of a particular kind with particular moral, cultural, and, perhaps, political requirements. It was right and proper to minister to the Jews. It was impolitic and awkward to tackle the question of Jewry. The first was a matter of urgency; the second was not. Moreover, the circumstances of the great majority of western Jews were such, as we have seen, that the issue of their status in society at large and the extent to which it was materially and morally tenable was in any case essentially academic at this time. It was therefore a matter which, if it was to be of concern to anyone, would be so only to those especially inclined by their nature, or by their occupation, to think in terms of general categories and, so far as possible, to place theory before practice—men on the margin of society, or alien or new to it, or at odds with it, men of the academy, but students and untenured academics, not members of the regular professoriate, and not men of affairs, not men of comfortable and established position, or, if established, then men who had been disturbed in their enjoyment of position and status by some internal or external event or shock and rendered restless and thoughtful.

The population of these classes of men and women was certainly somewhat larger among western Jews at the end of the century than in the general population; but in absolute terms it was none the less very small. The fraction that was inclined to take up the issue of Jewry at all was smaller still. And the numbers disposed to swim hard against the dominant current of Jewish opinion minute.

The students are an important case in point. The main reaction of Jewish university students to the rising anti-Semitic pressure in Germany and Austria was defensive and apologetic. Even at its most intense and—in view of the social counter-pressures—bravest, and even when latent national sentiment had in fact been electrified by the continuing offence to it and by the exposure of their social and psychological weakness—it remained self-protective. 'Jewish depravity is put forth in anti-Semitic propaganda with such conviction and zeal', concluded a group of Jewish students in Breslau in 1886, 'that the young Jew himself begins to doubt the righteousness of his cause and the right of Jewry to exist at all, especially as most young Jews know very little about the ideas of Judaism and its undeniable merits in ancient and modern civilization.'[35] In practice, their response was to organize themselves, separately. In itself, this was a startling and brave departure. But at bottom, the rules of the game, as set by the non-Jews, were not in question and the aim was to demonstrate that the Jews were fit to join it. The exclusion of Jews from the duelling fraternities led to the formation of Jewish ones; and when it was resolved by the 'Aryans' that the Jews were not *satisfaktionsfähig*, duels were deliberately provoked. Culturally and ideologically the Jewish element remained entirely subordinate to the German. The colours of the Jewish fraternity in Breslau were black, gold, and red; its coat of arms centred on a figure representing Germania and included, besides a device representing the three great world religions intertwined, and another symbolizing friendship and mutual assistance, a German sword crossed by two sabres; one of its Latin mottoes was *nemo me impune lacessit*; its name was carefully neutral: 'Viadrina' (after the University of Breslau itself). Other such Jewish fraternities were set up: 'Badenia' at Heidelberg, 'Sprevia' at Berlin, 'Licaria' at Munich.[36] Initially all this was unconventional and even daring. But the young rebels duly became respectable *Alte Herren* and their radicalism could be absorbed eventually into the ethos without discomfort. In a word, separatism here was a tactic, and provisional by intention. It would not have occurred to the men of 'Viadrina' to press for it as a permanent condition, a state of affairs that was not merely necessary, but desirable and proper in itself.

Very different was the 'Kadimah' union of students in Vienna and a world away from the duelling clubs in that, as a tiny minority within a minority, it did wish—or, at any rate, consider—a decisive and irreversible change in status for the Jews. It was given a Hebrew name (*kadima* = forward). Its first manifesto (1883) was pugnaciously and (for the times) uncompromisingly nationalistic: 'For eighteen centuries, since the Jewish nation lost its independence, it has been exposed to incessant persecutions, the aim of which is the destruction of Jewry . . . Kinsmen! Reach out your helping hand to us in the firm conviction that you will have contributed to a great and exalted purpose, to the regeneration of the Jewish

---

[35] 'A Word to our Co-religionists.' Text in Adolph Asch and Johanna Philippson, 'Self-Defence at the Turn of the Century: the Emergence of the K.C.', Leo Baeck Institute, *Year Book III*, London, 1958, p. 122.                    [36] Ibid., pp. 134–6.

222    *The Love of Zion*

nation!'[37] Its founders derived their guiding ideas from Perez Smolenskin[38] (who lived in Vienna), and from Pinsker[39] (whom they tended to see as the indirect, but real begetter of their movement, and whose leadership in practical matters they were glad to accept). But it must be noted that all, with one exception, were new-comers from Eastern Europe and that the exception, the man who was the driving force in the group, was himself only one generation away from the East[40] and was far from being a member of established Jewish, German-speaking society.

Nathan Birnbaum (1864–1937) was a difficult, inconsistent, and temperamental man, a son of poor parents who was in process of emerging into the educated bourgeoisie, but was not yet of it, a man of independent and original cast of mind with a gift for polemical writing and a fine turn of phrase. 'Hat auch der einzelne Jude ein Vaterland, das Jüdische Volk hat keines', was one of his dicta.[41] It was he who popularized the terms *Zionismus* and *Zionistisch*.[42] His views changed and changed again over the years; in time he was to move from secularism back to religious observance and his final position on the Jewish Question brought him into the ranks of the very orthodox and the anti-Zionists. But one of the few fixed points in the flux of his ideas was opposition to the assimilation of the Jews into the surrounding society. For the Jews to adjust themselves, under the pressure of anti-Semitism, to the practices of peoples whom he judged to be of inferior cultural achievement was shameful, to his mind. For the rest, in this early period his views, broadly, were a variant of Pinsker's. The Jews needed a centre—as a way out of the morass; as a place for the 'superfluous' Jews of Europe, now and in the future; as a cure for that sickness of the people that was a result of its exile and dispersion; and as

[37] M. T. Schnirer, 'Gründung der Kadimah', in Ludwig Rosenhek (ed.), *Festschrift zur Feier des 100 Semesters der akademischen Verbindung Kadimah 1883–1933*, Vienna, 1933, p. 18.

[38] See above, pp. 46f.

[39] See Moshe Schnirer's letter to Pinsker, 25 November 1883. Druyanov, i, no. 61, cols. 127–8.

[40] Birnbaum's father was from Cracow. The other two leading figures were Reuven Bierer (from Lemberg) and Moshe Schnirer (from Bucharest).

[41] Adolf Böhm, *Die Zionistische Bewegung*, second edition, i, Tel Aviv, 1935, p. 138.

[42] There was some random use of 'Zion' in various forms to denote modern Jewish national sentiment and purposes before Birnbaum began to employ it systematically. See G. Kressel, 'Selbstemanzipation', in B. Dinur and Y. Heilprin (eds.), *Shivat Zion*, iv, Jerusalem, 1956, p. 76; and Alex Bein, 'The Origin of the Term and Concept "Zionism"', in R. Patai (ed.), *Herzl Year Book*, ii, 1959.

a legitimate moral and political defender of those who remained in the Diaspora. A variant of Pinsker's but a *western* variant: the establishment of such a centre, by ridding the Exile of its evils, would end the common hatred of the Jews and also, by so doing, enhance the Jews' own feelings of loyalty to the countries of their domicile and of friendship for their peoples. Birnbaum's Zionism did not run counter to local patriotism, as Zionism did, necessarily, in Russia, but parallel to it. The establishment of a Jewish *Gemein-wesen* (polity) in Erez-Israel and the protection of the immediate, local political, social, and economic interests of the Jews of Austria were fully compatible purposes and could be pursued in tandem. Birnbaum even contested elections to a seat in the Reichsrat as a Zionist in 1907. (He lost.)

The 'Kadimah' circle was unambiguously political in character; its interests were doctrinal and propagandistic and, appropriately, its principal achievement in these years was the establishment of a periodical (1885)—the first Zionist journal in a Western European language and, indeed, the first Jewish periodical of any significance to set the promotion of Zionism as its central purpose. They called it *Selbstemanzipation* in deference to Pinsker and by way of pin-pointing the heart of their position.[43] Like most such ventures, it was something of a *tour de force* to have brought it out at all and publish it regularly for long stretches of time. There was never enough money. The approach was highly unpopular. The circula-tion was small. Most of the contributors were obscure. After a year and a quarter, publication stopped, then renewed in 1890 and ran for four years (under Birnbaum, as before), then removed to Berlin for publishing purposes, although still edited (under another name: *Jüdische Volkszeitung*) by Birnbaum in Vienna. The journal was finally discontinued at the end of 1894.[44] But while it lasted it served not only to help its contributors to formulate and sharpen their own ideas, but to facilitate contacts with the like-minded elsewhere both by circulation of the journal itself and by its being offered as a vehicle for sympathetic contributors.

There were analogous circles of expatriate students from Eastern Europe in Berlin and Paris. Closest to 'Kadimah' and most directly involved in, and influenced by, *Selbstemanzipation* was the self-styled Russian-Jewish Scientific Society in Berlin. The Society's

---

[43] They had originally thought of calling it *Der Jude*, but that, one supposes, would have been too bold, even for them.                    [44] Kressel, op. cit.

founder, Leo (Arye Leib) Motzkin (1867–1933), was born near Kiev, where his father's family, exceptionally, had rights of residence, and where he himself, as a boy, had witnessed the horrors of the 1881 pogrom. In 1882, in his fifteenth year, he was sent to Berlin. Motzkin had a particular talent for mathematics and did extremely well at the gymnasium and, later, at the university. He was thus in a very precise sense a product of both worlds. He was fully equipped academically and intellectually by his Prussian schoolmasters and professors and thoroughly at ease in western urban society. At the same time, he was possessed of a sure, quasi-intuitive knowledge of eastern Jewry and of the forces hostile to it. His social vision was thus a dual one—determined by respect for the institutional virtues and proprieties of German Jewry and a countervailing bias in favour of the moral integrity of eastern Jewry. As with virtually all new-comers, he was at first immensely impressed by the former. 'What stability, what security, what solidity . . .', he said, in retrospect, recalling his feelings on arrival; 'even if I disliked the national self-effacement of the German Jews, I knew the value of their social and cultural work for the benefit of both the country of their domicile and for world Jewry.'[45]

Although Motzkin and his friends found the German Jews' way of fighting anti-Semitism, when they fought it at all, cowardly and apologetic, their own intentions were modest enough, not to say timid. The stated purpose of the group was 'to give Jewish youth from Russia, now in Berlin, an opportunity to acquaint themselves with the interests and needs of the Jewish people'. This was intentionally unprovocative, one of their purposes being to draw as many potential recruits as possible into their orbit. Some years later the aim was redefined and made somewhat more specific: 'to disseminate national-Jewish, Zionist thinking among academic [i.e. university] Russian-Jewish youth, to encourage Jewish learning and a Jewish way of life'.[46] The emphasis on 'science'—or, more accurately, on study and discussion—was intended to mark the difference between the purely philanthropic, narrowly conceived 'pro-Palestine' approach, and what they themselves were after, which was a thorough review of the Jewish condition, an effort to reinvigorate the people internally, a move away from small things

---

[45] 'Maẓav ha-yehudim be-Germania, ha-kongres ha-yehudi ha-ʿolami ve-ha-tenuʿa ha-ẓionit', *Sefer Motzkin*, p. 267.

[46] Bein, 'Arye Leib Motzkin', ibid., p. xli fn.

to great things. But the great things, in Ḥibbat Ẓion's contemporary condition of decline, could only be theoretical, cultural, and moral. The students' achievements, such as they were, were in fact chiefly in debate—often with analogous groups of socialists in Berlin— and in the simple radiation of radical ideas on Jewish issues along the periphery of German Jewry proper and in which they made a few recruits. Many of the members of the Russisch-Jüdischer Wissenschaftlicher Verein of Berlin were gifted men who later rose to prominence in the movement: Motzkin himself, Victor Jacobson, Shmaryahu Levin, Yosef Lurie, Selig Soskin, Nachman Syrkin, and Chaim Weizmann among others.

A similar circle of expatriate student Ḥovevei Ẓion had been founded in Paris (at the same time, as it happened). It was a much slighter affair. While their chairman, Serge Voronof, later achieved great fame for his efforts to rejuvenate the human individual by transplanting glands from primates, his effort to promote the rejuvenation of the Jewish people was less sustained; and, so far as Ḥibbat Ẓion was concerned, he and most of his colleagues soon dropped out of sight. But it is worth noting that before doing so they had urged Pinsker to convene a general assembly of Ḥovevei Ẓion from all countries.[47] This was a popular idea, constantly repeated, invariably in the expectation that from such a conference or congress new ideas and a fresh course of action would emerge. Nothing came of the proposal directly. But a conference of 'sociétés palestinophiles' was eventually convened in Paris in the middle of January 1894 under other auspices. The original initiative can be traced to the Shavei Ẓion group of New York and the auguries were not wholly unfavourable to begin with. It had the (qualified) blessings of Edmond de Rothschild, whose representative (Scheid) participated; there were delegates from France itself, from England, from the United States, from Germany, and from Austria. There were also some local Russian Jews, including at least one of the students who had belonged to Voronof's group. The Odessa committee sent no representative because its regulations did not permit it to do so, but expressly wished the others well. The conference was intended as a western Kattowitz: the topics of debate were co-ordination, co-operation, settlement, and examination of ways and means. It was agreed that Paris would be the centre of the new framework of operation and that the English delegates would

[47] Voronof *et al.* to Pinsker, 16 June 1889. Druyanov, ii, no. 897, cols. 693–6.

play a major role. But in the event none of the decisions made was followed up; and some months later the Baron killed the project off by deciding that his people would not participate after all. To his mind, it was all too noisy and public and would end by attracting the attention of the Turkish authorities—with calamitous consequences.

For the rest, with one or two exceptions, the little pockets of Hovevei Zion scattered in Western Europe and in North America were substantially like the societies within the Russian Pale: doctrinally unproductive, well meaning, devoted to the notion of the resettlement of Erez-Israel, and composed predominantly, if not exclusively, of recent arrivals from the Pale. Their members were either largely oblivious of their new surroundings, or else in process of undergoing a preliminary reaction to them. Fear of apostasy, dislike of the habits of established western Jewry, anxiety about their current status, fear (in the United States) lest the treatment being meted out to the Chinese be followed by analogous ill-treatment of the Jews—these prompted old thoughts in new forms and seem to have caused some of the new-comers to seek contact with the movement back in Eastern Europe. But otherwise, their societies were hardly more than simple extensions of the Russo-Polish movement itself, subject to slow erosion by the assimilatory currents that beat upon them. Such, for example, was the Benei Zion society, founded in Paris in the Autumn of 1889 'for the good of the settlement of Erez-Israel' and 'to acquaint members with the Jewish question and strengthen their pure-national and holy-patriotic-Jewish sentiment';[48] and such was the Hovevei Zion society of New York whose revised charter of 1886 set down its aims as the propagation of 'the patriotic idea of the settlement of the Jews in the Land of Israel' and the improvement 'of the condition of the Jews in Palestine by giving them instructions in agriculture and other industries'.[49]

Yet beyond this ill-knit network of small groups and scattered individuals, linked in one way or another to the movement's centre of gravity in the Pale, there also began to appear, here and there, a genuinely native, western product who owed little or nothing

[48] Druyanov, ii, no. 659, cols. 308-10. Significantly, their statement of purposes and regulations are in Yiddish.

[49] Marnin Feinstein, *American Zionism 1884-1904*, New York, 1965, p. 30. Cf. Shlomo Noble, 'Pre-Herzlian Zionism in America as Reflected in the Yiddish Press', in I. S. Meyer (ed.), *Early History of Zionism in America*, New York, 1958.

historically or culturally or psychologically to the traditional forms and issues of Jewish life in Eastern Europe and was often ignorant of its salient characteristics, and ignorant of the classic Jewish tradition too, to a marked degree.

Thus Colonel Albert Edward Williamson Goldsmid (1846–1904) was a man out of a different world—in fact, a character out of a different story. 'I am Daniel Deronda', he told Herzl when they first met.[50] Goldsmid was a serving officer in the British Army. His father had been a member of the Indian Civil Service (Chief Secretary to the Bombay Government), who became a convert to Christianity and brought up his son as a Christian without ever telling him of his origins. His father's death led to the truth coming out. Goldsmid, then a subaltern in the Army, was stunned; and his response was to revert. He became an observant Jew; he married a woman who, like himself, was a Christian of Jewish descent and who then reconverted; he called his children Rachel and Carmel and, as he made a point of informing Herzl, saw to it that they 'had a strict religious upbringing and learned Hebrew at an early age'. But he continued to serve in the British Army and achieved fairly high rank (Officer Commanding the 41st Regimental District in Cardiff in 1897). This presented him with no dilemmas, in his view. 'Israel is my father and Britain is my mother', he is reputed to have liked to say.[51]

Like so many others, Goldsmid's interest in the public affairs of Jewry was aroused by events in Russia. He visited Erez-Israel and joined in efforts to bring aid to Russian Jews. With his relative Elim Henry d'Avigdor he formed the Ḥovevei Zion association of England and was himself the dominant influence within it. But it was a peculiar influence. He did not really understand the movement as conceived in the heartland of Jewry. He gave his organization what would now be termed a Masonic or Boy Scout stamp. He was at first somewhat insensitive to the vital doctrinal distinction between Ḥibbat Zion proper and the view underlying the Hirsch project in Argentina. In 1892 he accepted an invitation to go out to Argentina to supervise the enterprise. There, characteristically, his first step upon arrival was to issue a message to the settlers which

[50] *The Complete Diaries of Theodor Herzl*, ed. Raphael Patai, trans. Harry Zohn, New York, 1960, i, p. 282.
[51] Josef Fraenkel, 'Colonel Albert E. W. Goldsmid', *Herzl Year Book*, i, New York, 1958, p. 147.

228 The Love of Zion

began 'Michael, of the people of Israel, called Lt. Colonel Albert Edward Williamson Goldsmid, sends greetings to the children of Israel' and to make his appearance among them in dress uniform driving in an open landau drawn by white horses.[52] His achievements were correspondingly slight. 'I had a long conversation with Colonel Goldsmid and Mr. d'Avigdor last Sunday', Aḥad Ha-ʿAm wrote after meeting them in October 1893. 'They are both good Ḥovevei Zion and have much [good] will, but it seems to me that their *ability* is much smaller than their will.'[53]

In the mild atmosphere of late Victorian England Goldsmid's conversion and his leadership of the 'Tents' (or local societies) of Ḥovevei Zion (including one at Cambridge University) could be relegated to the class of gentlemanly eccentricities. For a Jew born and bred and more or less solidly established in the social and professional life of one of the *continental* states of Western Europe such a shift to the unconventional was necessarily a weightier affair, if only because the issues involved were commonly held to be of so much more importance. To go further still and explicitly and publicly call the seemingly settled order of Jewish–Gentile relations into serious question took special courage and independence of spirit and suggested particular moral and intellectual sensitivity and an intense inner experience. Max Bodenheimer, the young lawyer in Cologne, the epitome of German-Jewish respectability, moved in isolation towards the conclusion that the Jewish condition was absurd and undignified and that the solution was political independence. He had lost, as he later put it, 'the purity of my sense of belonging to the German environment'.[54]

It was as if some sort of light had abruptly broken into me. The strangeness of it shattered all my being. I saw myself as a slave before whom the road to freedom had suddenly opened . . . It is almost impossible to describe the state of mind that dominated me in consequence of this idea. Only shortly before I had debated whether to cast the burden of Judaism off and find refuge from the hatred of Israel in new surroundings where none would know of my origins, and now of a sudden I was filled with a holy enthusiasm to work for the good of my people.[55]

So febrile a state of mind was foreign to the pragmatic and sober men in the Pale into whose heads the idea of a debate on 'whether

[52] S. Adler-Rudel, 'Moritz Baron Hirsch', Leo Baeck Institute, *Year Book VIII*, London, 1963, pp. 55-6.  [53] *Igrot*, i, p. 59. Emphasis in original.
[54] *Darki le-Zion*, p. 19.  [55] Ibid., p. 37. This was in 1889.

to cast the burden of Judaism off' never entered and who could scarcely have understood it, even in the case of a man like Boden-heimer, had they known how his thoughts had run. Besides, they were now weary. When the young lawyer heard about Pinsker and sent him a copy of his pamphlet *Wohin mit den russischen Juden?*, the tired response from Odessa was that 'if I were young enough to wait for the realization [of the plan] I would be happy to join you. I am afraid, to my regret, that because of the Jews' unlucky destiny, your plan's fate will be the same as that of mine of some years ago. Don't be alarmed. If I came too soon, you may be sure that you do not come too late.'[56]

Such men differed in other ways from the kind of people who were drawn to the movement in the East. They were usually younger: Bodenheimer was twenty-four when his ideas crystallized. By secular standards, they tended to be better educated. They were usually of a more questioning, critical, and imaginative bent of mind and their approach to the issues that concerned them was generally more systematic; it was also more formal. Their range of skills was greater and they were bolder in employing them. But above all, compared with their eastern brethren, they were in the technical sense free men; and they were drawn to the movement because they believed it promised greater freedom yet. By the same token, they were less easily disciplined, less consistent, and less humble. In many respects, Herzl himself was the classic exemplar of the type.

[56] Klausner, op. cit., p. 104.

PART THREE

---

*Political Zionism*

# 9

# *Herzl*

### i

IT is appropriate to speak of the advent of Theodor Herzl. He was the hero of the Zionist movement—its only hero. So he was seen by its members and its adepts; and so he saw himself. He looked the hero. He acted the hero. He displayed the virtues and qualities that typically suggest the hero. For his followers—and for himself —he was Carlyle's 'Ablest Man', the one who, if he is raised to the supreme place and loyally revered, provides the best government, the one who is the 'truest-hearted, justest, Noblest Man', and whose instructions, because he is so, 'must be precisely the wisest, fittest, that we could anywhere or anyhow learn'.[1] He had a hero's flaws— some so deep and plain to see that, on inspection, it becomes hard to understand the sources of his evident power for action and harder still to arrive at a just assessment of his role and contribution in and to the modern history of the Jews, let alone his qualities as a dispenser of political and social ideas. He both observed and imagined things; and the basis of his action was an unfathomable combination of the world as it was and the world as he wished it to be. Some sources of his errors and his failures are thus easily identified. The problem is to account for the ease with which so much of what he did accomplish can reasonably be explained in similar terms, which is to say, in terms of the elements of truth and error, well-founded judgement and wild surmise, solid knowledge, and sheer fantasy which all seemed to have coexisted in his mind and to have served, jointly, as the springs of his thought and action. For Herzl's achievement was immense and unique. Zionism as a true political movement and as an international force—however small, however weak and uncertain—is to all intents and purposes his invention and his

---

[1] Thomas Carlyle, 'The Hero as King', *On Heroes, Hero-Worship, and the Heroic in History*, Lecture VI, London, 1926, ii, p. 100.

creation. He cut through the inconsistencies and dilemmas that overshadowed and largely paralysed the social action of the Jews of Europe in a *Jewish* cause with a speed and thoroughness that are hard to credit. And before the full impact of the new divisions, inconsistencies, and dilemmas which he himself had implanted in the still largely amorphous body politic of Jewry could be registered —he died, suddenly, at the age of 44, after a mere eight or nine years of public life, leaving a stunned following, assured of his own posthumous glory while others coped with his legacy.


ii


Herzl was a child—and, indeed, a man—of the declining Austro-Hungarian Empire, a political structure that is exceptionally difficult to understand except in terms of its intricately connected component national parts. He was a largely assimilated, German-speaking, Hungarian Jew. He had three sets of forenames: the Hebrew Binyamin Ze'ev, the Magyar Tivadar, the German Theodor. He partook—unequally—of three cultures; and was in one way or another partly alien to all three. Technically, as it were, he was free to see himself, and to seek to make others see him, either as a Jew or as a Hungarian, or later as an Austrian, or again as a person to whom any two of the three ascriptions applied simultaneously. In reality, none applied to him without qualification. On his father's side there was only a single generation between him and the classic, unquestioning, observant Jewish community life of Eastern and South-Eastern Europe.[2] But although he went to a Jewish school for some years in his childhood, he was virtually without Hebrew or more than the most superficial and distant acquaintance with Jewish law and ritual—let alone the history, literature, and philosophy of the Jews—by the time he had reached manhood. Although born and bred in Budapest (in which his mother's family had long been resident), he belonged, by the accident of birth, to the limited class of Hungarian Jews who resisted the contemporary tide of Magyarization and retained a loyalty for the German language and a fondness, often bordering on romantic

---

[2] Herzl's father, Jakob, was from Zemun (Semlin), near Belgrade. The *ḥakham* (rabbi) of Zemun was Yehuda Alkalai (1798–1878) whom it is customary to class with Kalischer (see pp. 12 ff. above) as an original and independent, if only very moderately influential, 'precursor' of Zionism. Herzl's grandfather was one of Alkalai's followers. Cf. Y. Ẓevi Zahavi, *Me-he-Ḥatam Sofer ve-ʿad Herzl*, Jerusalem, 1965, pp. 264 ff.

love, for much that was associated with German culture and what was then fancied best in, and specific to, the German people. 'If there is one thing I should like to be,' Herzl himself noted in his diary at his life's very turning-point, at the height of the period in which his essential ideas on the Jewish question took shape, 'it is a member of the old Prussian nobility.'[3] By vocation and by profession, moreover, he could accurately be described as a man of German letters. And by adoption and by choice he was, plainly, a notable Viennese: first as a university student, then (after a brief interlude as a lawyer in the provinces) as a playwright (of limited talent and moderate success), finally as a journalist of high repute. But never for a moment did Herzl actually fancy himself an authentic German—of the Austrian or of any other variety—and his faintly mawkish liking for the Germanic coexisted in his mind both with the belief that anti-Semitism had originated and had its 'centre' (*Hauptsitz*) in Germany[4] and with his profound and unchanging sense that his Jewish origin was a vital and irreducible element both of his inner make-up and of his social situation.

Yet as a subject of the multinational, multilingual Austro-Hungarian Empire he was not at all an alien or an outsider in the sense that Lilienblum and Pinsker were (even technically) alien subjects of the Russian Empire. In the pre-eminently plural society of Austria-Hungary it was possible for the Jews—once they had been granted legal emancipation—to play a role and to derive indirect political and social benefit from their being one category of subjects (among many others) of which both the government and the various political groups which contended for power and influence within the state had to take into account. True, the issue was confused and the possibilities reduced by the fact that the closer individual Jews came to the centre of the political arena, the more reluctant they were, as a rule, to act openly, or even covertly, on behalf of any defined Jewish interest. (It was just this that Birnbaum's 'Kadimah' group had proposed to do.)[5] But on the non-Jewish side there was virtually no such blurring of the matter. Those who sought the Jews as allies, those who opposed them and sought to crush them, and those few who might be termed their friends all saw them as a major constituent of the social, economic, cultural, and, latterly, political fabric of the Empire, Wickham

---

[3] *Diaries*, 5 July 1895, i, p. 196.     [4] Ibid., 28 June 1895, i, p. 190.
[5] See above, pp. 222 f.

Steed, one of the best informed and most acute of contemporary foreign observers (he was correspondent for *The Times* in Berlin, Rome, and Vienna between 1896 and 1914), went so far as to state his belief that 'among the peoples of Austria-Hungary the Jewish people stands first in importance . . . Economically, politically and in point of general influence they are . . . the most significant element in the Monarchy.'[6] An exaggeration, but one with a core of truth. In any event, for a Jew to see his people in these terms and to say so publicly was to swim against the tide of vocal and dominant Jewish opinion, while putting himself in embarrassing *rapport* with non-Jewish opinion on a Jewish issue. For an assimilated Jew, which is to say, a Jew who had irreversibly and for all practical purposes adopted the language, culture, and social habits of the non-Jews, to do just this was exceedingly rare, as we have seen. It was particularly rare in Austria-Hungary because where German was both a national tongue *and*, as it were, the imperial lingua franca, adoption of the language, even the acquisition of literary proficiency in it, did not in itself have the same implications for a switch of national identity—or its rejection—that the adoption of the native language and culture implied in Germany proper or in France or in England. In a word, a great variety of intermediate positions between totally turning one's back upon one's origins and total identification with a nationally defined Jewry seemed possible. And, alternatively, while it was very unusual, it was not absurd, on the face of it, for a German- and Magyar-speaking, agnostic Jew to propound Jewish separateness without serious reference to, and in virtual ignorance of, the Jews' own language and literary and historical tradition. And indeed, an assimilated western Jew who had concluded, for whatever reason, that the Emancipation had failed, or was to be rejected, or both, had little choice. He could not easily rejoin those of his people who still lived in the pre-emancipatory state—in Austrian Galicia, for example. He lacked the language, the lore, and, of course, the religious faith. To revert to the poverty and technical primitiveness characteristic of the Jews of the East was unthinkable. He could barely communicate with them. He found much in their aspect that repulsed him. He could only return on condition that they met him half-way, so to speak—on the basis of a radical transformation of the Jewish condition in all respects, social as well as political. Even then, if he

---

[6] Henry Wickham Steed, *The Hapsburg Monarchy*, London, 1914, p. 145.

himself was not to remain an outsider within the body of his people, in mirror-image of his alien status among the non-Jews, he had to establish a tenable and sufficiently intimate relationship with those Jews who had remained within the orbit of their own specific culture—who were, in practice, as we have seen, those who had most immediate cause to subscribe to a thoroughgoing reconstruction of Jewry.

Herzl's simple and spontaneous solution to the conundrum was to offer himself as their leader. The boldness of his vision (of which more later)—and its essential artlessness—can thus not be properly understood except in relation to the role he set for himself. And his impact on the course of Jewish history cannot be accounted for without overriding attention to Herzl the public figure and the man of action, rather than the ideologue, to Herzl the brilliant leader, Herzl the organizer of the Jewish national revival, Herzl 'the King of the Jews'. It was there that his distinction and originality lay, rather than in his ideas—which were clear enough, occasionally ingenious, entirely the product of his own mind, but marred by the superficiality of his analysis of the condition of the Jews, and by the *naïveté* of his programme for action, and in no essential respect really new, even if Herzl himself did not at first know this.

### iii

Theodor Herzl was an exceptionally impressive and good-looking man. 'His natural, charming courtesy cast its spell upon me at that first moment', wrote Stefan Zweig of his initial meeting with Herzl when, as a youth of nineteen, he went to him, unannounced, to offer the eminent literary editor of the Vienna *Neue Freie Presse* his first short story for publication.

The character of the courtesy was French, but his majestic appearance unquestionably gave it something of the dignity of kings or great diplomats . . . He took [the story] from me, counted the pages of the manuscript, regarded the first page with great interest, leaned back in his chair. It was with a certain feeling of terror that I watched him begin to read in my presence. The minutes seemed to pass slowly; but this first view of his face, seen from one side, made a deep impression on me. It was a faultlessly handsome face. The soft, well-kept black beard gave it a clear, almost rectangular outline, into which the clean-cut nose, set exactly in the middle, fitted well, as did the high, slightly rounded forehead. But this beauty—perhaps almost too regular, too much like a work of art—was deepened by the gentle, almond-shaped eyes with their heavy black, melancholy lashes—ancient Oriental eyes in this somewhat French face in the style of Alphonse Daudet, in this face which would have seemed slightly artificial or effeminate, or suggestive of the beau, had not the thousand-year-old melancholy of his soul shone through it.[7]

It is clear that, in his maturity, at least, Herzl was aware of the impression he made on others. It is more than probable that it contributed to, and underlay, the sense of mission and special destiny which gripped him in the thirty-fifth year of his life and sustained him in all that he did until his death at forty-four—and which was clearly the principal driving force within him. But there was much else in his circumstances and in his personal physical and mental equipment to bolster his sense of special destiny or, at the very least, make it possible for him to play out the essentials of the role he set himself.

He was the single and beloved son of his parents; and the death of his only sister (when he was in his eighteenth year) and his own unsuccessful marriage bound parents and son together at a period in life when a common tendency is for parents and children to grow apart. Their moral support and approval were unvarying to the end of his life.[8] Without his father's generous financial support he would have been without the means to travel, to publish his newspaper, and to recruit the quasi-mercenary aid on which much of his political action in Constantinople depended. Herzl himself had a gift for clear, pungent, and witty exposition. He was something of a master of the literary style favoured in the Vienna of his time: brilliant in a rather brittle way and studded with paradox and arresting metaphor. He had made a small reputation for himself as a playwright and feuilletonist before he was thirty and in 1891 was invited to serve as Paris correspondent of the most prestigious of all Viennese newspapers, the *Neue Freie Presse*. In 1895 a special post was created for him—that of literary or feuilleton editor—to enable him to return to Vienna. And despite the implacable opposition to his ideas with which the *Presse*'s two Jewish publishers and editors, Bacher and Benedikt, faced him at every turn thereafter, cajoling him, threatening him if he did not desist, consistently refusing to

[7] Stefan Zweig, '"König der Juden"', in Meyer Weisgal (ed.), *Theodor Herzl*, New York, 1929, p. 56.
[8] Herzl's father died two years before his son; his mother outlived him.

refer to his political activities even in their news columns, and all in the knowledge that it was his post on the newspaper that guaranteed Herzl's initial entrée into the political arena and that he exploited it to the limit of its possibilities, his talents and personal prestige as an editor and littérateur were such that his chiefs never ventured to fulfil the threat of dismissal and were satisfied to leave it dangling over him. Soon after his return to Vienna the Prime Minister, Count Badeni, sought to provide him with a newspaper of his own if Herzl would undertake mild support of the government. All in all, on the strength of his abilities as a writer, he had made a substantial career for himself.

Herzl the intellectual was bright and sharp, however, rather than profound, and quick to abstract from life, rather than consider it in the round and in depth. 'Let life itself be your source, and not your brain', he was advised by Ernst Hartmann, a popular actor of the day. 'You are obviously gifted, you have talent, inventiveness, everything a playwright needs. But it seems to me that you ought to have a somewhat more respectful attitude towards humanity, you ought to look more deeply into it.'[9] His first essay (*c.* 1893) at a root-and-branch solution of the Jewish Question 'at least in Austria' was staggering in its combination of shallow thinking and high, even brilliant fantasy, to say nothing of the central role he conceived for himself. He, Herzl, would go to the Pope and enlist his aid for a great movement for the free and honourable conversion of Jews to Christianity.

Free and honourable by virtue of the fact that the leaders of this movement—myself in particular—would remain Jews and *as such* would propagate conversion to the faith of the majority. The conversion was to take place in broad daylight, Sundays at noon, in Saint Stephen's Cathedral, with festive processions and amidst the pealing of bells. Not in shame, as individuals have converted up to now, but with proud gestures. And because the Jewish leaders would remain Jews, escorting the people only to the threshold of the church and themselves staying outside, the whole performance was to be elevated by a touch of candour.[10]

Indeed, the cast of his mind is already apparent in the scheme: the sheer, almost insolent simplicity of the plan (which we have every reason to believe he propounded in all seriousness), the confidence in the power of transparent rationality to move other

[9] Quoted in Alex Bein, *Theodore Herzl*, Philadelphia, Pa., 1941, pp. 65–6.
[10] *Diaries*, i, p. 7. Italics added.

men's minds, the affection for the grand, theatrical gesture, the concern for detail and for staging; and, on the other hand, the astounding ignorance of, and insensitivity to his own subject-matter—the Jews themselves, let alone the painful, at times hideous, nature of their extended relations with the Roman Church; and finally, the readiness to abandon the plan without a tear and change course while the mind continued to grope for a solution and 'the [Jewish] question continually bored into me and gnawed at me, tormented me and made me very miserable.'[11]

A crank? All too easy to see him—and dismiss him—as such. But along with the extravagant vision there was an entirely uncrankish charm of manner, much wit, no little kindness, and a warm, winning, and, on occasion, self-deprecating sense of humour.

Some of you have probably heard that I want to found the Jewish State and have come here to have a look at this strange and amusing man who proposes . . . so unusual an enterprise . . . Others have probably heard of an extraordinary idea called Zionism which also promises to be an exceedingly amusing affair. Nothing certain is known about it. It is only said that all the Jews will suddenly pack their bags, leave the countries of their domicile, and sail away to a new and unknown country to settle . . . But in fact, ladies and gentlemen, Zionism intends no such wicked injury to our anti-Semites. Just imagine the clamour against the Jews disappearing from public life: what would remain!?[12]

And there was the professional journalist's eye for the social and political reality around him, for colour, for the opportunity to convert his material into an article at once incisive and gay, intelligent and witty, sarcastic where possible, and with half an eye, as was proper, on his readers in Vienna: on the Palais Bourbon as a political exchange and as a club; on socialism as the heir of Boulangism; on the verbal style of the French politician; on the impossibility of effective censorship and how the Parisian censors had saved a play from failure by forbidding its performance; and, before long, in much the same spirit, on the *Judenfrage* in its French mould.

In June 1892 a young Jewish officer in the French Army, a Captain Mayer, had challenged a notorious anti-Semite, the Marquis de Morès, to a duel, and was killed by a sabre thrust for his pains. The result was a sensation, a great public funeral, and a martyr's burial

[11] *Diaries*, i, p. 4.
[12] Address to the Österreichisch-Israelitische Union (an organization for the protection of Jewish civil rights), 7 November 1896.

with military honours. It may be said that there was something in the atmosphere of the affair that presaged the very much greater *affaire* that broke two years later and also hinged on the misfortunes of a Jewish *polytechnicien* and captain in the French Army.

Herzl duly reported the funeral, carefully linked duelling to Boulangism and the disappointed Boulangists to anti-Semitism, and went on to take the measure of anti-Semitism in France as a whole: 'Here the Jews are not thrown to the mob.' In the century in which the Jews were granted equality of rights the condition of the broad masses of the people had also improved beyond any expectation. Therefore, he argued, 'the French people still remain strangers to, and without understanding of, anti-Semitism.'[13]

It was his first published piece on the subject. Read plain, it was cautious, tentative, and, in so far as it offered a judgement, superficial and partly wrong. Its optimism was misleading. Read more carefully, the inner state of mind and the drift of his thinking on the subject is already apparent—notably in the wan irony of his opening reference to the pomp with which Mayer was buried, the great funeral cortège that followed his coffin, and the massed wreaths of flowers which hid it from sight.

Until recently [Herzl began his piece] there was a measure of decency in French anti-Semitism, one could almost say: courtesy . . . Even when it burst out against the Jews directly, it did not deny that they were human beings. For one coming here from other countries this was very surprising. In France the particular sin with which the Jews were charged is [only] that they are from Frankfurt [although] the injustice of the accusation is plain to see, for some of them are from Mainz and even from Speier. In money matters there is anger with them only if they have any. They are often called 'Israélites'—[a term] which must be seen in itself as [reflecting] an easier attitude. However, the Jews have been most fortunate of all in their death. When their brilliant lives, the subject of so much envy, duly come to a successful end, these Jewish humans are buried amongst the Christian humans. In the cemetery there is a remarkable degree of co-operation; it is a thoroughly mixed society, as if before death there had been no difference [between Jews and Christians] at all.[14]

Herzl had met anti-Semitism long before he got to France. He had been aware of it as a schoolboy, as a student, and as a young

---

[13] *Neue Freie Presse*, 3 September 1892.
[14] Ibid. The ironic comment on the charge that the Jews were from Frankfurt may be a reference to Drumont's taunt that the Alsatian Jews who moved into central France after 1870 were really from Cologne, Frankfurt, Hamburg, and Vilna.

adult. It was all around him in Hungary, in Austria, and in Germany. He had encountered it in all its forms, even the most vulgar. 'One evening I entered a cheap nightclub and drank a glass of beer. When I got up to leave and made my way to the door through the noise and the smoke, a fellow called "Hep, hep!" after me. A chorus of horse-laughs arose around him.'[15] And yet while 'The Jewish Question naturally lurked for me around every turn and corner [and] I sighed over it and made fun of it [and] felt unhappy, still it never really took hold of me.'[16] It was only in Paris that he had begun to think of it as a universal phenomenon, probably because only there could he regard it—and its proponents—with the cold eye of the comparatively uninvolved foreign correspondent and stranger in France who, yet, could not doubt on what side of *this* particular argument he himself stood. In Paris, as he noted in his diary, 'I could pass through the crowd unrecognized.' And his years in Paris were crucial to his development in another way: it was in Paris that 'I saw how the world is run.'[17]

Seeing 'how the world is run' in the intense, relatively open, highly personal world of *fin de siècle* French parliamentary politics left an indelible impression on Herzl's mind.[18] It served to mitigate his tendency—innate, as it would seem—to see and interpret the world in extravagantly generalized terms. It left him with a feel for the role of the individual in public affairs and for ever on the watch—and with a taste—for the secret, for what might lie behind the scenes, and for the intricacy of connection between private and public interests. And it taught him enough about the common varieties of behaviour on a central political stage to give him the initial confidence he needed when later he sought to operate upon such a one himself.

In a word, it was in Paris that he matured. He arrived at the age of thirty-one; he left at thirty-five. He had accepted the post of correspondent there, he wrote shortly before his return to Vienna, when his self-confidence was at its lowest ebb. Then 'Paris conquered me and shook me through and through.' There he had been subjected daily and hourly to 'hundreds of thousands of powerful stimuli' and became 'a different person, a different artist'.[19] It

---

[15] *Diaries*, i, p. 6.    [16] Ibid., p. 5.    [17] Ibid.

[18] He witnessed the unfolding of the Panama scandal among other great and unsavoury affairs of the day.

[19] Letter to Heinrich Teweles (of the Landestheater in Prague), 19 May 1895. A. Bein (ed.), *Igrot Herzl*, ii (May 1895–August 1897), Jerusalem, 1958, no. 4, p. 4.

was in Paris, finally, that he acquired a sense of his own powers and a passionate will to employ them in the matter which, ostensibly, he was so ill equipped to deal with, but which had 'gnawed' at him all the while. At first as an 'artist':

I was at the sculptor Beer who made my bust. During one of the sessions I described to him the modern Jew and his condition. And so I found myself engulfed in the white heat of great eruptions. [Und ich geriet dabei in die Glut der grossen Eruptionen.] When I left, the whole play shot upwards in me like a granite pillar; I began to write it the next day in indescribable excitement . . .

Herzl later called the play *The New Ghetto*. It took him 'three blessed weeks of ardour and labour', but none the less he failed to write himself 'free of the matter' as he seems to have hoped he would. On the contrary: 'The thought grew stronger in me that I must do something for the Jews.' For the first time since his arrival in Paris he visited the city's principal synagogue and was, as he noted, reminded there of his youth and, looking at the congregation, 'saw a family likeness in their faces: bold, misshapen noses; furtive and cunning eyes.' He considered writing 'a book for and about the Jews'; then, pressed by Alphonse Daudet to remember *Uncle Tom's Cabin*, turned to planning a novel. But the idea of a novel was dropped in turn. Instead, he drafted 'a practical programme' and noted in his newly begun diary that just how and why he had proceeded from one to the other 'is already a mystery to me, although it happened within the last few weeks. It is in the realm of the Unconscious.'[20]

The mystery remains—part of the larger mystery of Herzl's conversion (the term is appropriate) from a man privately disturbed by the phenomenon of anti-Semitism into one who tried to get to the bottom of the Jewish Question and resolve it—thereby endangering his professional reputation, as he was constantly reminded, incurring public anger and ridicule, cutting across the nervous grain of his own type and class, and being termed a Quixote, a St. Bernard the Hermit, the Mahdi of Pelikangasse, and, of course, King of the Jews. (He noted the epithets and recorded them without emotion in his diary.) The peculiar virulence of French anti-Semitism may well have shocked him; but the evidence does not support the theory that it was the Dreyfus Case—and in particular the scene of Dreyfus's public degradation at the École Militaire (which he witnessed as a journalist) when the mob screamed 'À mort! À mort les juifs!'—that changed the essentially conventional man of letters into a dissentient and an *exalté*. Dreyfus may have helped precipitate the change in the sense that the case (it was not yet an *affaire*) contributed to tipping the balance between the opposing drives within him. But the roots of his obsession lay deeper—that much is plain—even if they cannot now be laid bare.

Nor can it be demonstrated conclusively—for all that it is superficially plausible—that he saw himself as a (or the) Messiah. But there is abundant evidence that he had long been powerfully aware of the legend of the Messiah and was later fully conscious of the fact that some of the simpler and more ardent of his followers could hardly keep from seeing him as the annointed Deliverer himself. For the rest, it is only of the ambivalence of his feelings on the subject that we can be really sure. He first heard of Shabbetai Zevi, the 'false Messiah' of the seventeenth century, in June 1895: his curiosity was immediately aroused; the analogy was neither rejected nor exactly confirmed. Years later (June 1900) he noted in his diary—which served as a commonplace book as well—'The difference between myself and Shabbetai Zevi (the way I imagine him), apart from the difference in the technical means inherent in the times, is that Shabbetai made himself great so as to be the equal of the great of the earth. I, however, find the great small, as small as myself.'[21] During his visit to Russia the year before his death he remarked, 'Our people believe that I am the Messiah. I myself do not know this, for I am no theologian.'[22]

The delivery of the Jews from shame and bondage obsessed Herzl. He knew he was obsessed. He recognized the obsession as a source of strength. And it seems he took a keen delight in it. In a sense, it served him as the proof of the validity and importance of the enterprise upon which he had embarked.

For some time past I have been occupied with a work of infinite grandeur. At the moment I do not know whether I shall carry it through. It looks like a mighty dream. But for days and weeks it has possessed me beyond the limits of consciousness; it accompanies me wherever I go, hovers behind my ordinary talk, looks over my shoulder at my comically trivial journalistic work, disturbs me, and intoxicates me.[23]

---

[21] *Diaries*, iii, p. 960.
[22] Quoted in Joseph Nedava, 'Herzl and Messianism', *Herzl Year Book*, vii, New York, 1971, p. 26.          [23] *Diaries*, i, p. 3.

Thus the very first passage in his diary begun in May 1895. And like any sane man conscious that he is in the course of being propelled by powerful, semi-mystical drives, there is at first the fear of being taken for a madman—a fear redoubled by the perfectly clear-minded recognition of the incredible nature, the seeming extravagance and absurdity, of what he was about.

What do I have to say on the Jewish Question? [he wrote to Bismarck] Actually it is very hard for me to utter the word. For if I do, the first impulse of every rational human being must be to send me to the observation room—Department for Inventors of Dirigible Balloons.

Well, how shall I preface it? Perhaps this way: $2 \times 2 = 4$, $2 \times 3 = 6$, $17 \times 7 = 119$, unless I am mistaken. I have five fingers on each hand. And I am writing with violet ink. And now I shall finally risk it:

I believe I have found the solution to the Jewish Question. Not *a* solution, but *the* solution, the only one.[24]

[24] Ibid., p. 118. Bismarck never replied.

# 10

## *The Jews' State*

### i

HERZL did not set out to study his subject before pronouncing upon it. It did not occur to him to consider whether the Jewish Question might not be one with which he was insufficiently familiar. To his mind, it was not the facts that were in doubt, it was what was to be made of them. Nor did it occur to him to find out what, if anything, others had made of the Question. It was thus that his ideas were formulated and largely set before he had ever heard of Ḥibbat Ẓion and that he only heard of the movement when his own search for recruits brought him into contact with men who had real and first-hand knowledge of the Jewish social scene. Narcisse Leven of the Alliance Israélite Universelle told him in September 1895 that 'especially in Russia I would find many adherents'; and that in 'Odessa, for example, there had lived a man named Pinsker who had fought for the same cause'. Herzl noted in his diary that, unfortunately, Pinsker was already dead; and added: 'His writings are said to be worthwhile. Shall read them as soon as I have time.'[1] But months passed before he did so and it was not before February 1896, a few days before *Der Judenstaat* was published, that he finally read *Autoemancipation!* He promptly remarked on 'an astounding correspondence in the critical part, a great similarity in the constructive one'. But on balance he did not regret not knowing earlier what Pinsker had had to say because 'perhaps I would have abandoned my own undertaking.'[2] Moses Hess is referred to in his diary only in May 1897—along with Disraeli and George Eliot—as a 'representative exponent of the Zionist idea',[3] from which it is clear that even at the time he had only the haziest notions about him. He did not begin to read *Rome and Jerusalem* until 1898 on his visit

---

[1] *Diaries*, i, p. 243.　　[2] Ibid., p. 299.　　[3] Ibid., p. 548.

to Erez-Israel; and it was not until May 1901, on a long train journey, that he finally read the book through. In the event, Hess 'enraptured and uplifted' him. 'Everything that we have tried', he noted inaccurately, 'is already in his book. The only bothersome thing is his Hegelian terminology. Wonderful the Spinozistic-Jewish and nationalist elements. Since Spinoza Jewry had brought forth no greater spirit than this forgotten, faded Moses Hess!'[4]

But it is worth stressing that there was nothing unusual in a Central European Jew of Herzl's class, education, and experience of public affairs pronouncing confidently on the condition of the Jewish people, at any rate within the context of the *Judenfrage*. It was, after all, a question with which, in an important sense, he was familiar, with which he had lived throughout his life, and which formed the initial—and then often the sole—basis of his relations with other Jews, whether of his own class or any other. And it seems to have been enough for him that his own familiarity with the immediate and felt symptoms of a social issue did not prevent him from thinking afresh about its full extent and its ultimate origins, and from going so far as to question, and then sharply revise, his own opinions about it. Besides, he was a journalist and practised in the art of drawing rapid, clear, and reasonably valid, if essentially intuitive, conclusions from a mass of imperfectly digested evidence. This was how he had made his reputation; this was where much of his strength lay. And, although difficult to demonstrate conclusively, there seems no reason to doubt that he was fully aware that the force of his message was, above all, in its simplicity and that his own power, as its bearer, owed a great deal to his role as a great *simplificateur*. Herzl, as Clemenceau said of him in retrospect, was a man of action.[5] He distrusted subtlety, intricacy, verbal agility, compromise, demands for caution, concern for the views of others at the expense of one's own, and other such qualities that tend to obstruct rapid progress towards a stated goal. Nor, finally, did he think that antecedence in publication conferred any kind of privilege or authority.[6] He sensed quite rightly, that even if, in its bare

4 Ibid., iii, p. 1090.

5 'Clemenceau Remembers Herzl', Weisgal, op. cit., p. 26.

6 'This Birnbaum,' he noted in his diary just after the First Zionist Congress, 'who had deserted Zionism for Socialism three years before I appeared on the scene, poses obtrusively as my "predecessor". In his brazen begging-letters, which he wrote me and others, he sets himself up as the discoverer and founder of Zionism, because he has written a pamphlet like many another since Pinsker (whom, after all, I had not read either).' *Diaries*, ii, p. 584.

outline, neither his analysis of the predicament of Jewry nor his recipe for its salvation was in any vital, theoretical respect different from what had been propounded before, that the tone differed, that the climate of ideas and attitudes in which what he had to say had been conceived and in which the enterprise was to be carried forward was strikingly fresh, and, that, above all, both analysis and programme derived a particular force from the fact that the man who now propounded a solution to the Jewish Problem proposed to push his plans in practice with the same confidence and energy with which he had drafted them.

ii

Herzl's 'practical programme' was conceived in its essentials, made and remade, and given its definitive formulation in the course of the nine months between the spring of 1895 and the winter of that year. This is a short period, too short for the stages whereby his ideas evolved to be of much significance in themselves, the more so as the changes, such as they were, were less substantive than editorial and tactical: on the one hand, the labour of making and remaking his 'programme' helped him bring his ideas and his plans into sharper focus; on the other hand, he changed his mind about the audience to which he would address himself. Of course, the rethinking of what he had to say and the change of intended audience were connected one with the other: both processes followed from the fact that both in Herzl's mind and in Herzl's method argument and action were inseparable. Each of the successive formulations of his programme was drafted for immediate use, namely to win support for putting his plans into actual operation. Each was therefore conceived with a particular audience in mind. As hope of success dwindled in each case, a fresh audience came into view and an amended formulation was devised. And over all, each experience, each failure, impelled him marginally to revise his views and, in the end, radically to recast the form in which he presented them — and, once he had overcome his disappointment, to fortify himself for the stage that was to follow.

Herzl's plan required, as we shall see, the mobilization of a vast sum of money. This, together with his general social and political predilection for national leadership by a benign and high-minded aristocracy and an over-simple belief in the might of 'Jewish finance',[7] led him to begin by seeking out those two pillars of Jewish enterprise and wealth, Baron de Hirsch and the Rothschild family, first one and then the other. He met Hirsch, still the greatest (and best-known) Jewish philanthropist of the day, on 2 June. There had been a fortnight of uncertainty while Herzl waited for an answer to his request for an interview and he was keyed-up, unsure of himself, over-loaded with voluminous notes, and incapable of suppressing an urge to demonstrate that he was the millionaire's social and intellectual equal, not a mendicant, not another *schnorrer*. He lectured Hirsch on the Jews' lack of political leadership and on the futility of Hirsch's own programme for Jewish migration to settlements in Argentina. He spoke of an army, and of men being fired more effectively by ideas than by the prospect of material assistance, of going to the Kaiser, and of persuading the Jewish plutocracy to finance an exodus. But he did not get beyond setting out a third of what he had wished to say and Hirsch, it seems, did not know what to make of his visitor. He listened and he was polite. But he made it plain that he had not been won over by any of Herzl's arguments and, as he appears to have been reluctant to decide whether he should take Herzl seriously, he avoided even that minimal commitment by chaffing Herzl gently and by making sardonic remarks about Jews in general, both rich and poor. It was agreed that they would meet again, but it was clear the meeting had been a failure; and 'once home [Herzl] immediately rushed to [his] writing-desk' to write to Hirsch at great length, in an effort to expound more clearly what he had tried to tell him face to face. The letter was a carefully written attempt to keep Hirsch interested and to make a further meeting possible. Only its pugnacious undertone suggested he had already virtually written Hirsch off as an ally, and that his thoughts had already begun to turn elsewhere.

On 28 June, still from Paris, he wrote to the head of the Vienna

---

[7] Herzl combined great personal fastidiousness in money matters with what is hard not to describe as an ex-member of a duelling fraternity's revulsion from those less inhibited about money than he. This was of a piece with his conception of a just society led by a class of noble men whose social influence and standards would gradually percolate downwards. Hence the ambiguity in his attitude to the Jewish rich—a self-established, generally accepted, but (because it was founded on money) flawed aristocracy. And hence, perhaps, his tendency to make the same, vulgar mistake about the grandees of Jewry that so many contemporary anti-Semites made, namely that the rich, because they were Jews, constituted a significant class, bound by common ties, in a word, the 'Jewish financial force' of the literature on Jewry, when in fact they were a class only in the very narrow sense of having certain common attributes while being virtually devoid of significant common bonds.

branch of the Rothschild family, Baron Albert. 'I shall come to the point without preliminaries. I have composed a memorandum about the Jewish Question for the German Kaiser.' It would be delivered at the end of July or at the beginning of August, he informed the Baron, and he himself would be in Vienna in July. 'If you would like to know what is in the document, I shall read it to you.' If not, 'it will be quite sufficient for you to return this letter to me.'[8]

It is not clear how serious Herzl was about presenting a memorandum to the Kaiser at this stage. Conceivably, if he had made progress with the Rothschilds he would have wanted to go on to Berlin—with their help. In any event, his main concern was with the Rothschilds themselves and he went to a great deal of trouble to prepare himself for an encounter with them. He wanted 'half a day' with Albert Rothschild. (Hirsch had been asked for 'an hour or two' of his time.) He had in mind a gathering of 'the Family Council' at which he would read an 'Address'—a detailed exposition of his ideas. The notes for it, drafted between 13 and 17 June, come to some 25,000 words,[9] many times longer than his notes for the meeting with Hirsch. He worked out exactly what he would say and how he would say it. He intended to worry the Rothschilds, to flatter them, to inspire them. He hoped to appeal both to their good sense and self-interest as men of the world and of business, and to their sense of honour and *noblesse oblige*. It is of interest that in his draft he touched a passionate, even apocalyptic note which is sounded nowhere else so clearly (and which, with a view to maintaining a sober front, he might well have abstained from striking had he had the opportunity to meet the Vienna Rothschilds in person):

. . . we must finally end up at the bottom, rock bottom. What appearance this will have, what form this will take, I cannot surmise. Will it be a revolutionary expropriation from below or a reactionary confiscation from above? Will they chase us away? Will they kill us?

I have a fair idea that it will take all these forms, and others. In one of the countries, probably France, there will come a social revolution whose first victims will needs be the big bankers and the Jews.

Anyone who has, like myself, lived in this country [i.e. France] for a few years as a disinterested and detached observer can no longer have any doubts about this.

---

[8] *Diaries*, ii, pp. 189-91; *Igrot*, ii, no. 16, pp. 30-1.　　　[9] *Diaries*, i, pp. 129-83.

In Russia there will simply be confiscation from above. In Germany they will make emergency laws as soon as the Kaiser can no longer manage the Reichstag. In Austria people will let themselves be intimidated by the Viennese rabble and deliver up the Jews. There, you see, the mob can achieve anything once it rears up. It does not know this yet, but the leaders will teach it.

So they will chase us out of these countries, and in the countries where we take refuge they will kill us.[10]

Was there no salvation for the Jews? Only through 'a very old, very famous, well-tried' manœuvre: an exodus. He then went on to outline how the exodus was to be organized and the Jews to be resettled.[11]

Herzl waited for an answer and counted the days. On 4 July he noted, 'Albert R's reply, which was due today, has not come. Fortunately I did not degrade myself by excessive courtesy in my letter.'[12] (The letter was duly delivered to Baron Albert Rothschild, as Herzl later discovered, on 5 July, but Rothschild did not reply, nor did he return the letter.)

At the end of July he left Paris. His last two months there had been a period of growing inner tension. (11 June: 'I am shunning all my acquaintances. They tread on my toes, having no idea of the world I come from; this makes daily living terribly irritating.'[13] He still kept his ideas almost entirely to himself. His mind was continually racing ahead, day-dreaming, sketching plans for action (item number four: 'More publicity, on the largest scale. Make Europe laugh at it, swear at it—in short, talk about it'); noting down desirable recruits (the *wunder-rebbe* of Sadagora 'to be brought over and installed as something like the bishop of a province'); and inventing a state ('majestic professional marches for great festive occasions', 'tobacco plantations, silk factories', 'all officials in uniform, trim, with military bearing, but not ludicrously so').[14] His one attempt to put his ideas before a friend met with pity and ridicule and pained him terribly. The number of men with whom he found himself in tune even on the general issue of the condition of Jewry was tiny. Only one was in any sense notable: Max Nordau,[15] a German-speaking, Hungarian Jew, a journalist of note, the author

[10] Ibid., pp. 131–2.
[11] On 7 June he had noted in his diary: 'The Exodus under Moses bears the same relation to this project as a Shrovetide play by Hans Sachs does to a Wagner opera.' Ibid., p. 38.
[12] Ibid., p. 192.    [13] Ibid., pp. 73–4.    [14] Ibid., pp. 32–5.
[15] The others were two of the three Marmorek brothers.

of a number of extremely bold and pessimistic analyses of contemporary society of which the best known were *Die conventionellen
Lügen der Kulturmenschheit* and *Entartung*, a playwright, a short-
story writer—in a word, a man remarkably like Herzl himself,
except that he was grounded in traditional Jewish learning, of
superior literary gifts, of greater repute as a man of letters, and eleven
years older. Again, somewhat like Herzl, but over a longer period,
Nordau had been struck (as Hess had been) by the futility and
indignity of the emancipated Jew's attempt to escape his origins,
by the depth of the roots of anti-Semitism in modern society, and
by the sick and hysterical character of the anti-Semitic movement,
especially in Germany. Faint signs of this appeared even in those
of his writings which dealt with general social problems. For
example, ridiculing the vain and brutal attempts of established and
reactionary authority to cope with the ferment in society, he drew
attention to the fact that, meanwhile, 'the dark mass of the people
. . . entertains itself by plundering and killing the Jews during these
tedious consultations of its physicians; casting greedy glances at the
castles of the nobility while it is destroying the taverns and synagogues of the Hebrews.'[16] Now when Nordau and Herzl discussed
the Jewish Question—'Each took the words right out of the other's
mouth. I never had such a strong feeling that we belonged together.'[17] But Herzl still kept his own counsel so far as the *solution*
to the Question was concerned, even with Nordau.

Back in Vienna he was therefore ready to revise his tactics somewhat. 'I don't need the rich Jews—but I do need men!' he wrote
to Moritz Güdemann, the Chief Rabbi of Vienna. 'Damn it, they
are hard to find!'[18] He read Güdemann the 'address' he had prepared for the Rothschilds, but the rabbi's response was ambiguous:
Herzl the man captivated him; Herzl's ideas frightened him.[19]
However, it was through Güdemann that he made the acquaintance
of Narcisse Leven of the Alliance Israélite Universelle, and Leven,
sceptical and somewhat impatient with Herzl himself, told him,

---

[16] *Conventional Lies of Our Civilization*, English edition from the seventh German edition,
London, 1898, pp. 3–4.

[17] *Diaries*, i, p. 196.

[18] 21 July 1895. *Igrot*, ii, no. 20, p. 36.

[19] The Chief Rabbi later published a more or less open attack upon Herzl's views. Both
men were served by the same publisher and the latter informed Herzl that as soon as Güdemann's book appeared Albert Rothschild ordered thirty copies of it. On relations between
the two see Josef Fraenkel, 'The Chief Rabbi and the Visionary', in J. Fraenkel (ed.), *The
Jews of Austria*, London, 1970.

as we have seen, about Pinsker and about Hibbat Zion in Eastern Europe. It was also Leven who advised him to make contact with the Grand Rabbi of France, Zadoc Kahn (whom he described— inaccurately, as Herzl later found out—as 'an ardent Zionist') and who mentioned Colonel Goldsmid to him ('I will keep the Colonel in mind', Herzl noted).[20]

Others were sounded out, very occasionally with success. The chief economic correspondent of his own newspaper, sworn to secrecy, 'was gripped, shaken, did not consider me crazy at all, and actually had no objections from the point of view of finance and economics. The objections he did make only showed me that he took my outline completely seriously.'[21] But generally matters were otherwise. 'I noticed how Dessauer's eyes began to gleam. I arouse enthusiasm in everyone whom I tell about the Jewish cause.' But on the following day, he noted: 'Spoke to Dessauer once more. In the meantime he had become lukewarm. Finished.'[22]

He became impatient and noted in his diary: barely any progress, only 'various steps forward and backward'. Then, on 15 October he wrote, 'I definitely need a newspaper for the cause';[23] and a few days later, on an impulse, he asked his chief on the *Neue Freie Presse*, Moritz Benedikt, for support: he wanted 'a smaller paper', alongside the big one, as a vehicle for his ideas, or else 'a Sunday edition with "The Solution of the Jewish Question", by Dr. Theodor Herzl, on the front page' and a regular column 'The Jewish Question' thereafter to contain the public discussion that would follow. Neither Benedikt nor his colleague Bacher had ever admitted to a special concern for Jewish problems in their news-paper. Nor could Herzl have seriously believed that they would now transform themselves; and, indeed, Benedikt was politely hostile and promised nothing. None the less, Herzl himself was invigorated and cheered by what he recognized as the new bold tack he had adopted. 'I have set myself in motion. Everything up to now has only been dreams and talk. Action has begun because I shall have the *Neue Freie Presse* either with me or against me.'[24]

He was still pre-eminently the journalist. It was as such that he had made his name—evidence, in itself, of the power of the printed word, and underscored by the Prime Minister's flattering offer to establish a newspaper for him to edit if he would promise political

[20] *Diaries*, i, pp. 242–3.    [21] Ibid., pp. 240–1.    [22] Ibid., p. 246.
[23] Ibid., p. 244.    [24] Ibid., p. 247.

support. The urge to abandon caution and publish his views—if possible on the pages of the *Neue Freie Presse* ('if I now gained the prestige of the *Neue Freie Presse* for my cause, it would surely be victorious!'),[25] if not, elsewhere—was therefore a strong and natural one. Moreover, it was now to be sedulously fed by his own chiefs on the *Presse*, who, to humour him and to help wean him away for a while from the Prime Minister, encouraged him to think that they might end by giving him the freedom of their pages. As further bait, they advised him to take leave of absence to go abroad again, to Paris or London, to form a 'study group' to consider the entire issue in appropriate depth. And as this, as it happened, fitted well with the mild prospect of support in France and England that Leven had held out to him, the temptation to travel again was probably irresistible.[26]

The final—and, it may be, the decisive—influence leading to this change of tactic and pace at the end of 1895 was Herzl's father.[27] His son had kept him abreast of his plans and movements and Jakob Herzl soon informed him that he disliked the idea of an approach to the Jewish magnates, and to the Rothschilds in particular. It was undignified and unlikely to succeed. The Rothschilds would not listen to others' advice about what was good for them. Nothing that had occurred in Austria in recent times, not even the September elections in Vienna,[28] indicated an inexorable strengthening of the anti-Semitic movement. And if this was his, Jakob's, view, it was unlikely that the Rothschilds would think otherwise.

[25] *Diaries*, i, p. 256.

[26] There is no direct evidence that Benedikt and Bacher knew of Herzl's meeting with Leven, let alone of what Leven had said to him. But it is not impossible that Herzl himself had told them something of Ḥibbat Zion in Paris, if only as an indicator of potential support for his case. One way or another, there is abundant evidence that both his chiefs treated Herzl and spoke of him as a gifted, but naïve and priggish man—or, in the Yiddish slang term, a *shmock* (as Herzl himself recorded in his diary on one occasion).

[27] That Herzl's parents exerted a dominant influence at this and other points in their son's career is argued with great conviction, but not wholly conclusively, in Y. Z. Zahavi, *Me-hitbolelut le-zionut: mekor zioniuto shel Herzl*, Jerusalem, 1972, pp. 27–66.

[28] The anti-Semitic Christian-Social party led by Karl Lueger won its famous landslide election to the Vienna City Council in September 1895. Herzl saw his views confirmed. True, compared with the clamour of popular politics in Paris, it was a relatively calm affair. But that made it all the more sinister, to his mind. The 'looks of hatred everywhere' were unmistakable. On election day 'toward evening I went to the Landstrasse district. In front of the polling place a silent, tense crowd. Suddenly Dr. Lueger came out to the square. Enthusiastic cheers; women waved white kerchiefs from the windows. The police held the crowd back. A man next to me said with tender warmth, but in a quiet tone of voice: "That is our Führer!"' (*Diaries*, i, p. 244).

It was not to the grandees but to 'the little men' that he should turn, Herzl's father told him. Banded together, they would form 'a mighty river'. They were capable of setting up the Jewish state and they would do so. But if it was millions who were to be influenced, then a book or popular pamphlet had to be written and the idea of founding a Jewish state published 'throughout the civilized world'.[29]

Herzl's brief journey to Paris, to London, and again to Paris (from the middle of November 1895 to the end of that month) was decisive for all that followed. He set off in a new mood and with new tactical purposes. He sought out certain notables both within and without the formal structures of the Jewish communities in France and Great Britain. He was listened to attentively by all and made a number of important converts. He appeared for the first time on a semi-public platform and he undertook to publish his views in some detail in the press. He ceased to grope for a method; and, on the other hand, he began to find the role he had assumed ever more congenial. Virtually all his remaining doubts dropped away: he returned to Vienna with his mind made up, confirmed in his beliefs and in the task he had set himself, and publicly committed to both.

In Paris, Herzl met Zadoc Kahn three times, and then once more on his return journey through Paris back to Vienna. He read him his 'address to the Rothschild's' with all references to the family carefully eliminated. The Chief Rabbi then brought others to meet him and on each occasion Herzl set out his arguments and rebutted objections with mild, but steadily growing, impatience: his tone, on his own evidence, became sharper and moderately aggressive, his judgements on those he spoke to harsher. 'Zadoc Kahn is of the breed of *little* Jews'; 'Becker is a typical Jew from the Latin Quarter . . . He reeks of books and conventional patriotism.' He ridiculed their emphasis on their French nationality. 'What? Don't you and . I belong to the same nation? Why did you wince when Lueger was elected? Why did I suffer when Captain Dreyfus was accused of high treason?'[30] He also sensed and despised their timidity. When Zadoc Kahn recommended that he send his text to Edmond de Rothschild, Herzl was peremptory: 'Wouldn't dream of it.'[31]

[29] Jakob to Theodor Herzl, 26 October 1895. CZA, H II C1.
[30] *Diaries*, i, pp. 272, 273, 275.          [31] Ibid., p. 285.

In the end, he wrote French Jewry off, while noting with some relish that he was becoming a public figure even among them. 'I recognized the impression I had made on [Zadoc Kahn] most clearly of all when the door opened for a second and an elderly lady—presumably Zadoc's wife—peered in through the crack with curiosity. This moment revealed to me what he must have told people about me.'[32]

His one success in Paris was with Nordau whom he met once more and to whom, this time, he spoke without reserve. Nordau understood the argument 'in a flash', Herzl noted with elation, and 'as an adherent'.[33] This was overstated. Nordau never lost a measure of critical reserve and his adherence to Herzl was not as complete at that stage, even for immediate practical purposes, as Herzl at first believed. But Nordau did prove an ally. He promised support, spoke to Herzl of the need to translate the 'pamphlet' (into which the 'address' to the family council of the Rothschilds was now to be transmuted) into Yiddish and Hebrew 'for the Russians', advised Herzl whom to meet in London, and wrote a valuable letter of introduction for him to Israel Zangwill.

Thursday there will call upon you an intimate friend of mine, Dr. Herzl, LL.D., sub-editor of the Vienna 'Neue Freie Presse', which, as I dare say you know, is one of the leading papers on our continent. Besides, Dr. Herzl is a great scholar, and an author of renown in Germany. He has written several plays that have achieved considerable success.

So much for the author. The man is a thorough gentleman and a serious, if somewhat enthusiastic, mind. He has worked out a scheme for resolving the anti-Semitic question and is coming to London for the purpose of trying to secure for his plan the moral support of the leading Jews . . .[34]

Zangwill, four years younger than Herzl, had already made his literary reputation with *Children of the Ghetto* (1892) and was a man of considerable standing within the rather narrow circuit of the English Jewish intelligentsia of the times. He received Herzl well and arranged a series of meetings, the most important of which were with the editor of the *Jewish Chronicle* (Asher Myers), with Goldsmid, and with the Chief Rabbi (Hermann Adler), who passed him on, in turn, to the banker and Member of Parliament, Sir Samuel

---

[32] *Diaries*, i, p. 274.    [33] Ibid., p. 272.
[34] Nordau to Zangwill, 17 November 1895. CZA, A 120/61.

Montagu, potentially the most useful contact of all.[35] At Nordau's request, Zangwill also brought him to the Maccabeans, a society whose membership Zangwill himself once described as consisting of 'such Jews as are untainted by commerce'—authors, artists, and professionals.

Throughout, Herzl was well received in London and listened to politely and with interest. He seems to have spoken with even more self-confidence and decisiveness than in Paris. And the sharp side of his ambivalent attitude to the wealthy and powerful was much in evidence. He rejected a proposal that the question of setting up a study group—the nominal purpose of his visit—'must first be submitted to the prominent Jews: Lord Rothschild, Mocatta, Montefiore, etc.' He told his new friends that 'You can't make me yield to majorities', and that 'This is the cause of the poor Jews, not of the rich ones. The protest of the latter is null, void, and worthless.'[36] On another occasion he said, that 'Whoever goes along with me is welcome. I am first turning to the notable Jews who have made a name for themselves by their past efforts, but I do not need them. It will only please me if respected people join with me. But I am not dependent on them.'[37]

The results were promising, if not more. Montagu made no binding commitment, but was markedly friendly and sympathetic. The contrast with Hirsch could not but have been much in Herzl's mind. Simeon Singer, the rabbi of the well-to-do congregation at the New West End Synagogue, became his ally. The meeting with Goldsmid was particularly warm and Herzl took the Colonel to his heart 'like a brother'. The editor of the *Jewish Chronicle* asked for a pre-publication summary of his pamphlet. He met with no nastiness (as he had in Vienna and Paris), but rather with a great deal of sympathy—some of it cautious, but some of it enthusiastic—and this while conducting his conversations in German and French which few of those he met knew well and some did not know at all. All in all, he had good reason to be pleased and to recross the Channel in a greatly improved state of mind.

Back in Vienna, Herzl gave his pamphlet its final form in the course of the first half of the month of December. It took him another month before he found a publisher for it. Meanwhile, on 17 January, the résumé, entitled 'A Solution to the Jewish Problem', appeared on three and a half dense columns in the *Jewish Chronicle*

[35] On Montagu, see below, pp. 302 f.        [36] *Diaries*, i, p. 283.        [37] Ibid., p. 279.

—his first irrevocable 'step into the public arena'—accompanied by editorial comment. 'We may safely assert', wrote the *Jewish Chronicle*'s leader writer, 'that this is one of the most astounding pronouncements which have ever been put forward on the Jewish Question.' What he found most strange was that 'the plan had been promulgated at all and that its author is a man of Dr. Herzl's type . . . a distinguished journalist and littérateur of the first rank in Vienna, no dreamer of dreams but a practical man of the world whose position on the staff of the *Neue Freie Presse* commands attention for all that he writes'. The *Jewish Chronicle* was not convinced by Herzl's arguments, but nor did it dismiss them, let alone jeer. 'We hardly anticipate a great future for a scheme which is the outcome of despair . . . Dr. Herzl's picture is coloured with a hard brush, but we must admit sadly enough that he is in a position from which he has good means of discerning the truth.'

The sensation was mild, however. Two letters to the editor were published the following week and a third letter the week after, then silence. In Vienna, as the news and the gist of what he had to say trickled back, there was some ridicule ('the Jewish Jules Verne'), some expressions of concern ('you will do the Jews terrible harm'), very heavy pressure from his chiefs on the *Neue Freie Presse* to desist, and covert threats to dismiss him if he did not. The only encouragement was from Jewish students who had read the article in German translation and came to invite him to a meeting of their society. When he arrived they greeted him with long, tempestuous applause and plied him with questions. 'A regular state?', he was asked; 'a real state on its own territory, with its own laws, inhabited, governed, and administered by Jews?'[38]

It was laughter Herzl feared more than anything—being 'marked down for a fool'—when the pamphlet finally appeared. But he was barely less concerned for his livelihood and for the loss of status if forced out of his post on the *Presse*. On the other hand, to retreat was contrary to every one of his principles of conduct. 'I am not a little boy who backs out of something at the last moment', he told Güdemann who tried, in a friendly enough fashion, to encourage him to do so before it was too late.[39] Besides, the article in the *Jewish Chronicle* had committed him. 'My 500 copies came this evening [14 February]', he recorded in his diary, that extraordinary

[38] Erwin Rosenberger, *Herzl as I Remember Him*, New York, 1959, p. 14.
[39] *Diaries*, i, p. 293.

document, remarkable as much for its detail and accuracy as for the simplicity with which every item is noted down, with barely a thought for the vanity and weakness which are laid bare along with the virtue and determination. 'When I had the bundle carted to my room, I was terribly shaken.' And the following day: 'Oppenheim made some jokes last night at the office. He wants to have my pamphlet bound. "If you are *meshugge* [crazy], have yourself bound', he said. I must be prepared for this sort of thing. The grown-up street urchins will be at my heels. But a man who is to carry the day in thirty years has to be considered crazy for the first two weeks.'[40] Three days later he had pulled himself together, recovered his style, and, as his first act, sent a copy to the Prime Minister, Count Badeni. 'This pamphlet', he wrote in the accompanying letter, 'will presumably cause a certain commotion: laughter, outcries, wails, abuse, misunderstanding, stupidities, baseness. I face all these things with the utmost composure. *Les chiens aboient—la caravane passe.*'[41]

### iii

Pinsker's *Autoemancipation!* was the work of a tired and elderly man. It was written, it will be recalled,[42] in some haste and in anger. Its emphasis was on the diagnosis of the ills of Jewry. Western Jews were invited to recognize that there was no salvation for them in universal liberalism, any more than for their kinsmen in the East, and that Jewry could redeem and liberate itself only if it took its affairs into its own hands. And since only the westerners were free to act, because only they had the experience and the resources and the influence, the heavier responsibility was theirs. Pinsker's *programme* was sketchy, almost perfunctory: the western leaders would call a congress and set up a directorate to find a haven and to manage the migration. The details would be worked out by those who responded. The main thing—and Pinsker's immediate purpose—was to stimulate that response. He saw no role for himself; in fact it did not at first occur to him that there should be one. It was only under pressure, as we have seen, and, indirectly, because there was no response of any consequence in the West, that he reluctantly took the lead among his own people in the East.

There is thus a sense in which the advent of Herzl can be seen

[40] Ibid., pp. 299–300.    [41] Ibid., p. 302.    [42] See above, pp. 126 ff.

as a much delayed, fortuitous, and of course unconscious response to Pinsker's summons. The more so as their thinking on many points, theoretical as well as practical, was remarkably alike. But there were three cardinal differences between them. The first was that Pinsker had intended his pamphlet as a single and discrete act—he called it a *Mahnruf*, a warning. It was for others, those who, as he hoped, would learn the lesson he wished to teach, to take the next step. Herzl, on the other hand and as we have seen, wrote his pamphlet as one move, one attempt among others (and after other moves had failed), to set his campaign in motion. The second difference was in the role each conceived for himself in what was to follow. While Pinsker gave no thought to it, in Herzl's case it was crucial to his thinking, and to all that he did in practice, that the central and leading role was his. The third difference was that Herzl's emphasis was on prescription, rather than diagnosis. He called his pamphlet *Der Judenstaat: Versuch einer modernen Lösung der Judenfrage*—commonly translated *The Jewish State*, but better rendered *The Jews' State: An Attempt at a Modern Solution of the Jewish Question*.[43]

*Der Judenstaat* is the length of a novella—some 30,000 words. It is written in a clear, light style by a man intent on getting it read. Its author is at pains to be absolutely unambiguous. 'The idea which I have developed in this pamphlet', reads its first sentence, 'is a very old one: it is the restoration of the Jewish State.' It is devoid of pathos. 'I do not intend to arouse sympathetic emotions on our behalf. That would be a foolish, futile, and undignified proceeding.' Its argument is intended to be set (and judged) within the terms of the forward-looking, practical, scientifically and socially advanced, optimistic, and liberal current of contemporary thinking. 'Whoever would attempt to convert the Jew into a husbandman [i.e. Baron de Hirsch] would be making an extraordinary mistake.' The peasant's tools and often his costume are identical with those of his earliest forefathers. 'His plough is unchanged; he carries the

---

[43] Seventeen editions of *Der Judenstaat* were published in Herzl's lifetime, that is, between 1896 and 1904: five in German, three in Russian, two in Hebrew, two in English, and one each in Yiddish, French, Romanian, Bulgarian, and German printed in Hebrew characters. In all editions over which he had some control he made a point of using his academic title (Doctor der Rechte), presumably, by way of emphasizing his utter seriousness and the distinction he wanted drawn between Herzl the propounder of a solution of the Jewish problem and Herzl the fashionable journalist and playwright. See H. Avrahami and A. Bein, 'Ha-hoẓa'ot shel "Medinat ha-yehudim" le-Teodor Herzl', in Daniel Carpi (ed.), *Ha-Ẓionut*, i, Tel Aviv, 1970, p. 465 and fn.

seed in his apron; mows with the . . . scythe and threshes with the . . . flail. But we know that all this can be done with machinery . . . The peasant is consequently a type which is in course of extinction . . . It is absurd and, indeed, impossible to make modern peasants on the old pattern . . .'

*Der Judenstaat* assumes the underlying harmony of human interests, the ultimate compatibility and conjunction of social forces, even those which are, on one level and in the short term, unalterably and bitterly opposed.

The [organized and self-initiated] departure of the Jews will involve no economic disturbances, no crises, no persecutions; in fact, the countries they abandon will revive to a new period of prosperity. There will be an inner migration of Christian citizens into the positions evacuated by Jews . . . The Jews will leave as honoured friends; and if some of them return, they will receive the same favourable treatment at the hands of civilized nations as is accorded to all foreign visitors.[44]

*Der Judenstaat* appeals throughout to the reason, the imagination, and the instinctive virtue of its readers. It seeks to anticipate their views and correct them. All in all, it is an orderly and workmanlike piece of writing: the problem, its solution, the method whereby matters are to be advanced, the legitimacy of the proposed means to advance them, the likely character of the result, and finally the answers to probable lines of criticism are all clearly and explicitly laid out.

For Herzl was at pains to persuade his readers that his was a down-to-earth, sensible, *feasible* plan. It was not Utopian. A Utopia may be an ingenious piece of machinery, he says; the problem is always to show how it can be set in motion. But here there was no doubt of the existence, nor of the identity, of a very powerful propelling force: the misery of the Jews. And thus the real questions were how best to employ it, to what machinery it was best harnessed, how that machinery was best constructed. Of course, he wrote, the plan would seem absurd if a single individual attempted to execute it.

But, if worked by a number of Jews in cooperation, it would appear perfectly rational and its accomplishment would present no difficulties worth mentioning. The idea depends only on the number of its supporters . . . It depends on the Jews themselves whether this political pamphlet remains for the present a political romance. If the present

---

[44] *The Jewish State*, trans. Sylvie d'Avigdor (1896), revised trans. Israel Cohen (1934), Introduction.

generation is too dull to understand it rightly, a future, finer and better generation will arise to understand it. The Jews who wish for a State shall have it; and they will deserve to have it.[45]

The source and context of the Jewish Question, in Herzl's view, are the pressure under which all Jews, in all countries, are subject. The pressure varies in degree and kind, but the phenomenon is a general one. 'In our economically upper classes it causes discomfort; in our middle classes continual and grave anxieties; in our lower classes absolute despair.' 'The nations in whose midst the Jews live are all either covertly or openly anti-Semitic.' Why this should be so is not of great interest to Herzl. On the rise and growth of modern anti-Semitism, he is brief and superficial: 'Its remote cause is our loss of the power of assimilation during the Middle Ages; its immediate cause is our excessive production of mediocre intellects who cannot find [a social and economic] outlet downwards or upwards.'[46] It is in this connection that his familiarity with the condition and *mores* of upper middle-class western Jewry exclusively is most marked—and with it his limited, unhistorical, and, in some ways, self-contradictory view of the nature and sources of Jewish nationhood. On the one hand, there is a faint, but constant echo of ancient dignities. It is a 'new Jewish State' that he wishes to advance. Yet, on the other hand, 'we have honestly endeavoured everywhere to merge ourselves in the social life of surrounding communities'; and, in another passage: 'We are one people—our enemies have made us one without our consent.' But in fact Herzl's interests lie elsewhere. Origins are less important to him than consequences. 'Everything tends to one and the same conclusion, clearly enunciated in that classic Berlin phrase: *Juden raus!*' ('out with the Jews!'). The Jewish Question is therefore an immediate and practical one. 'Are we to get out now, and if so, where to? Or, may we yet remain? And how long?' His own answer is that they— or, at any rate, most of them—cannot stay. The pressures are rising. The logic of the Jewish social situation is inexorable. 'When we sink, we become a revolutionary proletariat, the subordinate officers of all revolutionary parties; and at the same time, when we rise, there rises too our terrible power of the purse.' The Jews cannot wait for 'the ultimate perfection of humanity'. Assimilation— which he himself does not desire (for 'Our national character is too

[45] *The Jewish State*, Preface.          [46] Ibid., chapter 2.

historically famous, and in spite of every degradation too fine, to make its annihilation desirable')—is out of the question, if only because the Jews will not be left in peace long enough to allow them to merge with the surrounding peoples. Nothing is to be gained, however, by petty attempts to transfer a few thousand Jews from one country to another. 'They either come to grief at once, or prosper; and then their prosperity creates anti-Semitism.' So they must leave, but leave in great numbers and in an orderly and planned and purposeful manner. And they must enter not another people's country, but their own.

Distress binds us together and, thus united, we suddenly discover our strength. Yes, we are strong enough to form a state and, indeed, a model state. We possess all human and material resources necessary for the purpose . . .

Let sovereignty be granted us over a portion of the globe large enough to satisfy the rightful requirements of a nation; the rest we shall manage for ourselves.[47]

Herzl's plan, as he himself put it, was 'simple in design, but complicated in execution'. It was of two parts: assumption of responsibility for Jewish national affairs by a political body to be called the Society of Jews; and management of both the exodus of the Jews and their resettlement by a technical body to be called the Jewish Company. The first was to treat with governments, seek to obtain their consent to an assumption of Jewish sovereignty 'over a neutral piece of land', and then administer the territory as a provisional government. The second was to take the form of a Chartered Company, established in London under English law. It was to be endowed with a large working capital and designed to assume responsibility for the liquidation of the migrants' assets in their countries of origin and then provide land, housing, and employment in the new country in exchange. It was to promote industry and commerce—all in an enlightened and progressive spirit exemplified by insistence on a seven-hour working day, severe restriction on women's labour, attractive and healthy housing, good schools 'conducted on the most approved modern systems', and whatever else could be devised to contribute to the establishment of a decent life in the new country. It is to the Jewish Company that the longest chapter in *Der Judenstaat* is devoted.

It is characteristic of Herzl's fertile mind and of his strong belief

[47] Ibid.

that the Jews' state should be founded on clearly formulated principles of social justice that he goes into considerable detail on some points in his pamphlet. Thus on the 'workmen's dwellings' which the Company is to erect:

They will resemble neither those melancholy workmen's barracks of European towns, nor those miserable rows of shanties which surround factories; they will certainly present a uniform appearance because the Company must build cheaply . . . but the detached houses in little gardens will be united into attractive groups in each locality. The natural configuration of the land will arouse the ingenuity of those of our young architects whose ideas have not yet been cramped by routine . . . The Synagogue will be visible from long distances, for it is only our ancient faith that has kept us together.[48]

Herzl is also at pains to explain just how he envisages the migration of the Jews to their country—the process whereby they will be given a new home 'not by dragging them ruthlessly out of their sustaining soil, but rather by transplanting them carefully to better ground'. He touches on how they will travel, in what groups, who will lead each group, how the aged will be cared for ('. . . we shall not relegate the old to an almshouse. An almshouse is one of the cruellest charities which our stupid good nature invented'), how the sites for towns will be selected, and what he expects will impel middle-class Jews to stir out of their existing relative comfort ('the bright, young, and ambitious professionals will be attracted by the opportunities provided by the Society and the Company; and they will draw the others after them').

In contrast to the many pages devoted to the mechanics and finances of the exodus, the discussion of the workings of the political instrument he had in mind, the Society of Jews, the 'organ of the national movement', is brief. It is to be created before all else. It will be composed of the 'energetic' Jews who support the cause and who, by attaching themselves publicly to it, will provide it with the moral and political authority to negotiate with governments on behalf of the Jewish people. It will therefore be both a voluntary and a self-appointed group; and Herzl justifies this seemingly arrogant assumption of public responsibility by an ingenious application of an established principle of Roman law whereby any man may step forward to safeguard the property of another who is in distress, even without the latter's express warrant. The analogy is clear.

[48] *The Jewish State*, chapter 3.

The Jewish people are at present prevented . . . from conducting their political affairs themselves. Besides, they are in a condition of more or less severe distress in many parts of the world. They need, above all, a *gestor*. This *gestor* cannot, of course, be a single individual. Such a one would either make himself ridiculous or—seeing that he would appear to be working for his own interests—contemptible.

The *gestor* of the Jews must therefore be a corporate body. And that is the Society of Jews.[49]

The Society would do much more than negotiate. It would promote scientific study of the demography, economic resources, and public opinion of the Jews. It would investigate the country in which it was hoped to settle. It would set out preliminary outlines for administration and legislation. And 'internally, that is to say, in its relation with the Jewish people, the Society will create all the first indispensable institutions; it will be the nucleus out of which the public institutions of the Jewish state will later be developed.' Finally, the Society would resolve the cardinal issue of where the Jews are to migrate to, where the state is to be established. 'Shall we choose Palestine or Argentina?', Herzl asks. 'We shall take what is given us and what is preferred by Jewish public opinion.' The Society will negotiate, investigate the alternatives and the public mind, and then judge.

What could the Jews offer in exchange? And where should their preference lie? He was very clear on both points in his 'address to the Rothschilds', written about half a year before the pamphlet. He believed the Society of Jews, with the Jewish 'power of the purse' at its command, would be able to grant 'financial advantages' to the 'receiving country'—not in the form of a regular tribute (that would be undignified and, in the event of cessation of payment, a source of conflict), but in the form of loans. Moreover, the entry of the Jews into their new country would 'divert streams of wealth' to the entire region, and precipitate 'an unprecedented commercial prosperity' all round. 'This', he had planned to tell the Rothschilds, 'will, of course, be adequately explained to them [i.e. the governments concerned] during the negotiations.' It was his belief that all states would benefit, both those which the Jews would leave and those into whose neighbourhood they would arrive. And since this could be clearly demonstrated to them, there was every reason to believe that a plain statement of the case would bring them round.

[49] Ibid., chapter 5.

As for the country he had in mind, he had, indeed, thought of Erez-Israel. He noted that it 'would have in its favour the facts that it is the unforgotten ancestral seat of our people, that its name would constitute a programme, and that it would powerfully attract the lower masses'. But on balance, and although he was opposed neither to one nor to the other on principle, he tended towards South America—or specifically to an empty part of Argentina which he hoped the Republic would be willing to dispense with. The climate of Erez-Israel was not one which most modern Jews were comfortable in, it was not a country in which it would be easy to apply the modern economic techniques he had in mind, and it was too close to Europe for his taste: 'In the first quarter-century of our existence we shall have to have peace from Europe and its martial and social entanglements if we are to prosper.'[50]

But in *Der Judenstaat* Herzl is at once bolder and more cautious. (It is likely that his return to Vienna, in the summer of 1895, having brought in its wake a reacquaintance with Jewish public opinion, led him to tread more gingerly on the delicate topic of Erez-Israel and reconsider his views.) He speaks, very briefly, of both possibilities. But he speaks at slightly greater length and to more purpose of Erez-Israel. In a passage in which, with characteristic fervour and ingenuity, earlier reservations are put aside, all aspects of the question, as he saw it, the emotive, the tactical, and the regenerative, are tied together, and the outline of his diplomacy in the years to come is firmly laid down.

Palestine is our ever-memorable historic home. The very name of Palestine would attract our people with a force of marvellous potency. If his Majesty the Sultan were to give us Palestine, we could in return undertake to regulate the finances of Turkey. There we would form a portion of a rampart of Europe against Asia, an outpost of civilization as opposed to barbarism. We should, as a neutral state, remain in contact with all Europe—which would have to guarantee our existence. The sanctuaries of Christendom would be safeguarded by assigning to them an extra-territorial status such as is well known to the law of nations. We should form a guard of honour about these sanctuaries, answering for the fulfilment of this duty with our existence. This guard of honour would be the great symbol of the solution of the Jewish Question after eighteen centuries of Jewish suffering.[51]

[50] *Diaries*, i, pp. 133–5.
[51] *The Jewish State*, chapter 2.

# 11

## *Diplomacy*

### i

THE primary purpose of *Der Judenstaat* was tactical: to make the issue public and to draw new allies. Characteristically, Herzl grasped at the first straws in the wind and made the most of them. 'Here in Vienna', he wrote to Colonel Goldsmid barely a fortnight after publication of the pamphlet, 'the essay I have published has gained me the greatest of hatreds and the warmest of friendships. The Zionists of Vienna and Berlin have proclaimed their enthusiasm for my plan. The money-men praise and denounce me in the sharpest possible way. The anti-Semites treat me fairly. At all events, the discussion is now open and, it seems, will soon reach the parliaments.'[1] This was not wholly inaccurate; but it was decidedly hyperbolical for, as became evident in the course of the spring of 1896, the support his pamphlet would gain him was not of the nature, nor of the extent, nor again from within the circles, that he had counted on.

The general, non-Jewish public and the great figures of state whom Herzl had hoped to arouse on the grounds that the Jewish problem was *their* problem as much as anyone's virtually ignored *Der Judenstaat*. In part, no doubt, this was due to the fact that the subject received only very moderate attention in the press. His own newspaper, the most important in Vienna, carefully—almost zealously—abstained from any mention of his pamphlet or of any other of his activities. The comment in those Austrian and German newspapers that did trouble to notice *Der Judenstaat* was mostly unfriendly and sometimes nasty. Privately and informally there was some mild curiosity about Herzl and his ideas, such curiosity as odd behaviour by any well-known figure generally excites. But more lasting interest was displayed almost exclusively by those

[1] 27 February 1896. *Igrot*, ii, no. 44, p. 66.

with a prior, fixed professional, or ideological, or, in one notable case, mystical concern with the Jews. Among these was the Papal Nuncio in Vienna (Agliardi), a notable anti-Semitic editor and deputy in Hungary (Ivan von Simonyi), and the chaplain to the British Embassy in Vienna (William Hechler). The chaplain had long before predicted the re-establishment of a Jewish kingdom in Erez-Israel, had set 1897 as the final date for the event, and was quick to see in Herzl's advent important and tangible confirmation of his prophecy.[2] Herzl himself methodically noted and explored all leads and made what use he could of each. The Nuncio was duly visited,[3] Herzl drawing the correct conclusion from the conversation that 'Rome will be against us.'[4] It was evidently to von Simonyi that Herzl was referring when he wrote to Goldsmid that 'anti-Semites treat me fairly'—and who thus served him as grounds for his argument that established western Jews were wrong to fear his ideas as likely to provoke fresh anti-Semitic abuse. Hechler was more important: he seemed capable of opening up a path which would lead Herzl, ultimately, to the German Emperor. And in the event, he did become, as we shall see, a minor, but real, if peculiar, ally.

The Jewish reaction was stronger. But here again it was disappointing, on the whole. The response of those to whom Herzl had looked for support in the first instance—the rich and the truly prominent in France, in England, in Austria, in Hungary, and in Germany—was often hostile, only rarely warm, at best muffled and indecisive, or carefully non-committal. 'I have read your *Judenstaat* with lively interest', wrote the Chief Rabbi in Paris. 'You have posed a question of the highest importance and to have launched the idea is a great deal in itself. The future will show whether it is practical.'[5] Generally, those who were disinclined to an interest (let alone a display of interest) in the Question of the Jews remained unmoved by *Der Judenstaat*. Those who were opposed to a Jewish

[2] In 1896, conceivably after hearing of Herzl, Hechler published in Vienna a fly-sheet headed *Die bevorstehende Rückkehr der Juden nach Palästina* citing Biblical and other authorities for anticipating the restoration of the Jews and setting down the duties of Christians in this regard. It is evidently a translation of a fly-sheet he had published in English in London twelve years earlier.

[3] With some embarrassment: 'I entered the Nuncio's quarters on the "Am Hof" square, looking around furtively, like a man entering a house of ill repute . . . Anyone who saw me enter there could easily have misunderstood my errand.' *Diaries*, i, pp. 352–3.

[4] Ibid., p. 354.

[5] Zadoc Kahn to Herzl, 11 May 1896. CZA, H VIII 420/1.

nationalist position, whether on principle or out of fear, or both, were unimpressed by, and often contemptuous of, Herzl's analysis. Many, as expected, were provoked by the pamphlet's shockingly direct title and its simple statement of purposes. 'The idea is very singular', wrote Dr. Ludwig Ernst. 'It is not at all clear how to take it: seriously enough to be concerned or lightly enough to be amused?'[6] The *Jewish Chronicle* preferred Hirsch to Herzl because Hirsch confined himself to *Russian* Jewry. It also felt that the absence of a religious element in the scheme 'rendered [it] cold and comparatively uninviting'. Nor could the *Chronicle* approve of the author's 'odious' (if not baseless) theory that where there were Jews there was anti-Semitism.[7] Baron de Hirsch himself did not react. Nor did the Rothschilds.

All in all, *Der Judenstaat* made Herzl few thoroughgoing converts to the national cause, although some men with repressed or dormant sympathy for a bolder approach were aroused by the pamphlet and then confirmed by an encounter with Herzl himself—Leon Kellner, later Herzl's very good friend and literary executor, for example.[8] In a few cases, headed by his first great recruit, the result was to confirm the effect of the personal encounter.

I have read your *Judenstaat* twice [wrote Nordau on 26 February] . . . This is only my impression very briefly: from an objective point of view the pamphlet can be discussed from several aspects. From a subjective point of view it is, simply—great. If you had never written a line previously and were never to write again, this single pamphlet would assure you a permanent place among the heroes of all times. It is a heroic act for an artist in love with style to have dispensed with all verbal glitter in favour of concision and modesty in presentation of the argument. It was heroic beyond description to have burnt all your bridges behind you. You have ceased to be a 'German author', an Austrian patriot. In future you will be able to wield influence only by arousing the deepest human feelings in the reader . . . It was particular courage to have admitted to feelings that other Jews had pushed back into the depths of their unconscious. Uriel Acosta did less, Luther at Worms did not do more . . . What will come of the pamphlet I do not know; but that you have revealed yourself in it, that I do know.[9]

[6] Ludwig Ernst, *Kein Judenstaat sondern Gewissensfreiheit*, Leipzig and Vienna, 1896, p. 5.
[7] *Jewish Chronicle*, 24 April 1896.
[8] Paula Arnold, 'Teodor Herzl ve-Leon Kellner', *Shivat Zion*, iv, 1956, p. 120 and *passim*; and Paula Arnold, *Zikhronot be-ahava*, Jerusalem, 1968.
[9] S. Schwartz (ed.), *Max Nordau be-igrotav*, Jerusalem, 1944, app. v, no. 2, p. 295.

Goldsmid's response was, in its way, almost as warm. 'As you know,' he wrote to Herzl, 'I am an unwavering believer in the Idea that the Salvation of Israel can only be worked out by the realization of the National Idea and that its corollary is the Salvation of Humanity. I am also firmly convinced that the only possible locale for a permanent State of Israel is in the *Erez-Israel*.'[10]

But Goldsmid was, of course, a Ḥovev Ẓion of long standing and, by and large, those who expressed firm support or, in the full sense, rallied to Herzl, were similarly from the ranks of the converted. Some, like Goldsmid, were evidently impressed by the clarity and strength with which Herzl expounded his theme. Some were intrigued by the comparatively rare phenomenon of a man who was prominent in the non-Jewish world entering the arena of Jewish affairs in so determined a fashion and with so radical a purpose in mind. And Herzl's emergence as a significant, if still ambiguous, figure on the movement's horizon[11] was most rapid in Vienna where he was best known and where his views were at their most powerful because they were, so to speak, in their natural habitat. Both the leading members of the Zionist circle in Vienna— all excited, but some (notably Birnbaum) unmistakably jealous— and the students of Kadimah and several other societies of Jewish students rallied to him almost immediately. It was, furthermore, from among the Viennese recruits that an entourage and a personal staff began to form.[12] But his pamphlet was duly noted in Berlin both by members of the Russian-Jewish study circle and by a more strictly German-Jewish group of Ḥovevei Ẓion led by Heinrich Loewe and Willy Bambus. Some disliked what they regarded as his utopianism. Some resented his equating of Erez-Israel with Argentina. But in general, the tendency there was to welcome him as a valuable reinforcement to themselves, even when mildly offended by what appeared to be his presumptuous disregard of Pinsker.[13] None seemed to have had an immediate sense of the

---

[10] Goldsmid to Herzl, 23 February 1896. CZA, H VIII, 285a/2.

[11] It was also at this time (March 1896) that Herzl was examined by his family doctor and 'a heart ailment caused by excitement' was diagnosed.

[12] For a printed statement of support see CZA, H V, A1. One who soon became, in effect, a member of Herzl's staff of young assistants later recalled that people began to visit the local Rembrandtstrasse offices of Ḥibbat Ẓion in the hope of glimpsing Herzl and hearing him speak. Erwin Rosenberger, *Herzl as I Remember Him*, New York, 1959, pp. 23-4.

[13] For example: Rabbi J. Rülf, 'Der deutsche Staatsbürger jüdischen Glaubens', *Zion*, 17 May 1896, pp. 109-14.

role he himself intended to play and of the influence he was soon to wield.[14]

The reaction was warmer in Cologne where Max Bodenheimer and David Wolffsohn[15] had formed an independent society of Hovevei Zion in 1893, but had made virtually no progress apart from helping to pull a number of local settlement societies in various parts of Germany into a weak general federation the year after. It was Bodenheimer's view that the trouble with the existing societies lay precisely in the fact that they put the establishment of agricultural settlements in Erez-Israel at the top of their list of priorities, rather than seeing that settlement 'was only one of the means of promoting and expounding the renaissance of the Jewish people as a whole'.[16] As his impatience grew, this impeccably respectable *Rechtsanwalt* found himself considering (if, admittedly, later to reject) much wilder schemes for drawing the cart out of the mire — among them one devised by a young man named Beilendorf to settle the relatively empty trans-Jordanian part of Erez-Israel and make 'fresh and cheerful' war against the bedouin if they tried to interfere with plans to set up a Jewish state.[17] So in Cologne Herzl's *Judenstaat* fell on ready ears. 'It opened up a new epoch', wrote Bodenheimer. 'Herzl expressed openly all that was beating in our hearts. We felt that [within] this man there was something more than a deviser of utopias. We imagined him to have the genius of a statesman, to be the leader that our own people had lacked until now.'[18] Wolffsohn noted that reading *Der Judenstaat* had 'made me a new man'.[19]

Thus, at any rate, in retrospect. In fact, some months passed while they took stock of Herzl and he of them. Wolffsohn travelled

---

[14] Cf. Richard Lichtheim, *Toldot ha-zionut be-Germania*, Jerusalem, 1951, pp. 83–4; and Motzkin's comments, *Stenographisches Protokoll der Verhandlungen des XVII Zionistenkongresses*, 1931, p. 253.

[15] On Bodenheimer, see above, pp. 228 f. David Wolffsohn (1856–1914) was a Lithuanian Jew who had moved to Memel, then to Lyck, and finally, after many intermediate stages, to Cologne where he became a prosperous timber merchant. In Memel he had been a pupil of Rabbi Rülf and in Lyck he had known David Gordon well. He had thus come under the influence of two very prominent members of Hibbat Zion long before he moved to Germany proper. He was pulled back into the movement by Bodenheimer, contributing an intimate knowledge of, and feel for, the heartland of European Jewry which Bodenheimer, like so many other westerners, lacked. Herzl, to whom Wolffsohn soon became devoted and whom he succeeded as president of the movement, portrayed him as David Litwak in his novel *Altneuland*.     [16] Letter to Goldsmid, 16 November 1895. *Darki le-Zion*, p. 248.

[17] Ibid., p. 60.     [18] Ibid., p. 58.

[19] 'David Wolffsohn', Alex Bein, *'Im Herzl u-ve-ikvotav*, Tel Aviv, 1954, p. 126.

to Vienna in May to meet him and returned with a glowing report. He also painted a picture of a man who was virtually unaware of the extent to which others had anticipated, and now shared, his views. When Bodenheimer gently called all this to Herzl's attention and invited him to meet and address the forthcoming conference of German settlement societies[20] Herzl frankly admitted to his ignorance ('It is possible that I would not have written at all had I known the literature'). But he also somewhat circuitously declined the invitation. Indeed, without ever saying so explicitly, he lost no time in making clear that he was not prepared to be drawn into the existing framework of 'pro-Palestine', essentially philanthropic settlement societies. In the first place, he was opposed to their methods.

I have grateful admiration for what the Zionists have done up to now, but I am fundamentally opposed to infiltration [i.e. the channelling and settling of migrants on a small scale with or without the express sanction of the Ottoman authorities]. If infiltration is allowed to proceed, it will only increase the cost of the land and it will become harder and harder for us to buy it. The idea of a declaration of independence 'as soon as we are strong enough over there' I consider impracticable because the Great Powers would certainly not recognize it, even if the Porte had weakened enough [by then].

In the second place he had plans of his own. 'My programme, on the other hand, is to halt infiltration and to concentrate all energies on the acquisition of Palestine under international law. This requires diplomatic negotiations, which I have already begun, and a publicity campaign on the very largest scale.'[21]

If they were of his mind, Herzl was telling them in effect, there was much they could do; and detailed advice and requests for specific action soon flowed—as it did in all cases where he felt a recruit had been gained. But there was no real room for debate with him on either ends or means. The fact was that without ever putting the point explicitly and, quite possibly, without ever being fully aware himself of all that was implicit in the issue, Herzl was from the very first clear in his own mind about the terms on which he would accept and judge adherents to his cause. These were first and foremost unwavering agreement with him on his general pro-gramme and full confidence in his, Herzl's, own capacity to bring

---

[20] Bodenheimer to Herzl, 20 May 1896. *Darki le-Zion*, pp. 248–9.
[21] Herzl to Bodenheimer, 24 May 1896. *Igrot*, ii, no. 88, pp. 103–4; *Diaries*, i, p. 355.

it to fruition. Since his approach in general and what he specifically had in mind to do in particular ran counter to what had been customary in Ḥibbat Zion for many years, and since he was openly critical of the old style, and since, finally, his own programme for action was clearly bold, while its details were unknown or carefully wrapped up in such generalities as 'diplomatic negotiations', this issue of confidence in him personally was crucial from the start. Naturally, the more alarmed Ḥovevei Zion were by Herzl's boldness and the more disconcerted or irritated they were by his ignorance of, let alone his lack of explicit respect for, all their previous labours, the sharper it loomed. Even the most favourably inclined asked themselves whether he was, truly, the man of the hour. Nor was there any obviously undeniable evidence that he was. Hence the unmistakable relief and sense of doubts allayed in Bodenheimer's account of his first meeting with him rather more than a year later.

I knew at once that he would be our leader . . . His appearance filled me with joy and pride. A splendid man. It was thus, roughly, that as a pupil in the top class of the Gymnasium I had imagined Hector, the hero of Troy. More than anything it was his eyes and his mouth that captured my heart. Spirit and courage and kindness, strictness, softness, and humility were all combined in him.[22]

It was for just these reasons that Herzl's ties with eastern Jewry, to the overriding importance of which he himself was still insensible, were put at immediate risk by the radical and unprecedented nature of his aims and method. For of all the centres of Jewry it was the great conglomerate of Eastern European communities that he knew least about, while, of course, both the problem with which Ḥibbat Zion had attempted to grapple and the bulk of the human energy devoted to its solution were firmly located in, and constituted by, the Jews of the East.

The news of Herzl and *Der Judenstaat* travelled fast in Eastern Europe and the local Jewish press, now predominantly favourable, or at least charitably disposed to Ḥibbat Zion, was prompt to report the gist of its contents and something of the reactions to it elsewhere. Initial interest lay in the fact, that, as *Ha-Meliz* put it, here was a spokesman for the national cause who could not be lightly dismissed as yet another ignorant Polish Jew. Herzl was undeniably

[22] *Darki le-Zion*, p. 71.

K

'a European from head to foot by any standard'; that a man of his quality and renown had joined the Zionists and, more generally, that 'this dear soul had returned to the maternal bosom', was therefore an event. More than that, it might well serve as a signal and as an example to others.[23]

Yet, as the significance of what Herzl was actually saying sank in, doubts rose and there was some hostility. *Ha-Magid* had hastily announced the preparation of a Hebrew translation (within six weeks of the publication of *Der Judenstaat* in Vienna). But then the same paper, much diminished after the death of its greatest editor, David Gordon, wavered about the position to adopt. By July it was hoping that Dr. Herzl 'would soon conclude that the time had not yet come [for what he had in mind] and that our labours should be devoted to the expansion of settlement in the Holy Land by natural and practicable means'.[24] *Ha-Meliz* took refuge in similar banalities. On the one hand, the 'Zionist movement in Austria' was 'very odd' and its members were dreaming 'the pleasant dream that Herzl had dreamed up for them'; on the other hand, it had to be said that dreams were precious and that the settlements in Erez-Israel were themselves the handiwork of dreamers.[25] *Ha-Zefira* was cooler still. Sokolov, its most important editorial figure, opposed the preparation of a Yiddish edition of *Der Judenstaat* lest the common folk be deceived or confused by its fancies.[26] But like all Jewish papers it carefully reported the reactions of others, such as the observations of a contributor to a non-Jewish daily in Warsaw who argued in the classic anti-Semitic vein that while Dr. Herzl was correct in his belief that the Jews were in for bad times, his hopes of a solution were groundless because the Jews, as a people, were incapable of sacrifice in any noble cause.[27] The Russian-language *Voskhod*, which had come over in recent years to a position

[23]  *Ha-Meliz*, xlix, 1896, reprinted in *Ha-Magid*, 19 March 1896.

[24]  *Ha-Magid*, 12 March, 26 March, and 9 July 1896. In the event, *Ha-Magid* dropped its plan to publish *Der Judenstaat* and the first Hebrew edition was published by others (in Warsaw) in September of that year. It carried an introduction mentioning Nordau's and Bernard Lazare's support for Herzl's ideas, while criticizing him for his poor view of Ḥibbat Zion. This was explained as a function of Herzl's ignorance. It was also stated, for the benefit of the Russian censor, that so far as Russian Jewry was concerned, 'clearly nothing great or small can be done about [Herzl's programme] without the approval of authorities.'

Russian-language editions were passed by the censor and published in Odessa and St. Petersburg in July and September 1896 respectively.

[25]  *Ha-Meliz*, 9 August 1896.

[26]  *Ha-Zefira*, 228, 1896. But *Der Judenstaat* did appear in Yiddish in Galicia in that year.

[27]  *Ha-Zefira*, 16 April 1896.

of moderate support for Ḥibbat Ẓion, but was still anxious to maintain such shaky bridges between Jew and Russian as could still be said to be intact, was most hostile of all. This Herzl, wrote one of its regular contributors, 'proposes no more and no less than the foundation of a special Jewish state with a king, ministers, gendarmerie, an aristocracy, and a populace, in brief all the attributes of a modern state'—a programme that was 'utterly naïve'— while he himself, presumably, intended to be 'Jewish envoy to the royal court in Vienna'.[28]

The greatest of contemporary Jewish publicists was silent, however, and remained so until after the first Zionist Congress in the following year. The only suggestion of Aḥad Ha-ʿAm's position at this stage was a sober and politely critical review of *Der Judenstaat* published in his new journal *Ha-Shiloaḥ*, but written by another, Dr. David Ẓevi Farbstein, a naturalized Swiss Jew of impeccable academic qualifications—and very likely chosen by Aḥad Ha-ʿAm for those very reasons.[29] Farbstein's central point—phrased in the cool, precise language in which Aḥad Ha-ʿAm habitually refashioned the work of his contributors—accorded roughly with the master's teachings. Herzl's view of the Jewish predicament was only half-true. He saw the Jewish problem exclusively in national terms; he discounted the socio-economic basis of anti-Semitism, namely the effect of the Jews' economic role in society. So doing, he sought to make it possible for the Jews to escape the hatred which their condition and their unhappy relations with the surrounding population inspired by establishing them in their own country where there would be none to hate or oppress them. But in fact what was needed most was a radical change in the inner social and economic life of the Jews and it was only to the extent that a Jewish state would make such a change possible that it was

[28] Shmuel Gruzenberg, *Voskhod*, 8, 1896, pp. 212–14. Cf. Y. Slutsky, *Ha-ʿitonut ha-yehudit-rusit ba-meʾa ha-teshaʿ-ʿesre*, Jerusalem, 1970, p. 195.

[29] Aḥad Ha-ʿAm's biographer believes that the silence may have been due to the preparations for bringing out *Ha-Shiloaḥ* and to the fact that for much of the time—until May 1897—he was in Berlin, not in Odessa, and may not have been willing to take a stand until he had felt the collective pulse properly. On the other hand, *Ha-Shiloaḥ* did include short pieces on current events from its fourth number (at the beginning of 1897) on and, since the noise of controversy over Herzl and the impending Congress rose substantially in the spring of that year, some direct reference to one or the other would have been natural. Cf. Arye [Leon] Simon and Yosef Eliahu Heller, *Aḥad Ha-ʿAm: ha-ish, po-ʿolo ve-torato*, Jerusalem, 1955, pp. 47–8. Farbstein himself later joined Herzl and helped organize the 1897 Congress.

necessary and desirable. 'It was not by means of the state alone, but by the cultivation of its *land* that our people's way of life would change for the better.'[30] All this was from afar: judgements on the basis of the pamphlet and of reports at second hand from Vienna.

The first Russian Zionist of any prominence to meet Herzl face to face was Menaḥem Ussishkin.[31] By his own account he had been sent a copy of *Der Judenstaat* in May 1896 with a request from the Ḥovevei Ẓion in Vienna to distribute it; and he had refused. There was nothing in the theoretical part that would be new to Russian Jews who had read Pinsker and Lilienblum; and the practical part, he told them, was very superficial. Asked to reconsider on the grounds that the author was a most important man who could be of great help in the common cause, Ussishkin replied that 'the Jews of Russia know nothing of the author; let him first demonstrate activity'—by which he meant devotion and seriousness of intent. Passing through Vienna at the end of June, Ussishkin was pressed to call on Herzl, refused, and then relented when Herzl set out to mollify him. But months passed before Herzl had succeeded in bringing him into his orbit, and then it was done incompletely and with some show of reluctance on Ussishkin's part.[32]

There were certainly genuine doubts at work here along with injured vanity and resistance to the new man, the upstart. There was the knowledge that Baron Edmond de Rothschild was opposed to Herzl. And there was his disturbing semi-alien character—that which, in other respects, was the source of much of his strength and of his influence and, on one reading, his value to the movement. Yeḥiel Tchlenov,[33] a milder and more cautious man than Ussishkin, was at first delighted with *Der Judenstaat*—which he took to be a sign of the 'awakening of western Jewry'. But there was soon concern as well, fear that the new current of ideas would fail to enter into the general and accepted path, that the new men's 'hearts would not beat in time with ours', and that what had been achieved thus far with much pain and effort would hold no charms for the new Zionists with their new slogans—'or rather the old slogan in its new form proclaimed in Vienna'.[34] This was certainly of a piece with the reaction of many other leading eastern Ḥovevei Ẓion,

---

[30] *Ha-Shiloaḥ*, i, pp. 177–82.   [31] See above, pp. 75f. and 185f.

[32] 'Pegishati ha-rishona 'im Herzl', *Sefer Ussishkin*, Jerusalem, 1934, pp. 352–3.

[33] See above, pp. 75f.

[34] Yeḥiel Tchlenov, 'Ha-kongres ha-ẓioni ha-sheni ve-ha-veʿidot she-kadmu lo', in Sh. Eizenstadt (ed.), *Yeḥiel Tchlenov*, Tel Aviv, 1937, p. 101.

notably in Odessa. That a man of Herzl's status and type had joined the movement was gratifying; but equally, he irritated and disturbed them—because he stood in such contrast to themselves in thought and manner and because, in sum, he was manifestly free of the great socio-political pressure to be reasonable and moderate under which virtually all Russian Jews who voiced opinions on public affairs were accustomed to labour. The moderate change in attitude to Herzl to one somewhat less negative prior to the great personal confrontations and the really radical change that took place in the year that followed occurred less under the direct impact of Herzl's own activities on the broad stage on which he had chosen to perform (and to perform alone), than indirectly under the influence of those members of the movement to whom his new approach and his fresh and masterful personality made a particular appeal. It was through these allies, in turn, that he gained the position from which he could assert his leadership of the movement as a whole, ultimately reordering and refashioning Hibbat Zion from top to bottom with very little loss of total membership, with no loss worth mentioning of such momentum as it had retained from earlier and more hopeful days, and generating a remarkable release of the latent energy that had been stifled by its internal and external circumstances.

Herzl's initial allies in eastern Jewry did not amount to a definable category or sector of Hibbat Zion—except that, on the whole, few among them were regular and prominent members of the inner Odessa circle and most were of the second and third rank. Some were on its fringes. Some were leaders of the movement or lesser activists in what might be termed the outlying regions,[35] in Galicia and in the Balkans, for example, although there too the initial reaction of the established leadership was extremely cautious.[36]

[35] For the response of Hovevei Zion in Lemberg (Lvov) and Cracow see N. M. Gelber, *Toldot ha-tenu'a ha-zionit be-Galizia 1875-1918*, Jerusalem, 1958, i, pp. 286-9. For one roundabout way word of *Der Judenstaat*'s publications reached Erez-Israel see Leib Jaffe, *M'imei aviv: pirkei zikhronot*, Jerusalem, 1938, p. 21.

[36] Karpel Lippe, the leading figure in Romanian Hibbat Zion, writing in *Zion* (Berlin) in August 1896 (pp. 193-6), welcomed the progress that the Jewish national idea was making even among assimilated Jews, but pointed out that the Jews in Erez-Israel would have to continue to live with the fact of Ottoman power and could settle in the country only as Turkish subjects. The most they could hope for was local government. In any case, a Jewish *state* was out of the question because it was incompatible with the dictates of religion. I. Klausner, *Hibbat Zion be-Romania*, Jerusalem, 1958, p. 302. Lippe had made much the same points in a letter to the Warsaw Hibbat Zion society twelve years before. See above, p. 169.

Others were private individuals disposed to sympathy with Ḥibbat Ẓion but whose capacity and will for action had not been properly tapped thus far. A few were eccentrics, such as the brilliant Aaron Marcus, a Jew from Hamburg who had moved east to Galicia, turned ḥasid, and who wrote to Herzl that his 'pamphlet came like a lightning bolt in the darkness of night in both camps, assimilationists and ḥasidim' and congratulated him on his

beneficial critique of philanthropy in general and von Hirsch in particular. We are angry with this man who with his money and his Turkish connections could have brought about the colonization of Palestine in your sense, but who allowed himself to be convinced by the spineless Rabbi Jellinek that it was necessary only to lower the Polish Jews' mental level, his disgusting mania for thinking, to turn him into a peasant and a lowly manual labourer, in order to make the Jewish Question disappear, to liberate our Aryan brothers, that monstrosity of Christian-Germanic stupidity, from the trouser-selling youths who cannot, it is true, fulfil their task as men, but do at least know how to fulfil it as bank directors.[37]

What they all had in common was the will to respond to the friendly, gentlemanly letters in which Herzl's thanks were interspersed with detailed advice about the form support should take if it was to be useful to him and hints, and, on occasion, promises, of the support he would lend his correspondents in turn.[38] At this early stage he particularly wanted written resolutions of popular support to present to the Society of Jews which he hoped to found in London when he travelled there in July, but also consolidation of local support through propaganda and the clarification of the ideas he stood for by word of mouth and by republication and translation of *Der Judenstaat*. But, as with supporters closer home (with the one great exception of Nordau), there was no question in his mind of *consulting* his new friends, only of encouraging and stimulating them to act and of keeping their interest alive with spare references to his travels and hints of the great affairs that were in hand.[39]

One of the new, self-selected links with eastern Jewry deserves

---

[37] Marcus to Herzl, 27 April 1896. *Herzl Year Book*, i, 1958, pp. 187–9.

[38] From the start Herzl was concerned to use such influence and means as he possessed to assist and reward those who accepted his leadership. Cf. his diary entry for 17 March 1896 (*Diaries*, i, p. 314) and his punctilious response to Birnbaum's request for help, 26 April 1896, *Igrot*, i, no. 77a, p. 90).

[39] Cf. for example, letters to Leopold Goldschmied (Misslitz, Moravia); Gerszon Zipper (Lemberg); and Reuven Bierer (Sofia), *Igrot*, ii, nos. 65, pp. 80–1; 69, p. 83; and 92, p. 108.

particular mention. Professor Zevi (Gregory) Belkowsky (1865–
1948) had been an early member of Hibbat Zion in Odessa, his
native city—where his father had died of wounds inflicted in the
1881 pogrom. Refusing an invitation to teach at the local university
upon graduation because it was conditional on conversion to
Christianity he moved to Bulgaria in 1893 where he assumed the
Chair of Roman Law at Sofia. But he remained in close contact
with the Odessa centre of the movement, as well as becoming prominent in the Bulgarian branch. The effect of Herzl's pamphlet on
this earnest, devoted, but, on the whole, rather simple man was
particularly rapid and powerful and his response, with that of his
colleagues in the 'Zion' society in Sofia, was prompt. A resolution
pledging the society's support for the ideas embodied in *Der
Judenstaat* and loyalty to Herzl as its new spontaneously accepted
leader was drawn up and sent to Vienna. And Belkowsky wrote to
Herzl on behalf of all, that 'We are all tensely awaiting further
developments, which is to say, the foundation of the institutions
which you envisage, and we would ask you to keep us informed of
all that transpires.'[40] The more immediate and particular fruit of
Belkowsky's adherence to Herzl, however, was his intervention
on Herzl's behalf within the heart of Hibbat Zion, in Odessa itself.
At the regular conference of the committee early in July of that
year he tried to force the official leadership to overcome their
timidity and take a position on an issue which, apart from all other
considerations, was manifestly 'political'. He was not completely
successful. Fearful of the authorities, the committee delegated
'Mizrahi', the religious wing of the movement, which operated
without official sanction and was therefore, in any case, illegal by
default, to respond directly to Herzl's wish for contact with the movement in Russia; and meanwhile Belkowsky himself was delegated to
transmit to Herzl the committee's good wishes. Considering that
the doubts, suspicions, and plain fear of the new man of whom they
knew so little had not been more than marginally allayed, this was
no mean achievement for Belkowsky; and the concession to him was
balanced in the minds of some of those attending the meeting by
a parallel decision to republish Pinsker's *Autoemancipation!*[41]

---

[40] Belkowsky and Herbst to Herzl, 23 March 1896. *Ha-'Olam*, l, 29 August 1940, pp. 782–3.

[41] Klausner, *Mi-Katoviz 'ad Bazel*, ii, pp. 349–50; Izhak Nissenboim, *'Alei heldi*, Warsaw,
1929, p. 111. Ussishkin, the most powerful personality in the group, did not attend this
meeting.

ii

The links which Herzl established with Ḥibbat Ẓion in Eastern Europe in the spring of 1896 were thus somewhat oblique and limited. They were mediated by those members of the movement who had come forward on their own account and initiative to express their support; and they were left unexplored, and unexpanded to their full extent, owing to Herzl's own view of them as decidedly secondary to what he was most intent on—his contacts with the notables in Western Europe, with those he was fond of calling the 'upper Jews'. Accordingly, he took these very moderate successes in the East in his stride without either fully grasping the nature of the impact that he was making, or sensing what the support of great numbers of eastern Jews might come to signify for him in the future. Only later in the year, during his visit to the East End of London, and from then on by a process of gradual initiation into their qualities and *mores* that culminated in his journey to Russia the year before his death, did he come to see what had occurred. In the meantime, he noted these preliminary indicators of his coming advance to a position of national leadership unprecedented in modern times with some complacency. For the effect of these small successes was first and foremost to confirm in his own mind both the validity of his general analysis of the Jewish condition and the correctness of the tactic he had chosen to precipitate a change. And it was here, for the time being, that their importance lay. 'I had exposed myself, fully aware of the risks, to jeers and hatred. But I have already seen my reward: our people's poor see me as their friend. Cries of approval come to me from Russia, Galicia, Romania, Bulgaria, Hungary.'[42]

Herzl's mind was set upon direct political action. The form this action was to take was determined in part by his notion of what opportunities there were to advance the national purposes, in part by his ideas about the means that were required to seize them, and in part by his conception of the role he himself was to play. Briefly, he was out to induce the men in whose power it was—or seemed to be—to rearrange the political and territorial order in the Near East to do so. This could be done, he believed, by rational argument and by demonstration of where each statesman's interests lay. Where there was no immediately apparent interest, or where political

---

[42] Herzl to Martin Hinrichsen, 8 April 1896. *Igrot*, ii, no. 71, p. 85.

interests appeared to conflict with those of the Jews, a political or
material interest of the requisite nature had to be created. This
brought Herzl to seek out likely members of a second circle of men
in whose power it was either to bring their own influence to bear
upon the central figures or to create *an initio* the material induce-
ments that would deflect the great men from their present course.
Finally, he needed minor allies, men who wielded neither political
nor economic power of their own but did possess *access*: knowledge
of the characters and concerns of the great, and the ability to usher
Herzl in before them. Rational argument, a statesman's—indeed,
any man's—proper regard for his own interests, and the minimal
considerations of decency and *noblesse oblige* which are present in
the minds of all but the worst of men would then all operate. He
himself, by putting the arguments, as outlined in *Der Judenstaat*,
in their plainest and most persuasive form and by patiently setting
up the whole intricate system of levers of influence and interest
would then create the political machinery by which the Jewish
state was to be established. Given sufficient deftness and energy,
the smaller levers would work the larger until, finally, the gate into
Erez-Israel was opened and eastern Jewry, under its new leadership, would pour through.

In the centre of the web and in effective control of the object
of the enterprise was the Sultan. But Herzl was almost equally
interested in the support of the German Kaiser and of the Marquess
of Salisbury (who was both Prime Minister of England and Foreign
Secretary) as the leading figures of two of the three great powers
most concerned with, and influential in, the Near East. Nor did
Herzl entirely discount the possibility of inducing the Russian
government to support him, for all that the Ottomans perceived
the Russians as their major opponent and that it was settled Russian
policy towards its own Jewish subjects that had pushed the condition of the bulk of European Jews beyond tolerable limits.

Herzl's knowledge of the diplomacy of the Near East was superficial and he knew nothing at all of the way in which the Ottoman
Empire was ruled and of the considerations by which its rulers were
governed in turn. He believed that if the Jews—in effect, western
Jewry—were to employ its one great and notorious asset, its financial
resources, to help ease the financial difficulties for which the Ottoman government was equally notorious there would be grounds for
an alliance. This community of interests could be either initiated,

or confirmed, or both, by other means: for example, by the Jews playing the role of mediators between the Turks and another unfortunate people, the Armenians. Much less clear were Herzl's ideas about the role the European powers might be induced to play in this context. If they brought their influence to bear on Constantinople in the desired direction, they stood to gain, he thought, by the prestige that would accrue to them for having had a hand in the birth of the new state. More generally, as both the British and the Germans were intent on the preservation of the Ottoman Empire, any development that improved the economic and political stability of the Empire—in this case by the injection of Jewish capital, enterprise, and skilled labour—ought, he believed, to be viewed by them with favour. If the powers did support his plans the problem of the Jews would be *ipso facto* internationalized—that is to say, converted into a matter in the solution of which all were explicitly and publicly interested. That in itself would promote a climate of ideas in which the ancient framework of prejudices in which Jews and Gentiles alike viewed the Jewish problem would begin to erode. In fact, each advance, each convert that he made among the great men of the world would serve to widen the breach he had already made among the Jews. Nothing would do so much to bring the Jewish plutocrats of Western Europe round as evidence that their own rulers supported him. And since, ultimately, the prospects of making palpable progress depended on the willingness of the great Jewish financiers of Paris and London to deliver the *quid pro quo* that would be offered the Sultan for his agreement to the return of the Jews to Erez-Israel in great numbers, and as of right, and with a view to setting up their own autonomous regime, all three fronts had to be attacked at once and an advance on one front instantly exploited for an advance on one or both of the others. Meanwhile, nothing liable to disturb the delicate balance of his scheme could be tolerated: no 'infiltration' into Erez-Israel itself, no dissipation of energy on lesser matters, and no leakages of information except when deliberately decided on for a good purpose.

So far as the Jewish plutocracy was concerned, he was well aware what little progress he had made. He had failed to reach the Rothschilds; he had made no impression on Hirsch. But he had had a better hearing in London and something like a half-promise of support from Montagu. He hoped that the ground he had gained in Eastern Europe would help establish him and, in a sense, validate him, in the eyes of the rich and that things would now be easier. Reports of Rothschild's disfavour kept filtering through from Herzl's contacts in Paris and, indirectly, from his new friends in Hibbat Zion; but he had not given up all hope of inducing Baron Edmond de Rothschild to change his mind or, at the very least, refrain from wielding his vast influence against him. Nor had he lost hope of bringing Hirsch round; and had just written to Nordau to ask him to put out feelers in Hirsch's direction when he heard (21 April) of the latter's death. And meanwhile, he set about making the most of his opportunities, such as they were, in the other sphere in which he sought to act. These were opportunities opened up, but at the same time severely limited, by the men through whom this fairly well-known, but by no means powerful, journalist and playwright sought to make his entrée into the realm of high politics. Of these the two most important were Hechler, the chaplain to the British Embassy in Vienna, by means of whom Herzl hoped to open the way both to Lord Salisbury and to the Emperor Wilhelm II, and Philipp de Newlinski, an Austrian-Polish ex-diplomat of mildly unsavoury reputation who was prepared to use his excellent contacts in Constantinople to help usher Herzl into the inner circle of the Ottoman government.

All this—Herzl's estimate of his opportunities and the means by which they were to be seized—was put to the test almost immediately and in a remarkably short period of time. In the course of the sixty days that elapsed between 22 April and 21 July 1896 (neatly contained within the third book of his diary)[43] he touched upon all points of his political compass and put each one of his ideas to the test. The scale and strength of the political barriers by which Zionism was hemmed round were revealed and, in microcosm, the fortunes of the Herzlian movement as it evolved to the end of his lifetime and beyond it until the outbreak of the First World War were played out. To put the matter differently, Herzl's experience in this period was decisive for all that followed—although, as was often the case with him, some time passed before he had entirely grasped its significance.

William Hechler ('Next to Colonel Goldsmid, . . . the most unusual person I have met in this movement so far'[44] had come to Herzl on his own initiative and had suggested that he bring Herzl's ideas and

---

[43] *Diaries*, i, pp. 327–431.     [44] Entry for 16 March 1896, ibid., p. 311.

ultimately Herzl himself before some of the German princes, including, possibly, the greatest of them, the Kaiser. Hechler's credentials for the task, apart from his chaplaincy at the British Embassy in Vienna,[45] consisted in his having served as tutor to the son of Friedrich, the Grand Duke of Baden, and in still being on excellent terms with the family. The Grand Duke, a considerable figure in his own right, was the son-in-law of the late Wilhelm I, the first Kaiser of Germany, and by virtue of that fact uncle (by marriage) of the present Kaiser, Wilhelm II. In Herzl's eyes the middle-aged, excitable Anglican priest with his long grey 'prophet's' beard, and a 'Zionist song' of his own composition, his organ-playing, and his requests for travelling expenses was none the less a crank, 'an improbable figure', and, so he feared, would others see him. He was therefore, possibly, a man who might do him more harm than good by putting the intensely serious business Herzl was about in an absurd light. And there was the greater danger that his every word would be discounted on the assumption that the Jews had put him up to it. Such, indeed, was the Kaiser's first reaction when he was told about Hechler's new ideas.[46]

Herzl was frank about his purposes.

I told [Hechler]: I have got to establish direct contact, a contact that is discernible on the outside, with a responsible or non-responsible states-man—that is, with a minister of state or a prince. Then the Jews will believe in me, then they will follow me. The most suitable man would be the German Kaiser. I must be given help if I am to carry out the task.[47]

---

[45] Hechler seems to have informed Sir Frederick Monson, the British Ambassador, about Herzl and made an attempt to use his position to get Herzl a hearing in London. If so, he failed. The Embassy might have been expected to take some interest in Zionism on general grounds, but does not seem to have done so. No trace of the subject has been found in their dispatches for the period, nor, for that matter, in the dispatches of the other British Embassy which might have been curious about Zionism—the Embassy in Constantinople. However, questions of land purchase in Erez-Israel by Jews of British nationality and consular interventions on their behalf with the Turkish authorities were reported. See, for example, the memorandum in which it was proposed that the British Consul in Jerusalem (Dickson) 'point out to the Mutasarrif that Messrs. Rothschild and E. Franklin, being persons of high standing resident in England, cannot fairly be classed with the category of Jews prohibited by the Turkish government from holding real property in Palestine'. The issue was a refusal to register property acquired by the Anglo-Jewish Association for a school in Jerusalem. PRO, FO 195.1973, 10 December 1897, no. 522.

[46] Hechler to Grand Duke of Baden, 18 April 1896. 'Herzl, Hechler, the Grand Duke of Baden and the German Emperor', *Herzl Year Book*, iv, pp. 213-14. Also entry for 23 April, *Diaries*, i, p. 329. Hechler, who was of part-English and part-German descent, was greatly troubled lest he be suspected of having Jewish blood.

[47] Entry for 16 March, *Diaries*, i, p. 312.

Herzl promised him his travelling expenses, prepared himself for the meeting by observing the Kaiser carefully when the monarch visited Vienna the following month, and waited, with little confidence, to see what Hechler would do. The chaplain was almost as good as his word. He followed the Kaiser from Vienna to Karlsruhe, the Grand Duke's capital, and if he made little headway with the Kaiser himself, did very well with the Grand Duke. It was agreed that Herzl would be received in audience.

Herzl's interview with the Grand Duke of Baden on 23 April 1896 was his first venture out before one of the notable figures of contemporary Central European society. As such it corresponded to his first attempt in the previous year to put his arguments before one of the notables of Jewry: his interview with Hirsch. He had since become much more self-assured in his contacts with Jews, even with the greatest among them. But now, faced with the prospect of putting his case to a man on whose loyalties he had no natural claim and who, moreover, fairly epitomized Herzl's own fantasy world of a valorous, Germanic nobility, he was nervous and self-conscious in the extreme. 'I shall be cool, calm, firm, modest, but determined, and speak the same way', he wrote in his diary, sitting in the train on his way to Karlsruhe.[48] After the interview he recorded every shift in his own state of mind with pitiless precision.

> We were led into the first waiting-room. It was the Adjutants' Hall. And this did take my breath away. For here the regimental flags stand in magnificent rank and file. Encased in leather, they rest solemn and silent; they are the flags of 1870-1. On the wall between the flag-stands is a painting of a military review: the Grand Duke parading the troops before Kaiser Wilhelm I. One might say that only now did I realize where I was.[49]

The meeting went well. The Grand Duke was attentive, interested, and sympathetic. But his response to Herzl's request for intercession with the Kaiser was non-committal; and his replies to Herzl's and Hechler's further probing were mostly in the form of pronouncements of mixed quality on such topics as the contemporary diplomatic scene, the Russian Emperor's true attitude to his Jewish subjects, 'the decline of parliamentary government', and, with greater authority, on his own attitude to the Jews of Baden. By the end of the long talk Herzl's nervousness had worn off, the Grand Duke shook his hand (he had not done so at the

---

[48] 22 April, ibid., p. 328.  [49] 23 April, ibid., pp. 331-2.

outset), and it was agreed that Herzl would keep him informed of future developments. The only immediately usable gain was Friedrich's explicit consent to 'a few trustworthy men in England' being told that he took an interest in the matter. Still, Herzl judged the meeting a success. The cause had taken 'the greatest stride towards realization' thus far, he wrote to Nordau. 'I think I am not mistaken when I say: the matter has become serious'[50]—the more so as the second step was already in hand.

In June he would travel to Constantinople. There he hoped to be received by the Sultan and have an opportunity to set out the outlines of his plan for the purchase of Erez-Israel in exchange for the thorough reordering of Turkish finances. But this prospect brought him back sharply to a consideration of those within whose power he believed it was to supply the *quid pro quo*; and he resolved, with great reluctance, on a second approach to the Rothschilds. Nordau was now pressed to go and sound Edmond de Rothschild out, with great caution and discretion, making out, if possible, that the initiative for the meeting was Nordau's own. The meeting, arranged by the Chief Rabbi Zadoc Kahn, took place in mid May. 'I was at his place for exactly 63 minutes', Nordau reported. 'During this time Rothschild spoke for 53 minutes and I, with an effort and some lack of courtesy, for 10 minutes . . . He likes to listen to himself and hardly lets the man he is talking to utter a word.' But in any case, Nordau's errand was a hopeless one. The Baron was immovable. 'Rothschild wants to know absolutely nothing at all about the matter, he wants no share of it, and he will give no money for it.' His reasons were of two kinds. The plan was inherently unworkable because the Sultan feared Russia and Russia would never allow Palestine to fall under Jewish influence; and because, while the Sultan did need money and might make vague promises, his promises were worthless. He, Edmond de Rothschild, was in favour of leaving the Sultan alone.

The reasons for Edmond de Rothschild's general opposition to Herzl's Zionism were sharper still. He thought Herzl's initiative both dangerous and harmful. Dangerous, because as a consequence of what Herzl was doing the anti-Semites would argue the Jews' lack of a fatherland and the hypocrisy underlying their show of patriotism in the countries of their domicile. Harmful, because Herzl was interfering with Rothschild's own settlement work in

---

[50] Herzl to Nordau, 6 May. *Igrot*, ii, no. 79, pp. 92–3.

Erez-Israel. No one knew better than he how difficult it was to keep them going. 'A mass migration of Jews would arouse the enmity of the Bedouin, the mistrust of the Turkish authorities, the jealousy of the Christian colonies and pilgrims, and would undoubtedly lead to the suppression of the [Jewish] settlements which had already been established.'[51]

There was nothing to be done. 'We shall pass over him,' Herzl noted in his diary, 'and on to the order of the day', adding, with *Schadenfreude*, 'After this, there is something comical about today's dispatches from Paris which report street demonstrations against the Jews and in particular the Rothschilds. In front of the same house on the Rue Lafitte where on Friday E.R. had rejected my friend Nordau, the mob cried on Sunday: "Down with the Jews!"'[52]

The next great item on 'the order of the day', the journey to Constantinople, was the boldest, the most improbable, and the most important of all the moves that Herzl had made thus far. It is important to see that it was made far outside the relatively safe circle of Jewry; and at a considerable distance in both geographical and political terms from the ground with which he was familiar. It was a move, as Edmond de Rothschild had correctly pointed out, that put much of what had been accomplished in Erez-Israel at risk because it entailed calling a spade a spade and telling the Turks what he and some of his friends were really after and leaving the present rulers of the country to see in Herzl's approach so much confirmation of what they had judged the underlying purposes of the new *yishuv* to be all along. Indeed, the probability of failure was so high and the warnings he received from the outset (even from those on whom he was relying to help him) were so many and so similar, that the sheer insolence—or innocence—of Herzl's attempt to confront the Sultan of Turkey and put his proposals before him as a basis for *negotiation* is breath-taking. Nor is it easy to explain except as the product, in some sense, of a mind that was so given to concentration on ends that it was often virtually closed to a sober consideration of the means available for their achievement.

Herzl did not really grasp that in the middle of the last decade of the century the famous question of the future of the Ottoman Empire was posed, if at all, more out of settled habit than out of immediate concern. Despite an occasional spasm of international

---

[51] Nordau to Herzl, 15 May 1896. CZA, H VIII 614.   [52] Entry for 18 May.

interest and anxiety over such matters as the bitter treatment of the Armenians or the contemporary insurrection in Crete, none of the great Powers was prepared to incur the incalculable risks involved in the collapse and partition of the Ottoman Empire. In any case, the genuine international crisis points and the focuses of major diplomatic interest were all well away from the Empire in the last years of the century and after: in the Sudan, in central and southern Africa, and, above all, in the Far East. Nor did Herzl take the measure of the extent to which the arrest of the Empire's decomposition was due, as Professor Medlicott has put it, 'above all, perhaps [to] the tenacious, unsleeping defence of his authority by the sultan ʿAbd al-Hamid in the 1880's and the 1890's'.[53] He did not have more than the most superficial notion of the kind of man ʿAbd al-Hamid was, of what his purposes were, of what he believed in, of how he ruled. Yet the Sultan wielded much real power, had great political experience (he had been on his throne for twenty years when Herzl travelled to Constantinople for the first time), and had established a method of government suited, no doubt, to his predilection for the secret and the devious, but founded on a system of shadowy and shifting centres of authority too intricate for any but the most experienced and assiduous foreign observer to master. Even then, to the experts, it was a source of constant frustration and irritation well epitomized in this extract from a contemporary memorandum from the Chief Dragoman of the British Embassy to his Ambassador.

The general impression left upon me by the whole conversation is that the Sultan is sheltering himself behind the Porte for anything left undone, and that the system of administration is so disorganized and out of gear that no real amelioration is possible: the Grand Vizier may give as many orders as he pleases, but as any subordinate can neglect them and appeal direct to the Sultan, there is an end of the matter. The Sultan in the meantime can always say he instructed the Grand Vizier and he is therefore not to blame. No minister has any intercourse with the Sultan, except those who for personal reasons blindly follow his policy of inaction and retrogression, the rest, among them being the Grand Vizier, being mere cyphers without a vestige of authority.[54]

[53] *New Cambridge Modern History*, xi, Cambridge, 1967, p. 340.
[54] Block to Currie, 3 March 1896. PRO, FO 195.1926. 'Inaction and retrogression' was an exaggeration, but the 'duplicity' of the Sultan was an unshakeable part of the diplomatic conventional wisdom of the times. The Austrians even went so far, on one occasion, as to reveal their espionage activities in the course of confirming it in others' minds. 'Count

As opposed to the Sublime Porte, the official government structure, there was the Sultan's palace secretariat at the Yildiz Kiosk, led by the First and Second Secretaries, the guardians of access to the sovereign, his most important and intimate advisers, offices that over time were filled by men of a great variety of ability and character: some honest, all capable, some deceitful, a few cruel, and one or two, in the words of an observer of unique authority, 'ignorant and servile, but grasping and corruptible in the extreme'.[55] Least of all did Herzl have any notion of the unrectifiably inferior role allotted the Jews in the Muslim cosmology, or, for that matter, of the idea of land over which Muslims ruled being generally seen by them as inalienable. He knew nothing of Islam; and, for a professional journalist and littérateur, was remarkably insensitive to what was not immediately visible in an alien culture.[56] (It could also be said that he was in this respect fairly typical of his own times and class.) When he was told that the Sultan's approach to the question of Palestine was indissoluble from his own role of Caliph, Herzl noted the point without ever trying fully to understand it. But it was capital. Arminius Vambéry, who probably knew 'Abd al-Hamid better than any other European, did not think that he 'was . . . at all an unshakable believer, but [rather, that] keeping in view his character as a successor to the Prophet he accommodated himself in public life to the duties of a pious Mussulman'.[57] Here, over and above the straightforward political opposition to the creation of yet another national minority problem already alluded

Goluchowski . . . told me in confidence that he had quite recently been placed in possession of an original document, directly emanating from the Sultan, in the shape of an instruction for his guidance to the Grand Vizier, charging him to give such and such assurances to the Foreign Ambassadors, while at the same time carefully guarding against acting on these assurances. Count Goluchowski, in warranting this to me, quoted in part the Eastern phraseology of the Imperial paper, and observed that it was the first time he had had the chance of seeing "in black and white" so interesting a proof of the duplicity of Abdul Hamid.' Rumbold to Salisbury, 8 January 1897. PRO, FO 7.1255.

[55] Arminius Vambéry, 'Personal Recollections of Abdul Hamid II and Court', *Nineteenth Century and After*, lxv, June 1909, p. 992. The reference is to Tahsin Pasha.

[56] Cf. the exchange in Herzl's novel between Kingscourt, the Christian, who found it 'odd that you Mohammedans should not regard the Jews as interlopers' [in the Old–New Land], and the Muslim protagonist, Reshid, who argued that 'the Jews have brought us wealth and health; why should we harbour evil thoughts about them?' *Altneuland* (first published in 1902), bk. III, chap. 1.

[57] Op. cit., *Nineteenth Century and After*, lxvi, July 1909, p. 73. See also Ali Vahbi Bey (ed.), *Pensées et souvenirs de l'ex-sultan Abdul-Hamid*, Paris, 1914, pp. 14, 18–19, and *passim*. Some dates in this anthology are plainly wrong, but the content generally rings true.

to,[58] were the sources of the Sultan's refusal to countenance Zionism. While the technical grounds for the claim of the Osmanli Sultans to the Prophet's succession were extremely poor, the *fact* of their rule and sovereignty over much of the Muslim world and over all the Muslim holy places was decisive for their acceptance as Caliphs (literally: successors) by the Believers. This alone made it impossible for the Sultan to contemplate an impairment of his authority over, or of Muslim preponderance in, Palestine.

To set against these virtually insuperable obstacles—the more formidable for his being almost unaware of them—Herzl had few resources of his own. Who was he? Whom did he represent? Why should anyone bother to listen to him, let alone *negotiate*? Part of the answer to all three questions was that he was a senior member of the staff of the *Neue Freie Presse* and that, fortunately for him, the Turkish government, and the Sultan himself in particular, paid a great deal of attention to what was thought and written about them in Western and Central Europe.[59] Herzl was well aware that his post on the principal Vienna daily provided him with an invaluable visiting-card. The second of his two interviews with the Grand Vizier was entirely on that basis and was a straightforward exercise in journalism. Hence his own ambivalent attitude to his journalism and his willingness to suffer the mild, but constant humiliation of serving a newspaper that studiously ignored all that he himself was doing. The rest of the answer can only be guessed at. There was a certain ambivalence towards the Zionists in the attitude of the Turks themselves. The Jews were not the only migrants and settlers from Europe; there were the Christians, backed by their governments and church organizations, as dangerous in Turkish eyes as the Jews, if not more so, and much more difficult to handle. The Jews could therefore be seen as a counterpoise to them.[60] There was the uncertainty about Herzl's precise status— seen, as it probably was, in the light of the fanciful notions about Jewish cohesion and power that were only moderately less fashion-

---

[58] See Chapter 4 above, pp. 105 f.

[59] Cf. British Embassy dispatch, 21 July 1896, PRO, FO 195.1972, no. 326; and Sir Edwin Pears, *Forty Years in Constantinople*, London, 1916, pp. 115-19.

[60] The French and the Russians in particular saw the Jews as competitors in the matter of land purchase for example. Cf. Tischendorf (German Consul in Jerusalem) to Hohenlohe, 19 June 1897. Mordechai Eliav (ed.), *Ha-yishuv ha-yehudi be-Erez-Israel bi-re'i ha-mediniut ha-Germanit*, Tel Aviv, 1973, no. 163, p. 131; and Vambéry, *Nineteenth Century and After*, lxv, June 1909, p. 987.

able in Constantinople than in the capitals of Europe. There was the figure Herzl himself cut, his commanding presence, his transparent honesty of purpose, his intensity. It could not have been very easy to refuse to listen to him and not to take him at something like his own estimate. Even the most sceptical of Ottoman officials might have thought it reasonable to treat him with caution. Something of the stir he had already caused must certainly have been reported to the Porte, and possibly to the Sultan, if only because the Zionist movement had long since become an established subject of concern to—and, therefore, of surveillance by—the Ottoman government. Yet, in themselves, these were negligible factors. The key to the puzzle why Herzl's visit to Constantinople was not the complete failure the general circumstances seemed to entail cannot be divorced from the question of the character and role of his go-between and the terms in which the latter presented Herzl to the Ottoman government.

Philipp Michael de Newlinski (1841–99) was a member of the Polish *szlachta* whose family estates had been confiscated by the Russians as punishment for their involvement in the 1863 rebellion. He had been a lawyer in Russia, an official of the Austrian Embassy in Constantinople, and of the Foreign Ministry in Vienna, and then a journalist. When Herzl met him he was the editor of a small news agency specializing in Balkan and Levant political affairs which served him as an instrument and cover for other purposes. Amongst other things, he was a spy. At various times he had given confidential political service not only to the Austrians, but to the Russians, the Turks, the Serbians, the Bulgarians, and the Romanians. He was suspected—and to some extent feared—by all. Had it not been for his high style of living and the great expenses he incurred, and his consequent thirst for money, he would have flourished. Everybody paid him—except, it seems, the British who regarded him with particular dislike and saw him primarily as an agent of the Turks. He 'receives a permanent salary of 18,000 frs. per. ann. from the Sultan', the Chief Dragoman reported, 'besides travelling expenses and liberal presents, and is completely in the pay of the Yildiz . . . Every year he is summoned here, often through incidents created by himself in the hope of obtaining some secret mission from which he derives considerable pecuniary benefit.'[61] He was, in short, a man

---

[61] Block to Herbert, 21 May 1896. PRO, FO 195.1927. See also N. M. Gelber, 'Philipp Michael de Newlinski', *Herzl Year Book*, ii, 1959, pp. 113–52.

with great political experience, excellent sources of information, few scruples, if any, about receiving payment for political services rendered, and with first-rate access to the highest levels in Constantinople, not excluding the Sultan and his powerful and notorious Second Secretary, Izzat Bey. At the same time, he was not, *pace* the British Embassy, anyone's creature. He was of high intelligence, acute judgement, independent views, and more than occasional flickers of sympathy for political causes that were not his clients'. Herzl, probably rightly, never entirely discounted Newlinski's professions of sympathy for Zionism and could therefore never make up his mind whether to trust the man or not and, if at all, how far. He did not know the full extent and the precise nature of Newlinski's connections with the Turks. It did not occur to him, as it does now to us, with hindsight, that part of his brief may have been to spy on Herzl. Nevertheless, he did perform the invaluable service of ushering Herzl in before highly placed Ottoman officials and he did give Herzl accurate political intelligence and a great deal of good advice, the most important items of which were shrugged off.

He told me he had read my pamphlet before his last trip to Constantinople and discussed it with the Sultan. The latter had declared that he could never part with Jerusalem. The Mosque of Omar must always remain in the possession of Islam.
'We could get around that difficulty', I said. 'We shall extra-territorialize Jerusalem, which will then belong to nobody and yet to everybody—the holy place which will become the joint possession of all believers. The great *condominium* of culture and morality.'[62]

The important thing was that he did, truly, seem to have access to the Sultan and was prepared to help Herzl to be received by him in audience. These were grounds enough for preferring him to another candidate for the function of go-between whose access seemed more limited and of whose venality Herzl had no doubt at all.[63]

'Great things need no solid foundation', reads a well-known entry in Herzl's diary. 'An apple must be put on a table so that it will not fall. The earth floats in mid-air. Similarly, I may be able to found and stabilize the Jewish State without any firm support. The secret

---

[62] Entry for 7 May 1896. *Diaries*, i, pp. 345–6.
[63] This was Dionys Rosenfeld, editor of the *Freie Osmanische Post* published in Constantinople.

lies in motion.'[64] His sense of being propelled by inner and outer forces—from within himself and from within the Jewish masses and by virtue of their needs—was reinforced on the eve of his arrival in Constantinople. He had informed his new friends in Sofia that he would pass through and that he would welcome a brief meeting at the station in transit. But when the train pulled in, it was a crowd that awaited him,

men, women, and children, Sephardim, Ashkenazim, mere boys, and old men with white beards . . . A boy handed me a wreath of roses and carnations—Bierer made a speech in German. Then Caleb read off a French speech, and in conclusion he kissed my hand, despite my resistance. In this and subsequent addresses I was hailed in extravagant terms as Leader, as the Heart of Israel, etc. I think I stood there completely dumbfounded, and the passengers on the Orient Express stared at the odd spectacle in astonishment. Afterwards . . . I kissed Bierer farewell. They all pressed about me to shake my hand. People cried 'leshonoh haboh birusholayim [next year in Jerusalem]'. The train started moving. Hat-waving, emotion.[65]

Herzl arrived in Constantinople on 17 June. He left late on 28 June. It says something for his energy and, too, for Newlinski's ability to open doors, that he saw the Grand Vizier, Halil Rifat Pasha, the day after his arrival and the Sultan's Second Secretary, Izzat Bey, the day after that. The Grand Vizier listened politely, asked sensible questions, and shrugged off Herzl's refusal to be specific about the financial recompense he had in mind. 'I said I could state the scope of our proposals only to His Majesty. Should they be accepted in principle, Sir Samuel Montagu would submit our financial programme.'[66] But it was clear that Rifat Pasha disliked the project. Izzat Bey, an Arab, one of the most powerful men in the Empire, loathed and feared throughout the Turkish governmental system and believed by some to have had a particular responsibility for the Armenian massacres, made his meeting with Herzl conditional on it being limited to courtesies. But in private, according to Newlinski, Izzat Bey was friendly and gave advice: the Jews should first acquire some other territory, then offer it, along with additional payment, in exchange for Erez-Israel. 'It shows', Herzl noted, 'that he is thinking with us and for us'; and added in his diary, on the strength of what Newlinski had told him, that Izzat himself 'declines a

[64] 12 May 1896. *Diaries*, i, p. 348.
[65] Entry for 17 June. Ibid., p. 368.   [66] Ibid., p. 376.

personal share in [the transaction]. But he has his family in Arabia, numbering 1,500, for whom something would have to be done.'[67]

In the course of his twelve days, Herzl saw a great many other people of the Court and of the Sublime Porte. Most were reserved. Some were friendly. The friendliest was Mehmed Nuri Bey, the Secretary-General for Foreign Correspondence, or chief official of the Foreign Ministry, the son of a Frenchman called Châteauneuf (Herzl wrongly took him for an Armenian), a man of great intelligence and ability, and the Palace spy within his Ministry. Ostensibly, this was encouraging. Yet it was hard to assess the real significance or purpose of the man when the opposition to the project of his master the Sultan was so clear. 'Under an agreeable, cultivated and even refined exterior', it was noted in a British Embassy report some years later, Nuri 'is corrupt and unscrupulous in the extreme'.[68] Even Newlinski warned Herzl against being carried away by the good impression he made.

How far Herzl was out of his depth in Constantinople may be seen in his sole and very mild attempt to play politics on his own. On the strength of Newlinski's advice he deliberately went to see the Chief Dragoman of the Russian Embassy *before* seeing the Grand Vizier. This was on the grounds that Russia had 'gained the upper hand in the Yildiz Kiosk'. It is not clear what basis there was in fact, if any, to support the idea. Probably very little. Since the early 1880s the most influential foreign power in Turkey had been Germany and so, on the whole, it remained until the World War. The origins of Newlinski's wish to have Herzl pay the Russians a visit probably lay in his own connection with their Embassy.[69] But irrespective of the state of the play of palace intrigue in June 1896, the notion that the support of any foreign power would advance his dealings with the Turks was inherently fallacious. If the Turks knew of his visit to the Russian they cannot have liked it. And more fundamentally, Herzl's notion that one or more of the Powers could be persuaded to press the Ottomans to treat with him failed to correspond to what lay at the heart of the transaction he was proposing, namely that Jewish financial resources be used to relieve the Turks of the onerous and humiliating system under

[67] *Diaries*, i, p. 383.

[68] G. P. Gooch and Harold Temperley, *British Documents on the Origins of the War, 1898-1917*, v, p. 13.

[69] According to the British (PRO, FO 195.1927, no. 311), Newlinski was in the pay of the Russian Embassy in Constantinople at this time, as well as in that of the Turks.

which a large part of the national revenues was ceded to the servicing of the national debt. It was a system onerous to the Turks, but not to the foreign governments.

In any event, the authoritative Turkish response to Herzl's proposals arrived without delay at the end of the first full day of his stay in Constantinople, on 18 June. Newlinski bore the message. There was no question of Herzl being received by the Sultan. Furthermore:

> If Mr. Herzl is as much your friend as you are mine, [the Sultan had said] then advise him not to take another step in this matter. I cannot sell even a foot of land, for it does not belong to me, but to my people. My people have won this empire by fighting for it with their blood and have fertilized it with their blood. We will again cover it with our blood before we allow it to be wrested away from us. The men of two of my regiments from Syria and Palestine let themselves be killed one by one at Plevna. Not one of them yielded; they all gave their lives on that battlefield. The Turkish Empire belongs not to me, but to the Turkish people. I cannot give away any part of it. Let the Jews save their billions. When my Empire is partitioned, they may get Palestine for nothing. But only our corpses will be divided. I will not agree to vivisection.

Herzl's first response was characteristic. 'I was touched and shaken by the truly lofty words of the Sultan, although for the time being they dashed all my hopes. There is a tragic beauty in this fatalism which will bear death and dismemberment, yet will fight to the last breath, even if only through passive resistance.'[70] Nevertheless, he pulled himself together very rapidly and set about obtaining some sign from the Turks that they were, at least, still listening: he continued to press for an audience of the Sultan, if necessary as a representative of *Neue Freie Presse*; if that was not possible, he proposed the negotiation of a loan that was large enough to be of value, but still small enough not to require a major concession; finally, as a last resort, 'with reluctance and secret shame', he asked for a 'visible token' for the benefit of 'my people in London' —a decoration.

The supplementary Ottoman response came bit by bit by sign and by word. No gates were closed to him while he remained in Constantinople. A variety of Turkish officials of senior and middle ranks continued to receive him. And each day Newlinski brought fresh reports of what had been said or hinted at in his connection

[70] *Diaries*, i, pp. 378-9.

at the Yildiz and at the Porte. Then, more specifically, there was a request that Herzl demonstrate goodwill (and, by implication, his powers) by rendering a service: he could undertake to help soften criticism of ʿAbd al-Hamid's treatment of the Armenians in the European press and try to persuade the exiled Armenian leaders to submit to the Sultan's authority in return for unspecified concessions. Later there was a request for a loan of two million pounds on the security of the revenue of the Turkish lighthouses.

At one point there was a message from the Sultan not to leave Constantinople because there would be something to say to him before his departure and on his very last day in Constantinople there was a formal visit to the Sultan's treasures and palaces at the invitation of the Master of Ceremonies and in the company of an aide-de-camp. Lastly, there arrived the decoration: Commander of the Mejidiye Order.[71] In sum, he was challenged to show what he could do for the Turks; and, in exchange, he had been given some of the evidence he needed to show that negotiation was in progress. Nothing had been promised. On the contrary, his project had been expressly turned down. But it seemed to him, none the less, that he had cause to say and feel, that 'a stake had been driven in'; and he was now heavily encouraged by Newlinski to think that if he did help with the Armenians and did obtain the loan he would at least be on his way to achieving his goal. The upshot was that Herzl left Constantinople in good heart and that the further Turkey receded behind him in space and time the more promising and tangible his achievement came to seem to him. Both his judgement on what had transpired at Constantinople and his temperament impelled him to press forward without delay. So soon after his return to Vienna he turned down an offer of a second audience with the Grand Duke of Baden ('I don't need the Grand Duke at the moment') and moved on to London. 'This time fine weather,' he noted on arrival, 'and everything enchanting.'[72]

There is no reason to doubt that at some stage during Herzl's stay in Constantinople the Sultan changed his mind and decided to do just what Herzl, after the initial disappointment, had asked for:

[71] However, 'The granting of Turkish decorations during Abdul Hamid's time . . . had become so common that any value they may ever have possessed had ceased to exist in the minds of respectable people.' Sir Edwin Pears, *Forty Years in Constantinople*, p. 143.

[72] 3 July, 5 July 1896. *Diaries*, i, pp. 405, 406.

to enter into a relationship that committed no one, but that left all options nominally open—a flirtation, Herzl had called it. If Newlinski is to be believed, reports on Herzl had been asked for by the Sultan and opinions had been offered. After the consultation came the decision. The loan Herzl was asked to raise was of the amount which he himself had suggested: two million pounds. The decoration he had asked for was conferred (although Newlinski told him he would have got one anyway). The idea of Herzl acting as a mediator between the Sultan and the Armenians was not new. It had been broached by Newlinski long before they had set out for Constantinople together. Newlinski had had a brief from the Sultan to enter into contact with the Armenians,[73] he had not succeeded, and needed help. It was his idea to use Herzl. Taken together, all this suggests that the Sultan, conceivably on the advice of Izzat Bey, had seen (or been shown) how Herzl, at very little cost to himself, could be useful to him. The resolution to exploit him then followed. This may have been moderately incautious, for it did entail encouraging a man whose purposes were undeniably contrary to his own. But since Herzl appeared in Constantinople as an *individual*, not as the leader of a movement, and since some of the Turks (on Newlinski's evidence) thought his plan no more than fantasy, the danger could not have seemed great, if it was recognized at all.

But thus, in a roundabout way, Herzl did achieve one of his central aims: he had negotiated. He had come to the Sultan in the name of the Jews, but without formal credentials, with no visible backing, with barely more than a name or two to refer to. He had made an offer which had been rejected, but he had not been turned away and he had not been laughed at. He had made a second offer which had been taken up. He had made a demand—a paltry demand, but nevertheless a demand—which had been met. And above all, the principle that Jewish financial and—within its inherent limits— political power could be placed at the disposal of the Turkish government in exchange for political concessions by the Turks had been implicitly accepted. And that counted for a great deal even if the specific concessions which he had asked for on behalf of the Jewish people had been ruled out. What had occurred was something quite new, something which was qualitatively different from the old-style intercession and petitioning (or *shtadlanut*) on behalf

[73] Block to Herbert, 21 May 1896. PRO, FO 195.1927.

of Jewish individuals and Jewish communities. It differed too from the threatened use of financial power by individual Jews, by the Rothschilds, for example, on behalf of others. For it was not the expression of a notable Jew's private moral duty; and the power ostensibly in question was not Herzl's to wield.

The basis of Herzl's position was twofold. In the first place he evoked, more or less deliberately, that very sense and, to some extent, fear of Jewish power which the anti-Semites of the day, for diametrically opposed purposes and in a totally different spirit, played upon. In the second place, his entire programme was founded on the idea that such power as the Jews possessed could be legitimately and effectively employed in a cause defined by and for the Jews themselves—not a universal cause, not a cause of any one of the nations within which they lived or of the governments to which they were subject, but one specific to the Jews themselves. This simple view of the Jews as a people that could play an independent political role came naturally to Herzl. And the Turks had not really questioned it. This may have been because, under the Ottoman system, the Jews constituted a recognized ethno-religious community with a certain amount of self-rule in any case. It was consequently reasonable for them to have interests of their own, even if their interests were objectionable. In addition, Herzl's view of the Jews as a people capable of playing a political role of their own choosing corresponded, ironically, to what anti-Jewish forces in Turkey had long claimed. And, of course, it corresponded more markedly still to what the European anti-Semites argued. However, this last factor sufficed to make his views immensely disturbing to most of the Western European Jewish notables he was trying to win over. And thus an important part of the basis of the progress he had made in Constantinople and, on a deeper reading of the matter, his principal achievement there, became an immediate impediment to his further efforts in London and Paris. In Constantinople he had been spared a confrontation with the full force of Ottoman policy and deflected from a true estimate of the long-term opportunities for Zionism, given the diplomatic and territorial *status quo* in the Near East. In London and Paris everything impelled him to force the issue. As a consequence, his first important failure occurred not where, in a sense, it properly belonged, in the Near East itself, but in what could be regarded as the lesser arena, in Western Europe.

### iii

It was unfortunate for Herzl that so much of his plan hinged on the support of established members of the Jewish community in England. He had been warned not to misinterpret the courtesy with which he had been received the year before and not to rely on the polite and limited, if perfectly genuine, interest he had aroused. 'I have myself drawn attention to your scheme from the pulpit', wrote Rabbi Simeon Singer, his first and staunchest recruit in London. 'But I cannot disguise from myself the exceeding difficulty of producing anything like a sustained interest in the question. Antisemitism does not yet supply in these parts a sufficient spur to action along the lines indicated by you.'[74] Zangwill and Wolf warned him

not to come to London with too sanguine expectations of doing more than sowing the good seed . . .

People in England still think the idea not practicable and many object to it altogether while the formation of the Committee is very doubtful. Who could grapple with the work involved unless rich men devote their lives to the task?[75]

But the one rich man on whom Herzl was counting refused to give him clear backing. Sir Samuel Montagu did not think 'the intervention of a British subject' would help, Singer reported— given the poor relations between Britain and Turkey. Besides, there was no likelihood of the Turks being moved to make concessions by anyone. Only the partition of Turkey by the Powers would change matters. 'In that case alone is there a prospect of obtaining through the jealousy of each other among the Powers, the possession of Palestine for the Jews.'[76] Tell him 'No material sacrifice is being asked of him. He does not have to give a penny', Herzl replied.[77]

The faithful Singer duly reported the polite evasion that was the fruit of the banker's mixed feelings and genuine embarrassment.

I have again had a long conversation with Montagu. He says he dare not officially associate himself with a matter which is more or less abstract. What he is willing to do is to answer any concrete question of

[74] Singer to Herzl, 5 February 1896. CZA, H VIII 739/3. See also Singer to Herzl, 19 February 1896. CZA, H VIII 739/4.

[75] Zangwill to Herzl, 21 June 1896. CZA, H VIII 947/5.

[76] Singer to Herzl, 11 May 1896. CZA, H VIII 739/7.

[77] Herzl to Singer, 26 May 1896. *Igrot*, ii, no. 90a, pp. 105-6. Herzl explained his reluctance to write to Montagu directly as stemming from his poor English.

finance you may desire to put to him, and in so far to help [*sic*] in putting the advanced scheme on a sound basis. I think you will have to rest satisfied with this assurance.[78]

So despite the encouraging messages he had sent from Constantinople ('I have great things to relate', he wrote to Goldsmid), his reception in London began poorly. Lucien Wolf did interview him for the *Daily Graphic*, but Montagu and Goldsmid were not immediately available for talks and even Singer suggested it would be well if he set about obtaining an interview with Lord Rothschild as a major piece of business. A half-hearted attempt to get the local correspondent of the *Neue Freie Presse* to use his City connections to help raise the loan the Turks had asked for was abortive. So was a long talk with two representatives of the Anglo-Jewish Association in which he tried to win them over. He was prepared to abandon the leading position he had assumed if it would help bring the various local Jewish groups together, he told them. And he was willing to begin with a study group, rather than the full-fledged 'Society of Jews', the establishment of which, along with the loan, was his principal aim in London. But they were not moved. The one, Claude Montefiore, 'said with gravity that I was demanding a revolution in all the ideas he had held up to now';[79] the other, David Mocatta, wrote to him the next day that, 'personally, I fear I can be of little assistance to you, as I have a strong conviction that the plan of a "Jewish State" is neither practicable nor desirable.'[80]

His attempt to follow through with his undertaking to the Turks to try to conciliate the Armenians on their behalf was no more successful. A meeting in London with Avetis Nazarbekian, a leader of the Hunchaks, a revolutionary party much influenced by Narodnaya Volya, led to no results. The atmosphere was heavy with distrust. Few of his own friends, not even Nordau, would support him on so awkward and distasteful a matter as co-operating with the Turks, even benevolently, in the Armenian connection. Herzl himself was unhappy and unsure of himself in the role of mediator and glad to drop it entirely when, in August of that year, there was a fresh round of Armenian rebellion and Turkish repression and reconciliation was out of the question. In any case, the Hunchaks were in decline and were soon to be replaced in the forefront of the Armenian national movement by the Dashnaks.

---

[78] Singer to Herzl, 2 June 1896. CZA, H VIII 739/8.
[79] *Diaries*, i, p. 408.     [80] Mocatta to Herzl, 6 July 1896. CZA, H VIII 572.

Altogether, the descent from the lofty plane on which politics had been talked in Constantinople down to what seemed to him to be the petty and often personal level on which the discussion with established English Jewry had to be conducted was painful and irritating and only mildly arrested by the comparative warmth of the reception accorded him by the Maccabeans. He spoke before them from a carefully prepared text which he read in an English translation. (Questions were answered in German and French.) Zangwill responded, not unsympathetically, but in a manner indicating that he was anxious to show off his wit in the traditional after-dinner style. Lucien Wolf was somewhat more serious. Neither Montagu nor Goldsmid turned up. Nor did Nordau come from Paris as Herzl had hoped he would. So he was neither in his element culturally, nor speaking directly to the men whom he most needed. But on the other hand it was a forum that was not to be despised. The speech was duly reported at length in the *Jewish Chronicle* along with a leading article—doubtful in tone rather than hostile—about 'the Viennese enthusiast'; and Herzl himself judged the occasion a success. It was his first full-dress *public* statement. Hitherto he had tended to avoid making public speeches.[81]

The talk still reads well: serious, but not heavy; firm, but not over-assertive or arrogant; with a light touch and an attractive hint of the speaker's sense that the subject was greater than himself. In part, he was out to make the point that real progress had been made: the plan for a Jewish state had been discussed with persons in authority; the response to his own pamphlet had been much greater than he himself had hoped for; the validity of his analysis had been established. 'The Jews wished to be delivered from the dread of periodically recurring persecution.' Even where they do not suffer, their happiness is mixed with fear. 'Today I know and tomorrow the world will know that the Jews wish to have a state wherein they may at last live and thrive as free citizens.'

In part, the speech was a response to criticism. He indirectly denied the contention that his actions were likely to endanger the existing settlements in Erez-Israel. He assured his listeners that the Sultan was not hostile. He explained why the methods of Ḥibbat Zion were inadequate and, ultimately, likely to do no more than transplant into Erez-Israel itself all the problems attendant on Jewish minority existence anywhere.

[81] Cf. Herzl to 'Jung-Israel', Berlin, 9 March 1896. *Igrot*, ii, no. 52, p. 71.

But beyond these points there was a distinct reflection of his own discomfort and anxiety lest he himself be misunderstood and his motives misconstrued. 'I am only a literary man', he told his audience. The idea of embarking on a great political enterprise had come to him suddenly. He was himself astonished to find himself now making speeches or negotiating with reigning sovereigns, let alone with *financiers*. The latter point was the most acute. Herzl's detestation of the 'money-men' was partly straightforward—part and parcel of his social views—and partly a function of the hateful triangular association of the Jews, money, and evil which contemporary French and German anti-Semites had so successfully promoted and propagated in the common mind. This revulsion from Jewish money coloured all he said and did during this visit to London and later to Paris—the more so because, of course, it was on Jewish money and, to some extent, on the hated legend of Jewish money, that his strategy depended. Certainly, he told the Maccabeans, it would be nicer if we could set out on a romantic conquest of the country; only one would have to be twenty years old to think that possible.[82] This *malaise* helped propel him towards a break with those whom he had come to see.

To put the matter at its simplest, the key to the money was in Montagu's hands; but the key to Montagu, as Herzl discovered, was in Edmond de Rothschild's. Sir Samuel Montagu was twenty-eight years older than Herzl. He was, with the London Rothschilds, walking proof of the heights a Jew could attain in England without sacrifice of principle or of loyalty to tradition. He had been a Liberal Member of Parliament since 1885 and a Baronet since 1894. He was a Justice of the Peace and had a country seat in Hampshire. In 1907 he would be created a Peer (as Lord Swaythling). But he remained an observant Jew, as Herzl had noted when they first met. He was founder and president of the Synagogue Federation and

---

[82] He had noted in his diary in May: 'Two fellows from the *Kadimah*, Schalit and Neuberger, called on me. At the University of Vienna the assimilationists seem to be gaining the upper hand again. At the *Lesehalle* no one wants to hear about Zionism. They also told me that a proposal was afoot to recruit a volunteer battalion of one or two thousand men and to attempt a landing at Jaffa. Even if some might have given up their lives in the attempt, Europe would start paying attention to the aspirations of the Jews.

'I advised them against this fine Garibaldian idea, because these thousand men, unlike the men of Marsala, would not find a nationally prepared population awaiting them. The landing would be suppressed within twenty-four hours, like a schoolboys' prank' (*Diaries*, i, pp. 355-6). For an annotated text of Herzl's address to the Maccabeans, see *Bifnei ʿam veʿolam*, i, pp. 13-22.

long a member of the Board of Deputies of British Jews. He had visited Erez-Israel in 1875 and, with Lord Rothschild, was founder of the first modern school in Jerusalem. He had been one of the first great Jewish philanthropists to try to organize aid for Russian Jews in the early 1880s and had visited Russia in 1886 to see what could be done for them on the spot. But he was cautious, even then: like Hirsch, his first instinct was to *discourage* emigration and to seek a local and moderate solution. So, now, with Herzl whom, after a pause, he had invited to meet him at the House of Commons. He was friendly; and Herzl, frankly impressed by the surroundings ('I begin to understand why the English Jew should cling to a country in which they can enter this house as masters'),[83] softened. But Montagu's reservations were not modified by what Herzl told him of his journeys to Karlsruhe and Constantinople and his doubts were restated at a second meeting in which they were joined by Goldsmid.

There were practical objections to Herzl's project. The Sultan was not to be trusted, they thought. Once he had got his loan he 'would kick the Jewish immigrants around'. Then there was a larger and more readily available (and politically more neutral) source of funds than any they could raise: Baron de Hirsch's legacy which was reputed to amount to ten million pounds sterling, and had been set aside for philanthropic purposes specifically. But the main objections ran deeper and were partly of principle. Writing to Herzl a year later Montagu recalled what he had told him in July 1896.

I do not think that Jews should act internationally on political matters. I do not think that Jews can be established in Palestine excepting by the voluntary combination of the great powers or by some leader who would command the confidence of the Jewish race. I would not like to see a very large number of Jews placed under Turkish rule at the present time.[84]

He therefore laid down three conditions for his support. The Powers must agree. The Hirsch foundation must make its resources available. And Edmond de Rothschild must join them.

If Herzl resented the very broad hint that it was Edmond de Rothschild they preferred as their leader, he did not show it. He was evidently at pains to make it absolutely clear that in this matter— as on questions of money—he was driven by no improper, ulterior motive. He would not be an obstacle to progress, he told them; he would withdraw if Rothschild was prepared to join the movement.

[83] *Diaries*, i, p. 411.     [84] Montagu to Herzl, 14 July 1897. CZA, H VIII 575/5.

It was clear enough, and became clearer still as Herzl's visit drew to a close, that the differences between Herzl on the one hand and his new contacts in London on the other centred as much on the approach towards the existing, piecemeal settlement of Erez-Israel—the 'infiltration' to which Herzl objected—as on the larger issues of a Jewish state and of Jewish political action. And since Edmond de Rothschild was now both the pre-eminent symbol and, to a very large extent, the actual director of the enterprise in its current form, it was inherently improbable that he, Rothschild, would now change his mind. On the face of it, therefore, it looked as if one of the conditions which the two English Jews set Herzl was incapable of fulfilment; and the grounds for Herzl's suspicion that their fulfilment was not desired, let alone expected, were laid. But at heart the matter was more complex.

Many of the English Jews whom Herzl was meeting, Montagu and Goldsmid among them, were attracted by his vision, his boldness, by the man himself. Some, like Zangwill, welcomed 'anything that makes Jews think . . . [because] the race needs a renaissance, whether political or spiritual or both'.[85] At the same time, the instinct of the more cautious—and they were the majority, and caution, for sound historical reasons, has long been the deepest-rooted of all Jewish social responses—was to steer clear of changes liable to put Jewish security and achievements at risk. Change stimulated by the deliberate intention of the Jews themselves was doubly suspect. And responsibility for the precipitation of change was to be avoided. They were, of course, right in seeing that Herzl's programme implied a momentous departure from the established pattern of relations between Jewry and the non-Jewish world. And it was easy, and not unreasonable, for them to believe that this departure did put a great deal at risk, even if they, or some of them, could see its advantages as well. How then was the issue to be resolved and who was to resolve it? This ostensibly formal issue was as difficult to handle as the one of substance. For it was beyond the bounds of the experience and imagination of men of their generation and background to devise a workable and fully legitimate method whereby the decision to move in the new direction could be debated and, if necessary, taken. Hence their insistence on the responsibility being assumed by a 'leader who would command the confidence of the Jewish race' even when it was evident to all con-

85 Zangwill to Gustav Cohen, 27 September 1896. Schwadron Collection, 12B.

cerned that there were no national institutions capable of determining the identity of such a latter-day Exilarch beyond reasonable
question: no parliament, no rules of election, no hereditary line.
The only class of candidates even remotely acceptable to such men
as Montagu, along with countless thousands of his contemporaries
throughout European Jewry, was a member of the one great
universally known family, the Rothschilds. A Rothschild had not
only great political and material resources of his own which he
could wield in a national cause; he had too, by virtue of legend
and customary thinking, an ascriptive right to exercise leadership.

In these circumstances, Herzl might have been right to judge the
journey to England a failure and in the nature of an anticlimax after
the modest progress made in the Levant. But in the event, his conclusion was less simple. 'I am satisfied with the result of my trip to
London', he wrote in his diary as he waited at Folkestone to cross
over to France where he was to meet Edmond de Rothschild. 'The
conditional promise of Montagu and Goldsmid to join in with us
. . . suffices for the present.' It may be that, as in Constantinople,
his energy and haste were mixed with a tremendous patience: so
long as there had been no complete break nothing had been totally
lost. But the more important reason was that elsewhere in London
he had been accorded a personal triumph and armed with a card
that he believed he could play—and would play with relish—
against the rich Jews who were withholding their support.

On 12 July Herzl had been invited to speak in the Jewish Workingmen's Club in Whitechapel in the East End of London—in
Montagu's parliamentary constituency, as it happened. It was an
appearance that Montagu, Goldsmid, and others had not wanted
him to make and only the *Hakham* (Sephardi Chief Rabbi), Moses
Gaster, among the notables of London Jewry, was present. The
audience that crowded into the club was overwhelmingly East
European. The predominant language was Yiddish. The ambience
was as in Sofia when Herzl passed through: warm, effusive, adula-
tory, expectant. Herzl spoke extemporaneously (in German). He
evidently felt much freer here than he had among the Maccabeans.
The content of his speech was stronger, the tone more passionate,
his sense of the audience more acute. Our emancipation has been
incomplete, he told them, and it is now evident that the other
nations do not want it completed. The solution to the problem of

L

the Jews must therefore be founded on the Jews' own nationality. And all efforts must be concentrated on achieving national recognition—because we are a nation, although an oppressed one. He conceded that he had been wrong about Erez-Israel—it alone was the country in which the Jews wished to establish their state. What if it was barren? It had once been fruitful; we would make it so again. We would show up the lies that had been told about us: the people of the East End of London knew very well how hard the Jews could work. The legend that the Jews took no part in the creation of natural wealth would be destroyed. As for the methods —there were, here in England, men who knew all that was needed about the modern techniques of settlement. They would know how to conduct the enterprise. He himself would do what he could to mobilize them and he would be glad to transfer the leadership of the movement to other shoulders. But, equally, if none came forward to assume it, he himself would know how to rouse the masses.

Herzl's impact on the crowd on that hot Sunday afternoon was electric. He was cheered wildly. Hats were waved. The hurrahs followed him into the street. The crucial effect of the triumph, however, was on himself. 'Now it really depends only on myself whether I shall become the leader of the masses', he concluded. He had acquired, he thought, an instrument whereby he could put pressure on the notables. For they would want him to abandon his leadership and, in exchange, they would be prepared to assume that leadership themselves.

But there was more to the experience than that. Three days later, reflecting on it, he noted that

As I sat on the platform of the workingmen's stage on Sunday I experienced strange sensations. I saw and heard my legend being born. The people are sentimental; the masses do not see clearly. I believe that even now they no longer have a clear image of me. A light fog is beginning to rise around me, and it may perhaps become the cloud in which I shall walk.

But even if they no longer see my features distinctly, still they divine that I mean very well by them, and that I am the man of the little people.

Of course, they would probably show the same affection to some clever deceiver and impostor as they do to me, in whom they are not deceived.

This is perhaps the most interesting thing I am recording in these notebooks—the way my legend is being born.

And while I was listening, on that people's tribunal, to the emphatic words and the cheering of my adherents, I inwardly resolved quite firmly to become ever worthier of their trust and affection.[86]

Thus fortified in his intention 'to unite the poor in order to put pressure on the lukewarm and hesitant rich', Herzl reached Paris and at long last delivered his 'Address to the Rothschilds' at the Baron's office in the rue Lafitte on 18 July.[87]

The meeting got off to a very bad start and remained a dialogue of the deaf to the end.[88] Herzl, on his own evidence, was touchy and aggressive: irritated by the atmosphere of servility surrounding Baron Edmond and irritated again by the millionaire's comfortable assumption of authority. Rothschild himself was frightened: frightened of this wild unknown man, this 'new Bernard the Hermit' who would upset the masses and the familiar and established order of things, who would upset the Turks too, and generally do the Jews harm everywhere by encouraging the anti-Semites to raise the cry that they should be made to leave for their own country. Besides, who would control 'the influx of the masses' into Erez-Israel? Who would provide for 'the 150,000 *schnorrers* [beggars] who would be the first to arrive'? Then there was all this noise about the ultimate purposes of the enterprise. 'I felt,' he related years later, 'that the colours could be raised over a house only after it had been built, and that there was no point in hoisting the flag when there was still no edifice and when even the land for the edifice had not yet been provided. That was the reason for my opposition to Herzl.'[89]

It was Herzl who brought the argument to a close, fully conscious of the drama of the moment. ('I picked up my umbrella from the floor and rose.') 'You were the keystone of the entire combination', he told Rothschild. 'If you refuse, everything I have fashioned so far will fall to pieces.' It was time for a straight answer, he said, yes or no. He had offered to turn the direction of the entire enterprise

---

[86] *Diaries*, i, pp. 421–2.

[87] See above, pp. 249–51.

[88] The only detailed account is Herzl's (*Diaries*, i, pp. 426–30). The private Rothschild archives are inaccessible. But hostile hearsay reports in letters from people close to leading Jewish personalities in Paris indirectly bear out Herzl's account. So does the little that the Baron related to Isaac Naiditch many years after the event. (Cf. Isaac Naiditch, *Edmond de Rothschild*, Washington, D.C., 1945, pp. 25-6.)

[89] Naiditch, op. cit., p. 26. 'But history has shown', he added, 'that it was Herzl who was right and not I.'

over to Rothschild. Now he would have to embark on what neither of them had wished for: 'mass agitation'.

There was no direct response. There is nothing to suggest that Rothschild and the men around him so much as dreamed of being drawn into his scheme. In any case, as matters were seen in Paris, what substance was there to this scheme, this enterprise, the control over which he was prepared so grandly to surrender to them? They only feared him somewhat—as a trouble-maker, as a possible rabble-rouser, as a man who would wilfully or blindly upset the delicate balances on which the Jewish position rested almost everywhere. They were not even sure there were real grounds to fear him. 'M. Leven croit qu'en fait il n'y a pas grand' chose à redouter de l'agitation nationale de Herzl [;] il serait seul à se prendre au sérieux, à s'agiter et n'a personne ou à peu près derrière lui.'[90]

---

[90] [Meyerson?] to Zadoc Kahn, 2 August 1896. CZA, A 51/4. Narcisse Leven, a co-founder of the Alliance Israélite Universelle and president of the Jewish Colonization Association, had been present at the confrontation between Edmond de Rothschild and Theodor Herzl.

# 12

## *Turning-point*

i

NEVER pray for a new king, runs a Yiddish proverb. (*Men tor nit betn oif a nayem melech.*) It was soon clear to the Jews of Russia and Poland—as to countless other subjects of the Tsar—that there was no more to be hoped for under Nicholas II than under his father. The profoundly hostile spirit which informed the Russian government collectively and most members of the governing class individually in their approach to the Jews had been affected neither by time nor by experience. Pobedonostev,[1] who had been tutor to Nicholas II as he had to Alexander III, was still extremely influential in the early years of the new reign. The Tsar himself, a smaller man both physically and mentally than his father, regarded the Jews with, if anything, greater loathing. The vast cumbersome machinery of government, from Court, Ministries, and Senate in the capital down through the provincial governors to the lowliest village police officers, continued to bear down upon them as before. The pogroms were not renewed for the time being,[2] but the intricate structure of administrative pressures and harassment to which the Jews were subjected was maintained intact and gradually improved upon. Old edicts and rulings were reinterpreted and refined; new ones were issued to cover unanticipated gaps and anomalies in the system evolved under Alexander III. The problem of how to resolve the contradiction between what was implied by the principle that the lives of the Jews must be constricted and the implications of the conviction that the propertied and the skilled deserved to be favoured over (and, if need be, at the expense of) the poor, the unskilled, and

---

[1] See above, pp. 49 ff.

[2] Attacks by mobs out for plunder did occur from time to time, serving to keep memories of the early 1880s alive; but they were not encouraged, and were usually put down, by the authorities. For a typical account, see *Ha-Magid*, 20 May 1897.

the illiterate was never successfully met. But the effort to meet it was unremitting. For the Jews themselves the results ranged from the merely vexatious and personally humiliating to the economically penal. For example, by the terms of one modification of the rules, Jewish soldiers were forbidden to spend their leave outside the Pale of Settlement regardless of where they were serving. By the terms of other rulings, the categories of artisans entitled to live outside the Pale were successively narrowed—galosh-makers one year, ink-makers another, piano-tuners and land surveyors the third. In 1897 razzias were conducted in the streets of Moscow and persons of 'Semitic physiognomy' were arrested in broad daylight and deported to the Pale. And most drastic of all measures taken in the early years of Nicholas II's reign, and most immediate in its impact, a state liquor monopoly was introduced into the western provinces (1896). This had the effect (and the intention) of depriving almost 30,000 Jewish tavern keepers of their livelihood at one blow.

The chief consequence of these and similar measures was to accelerate the material ruin of Russian and Polish Jewry. To a marked degree the endemic poverty now gave way steadily to pauperism. In the last years of the nineteenth century the earnings of Jewish clothing-workers in the ten provinces of Russian Poland were commonly less than 6 roubles or 12 shillings a week (at the rate of exchange current at the time); often they were as low as 2 roubles. A seamstress might earn £10 a year; a lace-maker less than half that. In the Ukraine conditions were often worse: in Volhynia even a master tailor generally earned no more than £12 to £20 per annum, the earnings of a master shoemaker might be £10, and a seamstress was lucky if she earned half that. The numbers of the very poor, measured by the corresponding resort to charity, increased by almost 30 per cent within the entire Pale between 1894 and 1898. In some provinces the corresponding increase was close to 50 per cent. Broadly, by the end of the century, between a fifth and a third of the Jewish population in many of the great centres had been reduced to virtual beggary.[3] And all this, it must be remembered, was taking place against the general background of peasant and proletarian misery at one end of the Russian social scale and of a fresh crushing of hopes for a liberalization of the regime at the other. Accordingly, the fact that there ensued

[3] Lucien Wolf (ed.), *The Legal Sufferings of the Jews in Russia*, introd. A. V. Dicey, London, 1912, pp. 55-7.

among the Jews of the Empire—as among the Russians proper, but more intensely among the Jews and pervasively because of their special disabilities, their social isolation, and their higher standards of literacy—a sharp rise in conscious discontent and in receptivity to new and radical ideas requires no special explanation. And herein lay one reason why, despite the circumstance that the great migration to the West continued almost unabated, the questions posed and the issues debated within Russo-Polish Jewry ceased to be reducible, in effect, to the simple alternatives: to flee or to try to make a stand.

That the great wave of pogroms had abated and that persecution of the Jews was now conducted principally through the instrumentalities of law and administration may also have had a good deal to do with the somewhat greater variety of approach and the greater complexity of public issues commonly posed. Russia was, after all, in many respects, a *Rechtsstaat*. Up to a point the law could be fought with law. Jewish lawyers could plead Jewish cases in the courts. The fight (and the strikes) conducted by Jewish workers in Vilna in 1892–3 for a working day limited to twelve hours relied on an ancient statute dating back to Catherine II. The new social mood owed next to nothing to the efforts of those established Jewish notables who, under Alexander III, had argued for patience and greater efforts to prove the 'usefulness' of the Jewish communities within the general framework of Russian society. And it ran quite contrary to the ancient practice of bending doggedly with the storm and taking mental refuge in an inner life in which the traditional emphasis on study and prayer tended to cast all else out towards the edge of consciousness.

The most powerful of the newer trends of thought were generally as radical in respect of the traditional structure of Jewish society (still largely dominated by the rich and the learned, by the *gevir* and the rabbi) as they were in respect of the political and economic system at large. It was in this period that there appeared on the Jewish scene, in White Russia and Lithuania particularly, clandestine Marxist revolutionary groups. They were fully analogous to those which had begun to operate within the general population and came to be linked with them. But in themselves they were ethnically homogeneous. For the comparatively docile common folk of eastern Jewry this syndicalism was a striking departure—the more so because in practice social agitation by, and on behalf of,

Jewish workers was almost invariably directed against Jewish employers with whom the rabbis, out of ingrained habit, and the police, on general principle, both sided. It was thus that class divisions of a modern kind, sharper and more blatant than had been known before, appeared within the Pale. True, few Jewish employers corresponded to the notional capitalists of Marxist theory: most *bale-batim* were no more than petty bourgeois themselves. The real, complex social structure of eastern Jewry was no more amenable to simple class or Marxist analysis than was that of overwhelmingly agrarian Russia itself. But there did certainly exist Jewish capitalists, and the steady impoverishment of the Jewish artisan class in these years had helped to create a large reservoir of urban industrial labourers who could be fairly termed 'proletarians'.

The epitome of this new development of radical social democracy in eastern Jewry was the Bund, the 'General Jewish Workers' Union in Lithuania, Poland, and Russia', founded in 1897. (It is worth noting that this was a full year before the 'Russian Social-Democratic Workers' Party', out of which the Russian Communist Party proper later evolved and of which the Bund was for many years a largely autonomous, constituent organization, was founded.) Its relevance to our own subject is twofold.

In the first place the rise of a *Jewish* revolutionary workers' organization provided remarkable evidence of the isolation of the Jews within the national working class. For reasons of cultural affinity, the early Jewish adepts of Marxism found it much easier to operate among other Jews than within the general population. Furthermore, as Jewish and non-Jewish labourers rarely worked together in the same factories and workshops, joint industrial action was not practicable even if it had been socially conceivable. So while the rise of class-oriented movements tended ultimately to provide for the needs of those radical spirits who looked for a cause that was not ethnically or religiously defined, but could be held common to all subjects of the Empire, in the short run even socialists, if they were Jews, had with rare exceptions to operate within the confines of their own people.

In the second place, the rise of the Bund indicates the advanced stage which the long-standing process of secularization of Jewish life and the consolidation of ever more critical and sceptical attitudes to tradition had now reached. It is also true that, in retrospect, it can be seen that for many of its members the movement that coalesced as the Bund came to serve as a decompression chamber, so to speak, intermediate between social action within Jewry alone and the ampler stage of supra-national or 'all-Russian' politics. To take one example, Martov (*né* Tsederbaum), the future leader of the Mensheviks, had begun as a militant member of the Jewish social democratic workers' organization in Vilna, the most important of the local circles to which the origins of the Bund can be directly traced. And it is not uncharacteristic of the road which impatience with orthodoxy of any kind had taken many thousands of educated East European Jews in the course of two or three generations that Martov himself was the grandson of Alexander Tsederbaum, founder of the Hebrew journal *Ha-Meliz* and a notable proponent of the *haskala*.[4] But those, like Martov, who wished to end Jewish isolation by joining the general revolutionary struggle in Russia even at the cost of an abandonment of Jewish communal identity were still in a very small minority. Overwhelmingly, even for revolutionaries, there was no question of dropping out of the Jewish community. It was rather that the forms in which Jewish particularism and national feelings had come increasingly to be conceived by virtually all adherents to the drive for the modernization of Jewish life in these closing years of the century were not religious and legal, as had been traditional in the past, but secular and literary. There was thus set a loose framework of loyalties and goals in which all radical movements evolved and of which all partook.

These were the times of the full flowering of what had been begun by the *maskilim*. Mapu, Smolenskin, and Yehuda Leib Gordon were dead, and Mendele Mokher Sefarim (1835–1917) and Lilienblum (1843–1910), although still writing, were past their peak. But Shalom Aleichem (1859–1916), Isaac Leib Peretz (1852–1915), and David Frischman (1859–1922) were in their prime; Aḥad Ha-ʿAm was at the height of his powers and approaching the peak of his prestige; Mordecai Zeʾev Feuerberg (1874–99) had entered on his brilliant and pathetically short career; Micha Yosef Berdyczewski (1865–1921) had begun his most fruitful period; and David Pinski (1872–1959) and Shaʾul Tschernichowsky (1875–1943) had published their first stories and poems respectively. The greatest figure in modern Hebrew literature, Ḥayyim Naḥman Bialik (1873–1934), had made his appearance as well.

---

[4] It was the same Alexander Tsederbaum who had done most, by intercession in St. Petersburg, to obtain legal sanction for the Odessa committee in 1890. (See above, p. 175.)

It was the distinguishing mark of all the younger men that the crudely revivalist, archaistic strain present in the early literature of the *haskala* was absent from their writings. They were moderns; and this not least because all shared an intense concern with the social condition of the Jews which reinforced the powerful sense of national identity represented by their choice of language—Hebrew or Yiddish (or both), rather than Russian or Polish—in which to write. They expressed the new, essentially secular national feeling and they fostered it—as much by the celebration of certain aspects of Jewish life as by the criticism and ridicule of others. It was this secular nationalism which made the notion of a particularist Jewish variety of social democracy ideologically tenable and, indeed, acceptable to many thousands for whom a total abandonment of Jewish society was unthinkable.

In this cardinal respect, the origins of the Jewish revolutionary movement can be traced to sources which were akin, if not identical, to those of East European Zionism. The differences between the two were partly of emphasis—which is to say, on the extent to which the secularism was thoroughgoing in each case. The socialists wanted a clean break with the past. The Zionists wanted to reconstitute it. It was therefore possible for the latter, unlike the former, to make common cause with the liberal wing, at least, of orthodoxy. Then there was the question of the emphasis on social questions as such. The socialists took them to be fundamental, but were prepared to recognize that the Jewish predicament had peculiarities that were not wholly amenable to analysis in strict socio-economic and class terms. The Zionists were, of course, very far from disregarding the social condition of the Jews: it was a fundamental component of their view. But they believed that, in practice, the right order of things was the reverse. The reordering of Jewish life was conditional on national independence. Both parties, in short, believed in surgery. But while the socialists wanted to help anputate the autocracy and capitalism and their respective supporting systems from the body politic of Russia, the Zionists wanted to remove the Jews. It is true that these matters were never clear-cut. The Jewish socialists encountered rising resistance to their claim to special status within the social-democratic movement as a whole and to recognition as the primary spokesmen for the Jewish working classes. They were therefore under constant pressure either to lose themselves in the general revolutionary fight, or else to bolster the particularist and separatist tendencies inherent in the very existence of a Jewish sub-division of the organized socialist movement at the risk of breaking with it if need be. Among the Zionists, on the other hand, support for a national political solution as the *sine qua non* of a solution to the Jewish problem did not preclude consideration of general social questions. In time, there developed a powerful trend to socialism within the general context of Zionism. This answered to the needs of those Zionists whose sympathies were simultaneously with the all-Russian revolutionary struggle, whatever they may have thought of the prospects it held out for the Jews, and who for reasons of temperament or principle were unwilling to postpone the effort to determine the internal character of the Jewish state until after its actual establishment. A fair part of the later history of Zionism was a function of the many combinations and recombinations composed out of these and cognate elements.

All in all, so far as the Jews were concerned, the late 1890s in Russia were marked—coincidentally with the change of ruler—by an intensification of social and literary activity percolating into, and encompassing, ever larger segments of the Jewish population. Readiness to listen to new ideas and messages and the ability to absorb them were greater than ever before. So were the numbers of free-floating, half-secularized members of the Jewish intelligentsia who carried and disseminated, when they did not formulate, these ideas and recipes for social action. Issues became more sharply defined in the public mind. Alternative programmes became better known. And it was not the least significant characteristic of this process of political education that in some respects it took place independently of the general rise of political-mindedness, unrest, and clandestine activity throughout Russia and Poland, while in other respects it was in symbiotic relationship to it. Arguments for change indirectly supported each other regardless of their specific content. Arguments for caution and patience began to lose much of their traditional force. The fashion among the young, the educated, and the poor was more than ever before to look forward, rather than backward, to anticipate release, and to act to further it. The young, the educated, and the poor being large and growing classes, the existing state of affairs came to be ever less easily tolerated by ever greater numbers. In sum, there was a disposition, stronger than ever, to seek deliverance from the misery of the

Jewish condition. Yet, Herzl as the leader, and political Zionism
as the plan, of action were slow to make an impact. How is this to
be explained?

There was nothing in Herzl's programme that was directly and
explicitly relevant to general social and political conditions in
Russia. His own views, as we have seen, were, by the standards
of the times, progressive and leaned towards mild forms of state
and democratic socialism. Like the overwhelming majority of
Hovevei Zion, he was convinced that the business at hand precluded close attention to socio-economic issues, the more so as his
programme necessarily depended on winning the trust and co-
operation of reactionary and despotic states. In the context of life
within the Russian Empire this was a weakness, the same weakness
from which Hibbat Zion suffered when compared with the new
social democratic revolutionaries.

One source of the latter's strengthening appeal to all varieties of
radical Jewish opinion—as much to particularists as to universalists
—was that their cause could easily be presented as one of immediate
and practical significance. Even if the toppling of the autocracy
seemed distant, there was much to be done here and now. And
what one did here and now in Russia would, at the very least, help
determine what course the otherwise ineluctable revolution would
take. Beyond that, clandestine organization and sedition—in fact,
any action against the regime, at any level—tended to mitigate
accumulated frustration and pain. In contrast, the ruling ideas of
the Hibbat Zion movement were predicated on countless years of
patient preparatory work at the end of which stood a deliberately
ill-defined goal. The growing, tough, ostensibly realistic movement
for a social democratic revolution with its closely argued ideological
underpinning could be contrasted to the fading Hibbat Zion of the
Odessa school, with all the ambiguities of its timid approach to
modern Russia and the lack of rigour in its notions about what was
ultimately to be done in and about the remote country to which it
looked for salvation. The weak reaction which Herzl's ideas aroused
among the Hovevei Zion of Russia and Poland was thus due, in the
first place, to the fact that he did not, initially, offer *them* a sharp
enough departure from the old forms. Certainly, his theory was
striking in its simplicity and clarity. His goals could not be better
defined. His method was set out for all to see. But the action, in
Herzl's scheme, was to be taken by a group of western Jewish

magnates while the role of the easterners was limited to that of, at best, providing proof (in the form of 'petitions' of support) of the validity and legitimacy of the enterprise. Eastern Hovevei Zion were thus not called upon to do much more than applaud. And since they had been left passive and free to watch his activities in calm and from afar, the urge to regard them critically and somewhat patronizingly and to give vent rapidly to the suspicions a newcomer so easily and ineluctably arouses was generally too strong to resist.

In the second place, Herzl made no attempt to appeal directly to Russian Jewry or even, at this stage, to individual Russian and Polish Jews. He did not travel to Russia and Poland. His adepts there organized no public meetings: these were possible in London and Vienna and on the periphery of the Jewish Pale—in Bulgaria, in Romania, in Galicia, and in Bukovina—but not, of course, within the Autocrat's domain. The reaction to Herzl was therefore closely and functionally related to what was reported and written about him in the Jewish press, along with such news and comment and rumours as filtered through into Russia by word of mouth and by letter from Hovevei Zion resident or travelling abroad. The Russian-language press was, as we have seen, distinctly hostile. In any case, its attitude to Hibbat Zion even in its mildest form was at best lukewarm. But a careful reader of the major Hebrew journals, *Ha-Zefira*, *Ha-Meliz*, and *Ha-Magid* (the last now published in Cracow but available in Russia) could follow events well enough. Reports from Paris, London, Vienna, Lemberg, Czernowitz, Galati, and other centres of Jewish population in the West and the East were printed regularly; and if local correspondents were generally uninhibited in pushing their own views, most views were represented.

These journals, however, were little bastions of caution and worldly wisdom. Their editors were supremely conscious of their responsibility as guardians of the only true national Jewish institutions within the Pale. They took themselves very seriously, not without a measure of justice, as makers of opinion and promoters of judicious thinking on public issues. And they shared with virtually all men of learning and letters, modernists no less than traditionalists, a profound aversion to anything that smacked of a simple solution, of quick deliverance, of an easy appeal to the unlettered and incautious populace—anything, in a word, that smacked of Messianism, anything that evoked echoes of the dark days of Shabbetai Zevi and half a nation led astray. It was this which impelled them

to draw a line, instinctively, between, on the one hand, the proposal
to translate Herzl's pamphlet into the popular language, Yiddish,
and, on the other hand, to report on Herzl to their own readers with
a high degree of accuracy. For the typical reader of the Hebrew
press was a comparatively well-educated man, a sympathizer with
Ḥibbat Zion, if not an active member, a man who was often much
like themselves—in a word: an initiate. And it must have been this
same fear of the intemperate and the quixotic that underlay the
young Bialik's first and conventional reaction to the new man,
Herzl: a mildly satiric poem on a mystic who, no longer able to bear
the misery around him, abandons his studies, cries 'It cannot continue! No, I can no longer delay!', calls for his prayer shawl and
his pack, and goes off to see the emperor to tell him so. He never
reaches the emperor and ends up mad and blind.[5]

It was thus that what was most striking and radical in Herzl,
where he differed most markedly from the established leaders of
Ḥibbat Zion, and the respect in which political Zionism was soon
to be able to compete very powerfully with the movement to harness
the Jews to a revolution inside Russia were all precisely those
elements that most antagonized many of the most influential leaders
of opinion within Ḥibbat Zion. This became evident when reports
(some accurate, some not) of his travels to Constantinople, London,
and Paris in the summer of 1896 began to come through and it had
become evident that the author of *Der Judenstaat* intended to be
a man of action.

'Wonderful rumours about a "Jewish State" which Dr. Herzl
has thought of creating' was the sarcastic headline Naḥum Sokolov
gave his first, considered statement on the subject. It was hard to
know what to make of this man, he wrote, distinguished though he
might be in the world of letters. Who would have believed that the
author of so improbable an idea would have lost no time trying to
put it into immediate effect? And one by one Herzl's ostensive dis-
qualifications for leadership were ticked off by Sokolov: his origins
in the assimilatory branch of Jewry, his indifference to the question
of Erez-Israel *v.* Argentina,[6] his naïve reliance on 'spider-webs of
political intrigue' to achieve his purposes, the extreme radicalism

[5] 'Rabbi Zeraḥ' was sent to *Ha-Shiloaḥ*, but Aḥad Ha-'Am refused to publish it, possibly
to avoid trouble with the censors, but conceivably too because he was unwilling to make
light of the excitement Herzl was causing. Cf. Yeruḥam Lachower, *Bialik: ḥayyav v'iẓirato*,
Tel Aviv, 1944, i, pp. 232–3.

[6] In fact, Herzl had already changed his mind. See above, p. 266.

of his ideas, his simple-minded openness, his haste. But leaving aside questions of personality, there was the additional, dire fact that Herzl's purposes and Herzl's methods were *political*, while here (in Russia), as was clear to all, politics, so Sokolov assured his readers, pertained exclusively to the government.[7]

Sokolov returned to the theme of politics and, in particular, to the notion that the Jews wanted a *state*, some months later. Herzl was like a little boy playing with fire near a barn, innocent but extremely dangerous. The truth had therefore to be stated: all sensible men knew where the obstacles to the resettlement of Erez-Israel lay. All knew how frightened the Turks were of national plots and risings and the continual attempts to cut further slices off the Empire. Yet now the Turks were being told to their faces (by Herzl) that the Jews too were after a state of their own. Hence the new edicts limiting immigration. But the truth was otherwise.

We all know [wrote Sokolov] that all these thoughts are devoid of substance. We all know that of the nations that live under the protection of the government, there is only one that will not quarrel or threaten violence, one nation that believes heart and soul in its rulers, and that nation is the people of Israel. All our brethren want is to dwell in peace and work their fields. They seek neither states nor kingdoms. This is what the Turkish government must be told again and again for the sake of truth and peace.[8]

There were other irritants. Herzl, complained *Ha-Magid*, presumed to treat with the Sultan and the 'wealthy Jews of England' without deigning to consult 'the people themselves . . . to hear their views, to ask them about their needs, and to see whether they are, in fact, worthy of the roles of "heroes of the drama" which he has written, and whether they will not shame him when he puts them on the stage in sight of all the world. Dr. Herzl is a great writer, but a poor statesman.'[9]

The journalists were the only class impelled by long habit and by the logic of their profession to take a stand; and theirs, to all intents and purposes, was (and could be) the sole public response in Russia and on behalf of Russian and Polish Jews to Herzl's first

[7] *Ha-Zefira*, 8 July 1896.
[8] Ibid., 20 October 1896. Herzl's attention was called to the article by Michael Berkowicz, his Hebrew secretary. He replied at length, and in some anger, correcting Sokolov's factual errors (e.g. about not having been received by Rothschild) and restating his case. This was published in full along with a fresh response by Sokolov. Ibid., 1 November 1896.
[9] *Ha-Magid*, 30 July 1896.

moves. Therefore, too much should not be made of it. It was a surface response: quick, rather than considered, and in tune with fashionable opinion rather than the deeper, slower currents of thought. Nevertheless, it reflected the puzzle he had set Ḥibbat Zion quite faithfully. And it should be noted too that, all told, it did not differ markedly from the response his first moves had elicited in the West: a shifting combination of grudging respect, momentary excitement fading into disbelief, and retreat to a feeling that nothing good for the Jews was likely to come of the novelty. So the matter rested for a time while other, various, and contradictory views floated in from the outside. Belkowsky, as we have seen, worked to get the Odessa committee to take a stand in Herzl's favour. Another enthusiastic voice was that of Yehoshua Eisenstadt-Barzilai, a leading member of Benei Moshe, now living in Jaffa—and thus, again, like Belkowsky, an emigrant from Russia:

Do you hear the words of Dr. Herzl? [he called in a fly-sheet he drafted for circulation in Europe] Is not your heart warmed by what you hear? Does not your blood boil . . . Will you stand aside in [these] times of hardship? Will you be silent when our enemies give you no rest and vilify you without respite? Will you not muster your last ounce of strength to put the great idea that [Herzl] has put forward into effect?[10]

On the other hand, there were dark and frankly hostile reports from Paris, the contents of which soon became known.

Herzl has accomplished nothing real, either in Constantinople, or in London, or, of course, in Paris. The rumour that he spoke to the Sultan is false. It is not certain that he spoke to the Grand Vizier. His talk is of great affairs, but it seems to me that in the end only one of two things will come of them. He is either a true Ḥovev Zion, in which case when he sees that he has accomplished nothing . . . he will turn to the Ḥovevei Zion and co-operate with them. Or else, he is a Ḥovev Zion only in words, in which case when he has learnt that he is not much believed and that what he has done thus far runs contrary to the idea of Ḥibbat Zion, he will leave the camp. The idea of a gradual settlement of Erez-Israel is foreign to him; he wants to bring forth a nation in a single generation. Here [in Paris] everything possible has been done to deflect him and, especially, to show him how remote what he proposes is from all that is real and possible.[11]

10 CZA, A24/4/465a.
11 Ludvipol to Ussishkin, 19 July 1896. CZA, A24/4/455. Cf. similar letter from Avraham Ludvipol to the Benei Moshe Society in Jaffa, 3 August 1896. A. Druyanov (ed.), *Mi-yamim rishonim*, 1934, i, pp. 46–7.

For the well-meaning, the consequence of the often scrappy information and the violently contradictory views was confusion. 'Now
we cannot make out this matter of Dr. Herzl clearly. On the one
hand there are those who praise him to the skies, like Professor
Belkowsky; and on the other hand there are those who denigrate
him absolutely, like the writer Ludvipol in Paris . . . May I ask
you for your opinion?'[12] Possibly for this reason and because many
sensed that, regardless of his virtues, this new-comer, with his
rather grand manner, was likely to upset the infinitely delicate
balance on which all the affairs of the movement relied, people
mostly held their tongues, took refuge from the issue in passivity,
and kept up the long patient wait for new developments. A change
only came in the following year (1897) as the undercurrents
that were favourable to a drastic departure from the old forms
gradually came to the fore. It was precipitated, however, by
Herzl himself, from the outside, and not by an initiative from
within Russia.

ii

Despite Herzl's brave words about 'mass agitation', the crumbling
of his hopes in London and Paris was not followed by a dramatic
change of direction or pace. True, a new note of sorts was struck
in his instructions to his closest followers and in his own activities.
De Haas, who had replaced Singer as his chief contact in England,
was urged from time to time to keep popular interest alive, chiefly
through the press, occasionally through public meetings. At home,
in Vienna, Herzl agreed (September 1896) to his own election as
head of the local Zionist movement and began to take a closer
interest in its affairs; in November he made his first speech there.
He also began to respond rather more cordially and systematically
than before to the broadening stream of visitors to his home from
all parts of the Dispersion. He took careful note of what was written
about him in the Jewish press—not only in England, in Austria,
and in Germany, but, as we have seen, in Eastern Europe. And he
maintained all the new contacts which first *Der Judenstaat* and then
his growing personal reputation had gained for him by means of
a voluminous correspondence, each one of his own letters being

---

[12] Nissenboim to Ussishkin, 1 September 1896. Israel Shapira (ed.), *Igrot ha-rav Nissenboim*, Jerusalem, 1956, p. 59.

drafted with evident care and in an effort to put writer and correspondent into as precise a relationship as possible. But there was
not much more to it than that. Where a correspondent was capable
of helping him with a point of local information—on conditions in
Erez-Israel, for example—he was asked to do so. Where visitors
and correspondents tried to impress their own views upon him
Herzl politely but inflexibly restated his own position.

It is a fair question whether he could have reasonably gone faster
at this stage. His requests to de Haas—of whom more was demanded
than of anyone else—were virtually always of an *ad hoc* nature; but
then Herzl was conscious of the difficulty of giving detailed instructions at so great a distance. Bodenheimer and Wolffsohn were in
Cologne, a provincial centre where there was not the real base, nor
the significant targets, for action that existed in London or even
Berlin. In Paris, apart from the isolated figure of Nordau, he had
to face the hostility—or at best the friendly neutrality—of the best-
organized Jewish institutions anywhere. In Berlin there were only
the leading members of the Berlin group of Hovevei Zion to turn
to. They were not wholly unfriendly, but certainly they were not
his allies. In Vienna he had himself become the leading figure in
a small band of loyalists and there at least he had men to call on,
his *Mitarbeiter*, and he did begin to cast about for a course of action,
appropriate to local conditions. As for the more distant centres in
Poland, in Russia, in the Balkans, and in Erez-Israel itself, there
again, he expected little of them and asked less. When Belkowsky
wrote to him (20 September), after a visit to Odessa, that Russian
Zionists who did not dare to express support for him openly had
empowered him to tell Herzl where they stood, Herzl's own
response did not go beyond 'heartiest thanks for your courteous
letter' and a request that Belkowsky's friends in Russia be thanked
as well and given an assurance that he, Herzl, would continue to
labour in the common cause.[13] To his new Romanian supporters
he wrote some months later:

> If you want a *mot d'ordre* from me for Hovevei Zion in Romania, here
> it is:
> Organize yourselves, gather strength, and be prepared. Spread a net-
> work of local societies all through Romania . . . and keep me informed
> [of your activities].

[13] Herzl to Belkowsky, 24 September 1896. *Igrot*, ii, no. 135, p. 149.

If you will accept my leadership, as Zionists of various other countries have, I will keep you abreast, of course, of all important events.[14]

It is plain enough that this passivity, this seeming inability to take the gift of leadership that was offered him and turn it to good account, stemmed in part from the fact that he had no clear idea what use to make of the support offered him apart from storing up these allies against the future. The idea of going to the people, rather than to the magnates, had come to him as an intuition. He was a long way from having worked out how he should proceed in practice. His own fresh and brief experience of political organization on his native ground in Vienna had only served to discourage and depress him. He had found that the major administrative and financial burdens of the enterprise were his to bear; that his effective associates were few in number and that what he could expect of them almost with certainty was interminable and often fruitless debate; that many struck him as being of indifferent intellectual and moral quality, for the sincere among them tended to be inactive, while the active seemed only out to 'advance their careers through an editor of the *Neue Freie Presse*'; and that he would for ever have to cope with jealousy, unreliability, and ingratitude.[15] This was a harsh view and not entirely just. In so far as it did correspond to the true state of affairs, it was in some measure Herzl's own fault. It was rare for him, as has been noted, to consult the members of his immediate circle—which tended, with time, to take on something of the aspect of a court. If he knew his own mind, it did not follow that others knew it. Those who were moved to support him consistently were thus, perhaps inevitably, those who were young enough to be willing to subordinate themselves to him, or the self-consciously mediocre, or bigger men who were yet sufficiently distant from him geographically to be able to see him above all in abstract terms, not as a man of flesh and blood with whom daily business had to be transacted.

But in part, too, the furious decision taken in July to go to the people had been of a general, non-specific kind. None of the meagre cards which he actually held suited it; none of his accomplishments thus far, however small, was in line with it. Inertia alone might have sufficed to keep him going for a while on the old path towards

---

[14] Herzl to Pineles, 18 January. *Igrot*, ii, no. 180, p. 195. This was evidently in response to a long letter from Pineles, 4 January 1897. CZA, H VIII 642.

[15] Cf. *Diaries*, ii, pp. 448, 451, 466, 471–3, 481.

the old targets. But in any case, the intended change of strategy did not yet imply a changed conception of what targets were to be aimed at; and the bitter disappointments in London ,and Paris had not yet altered his view on what actually constituted 'political Zionism' and what tactics were appropriate to its purpose.

> Your letter has interested me so much, [he wrote to a leader of the Zionist party in Austrian Galicia who had begged him to devote much more of his time to the movement] that I should gladly talk to you about many matters; and I hope there will be an opportunity for that when I come to Galicia. I still do not know exactly when I shall be able to do so, but it is in my programme for the very near future. I may be obliged to travel quite soon—on our affairs, as always—to Paris and to other places, and this activity is at the moment more important than popular propaganda.[16]

In the event, Herzl did not travel to Lemberg (Lvov). He did draw his correspondent (Adolf Stand) into his circle; and he did give the younger man regular advice that was hardly distinguishable from instruction. But otherwise, as his letter frankly stated, he still had no doubt that the main effort lay in Paris and in 'other places', which is to say among the princes and the magnates.

On that score there did follow (22 July) a successful meeting with Prince Ferdinand (later King) of Bulgaria arranged by Newlinski; and the Turkish connection was maintained after a fashion through the Ottoman Ambassador in Vienna. But there was little else to show for his continual efforts. In September there was an abortive attempt, through Hechler, to obtain an audience of the Kaiser. There were similar and again unsuccessful attempts to meet a former Prussian Minister of War and to be received by Lord Salisbury. On another plane he began a correspondence with the eminent Danish-Jewish critic Georg Brandes, conceivably in the hope of drawing a second lion into the fold alongside Nordau, but it too was a failure: Brandes, the universalist, was uninterested in the narrowly Jewish.[17] Herzl's hope of bringing Sir Samuel Montagu round was never fully abandoned, although he made no progress there either. Nor did he entirely lose all hope that Edmond de Rothschild might change his views and he was assiduous in his

---

[16] Herzl to Stand (Lemberg), 23 September 1896. *Igrot*, ii, no. 134, p. 148.

[17] For the exchange of letters, November 1896 to January 1897, see Rafael Edelmann, 'Theodor Herzl and Georg Brandes', in Tulo Nussenblatt (ed.), *Theodor Herzl Jahrbuch*, Vienna, 1937, pp. 165-9.

cultivation of the only man in Paris who was at one and the same time close to Rothschild, of personal distinction himself, and moderately (if very cautiously) sympathetic to Herzl—the Chief Rabbi, Zadoc Kahn. Thus, when Zadoc Kahn hazarded the notion of a confidential meeting of established Jewish leaders ('les représentants les plus autorisés des grandes communautés juives') to discuss the issues which Herzl had raised 'from all aspects',[18] the response was warm. He was not a 'raging agitator', he wrote to the rabbi; and he was prepared to prove it by attendance at such a conference—if, that is, it was to be a truly practical affair.[19] However, nothing ever came of the idea, nor of others that the two men exchanged. In October the correspondence fizzled out. 'Dear sir, I have no advice . . . to give you', the rabbi concluded.[20]

There were other minor sources of discomfort. There was Newlinski whom Herzl could never finally make up his mind whether to trust fully or not. Bismarck, he was informed, had read *Der Judenstaat* after all, but had judged it a 'melancholy fantasy'. And he was infuriated to learn that a number of prominent Jewish bankers were proposing to participate in the large-scale settlement of Turkish financial affairs that had begun to be discussed, thus doing precisely what he had wanted of them, but for the wrong—i.e. purely commercial—reasons and to no political purpose whatsoever.

By the autumn of 1896, the failure to put his achievements, such as they were, to effective use and, above all, his failure to maintain the momentum of his initial venture into high politics were fully apparent to him. In the summer, still buoyant after his journeys in June and July he had written to Wolffsohn jauntily, 'The state of affairs is now as follows: *very propitious* in Constantinople, tolerable in London, bad in Paris.' Rothschild, in other words, was keeping everything back, including the Londoners. His own response, he wrote, was that 'I shall at once begin to organize.'[21] But by the autumn, as he took stock, he was for the moment, in his own words, 'demoralized'[22] by the bleak prospect around him; and as time went by the gloom deepened. 'I feel myself getting tired. More frequently than ever I now believe that my movement is at an end. I am fully convinced of its feasibility, but cannot overcome

---

[18] Zadoc Kahn to Herzl, 30 July 1896. CZA, H VIII 420/4.
[19] Herzl to Zadoc Kahn, 2 August 1896. *Igrot*, ii, no. 117, pp. 134–5.
[20] Zadoc Kahn to Herzl, 26 October 1896. CZA, H VIII 420/9.
[21] Emphasis in original. Herzl to Wolffsohn, 1 August 1896. CZA, H B58 (*Igrot*, ii, 115, p. 131).   [22] *Diaries*, ii, p. 481.

the initial difficulties.'[23] A sense of having sustained an irrevocable loss of momentum began to grow—to be traced, fundamentally, it seemed to him, to the opposition of the 'ignorant and mean' bankers, the 'miserable rascals' who had it in their power to help him seize the priceless opportunities that were briefly his for the taking.[24]

There was the general chronic need for funds. 'It is a vicious circle,' he wrote to de Haas; 'no funds no propaganda, no propaganda no funds.'[25] There was, of course, the basic refusal to put up money for the great transaction with the Turks. But almost as depressing and still more galling was the failure to find the paltry means (as he judged them) to mount what he was sure was the simple, promising, and feasible project of a newspaper—a 'great paper' that could be turned into an instrument of independent Jewish policy, and such as he himself was so obviously well equipped to run and which would release him from the continual, at times 'untenable', irritation and friction implicit in his post on the *Neue Freie Presse*. Its editors were as hostile as ever to his cause, yet it was to them he owed his livelihood and much of his public position. Herzl believed that a newspaper could be made a source of independent political power: 'governments negotiate with a great paper as one Power to another.'[26] He knew how sensitive the Turks were to the foreign press. He had been urged by the Prime Minister of Austria to found and run a newspaper that would support the government; and now, as elections approached, the proposal was renewed. But as there could be no question of a government subvention—as much for principle's sake as to ensure he was free to barter his support for the government's—he had to raise the money himself. He could get some 400,000 guilders from his family; but he needed a million. He put the project to the trustees of the Hirsch foundation (I.C.A.) through Zadoc Kahn and was turned down flat.[27] It was infuriating. 'This bagatelle (considering the greatness of the cause) is wanting—and this is why we shall have to sleep although it is daylight.'[28] At the beginning of 1897 he

[23] *Diaries*, ii, p. 504.
[24] Herzl to Gustav Cohen, 2 December 1896. *Igrot*, ii, no. 165, p. 176. Herzl to de Haas, 8 February 1897. Ibid., no. 189, p. 201.
[25] Herzl to de Haas, 15 December 1896. Ibid., no. 172, p. 183.
[26] *Diaries*, ii, p. 505.
[27] Zadoc Kahn to Herzl, 26 October 1896. CZA, H VIII 420/9.
[28] *Diaries*, ii, p. 504.

observed that 'the general torpor of the movement is gradually getting into my bones.'[29]

For all these bouts of gloom there was no loss of faith in the practicability of the Zionist enterprise itself, only an irritable, often petulant railing against the inadequacy, sluggishness, selfishness, or sheer poltroonery of those to whom he looked to help him carry it through. There was in Herzl none of the profound, if somewhat pathetic pessimism that moved Nordau to write him at this time: 'All my perceptions cause me to doubt whether Jewry still has sufficient virility to maintain its historic personality at the cost of a struggle for life and death. Certainly without such a struggle nothing will be achieved.'[30] Herzl was subject to depression, but not to romantic despair. Nor did his ill-humour ever dull the edge of his imagination and his *élan*. He remained consistently alert to every potential opening: cultivating an artist who had once painted the Princess of Hesse and who therefore stood a chance of becoming a court painter in St. Petersburg now that she was Empress of Russia; running a Zionist candidate in the Reichsrat elections but dropping the idea when it appeared that the campaign had been entered too late for satisfactory results; proposing to press the *Ḥakham* (Sephardi Chief Rabbi) in London to try to win over a Jewish diamond magnate from South Africa upon hearing that the latter had come to London; writing to the Grand Duke Vladimir of Russia for an interview upon hearing that he was in Berlin—on the strength of Prince Ferdinand of Bulgaria's assurance that Vladimir was the one man in Russia who might help; and so on, no matter how remote the possibility or, ostensibly, implausible.

The sources of Herzl's energy and absolute seriousness of purpose were first and foremost internal. But there is no reason to doubt that the ever widening circle of his correspondence, his rising notoriety, and the steady stream of visitors to his home in Vienna from throughout the Dispersion and from Ereẓ-Israel all served to raise his spirits when they flagged and to reinforce his own powerful, inner conviction of the role he should play. Indeed, in many eyes the role was already his. 'Hold your hands high, dear Doctor', Wolffsohn wrote to encourage him and to remind him of Moses whose flagging arms were held high by his men until the battle between the Israelites and Amalek had been won. 'Fight to the

[29] Ibid., p. 505.
[30] Nordau to Herzl, 10 October 1896. CZA, H VIII 614.

utmost. At the right time the right young men will not fail to appear in support and Israel's victory will have been won'.[31]

But apart from his inner belief and the heart put in him from time to time by members of his entourage, it may be supposed that there could, in fact, be no turning back for so intense and sensitive a man except at a price that he would probably have himself judged a public humiliation. In the twelve months since the appearance of *Der Judenstaat* the once fashionable playwright and feuilletonist had travelled too far and for too long outside the bounds of what in his milieu constituted ideological propriety to be capable of abandoning the effort to demonstrate the intellectual and material validity of his programme. The plan to convene a great public congress of Zionists encompassed a great deal more than such a demonstration; but it was at least, and in the first instance, that— which is perhaps why it had been in Herzl's mind for a very long time before the effective if somewhat anti-climactic decision to convene such a congress was taken.

The idea of calling 'a general assembly of Zionists' (*ein allgemeiner Zionistentag*) crops up in Herzl's correspondence and in his diary almost immediately after his return to Vienna from his journey to the Levant and to London and Paris.[32] But it is evident that he had not yet considered how it would be mounted, who would be invited to attend, what its programme would be, or any other organizational detail. His mind was really elsewhere, as we have seen. He was much more interested in Zadoc Kahn's idea of a secret conference of established leaders which he would 'rouse . . . to some action' on the strength of the 'further diplomatic success' he would have achieved by the time it convened.[33] A manifestly *public* congress was another matter, probably conceived—and that hazily—as a weapon to be held in reserve, an obvious tactic to be employed once one had set about 'mass agitation' in earnest. By November, however, the idea was firmly lodged in his mind and he had begun to think of it concretely, even if he was still in no hurry to act.[34] In January 1897, with the worst of his depression behind him, it is clear that he was really set upon it, if only because its attraction had grown *pari passu* with the dashing of virtually all other expectations.

---

[31] Wolffsohn to Herzl, 10 August 1896. CZA, H VIII 940/5.
[32] Herzl to Wolffsohn, 1 August 1896. *Igrot*, ii, no. 115, p. 131.
[33] *Diaries*, ii, p. 447.
[34] Herzl to Stand, 18 November 1896. *Igrot*, ii, no. 160, pp. 171–2.

The references to a congress in his correspondence and in his diary become definite and specific and at the same time, as was frequent with Herzl, very matter of fact—as if what he was embarking on was the most natural thing in the world. De Haas was informed that 'I intend to call a general assembly of Zionists in Switzerland this summer' and encouraged to give the item moderate preliminary publicity.[35] A month later he was informing his friends of the proposed venue (Zürich) and of the approximate date (the latter half of August), and had moved forward to a first consideration of some of the more intricate problems that he would have to face, such as what the Russian Jews were likely to think of it.[36]

The operative decision to convene the Zionist Congress was taken shortly after, on 7 March 1897, on the second of two days of conference in Vienna with a group of Hovevei Zion from Berlin. The occasion of the conference was an attempt by the Berliners, led by Willy Bambus, to bring Herzl and his associates in Austria into a co-operative, working relationship with the Berlin circle. Bambus was the leading figure and the prime mover in 'Esra', a society founded over a decade earlier on the classic basis, namely to facilitate and encourage the settlement of Russian Jews in Erez-Israel. It was run on determinedly philanthropic lines. Bambus and his friends were far less politically inclined than the other Zionist or proto-Zionist circles in Germany, Bodenheimer's and Wolffsohn's group in Cologne, and the Russian-Jewish studies society led by Motzkin in Berlin. For one thing they were not so consciously in revolt against, and were therefore more sensitive to, contemporary run-of-the-mill German-Jewish middle-class notions about the place of Jews in Germany and about what constituted the proper and possible basis on which Jews could be integrated into German society. They were also in close touch with the existing major sources of philanthropic assistance to the settlements in Erez-Israel, namely Baron de Rothschild and his representatives, the Hirsch foundation, and the Odessa committee. And beyond that they fancied, not wholly without justification, that they were men of a practical bent of mind. Some, like Bambus himself and his colleague Hirsch Hildesheimer, had devoted many years to the

---

[35] Herzl to de Haas, 3 January 1897. Ibid. i, no. 174, p. 185. See also Herzl to Bambus, 26 January 1897. Ibid., no. 182, p. 196.

[36] Herzl to Stand, 18 February 1897. Ibid., no. 193, p. 205. *Diaries*, ii, p. 517; and I. Klausner, *Mi-Katoviz 'ad Bazel*, ii, p. 354. Belkowsky was asked to inquire. The first reaction was that, of course, they could not attend for fear of antagonizing the authorities.

enterprise, and had acquired a great deal of experience. Their preference for the concrete over the imaginative—and hence for cows and vineyards in Erez-Israel over argument about the ultimate aims of the movement—was thus very strong. Still they were not all of one mind. Attitudes varied: all were aware of the sorry, invertebrate state of Ḥibbat Ẓion; therefore many (but certainly not all) valued the adherence of Herzl to a cause which in the German-speaking countries had yet to attract anyone of comparable prominence; some (but they were a minority) were positively impressed by his views and were beginning to be sympathetic to them. It was the latter category that had started the train of correspondence with him that led to the meeting. But they were not his men. They hoped to tame Herzl and to draw him towards them; and they wanted his help.

Specifically, Bambus and his friends came to Vienna to discuss the foundation of an agricultural bank to advance matters in Erez-Israel and, also, having heard of Herzl's own interest in a powerful journal for the movement, to gain his help for the conversion of their own monthly *Zion* into a bigger affair. Herzl was polite about the bank. He was, of course, more interested in the other project. Propaganda—that was the first requirement, he had already written to Bambus. He, too wanted to come to an understanding, he had written to them, and, really, the differences between them were only of 'nuances'.[37] It remains, that in Berlin they knew of Herzl's plan to convene a Congress and must have assumed that he would raise it at the meeting.

When the two groups[38] met, it seemed at first that the general optimism had not been misplaced. The matter of the bank did not come up for serious discussion, if at all.[39] There was no disagreement about the journal: it was resolved to establish a daily newspaper. Indeed, Bambus's support for such a project was indirect evidence of his own progress towards a conception of things akin to that of

---

[37] Herzl to Bambus, 26 January 1897. *Igrot*, ii, no. 182, p. 196.

[38] Among those who accompanied Bambus to Vienna were Nathan Birnbaum, who now lived in Berlin and edited the journal which the Berliners wanted built up, and Moritz Moses, who had attended the first conference of Ḥovevei Ẓion at Kattowitz in 1884. Birnbaum and Moses had also joined in one of the many abortive attempts to call a great general conference of Zionists at a meeting in Vienna in September 1893. The conference was to convene in Berlin a year later. Among those attending the earlier Vienna meeting were Belkowsky, Ehrenpreis, and Salz, who had now rallied to Herzl. CZA, A 171/16.

[39] The extremely sketchy protocol of the two days of talks (CZA, Z 1/34) carries no mention of it; nor does Herzl's account (*Diaries*, ii, pp. 518–20).

Herzl's. But of course the foundation or purchase of a newspaper depended on their collective ability to raise funds and in this latter respect it was soon clear that the prospects of getting beyond the point at which Herzl had been baulked were poor.

The second day of the conference (7 March) was devoted to Herzl's Congress. It was resolved to convene it on 25 August, in Munich, if that were possible, and, if not, in Breslau or in Zürich;[40] that the invitations to the Congress would carry Herzl's signature and that he would determine its form; and that an organizing committee (to include some people who were not present, among them Belkowsky in Sofia and Pineles in Galati, Romania) would be set up to assist him. Ideas for the agenda, all sketchy, some obscure, were advanced: among them addresses or discussions on the 'psychology and pathology of the Jews', on the 'general question of the Jews from a political point of view', and on theory and practice in Zionism'.

The atmosphere at this Vienna meeting was friendly, so much so that the two leading figures were evidently misled into thinking that there was identity of views where in truth there was moderate agreement marred by at least one very significant difference. Bambus had wanted two congresses, one 'internal', and the other 'external'; for with his ingrained caution and fear of anything suggesting bombast he preferred having sensitive issues, and questions of major principle discussed in private and only the comparatively mundane affairs of the *yishuv* discussed in public. But only the bald proposal for the 'two congresses' was noted in the brief protocol and Herzl, carelessly, but evidently in good faith, seems to have taken 'two congresses' to mean no more than that the (single) Congress would have both public and closed sessions. The upshot was that the Berliners departed, leaving Herzl confident that real progress had been made and that he had at last found a solid and capable ally, and resolved to press ahead with the organization of the Congress without delay.

iii

The decision to call a congress transformed the scene. Herzl had at last set himself and his friends a task that was within the bounds

---

[40] The date was later changed to 29 August, the venue, as we shall see, to Basel.

of the attainable. It was, moreover, a task to which his gifts and his experience were fully suited: his energy, his personal authority and persuasiveness, his sense of the theatre (both literal and figurative), and his many years as a parliamentary correspondent at the French Chamber of Deputies. But, above all, both adherents of the movement in all parts of Europe who had any pretension to a position of influence within it and its active opponents had at one stroke been presented with an issue on which they would now have to make up their minds and visibly, publicly commit themselves one way or the other.

Some months passed before the full significance of the call to a Zionist Congress and the blunt circumstance that Herzl was absolutely determined to have it held had fully worked themselves to the surface of consciousness in every case. The lines, the intensity, and the chronology of the ensuing debate varied from one locality to another. The processes by which support was gained or lost and the critical reasons underlying the ultimate decision in any particular case were often complex, if not, ultimately, unknowable. But the reasons for accepting or rejecting Herzl's call may now be judged secondary in import to the fact that a question had been posed to which the answer was reducible to a simple yes or no. This was new in modern Jewish affairs.

In effect, what now ensued was a campaign to capture visible support for Zionism in a manner that bears comparison with the conduct of a free parliamentary election, but where the circumstances were peculiar and unique. The public concerned was virtually without experience of regular, institutionalized national politics; the electorate was not clearly defined and, perhaps, not definable; only one party, the Zionist, openly competed for support; only the Zionist platform was coherent. Yet there was a clear issue before the public and a well-identified candidate with a known programme. The grounds for a decision one way or another might therefore be intuitive in any given case, or confused or even misplaced; but there were many cases in which they were explicit; and in the aggregate there was, by the standards of the times and within the limits of the still inchoate Jewish polity, a recognizable outcome.

From the first, there had been no doubt in Herzl's mind about what was to be aimed at. The Congress was to 'be a glorious demonstration to the world of what Zionism is and of what it wants'.

Apart from that, its immediate business was to make a unified Zionist movement possible.[41] This was a task to be invested with urgency: it was late in the day; opportunities had been lost. Detailed instructions to proved friends were issued from Vienna within days of the meeting with Bambus. The *Jewish Chronicle* in London was provided with a preliminary agenda in a little over a week. By the beginning of April the first formal announcement, complete with registration particulars and instructions, a draft agenda, and the gist of the aims of the Congress, had been drafted and dispatched to a large number of prominent figures, in many cases accompanied by personal letters from Herzl. The language was sedate, but there was no circumlocution about the underlying rationale. The Congress would consider the needs of those Jews who were in straits and seek a remedy; and, if it thought it advisable, appoint an executive committee to manage the affairs of the Jews until it was next convened. 'The matter of the Jews [*die Judensache*] had to be taken out of the hands of private individuals, however well intentioned. It was necessary to set up a forum before which anyone could be brought to give an account of what he is or is not doing in the matter of the Jews.'[42] Thus at the apex of the national pyramid. At its base, true to his fixed conceptions, Herzl's friends were asked to attempt the famous 'mass agitation'. All with the prospect of reaching the 'masses' were asked to foment public demonstrations, launch the signing of mass 'petitions' (or memorials), collect funds to cover the expenses of delegates (especially from Eastern Europe) who could not otherwise travel, and in every other way ensure the greatest possible public, popular backing for the principal actors on centre stage.[43] And these, to Herzl's mind, despite all he had experienced since his meeting with Hirsch two years earlier, could only be the notables of western Jewry. The difference was that it was not their money he wanted now, but their persons; and he did not doubt that the success of the Congress would depend first and foremost on the numbers and reputations of those who could be persuaded to attend. Accordingly, he began by returning to the ground that he had already covered in England, France, and Germany and while he did not neglect his new supporters in the

[41] Herzl to Bentwich, 9 March 1897. *Igrot*, ii, no. 199, p. 212.

[42] Ibid., no. 219, pp. 235-7.

[43] See for example Herzl to de Haas on stirring things up in the East End of London, 12 March 1897, ibid., no. 200, pp. 213-15; and Herzl to Stand, 11 April, ibid., no. 231, pp. 247-8.

East, it was to the former, initially, that he applied himself with his characteristic energy, imagination, and attention to detail.

Of all the growing number of men involved in the new movement —his creation, as he and all the men around him saw it—he alone was entirely and single-mindedly engrossed in its service. One of his new disciples and assistants later wrote of this period (with obvious awe, but without exaggeration): 'We consulted, resolved, decided—and then each one of us returned to his own affairs. Herzl organized the Congress on his own, entirely on his own, with his own money and labour . . . He attended to everything, nothing escaped him. There were times when he sat up all night with the students and did all sorts of jobs, even addressing the envelopes.'[44]

Herzl made no attempt to turn once more to those, like Edmond de Rothschild, who had already rejected his ideas flatly. The Congress had, after all, been conceived initially as a public rebellion against the established secular leaders of Jewry, and of Hibbat Zion in particular. But he did try to persuade those on the margin of the opposition to him, who were cautiously sympathetic to him, but who had none the less held back, to take the plunge—Goldsmid, for example. He tried by reasoned argument, by appeals to his sense of principle, by playing on his vanity ('You, Colonel, ought to enter the Turkish service as a general, like Woods, Kamphövener, von der Goltz, and other foreign officers, and in that capacity you would be in command in Palestine under the suzerainty of the Sultan'), and by repeating his offer to retire from the leadership if Goldsmid and his friends would promise to maintain the course he had set. But above all, he sought to make it absolutely clear that the decision to hold the Congress was irrevocable: 'The Munich Congress is a settled affair from which I can no longer withdraw. But it is a necessity as well.'[45]

Herzl repeated this statement of unalterable intent again and again at every opportunity. It served him, he believed, as the iron fist within the velvet glove of blandishment, and helped him to bear with the irritating need to deal with men who had already disappointed him, some of whom he despised. He knew he frightened them: a public congress of Jews was in itself a fearful thing to men who habitually trod softly. He hoped their fear of him would work to bring them over to his side, if only in an effort to restrain him.

[44] Yehoshua Thon, *Theodor Herzl*, Berlin, 1914, p. 26.
[45] *Diaries*, ii, pp. 532–3.

But the tactic failed almost totally. 'We mustn't talk too loudly of
the National Idea . . . publicity is a mistake, I think, at the present
juncture', was Goldsmid's characteristic response.[46] And early in
June the 'Headquarters Tent' of the Hovevei Zion in Great Britain
announced, without explanation, that it would have nothing to do
with 'the congress convened by Dr. Herzl'.[47] Montagu told him
that he was opposed to the Jews acting 'internationally on political
matters'.[48] Zadoc Kahn assured Herzl that he would be following
events with the greatest attention, but that as rabbis in France were
in some sense officials of the state, his own position was 'extremely
difficult'.[49] Güdemann, the Chief Rabbi of Vienna, after vacillating
a while longer, broke with him completely and published a violently
anti-Zionist pamphlet. A wild hope that Bacher, one of his chiefs
on the *Neue Freie Presse*, might change his skin was soon dashed
and Herzl found himself instead under heavy pressure from his
employers to desist from the entire project. (He refused, but it was
an additional source of stress.) Most serious and most unexpected
of all was the rapid defection of his newly won ally Bambus and his
colleague, Hildesheimer,[50] the alliance with whom had precipitated
the decision to convene the Congress. They had been alarmed by
the generally hostile reception to the idea of a congress in the three
chief centres of western Hibbat Zion—in Berlin, in Paris, and in
London—and in Munich itself where the official secular and
religious leaders of the local community were terrified of the
embarrassment which they believed the convening of a Zionist
Congress on their own doorstep would cause them. Bambus accordingly asked Herzl to reconsider holding two separate congresses,
one, the political, in private, and only the other, dealing exclusively
with settlement affairs, in public. And without waiting for Herzl's
response, he announced that, while it was true that there had been
talks on holding a congress at which general questions of concern
to Jewry would be discussed, nothing had in fact been decided and
Herzl's declarations and invitations were unauthorized. He was
therefore obliged to declare that, 'of course', he had never intended
to attend a Zionist Congress, but had held out the prospect of his

---

[46] Goldsmid to Herzl, 30 March 1897. CZA, H VIII 285a/8.
[47] *Jewish Chronicle*, 4 June 1897.
[48] Montagu to Herzl, 14 July 1897. CZA, H VIII 575/5. Cf. above, p. 303.
[49] Zadoc Kahn to Herzl, 30 April 1897. CZA, H VIII 420/12.
[50] This was Hirsch Hildesheimer, the son of Rabbi 'Azriel Hildesheimer in whom
Pinsker had put hopes and been similarly disappointed. Cf. above, pp. 169f.

presence and his participation only and solely in the event that the planned assembly would be devoted to a discussion of the manifold tasks of the Palestine aid project, particularly colonization.'[51] In June, after several weeks of rumbling protest, the Jewish community in Munich made its opposition explicit. On 6 July the five-man executive committee of the German rabbinate did what no other country-wide Jewish secular or religious organization had done: it formally and publicly condemned the 'efforts of the so-called Zionists to create a Jewish National State in Palestine' as contrary to Holy Writ, and drew a sharp distinction between legitimate efforts to assist Jewish settlers in the Holy Land, and the illegitimate purposes of the Zionists. The former implied no disloyalty by Jews to the country of their residence and citizenship, the country which they were required by Judaism to serve 'with the utmost devotion'. The latter, they implied, did. The rabbis therefore called upon 'all who have the welfare of Judaism at heart' to hold aloof from Zionism and abstain from attending the conference.

The upshot was that by the middle of the year it was abundantly clear that the Congress was not going to be the brilliant assembly of western Jews setting out to deal once and for all with the miseries of their poorer brethren that Herzl, like Pinsker before him, had wanted. Nordau, the only man of first-rate repute to join him, remained steadfast. But for the rest, there were only the members of his youthful entourage in Vienna enriched by a few older, middle-class men, a handful of students in France, more students in Berlin (many of whom were Russian, not German, Jews), de Haas in London, and some obscure figures from the East End and from lesser communities in the English provinces (Leeds, notably), and a scattered handful of other loyalists of whom Bodenheimer and Wolffsohn were the most important and promising. None the less, as the summer of 1897 wore on, there did occur a subtle change in the prevalent attitudes to the affair: higher regard for Herzl from his opponents and from the sceptics and a rise of confidence among his supporters. On 9 July the *Jewish Chronicle* headed its hostile leading article 'Dr. Herzl's Congress' and a week later it was reporting on 'The Proposed "Zionist" Congress'; but in the following month the ironic inverted commas were dropped and on

---

[51] Bambus to Herzl, 22 April 1897; and Bodenheimer to Herzl, 20 May 1897. Henriette Hannah Bodenheimer, *Im Anfang der zionistischen Bewegung*, Frankfurt a.M., 1965, pp. 34–5 fn. 9, and pp. 39–40. See also *Diaries*, ii, p. 544.

13 August the *Chronicle*'s Vienna correspondent was reporting matter-of-factly that the invitations to the delegates were ready for distribution and that 'the cards are very tastefully got up'. In August, on the eve of the Congress, Goldsmid wrote to Herzl in an apologetic and ingratiating tone that while he was still opposed in principle to the Congress, individual members of the English Hovevei Zion societies were free to attend and that, for his own part, 'I have watched with the greatest interest the whole movement and I think you are to be congratulated on the opposition of the German and American *Rabbonim*.'[52] Zadoc Kahn too wrote to Herzl in the same vein.[53] And Willy Bambus (but not his friend Hildesheimer) reconsidered his position and informed Herzl that he would attend the Congress after all. As for the mood and the growing pugnacity of Herzl's supporters, they are well epitomized by Nordau's comment that the German rabbis were opposed to Zionism because they evidently felt no need to revolt against their own servitude. 'There are degrees even in degradation', he told a questioner.[54]

This change of mood owed a great deal to the fact that the decision to call the Congress had touched off a furore. The Congress was intended to be a much more visible political act than Herzl's theoretical essay of the year before. Unmistakably, it was a venture into the pursuit of Jewish interests which lay well beyond the limits of communal, charitable, and strictly religious affairs. The opposition to it was therefore the more serious and the public debate upon it the fiercer. Nor were the Zionists backward. Nordau slashed at the Chief Rabbi of Vienna for daring to attack Herzl. Bodenheimer and his friends assailed the German *Protestrabbiner*, as they came to be called. Herzl took the lead and set the tone himself by, at long last, establishing an organ for the movement, the weekly *Die Welt*. (He relied entirely on his own and his father's resources. The daily newspaper that he had wanted was beyond their means.) 'Unser Wochenschrift ist ein "Judenblatt"', read the very first sentence of *Die Welt*'s first leading article; and its cover, with the same provocative intent, was yellow.[55] In brief, it was during the months

---

[52] Goldsmid to Herzl, 8 August 1897. CZA, H VIII 285a/11.

[53] Zadoc Kahn to Herzl, 29 August 1897. CZA, H VIII 420/16.

[54] *Jewish Chronicle*, 23 July 1897.

[55] *Die Welt*, 4 June 1897. *Judenblatt* ('Jews' paper') was the contemptuous term used by anti-Semites in Germany and Austria to describe periodicals owned or edited by Jews— like Herzl's own employer, the *Neue Freie Presse*.

M

before the Congress met that the lines separating the Zionists from others were first traced before a wide public. While many who had known little about Zionism were now made more fearful, others were drawn to it, often in spite of themselves, and of what they took to be their better judgement, impressed and even touched by the doggedness with which Herzl cast all he did in the strong light of dignity and forthrightness—worlds away from the atmosphere of cluttered thinking and self-mortification in which Jewish public affairs were generally conducted at the time.[56]

There was another factor. Despite the need to argue endlessly, to wheedle others, and to keep up his own spirits in the face of repeated disappointments and strain, Herzl did stick to his guns throughout. He refused to compromise over the nature of the Congress. He encouraged Bodenheimer to assume the leadership of Zionism in Germany when it became apparent that the established Hovevei Zion in Berlin were drawing back.[57] His essential response to the protests of the Munich Jewish community was unhesitatingly to arrange to move the Congress to Basel. At no stage did he lose his nerve. When he recognized an error he set out to correct it. And he was as ready as ever to look for the hidden advantage in what appeared a tactical defeat. He saw, almost from the first, that the rising clamour against him and his Congress could be of benefit. And his diary entries for the period suggest faintly, but unmistakably, that having braced himself to face the refusal of every Western and Central European figure of the front rank to attend (always excepting Nordau), he began to find the loneliness of his position and his consequent unquestionable and enhanced indispensability to the movement a source of secret satisfaction, if not exhilaration. For his influence over those who stuck by him grew steadily in this period and he emerged at the Congress itself even before it had fully assembled, a greater figure than he had been before, an established national leader. In the inchoate condition of Jewish national politics, this alone assured him of a substantial measure of power and influence and, in accordance with long tradition, it set him apart as a man whose doings had to be comprehended in the calculations of all others who had pretensions to a role in Jewish national affairs. It was this factor which had moved

Bambus and some of his colleagues to change their minds and attend the Congress. And it is of the greatest significance that they were at one here with those Hovevei Zion in the East who shared their doubts about Herzl and had additional reservations of their own, but who, in the end, saw no alternative to 'attending the Congress in order to see to it that the true interests of the matter for which we have laboured for more than fifteen years are assured'.[58]

iv

Herzl's connections with Hibbat Zion in Eastern Europe were, as we have seen, of two kinds: direct and fairly regular contacts, maintained either in person or by means of correspondence, with a small number of leading Hovevei Zion in the main Jewish communities on the periphery of the Russian Empire or just beyond; and a very sparse and random series of meetings with such Hovevei Zion from Russia itself as happened to be journeying, or living abroad. Into the latter category fell his meeting with Ussishkin and his own appearance before an audience of East European Jews in Whitechapel in the previous year. But those who were involved in the first category played a more important role. In the first place, they themselves, as prominent inhabitants of important regions of the Diaspora, by rallying to Herzl helped him to demonstrate the ecumenical character of the Congress. In the second place it was largely on them that he relied to represent him in the heartland countries of Russia and Russian Poland—from whose people he was cut off materially by sheer distance and by such particular circumstances as fear lest he incriminate them with the Russian police, but also psychologically by differences of outlook, culture, and language. They also helped to supplement what he could learn of the East from his entourage in Vienna (many members of which were originally from Poland or Russia themselves). Thus with Belkowsky in Bulgaria, as has been noted, and several others of whom the most important were Adolf Stand and Avraham Salz in Galicia, Mordechai Ehrenpreis in Croatia, and Aharon Kaminka in Prague.

In general, Herzl had never doubted that the main part of the eastern wing of Hibbat Zion within the Pale of Settlement, along

[58] Bambus, S. P. Rabbinowitz ('Shefer'), and S. Turoff to Y. L. Goldberg, n.d., CZA, A9/69.

with its broad, but ill-defined popular following—the 'masses' or the 'Russians', as he thought of them—would rally round him. Theirs, after all, was the concrete and immediate need for help; and the call to a great Congress of Zionists was therefore not one which they, conceivably, would turn down. He was aware that the response to all his public doings was still somewhat quizzical and far from being uniformly favourable. He had also expected them to be extremely cautious and their overt reaction, given the harsh terms under which Jewish public and private life was conducted within Russia, to be muted. What he had not anticipated was having to shift his main effort, the centre of gravity of his campaign, to the East. Still less had he expected the success of the Congress to turn ultimately on whether the 'Russians' would or would not come, and in what numbers. But in the event, much as he had misjudged the likely response to his call to the Congress in the West, so he misjudged the complexity of the issues in the East. Moreover, largely because of his method of acting through intermediaries and, too, because his original view of things had been so simplistic and in part ill founded, it took time—valuable time— before he sensed that all was not well and before he tried to come to grips with the problem personally. It was not until two months after the decision to call a Congress had been made that he first became concerned about the feeble response. It was not before the end of May that he made his first attempt to contact influential figures in Russo-Polish Jewry directly. 'It is only from Russia that I hear nothing', he complained to a veteran Ḥovev Zion in Bialystok; and then had a formal but very accommodating letter to Rabbi Mohilever written for him in stilted Hebrew to ask the rabbi to encourage his friends to participate. He especially wanted those who were familiar with the affairs of the *yishuv*, he wrote to Mohilever, and 'who also know the spirit of our people and our Holy Law and our history . . . and who must [therefore] come to our conference and express their views on our people's needs and future'.[59] By the end of June, after the decision to move the Congress to Basel, he was seriously worried.[60] On 24 July, now very late in the day, he asked Mordechai Ehrenpreis to prepare and print a Hebrew-language

[59] Herzl to Salz, 7 May 1897; Herzl to Chazanowicz, 24 May 1897; Herzl, Schnirer, and Kokesch (jointly) to Mohilever, 25 May 1897. *Igrot*, ii, no. 254, p. 270; no. 286, p. 297; and no. 291, pp. 300–1.

[60] Cf. Herzl to Ehrenpreis, 28 June 1897, ibid., no. 326, p. 323; and see also letter to Belkowsky, 8 July 1897, ibid., no. 334, p. 330.

version of the official invitation to the Congress and send it to a number of prominent members of the movement. 'You must emphasize in the strongest way', he instructed Ehrenpreis, 'that this Congress must definitely succeed, for if not the matter of Zion will be set back for years. But for it to succeed the Russians must come in large numbers.' On the same day he wrote directly to Aḥad Ha-ʿAm to urge him too to come to Basel.[61]

Reports that Herzl and his friends had called a Congress of Zionists were quickly picked up and reported in Russia. So were the quarrel with Bambus, the debates with Rabbi Güdemann and with the German rabbinate, the decision to transfer the venue from Munich, and all the other major starts and stops on the way to Basel. The reporting was full and facts were presented to the reader of the Jewish press with a fair degree of accuracy. The usual form was one of correspondence from abroad—which absolved editors from the need to take a position of their own. But editorial attitudes were made plain from time to time either in brief comments tacked on to the foreign correspondence proper, or else, but much more rarely, in full-blown leading articles.

The first press reactions to the call to the Congress were friendly, on the whole. If the assembly were to bring some unity to the movement, then surely, thought *Ha-Magid*'s correspondent, it was to be welcomed.[62] *Ha-Zefira* initially (and surprisingly, in view of Sokolov's well-known views) went further: nothing comparable had been attempted since the movement had begun and we were entitled to see it as a good augury, the 'beginning of redemption [*atḥalta di-geʾula*], for at last the many needs of our people have assumed a concrete form . . . and the Jewish question on which all had trodden . . . will now be discussed in public by the wise and the eminent'.[63]

Private reactions were mixed. A few of the veterans appear to have been rapid converts to the idea, among them Lilienblum, for whom it was the fact that Herzl was a relative new-comer to the movement and a westerner that was decisive. Here at last was a man of prominence who wanted to involve western Jewry in the re-establishment of the *yishuv* in Erez-Israel. Could such a one be

---

[61] Herzl to Ehrenpreis; and Herzl to Aḥad Ha-ʿAm, 24 July 1897. Ibid., no. 351, pp. 346–7; and no. 352, p. 347.

[62] *Ha-Meliz̧*, 21 April 1897.     [63] *Ha-Zefira*, 5 May 1897.

turned down? As for Herzl's political fantasies, if such they were, they would fade when Herzl himself ended, as he must, Lilienblum argued, by taking a road that the preponderant eastern Ḥibbat Zion would determine for him.[64] But most of the group headed by the Odessa Committee were opposed. The grounds were often virtually intuitive. 'Professor Belkowsky writes to me that Dr. Herzl proposes to call a conference of Ḥovevei Zion from all countries', wrote Izḥak Nissenboim upon first hearing of the plan and even before it had been announced formally in Vienna. 'Of course, we . . . in Russia cannot take part.'[65] Even men who were not unfavourably inclined were cool and cautious and wanted a great many questions answered.

There can be no question of Ḥovevim from Russia attending as *delegates* and agents of the societies of the Odessa committee, [wrote Ussishkin to Kaminka (in Prague)] for that is quite impossible for many reasons. But it is my view that it would be a good thing if the heads of the conference [i.e. the Congress] did invite a certain number of Russian Ḥovevim—some orthodox and some enlightened, some old and some young—all in a private capacity as people who know the Jewish people and its characteristics and know all about the *yishuv* from its very beginning. These will be the 'experts' who, as questions arise at the conference table, will show and teach the men of action and the men of speech what to say and what to do. Altogether, I must tell you that *most* of us do not expect the Munich conference to be of *real* use . . . [But] on the general question of people from Russia attending, you must write to Rabbi Mohilever.

Who has already agreed to attend? Will it be possible to read a report [at the Congress] in the Russian language?[66]

Herzl and his friends 'have hopes, but they have a programme too,' Ussishkin later wrote to Aḥad Ha-ʿAm, 'while we have hopes, but do not know what to do.'[67] But while Aḥad Ha-ʿAm shared his sense that the movement had run into the sands he was a great deal more sceptical about Herzl. Aḥad Ha-ʿAm did not oppose the Congress, but he could see little good coming of it. It was unlikely, he

[64] *Ha-Arez*, 24 February 1935.

[65] Nissenboim to Appel, 7 February 1897. Israel Shapira (ed.), *Igrot ha-rav Nissenboim*, Jerusalem, 1956, p. 80. Nissenboim stood very close to Mohilever; Appel was a leading Ḥovev Zion in Vilna.

[66] Ussishkin to Kaminka, 13 April 1897. CZA, A147/33/2 (emphases in original). Kaminka duly passed the gist of Ussishkin's letter on to Herzl. See CZA, H VIII 424/7.

[67] S. Schwartz, *Ussishkin be-igrotav*, Jerusalem, 1949, p. 62.

thought, to make an impression on European public opinion, except, unfortunately, upon the Turks—with the result that *their* opposition to the Jewish enterprise in Ereẓ-Israel would be the stronger. At best, the Congress might raise the prestige of Zionism in the eyes of the Jews themselves, particularly in the eyes of the rich who had tended thus far to regard the movement as an affair of the feckless in which it was beneath their dignity to participate.

But to hope for 'diplomatic' action—that, it seems to me, would be totally without foundation so long as there are fewer than 100,000 Jews working the land at the very least. And if you ask if so, what are we to hope for? [My answer is that] that is a question which can bring only a 'practical man' like you to despair. For my part, I still believe that a day will come when our eyes will open and we shall see what Ereẓ-Israel [really signifies] for us and in our spiritual life; and then we shall cease squandering our pennies on matters of no *substance*, but rather gather them together and make of them things that are small and complete and exemplary in Israel. Then the people will turn towards Ereẓ-Israel once more and thousands of our brethren, without the help of announcements and proclamations, will resettle in Ereẓ-Israel and live a good and decent life. Only then—and whether it will be in the twentieth century or the twenty-first is of no consequence—will the time come for diplomatic action.[68]

To which Ussishkin's irritated response was that 'in any event, there was more to be hoped for from some movement, however egregious, than from the despair which you and your friends on *Ha-Shiloaḥ* offer.'[69] In fact, Aḥad Ha-ʿAm had carefully avoided discussing the subject of the Congress in his journal. 'To be impressed and excited by the great deliverance is beyond me', he wrote to a friend; 'and to say outright what I think in my heart is superfluous. I am already held by many to be a pessimist who sees and prophesies nothing but evil; so what good would come of what I have to say?'[70]

The balance of opinion was thus slow to change. By and large, three months after the original call to the assembly, the leading members of Ḥibbat Ẓion in Russia had still failed to reach a consensus of view on the Congress. They were only clearer in their minds about its difficulties. There was, in the first place, the question whether it was *politic* for Russian Jews and Russian Ḥovevei

---

[68] Aḥad Ha-ʿAm to Ussishkin, 3 June 1897. Aḥad Ha-ʿAm, *Igrot*, second edition, Tel Aviv, 1956, i, pp. 220–1.     [69] Schwartz, op. cit., p. 63.
[70] Aḥad Ha-ʿAm to Michelson, 29 July 1897. *Igrot*, i, p. 247.

Zion in particular to attend such a Congress—in view of the possible repercussions on the *yishuv* in Ereẓ-Israel to which Aḥad Ha-ʿAm had referred, and also having regard to the precarious state of the movement in Russia itself, a movement dimly tolerated by the state, but only provided it abstained from doing anything likely to arouse the latent suspicions of the Russian police. It was in deference to these concerns that Munich had originally been chosen because the first choice, Zürich, had a bad name in Russian police books; and it was again with the notoriety of Zürich as a gathering place for anarchists and other species of revolutionaries that Basel was settled on when Munich had to be abandoned. Sensitivity to this, the police side of things, was to remain alive, as will be seen, up to the eve of the Congress itself and beyond it.

Then, as it became evident that, in an important sense, the affair was indeed to be what the *Jewish Chronicle* had called 'Dr. Herzl's Congress', the familiar doubts about Herzl came to the fore once more. For it was one thing to watch him on his travels from afar; it was another to enter into an alliance of sorts with him.

To Herzl's inherent disadvantage as the arch representative of those 'extreme Zionists who had come to us from without the Jewish camp and to whom Judaism was foreign to their spirit' as opposed to the 'moderate Zionists . . . who knew that Judaism was Zionism'[71] there was added the circumstance that overwhelmingly the established figures in western Ḥibbat Ẓion had rejected him outright. This was soon known and was very damaging to him in Russia. The very last thing that the Odessa circle wanted was a quarrel with their benefactor, Baron Edmond de Rothschild, or with any of those close to him. The hostility which Herzl had aroused in Western Europe affected the progress of his views in the East in another way. As already pointed out, it was on correspondents in the West, notably in Berlin and Vienna, that the periodicals friendly to the movement chiefly relied for their reports and for much of their comment on the entire subject. These were mostly men of the old school who reflected the traditional positions of Ḥibbat Ẓion. Accordingly, views critical of Herzl and the Congress, if not hostile to them, tended to predominate in print. Sometimes the tone was nasty: one such correspondent charged Herzl (without any justification) with contempt for 'Polish Jews' and with not having invited any to join him either in organizing the Congress

[71] *Ha-Magid*, 1 July 1897.

or even in attending it.[72] This was damaging; although such pieces had the saving characteristic that they provided Herzl's supporters with opportunities for public rebuttal.[73]

The deepest reservations in the East concerned Herzl's methods (rather than, as in the West, his aims): the 'noise' he made, the opportunities he gave the anti-Semitic press to publish canards, the neglect of what was modest and practical as opposed to an evident tendency to the grand and the ambitious:[74] and underlying them were old, mostly unspoken fears, of the dangerous man, the false prophet, the new Shabbetai Ẓevi who would stimulate unsatisfiable wants, loose the bonds of the Law and of authority, and end by leading the innocents to catastrophe. It was therefore easiest of all, even for those who were disposed to respond to the call to Basel, to postpone the making of a final commitment, the more so since, as the measure of the opposition which Herzl had aroused came to be taken, it was permissible to ask whether the Congress would ever assemble. But a change came when in the beginning of the summer it became evident that the answer to this latter question was positive beyond a doubt and Herzl began to press the Russians for a decision more directly.

In May, as has been seen, he had begun to seek out prominent figures directly. In the case of Mohilever this was at Belkowsky's suggestion and followed directly from recognition of Mohilever's key position as the leading figure in the orthodox wing of Ḥibbat Zion (Mizraḥi) into whose hands the contact with Belkowsky and through him with Herzl had been put by the Odessa committee.[75] Herzl's message, particularly the respectful reference to 'the spirit of our people and our Holy Law', was well received, and its contents promptly circularized by Mohilever's entourage with a fairly straightforward recommendation to attend the Congress.[76] At the same time, a very flattering letter was sent from Vienna to Lilienblum, of whose 'standing as a writer . . . and activities in the national movement these many years we know', inviting him to attend the Congress and to address it. In typical accordance with Herzl's belief in using every available carrot, Lilienblum was also invited

---

[72] Yehuda Leib Wintz in 'Letter from Berlin', *Ha-Meliz*, 9, 10 June 1897.

[73] Cf. *Ha-Meliz*, 2 July 1897.

[74] See, for example, 'Aminadav (pseud.), 'Pinkas katan', *Ha-Meliz*, 17 June 1897.

[75] See above, p. 279.

[76] Circular letter evidently written by Nissenboim on Mohilever's authority, 27 May 1897. Iẓḥak Nissenboim, *'Alei Ḥeldi*, Warsaw, 1929, pp. 113–14.

to serve as correspondent for *Die Welt*[77] which was just about to
come out. Ussishkin too was approached directly; and so was
Sokolov—on the grounds, in the words of the intermediary in the
case (Farbstein), that 'it would be advisable to invite him to keep
him acquiescent. He may do harm as he is the Jewish press mono-
polist in Russian Poland.'[78] So was Aḥad Ha-ʿAm, but with less
success and with the unfortunate result of instantly raising a wall
of misunderstanding between him and Herzl.

This last incident is of special interest because it shows the
inherent limitations of Herzl's attempt to mobilize support from
afar among people of whom he knew next to nothing. Ehrenpreis,
Herzl's loyalist in Croatia and, like Belkowsky, a key link between
Vienna and Russia, had written to Aḥad Ha-ʿAm (then in Odessa)
in July, pressing him to attend the Congress and asking the great
man for his views on current attitudes to the projected Congress
and for names of people in Russia who ought to be invited personally.
Aḥad Ha-ʿAm replied with his habitual precision that he did, indeed,
want to go to Basel, but could not yet promise to do so. Nor could
he tell Ehrenpreis much about trends of opinion in the movement
because he himself did not know much more of the matter than
appeared in the periodical press. He had not even known of the
move from Munich to Basel until he, Ehrenpreis, had told him of
it; and still did not know the reasons for the move because Ehrenpreis had not informed him of them. 'That being the state of affairs,
I am not entitled to talk about the subject lest I fall into error.' Yet
he could not constrain himself from pointing out that the organizing
committee in Vienna had not acted with due reflection and wisdom.

Here, for example, here in our city [Odessa], where the central committee of Ḥibbat Ẓion is located, Mr. Lilienblum was *alone* in receiving
an invitation to the Congress some weeks ago. You must admit that this
was—if we are to employ polite language—*tactless*. Do they really not
know in Vienna that there are other Ḥovevei Ẓion in Russia apart from
MLL? And if they do not really know to whom· they should write,
they should have waited until they did know and in the meantime write
to no one.

    [77] Kokesch (on behalf of 'Zion', the Austrian Zionist association) to Lilienblum, 28 May
1897. A. Druyanov (ed.), *Mi-yamim rishonim*, i. 2, p. 44. In the event, despite his sympathies,
Lilienblum did not attend the Congress. It is not clear why. He may not have been able to
raise the fare; but he may have felt that he ought not to compromise the Odessa committee
of which he was secretary.
    [78] Josef Wenkert, 'Herzl and Sokolov', *Herzl Year Book*, ii, p. 187 fn. 7.

He hoped that he would not be suspected of bearing any grudge. He only raised the point, he wrote, because he thought it reflected a general fault; and because it was probable that other men in other cities had been offended. Nor was that all.

Two or three weeks ago a certain student from M., Mr. B., came here and organized assemblies and meetings as a representative of the Vienna committee. His purpose was to encourage Ḥovevei Zion to go to the Congress, to send 'petitions', and the like, and from here he went on to other cities for the same purpose. Now it is my humble opinion that a man like that—who is still immature, and, apart from a degree of 'holy impudence' disproportionate to his years, unqualified to serve as a delegate in such a matter—is entirely incapable of raising the prestige of the Congress in the eyes of the sensible members of Ḥibbat Zion.[79]

Herzl made a clumsy attempt to mollify Aḥad Ha-ʿAm ('I have been informed that you have been expecting a special invitation to the Congress')[80] and failed. 'As I believe the Congress to be in any event a very important matter for our cause as a whole,' was the response, 'it could not have occurred to me that I should await a special invitation.' In any event, Aḥad Ha-ʿAm concluded, there was no real cause for worry in Vienna. 'We are told that delegates to the Congress are being elected in many of the great centres in Russia. With regard to *numbers*, therefore, the Russian contingent would be adequate.'[81]

The 'student from M., Mr. B.' who had so provoked Aḥad Ha-ʿAm was Yehoshua Buchmil, a student of agriculture at Montpellier. He had been a leading member of 'Avenir d'Israël', a small Jewish nationalist group at the local university mostly made up of Russian Jews like himself with some members from a number of other Eastern European and North African countries. No French Jews belonged to it. They had begun by seeing themselves as an integral part of Ḥibbat Zion, then rapidly developed bolder ideas of their own. Chief of these was a demand to subject the question of the continuing flow of public resources in aid of Jewish settlement in Argentina (as opposed to Ereẓ-Israel) to the will of Russian and Polish Jews—to be expressed one way or another in a national referendum to be held. But Buchmil's attempt to impress his views

[79] Aḥad Ha-ʿAm to Ehrenpreis, 8 July 1897 (emphases in original). Aḥad Ha-ʿAm, *Igrot*, i, pp. 234–5.
[80] Herzl to Aḥad Ha-ʿAm, 24 July 1897. Herzl, *Igrot*, ii, no. 352, p. 347.
[81] Aḥad Ha-ʿAm to Herzl, 28 July 1897. Aḥad Ha-ʿAm, *Igrot*, i, p. 246.

upon the established leaders of Ḥibbat Ẓion in Paris proved fruitless, and he subsequently found his way to Herzl. Herzl, already
heavily involved in the organization of the Congress, gave him an
entirely different reception—patient, friendly, interested, and
interesting—and ended by asking him to go to Russia to tackle
leading members of the movement directly and encourage them to
decide in favour of attending the Congress. To this Buchmil
agreed, apparently without much hesitation.

The idea of sending Buchmil to Russia as a personal delegate
seems to have come to Herzl spontaneously. But the problem of
bringing direct influence to bear upon Russian Jewry must have
been in his mind for some time. He was worried by the slow pace
of events, as we have seen, and Belkowsky had already written to
him early in May making just such a proposal to send a number
of itinerant proselytizers to do by direct confrontation what could
not be done adequately, if at all, by correspondence and handbills
and only very indirectly and unsystematically through the press.[82]
Herzl's close collaborator Moshe (Moritz) Schnirer was sent to
north Russia and Lithuania on such a mission. But it was Buchmil's
journey which was the more elaborate, the longer, and the more
successful. He visited Kishinev, Odessa, Kiev, Yekaterinoslav,
Bialystok, Elizavetgrad, and some two dozen other cities and towns
in south and west Russia. In Odessa he appeared before the Central
Committee of Ḥibbat Ẓion and obtained a valuable letter of introduction to other centres from Lilienblum who backed him from
the start. He met a great many of the other leading figures, among
them Mohilever, Mandelstamm, and Ussishkin. Meetings were
arranged for him in each locality and these, if they were not always
successful, were by all accounts well attended and often stormy.
Supporters and opponents were easily mustered. He himself was
a man of volatile temperament and limited respect for his seniors
and his unexpected appearance on the scene as Herzl's herald, along
with the debates which he precipitated and in which he himself
often played a central role, was not without an element of drama.
It is a fair conclusion that his mission added to the slow pressure
towards a decision.

Thanks to his ties with our city [Kishinev] (in which he had worked
as a youth) [Buchmil] soon found out what he needed to know about us

---

[82] See Belkowsky to Herzl, 8 May 1897. CZA, A 171/20.

[i.e. the local members of the movement] and we soon organized a secret meeting in the courtyard of a house in which our comrades Avraham and Shlomo Dubinsky lived. The courtyard was crowded with Ḥovevei Zion and after numerous arguments and objections from supporters of the Odessa Committee who were fighting everywhere against the convening of the first Congress so as to stop their position from being swept from under them, it was resolved to send one delegate from Kishinev to the Congress.[83]

The debate on whether to attend the Congress or not remained an open one until the end of July, or just a month before the Congress was due to convene. But for all the heat with which it was conducted and for all that it extended throughout the movement and was judged by many to be the greatest public question to face Russo-Polish Jewry since the issue of mass emigration first arose in 1881, it was devoid of clear lines and of accepted leaders of opinion. Nor did it touch on fundamentals. The immediate question posed was simple enough. But the grounds for acceptance or rejection of the invitation to Basel could not be. And perhaps because such grounds necessarily entailed views of the fundamental nature and causes of the *Judenfrage* in Russia and Poland (and indeed elsewhere), views which many still hesitated to formulate clearly and state openly, the public debate was a great deal less straightforward than the issue. At no time was there a real departure from the now well-worn paths of support for, and opposition to, the new wind blowing from Vienna: on the one hand there was fear of Herzl's adventurousness and impatience and his 'day-dreams', the dichotomies between the 'political' and the 'non-political' road to Zion and between the dangers inherent in the one as opposed to the relative safety of the other; and, on the other hand, there were the arguments that even if Herzl and his 'crowd' had erred in being hasty, i.e. guilty of *deḥikat ha-keẓ*, they were only saying what those in Russia had not had the courage to say outright, that it would be lamentable if this, the most powerful move in support of Zionism ever to emerge from the West, should not be met and aided by a parallel move from the East, and that the concentration of all efforts on settlement in Ereẓ-Israel had brought the movement as a whole to an impasse out of which it was vital that it now be extricated. All

---

[83] Yaʿakov Bernstein-Cohen, 'Zikhronot', *Sefer Bernstein-Cohen*, Tel Aviv, 1946, p. 119. For Buchmil's own account of his journey see Y. Buchmil, 'Ha-taʿamula be-rusia la-kongres ha-rishon', in L. Jaffe (ed.), *Sefer ha-kongres*, Jerusalem, 1950, pp. 93–105. See also Naḥum Slouschz, 'Le-toldot ha-ẓionut ha-medinit', *Ha-Toren*, Elul, 5682 [1922], pp. 60–7.

such points of argument as these, the staple of the debate, were in themselves inherently unsatisfactory. No one, least of all anyone in Russia, could as yet properly assess how the Congress might turn out, nor what its remoter consequences might be. Nothing of significance had been learned or written about Herzl since his travels of the previous year. Indeed, when all had been said and done, the strongest undercurrent in the debate was the anticipatory excitement of the event itself and for all but the coolest minds the question at hand was whether to allow oneself to be drawn into it.

. . . What do you think of Dr. Herzl's Zionist movement in general and of the Basel conference in particular [Lilienblum was asked]. The prospect is most encouraging, the heart, the senses, the Jewish soul are drawn by magic cords to this great and marvellous scene: the benefactors of the people will gather with the God of Abraham and the banner of the army of Israel in their hands! The ingathering of the Exiles, the renaissance of the people! Oh, how marvellous is the enchantment, how great is the idea, how sublime the thought! Thus I find myself dreaming of the Return to Zion and the Redemption of Israel. But . . . at times logic and cold reason speak otherwise and sad thoughts arise: who knows if we are not dreaming? . . . [Then] my main question is whether this movement bodes us, Ḥibbat Zion as it is here [in Russia] and the [Odessa] committee, no ill?[84]

However, when it had at last become clear beyond a doubt that the Congress would certainly be held and that to that extent the matter was out of their hands, discussions moved into a different channel. If they did resolve to go, it was asked in Odessa, should they go as a *body* and, if not as a body, how could they co-ordinate their moves, and, more fundamentally, what should they seek at Basel, what tactics should they adopt? Ussishkin's answer was that they must begin by sticking together. The Congress, he wrote to the Vilna association at the end of June,

can be of use if it concerns itself with matters which [the western Zionists] regard as of small weight and which we regard as of great weight and to that purpose we must try to have a certain number of our brethren attending . . . It would be well if those coming from Russia arrived in Basel two or three days before time, so too those of our brethren living abroad. Then all would consult jointly, draw up a general 'Russian' programme, and be of one mind in respect of all the questions coming up before the conference.[85]

[84] Shelomo Ha-Kohen to Lilienblum, 10 August 1897. *Mi-yamim rishonim*, i, p. 45.
[85] Ussishkin to Ḥovevei Zion, Vilna, 27 June 1897. CZA, A9/69.

It must be said that on this, as on other aspects of the debate within the inner circle of the movement, Herzl loomed over the discussions without being in any significant sense a party to them. The debate was internal; its leaders made up their own minds. Herzl's delegates and other intermediaries played an important, but limited role. They supplied details of the programme planned for Basel; they egged people on to make their decision. But they did not seriously influence the substance of the governing considerations; still less did they succeed in winning over any of the major figures by dint of direct persuasion. The upshot was that while, as the summer wore on, support for Basel among younger, less influential, and more easily influenced people did grow steadily and the balance over all did tip in Herzl's favour, many of the leading members of the movement, particularly those in Odessa, those, in effect, who, with justification, felt their responsibility most strongly, still hesitated. Accordingly, the *quality* of the prospective Russian delegation to Basel, as Aḥad Ha-ʿAm in his direct and acid way had warned Herzl, still remained unclear.

This last enclave of resistance fell on 28 July at Carlsbad. Several leading members of the Russo-Polish Ḥibbat Ẓion were abroad at the time, among them Avraham Greenberg, chairman of the Odessa committee, and S. P. Rabbinowitz ('Shefer'). Aharon Kaminka, Herzl's intermediary in Prague (himself a Russian Jew and an occasional member of the Odessa circle), seized the opportunity to bring them together with others who were close to Herzl—or close enough to him to serve as go-betweens: Johann Kremenezky (also originally from Russia) and Wilhelm Stiassny. There were present, in addition, two Ḥovevim from Riga, one from Rostov-on-Don, and one from Irkutsk, but it was the presence of Greenberg and 'Shefer' that gave the forum its weight. No time seems to have been lost on generalities. Their prime concern, said Greenberg, was to ensure that no harm was done them by the Basel Congress. Any Russian who chose to speak should therefore make clear that he did so in a private capacity. But that was not really enough and they had three specific demands corresponding to three fears: that nothing be said at Basel that might offend the Baron (whose firm opposition to the Congress had just been borne home upon 'Shefer' once more); that nothing be said to offend the Turks; and lastly that nothing critical of the Tsar's government be uttered. These were difficult demands to meet. It was impossible, as one of the

Viennese pointed out, to restrict the western delegates' freedom to speak their minds, quite apart from the fact that there were some who thought that it was positively desirable that the representatives of the Jewish people gathered in a unique assembly speak out with honesty and courage. Thus, the address to the Congress to be delivered by Nordau would deal with the general condition of the Jews. Was it conceivable that nothing would be said about *Russia*? At this the Russians retreated somewhat. They announced that they themselves would co-ordinate their position at Basel by means of a caucus of their own and they exacted a promise that Herzl would be spoken to and that the need to accommodate their fears and to maintain a high degree of 'moderation and caution' be impressed upon him and his friends.[86] There was no difficulty about this. Herzl had already given an undertaking to see to it that no tones displeasing to the Russian government would be heard at the Congress[87] and he willingly repeated it. He further promised that settlement affairs—and Baron de Rothschild by implication— be treated 'with respect, so far as possible'.[88] The plan to organize a caucus of Russian Ḥovevei Zion raised no objections and was therefore recognized implicitly as legitimate.

The open debate was at an end. There remained of course the larger but unnegotiated question whether the Congress was going to confirm—and celebrate—that discontinuity between the old Ḥibbat Zion and a new movement that could already be seen rising out of the former's ashes; or whether, as some, notably 'Shefer' in the East and Bambus in the West, plainly encouraged themselves to believe, matters could still be kept more or less within the old limits and along the old lines. 'We are going to Basel', they wrote, in order to ensure that 'the epitome of Zionism [remains] concern with Ḥibbat Zion, [namely] the expansion of settlement in the Holy Land and proper regard for the *yishuv* in the lands of the Diaspora'.[89] But they cannot have been too optimistic. 'It would have been a great deal more convenient if the Congress had never been convened at all', 'Shefer' admitted; 'but now that it has been convened, we must sweeten the pill and make every effort to prevent any harm being done to the *yishuv* as it stands at present and to our

[86] Protocol of Carlsbad conference, 28 July 1897; and the letter of 'Shefer' to Y. L. Goldberg, Vilna, 30 July 1897; in *Sefer ha-kongres*, pp. 404–5 and 415–17.
[87] Herzl to Ehrenpreis, 24 July 1897, *Igrot*, ii, no. 351, p. 346.
[88] Stiassny to 'Shefer', [8 August 1897]. *Sefer ha-kongres*, p. 417.
[89] Circular letter signed by 'Shefer', Bambus, and Turow, n.d., ibid.

activities in the future.'[90] All in all, the common mood among the veterans was one of resignation. 'Perhaps, after all, I too shall be there', wrote Aḥad Ha-ʿAm. 'It is possible that I shall be of some small use, for it is painful to see everything put into the hands of young people whose enthusiasm is greater than their understanding . . .'[91]

[90] 'Shefer' to Goldberg, 30 July 1897, ibid., p. 416.
[91] Aḥad Ha-ʿAm to Michelson, 29 July 1897. *Igrot*, i, p. 247.

# 13

## The First Congress

### i

THE Zionist Congress at Basel was an event without precedent. Therefore the dominant mood among the delegates was one of uncertainty. The questions who was to be there, how it was to be managed, what its precise results would be were in the minds of every man and woman travelling to Basel at the end of August; and the tension and the fear of disappointment were the greater for none being able to provide themselves with even an approximate answer in advance of the event. Hence the many contemporary accounts of excited discussions during the long train journey from the East as participants identified each other, of the sharp looks exchanged as groups from different countries met in Basel, and of the attention paid to every detail of organization as likely indicators of what could be expected.[1]

The arrangements had been well thought out and Herzl's hand and eye for detail and his concern to leave a strong impression of efficiency and order were apparent. There was a Congress bureau permanently manned with secretaries with knowledge of the requisite languages. The agenda had been printed beforehand, an illustrated postcard was available, and participants were provided with a badge devised by Bodenheimer (a blue shield with a red border bearing the inscription 'The establishment of a Jewish state is the only possible solution to the Jewish Question'; and in its centre the Lion of Judah surrounded by a Shield of David and twelve stars). The press was catered for. *Die Welt* was to be printed in an especially large edition. Herzl called formally at the offices of the Canton of Basel and was rewarded by the President of the Canton attending one of the sessions of the Congress. A preparatory meeting to settle questions of procedure was held two days before

[1] For example: *Ha-Magid*, 2 September 1897.

the plenary sessions of the Congress began, its most important single piece of business being the appointment of a seven-man committee headed by Nordau to draft the programme of the movement to set before the Congress. And finally, and characteristically, on the day before the Congress opened, a Saturday, Herzl attended the morning service at the local synagogue and was duly honoured by being called to the reading of the Law—for which he had prepared by having the Hebrew benediction which he was due to recite drilled into him beforehand.

The initial impression which Herzl made on the delegates assembling in Basel was favourable, but not remarkable. When he first appeared before them in a formal role, at the preparatory meeting, he said so little and that so gently that some raised the question whether they ought not to cast about for someone stronger than he to preside over the Congress proper. Later it occurred to them that he might be saving himself for what was ahead.[2] Probably, he was observing the people gathering around him as carefully as they were observing him. 'The fact is—which I conceal from everyone—', he had noted in his diary on the train that took him to Basel, 'that I have only an army of *schnorrers*.[3] I am in command only of boys, beggars, and prigs . . . Nevertheless, this army would be entirely sufficient if only success were in sight . . . So we shall see what the immediate future holds in store.'[4] It was with the same strong sense of the fragility of the enterprise and in the same vein of irritation that he listed the obstacles around which he would have to manœuvre, the groups he would have to avoid offending, the opponents he would have to take into account: his employers on the *Neue Freie Presse*, the orthodox Jews, the modernist Jews, the issue of his own status as an Austrian subject, the Turks, the Russian government, the Christian churches 'on account of the Holy places', the Ḥovevei Ẓion in Russia, and Edmond de Rothschild and his supporters, and the settlers in Ereẓ-Israel who depended on him—to all of which there had to be added the factors of envy and jealousy which he was always so quick to discern. It all amounted, he noted, to one of the labours of Hercules, but less because of intrinsic difficulties than because 'I no longer have any

---

[2] [Mordekhai] Ben-ʿAmi [Rabinowicz], 'Herzl ve-ha-kongres ha-rishon', *Sefer ha-kongres*, pp. 123-4.

[3] One wonders whether he recalled that this was the same term of contempt that Edmond de Rothschild had used at their meeting the year before. Cf. above, p. 307.

[4] *Diaries*, ii, p. 577.

zest for it'.[5] Plainly, as the time for the Congress drew near, he had become afraid of failure. He was sure he had done all that could be done to make the Congress a success. Now, on the eve, things were out of his hands. 'I have fashioned a Congress for the Jews, and let the people help themselves from this point on if they really want to', he had said to Bacher before leaving Vienna. 'As for myself, there are times when I have had more than my fill of the whole thing.'[6]

The Congress opened on Sunday morning, 29 August 1897, in the concert hall of the Basel Municipal Casino. Herzl had insisted on the delegates attending the opening session in formal dress, tails and white tie, and begged Nordau, who had none the less turned up in a frock coat, to go back to his hotel and change. 'I told him: today the praesidium of the Zionist Congress is nothing at all, we still have to establish everything. People should get used to seeing the Congress as a most exalted and solemn thing.' Nordau allowed himself to be persuaded and Herzl 'hugged him gratefully'.[7] In the event, all went off very well and he was pleased that he himself had been 'quite calm, as one should be when events occur as planned'. For most, if not all, of those present it was a profoundly moving occasion.

When I went to the Casino [a member of the Odessa committee recalled] I was so excited my legs were weak and I stumbled . . . The delegates greeted each other warmly. They conversed quietly. Tremendous anticipation . . . Suddenly the hall was quiet . . . Old Doctor Lippe of Jassy mounted the rostrum, covered his white head with his hat, and made a blessing . . . Many eyes filled with tears . . . Herzl mounted the rostrum calmly . . . Not the Herzl I knew, the one I had seen only the previous evening. Before us was the splendid figure of a son of kings with a deep and concentrated gaze, handsome and sad at one and the same time. It was not the elegant Herzl of Vienna, but a man of the house of David risen all of a sudden from his grave in all his legendary glory.[8]

ii

Between 200 and 250 men and women from 24 states and territories attended the Basel Congress. The official *Präsenz-Liste* included 199 names, but is known to be incomplete—for a number of Russian

---

[5] *Diaries*, ii, pp. 578–9.     [6] Ibid., p. 576.
[7] Ibid., p. 581.     [8] Ben-ʿAmi, op. cit., p. 124.

subjects wanted their names left out for fear of arrest on their return home.[9] Others neglected to register. And a further source of confusion lay in the fact that no clear distinction was drawn, or could be drawn, between the several varieties of participants. About a third of the number were delegates in the full sense that they had been duly elected to represent their local communities or Hibbat Zion and Zionist societies;[10] there were those who had been specifically invited; there were some who had come in a dual capacity—Sokolov, for example, was both a representative of the press and a notable in his own right; a few of the participants had come with their wives and some with their daughters—and these were not distinguished from women who participated independently (among them, for example, a Mrs. Rosa Sonnenschein, editor of the *American Jewess*, New York); and there were a number of non-Jews, among them Hechler, who figured as 'guests' of the Congress; and finally there were the spectators seated in the public gallery and numbering many hundreds. It is probable that some of the latter belonged on the floor of the hall. Ahad Ha-ʿAm, who had refused formal election as a delegate, did attend, but took no part in the proceedings. None the less, he was treated as the important and representative figure he was and his picture was duly included among the 162 portraits that made up the commemorative collective photograph. In any event only two distinctions were drawn in practice. One was between the Jews and the non-Jews (the latter were not expected to participate in the proceedings); the other was between the men and the women (the latter not being entitled to vote).[11] Little importance was attached to the forms of selection, not excluding self-selection, at this foundation Congress.

I do ask you [Herzl had admonished Belkowsky] not to stop anyone from attending the Congress. Of course, the official delegates will appear, speak, and vote with an entirely different [measure of] authority than

---

[9] In the event, none was arrested. The Vilna delegates, however, noted on their return that the secret police began to take more interest in them than before and an elaborate cover had to be organized, and the local police commandant bribed, before a meeting of local Zionists could be called and the Congress reported on. Yehuda Leib Goldberg, 'Derekh laʿavor geʾulim', *Sefer ha-kongres*, p. 129.

[10] See Haiyim Orlan, 'The Participants in the First Zionist Congress', *Herzl Year Book*, vi, pp. 133–52.

[11] Women were given full voting rights, however, at the Second Congress in the following year.

those who have been sent by no one. But their presence is absolutely desirable. The greater the numbers of participants at the Congress, the greater will be the demonstration that we intend it to be.[12]

Who were the participants? Taken together,[13] they were an assembly of educated, middle-class Jews: roughly a quarter were men of business, industry, and finance, and the next three largest categories, each approximating a sixth of the total, were men of letters, members of the professions, and students. There were also eleven rabbis, a synagogue cantor, a farmer, a sculptor, two stenographers, and a printer. (The occupations of the remaining fifth to a sixth of the total are unknown.) Overwhelmingly, they were liberal and modernist in their social and religious tendencies. There were some agnostics. There were a few socialists, notably among the Russian-Jewish students from Berlin. But most were much less interested in social problems than in the Problem of the Jews and, having been brought up in the tradition, had an ingrained respect for—or, at the very least, a certain wariness of—religious orthodoxy. However, orthodoxy proper was hardly represented. None of the rabbis present was in any sense a man of prominence and authority within it. There was only Rabbi Mohilever's grand-son to represent the one considerable figure in that still dominant wing of Jewry who had been a staunch Hovev Zion throughout and who was now prepared, if cautiously, to welcome a fresh initiative. Herzl, who tended to believe that the rabbis held the key to the hearts of 'the people', made what he could of this and had Mohi-lever's long letter of greeting to the Congress read out in full in plenary session.

Very few of the participants were men of note outside Jewry. Only Nordau had what could be fairly termed an international reputation. Herzl and Zangwill were both writers of repute (Zang-will rather more than Herzl), but neither was a major figure in their respective worlds of letters. There was also an untenured professor of mathematics at Heidelberg (Hermann Schapira). But of none of the other participants could it be said that they lent lustre to the Congress by virtue of the status they had achieved among the Gentiles. Accordingly, the *quality* of the Congress had to be judged in terms of the status of its members within the Jewish world itself;

---

[12] Herzl to Belkowsky, 30 June 1897. *Igrot*, ii, no. 327, p. 325.
[13] The breakdown that follows is based, with modifications, on the data collated by Orlan, op. cit.

and so judged, its salient attributes were two. It was, in the first place, an assembly in which East European Jewry predominated. About half of the participants had come to Basel from Russia, Romania, Serbia, Bulgaria, Austrian Poland (Galicia), and Bukovina. The largest of all groups was, in fact, that from the Russian Empire (Russia, Russian Poland, Lithuania, and Latvia)—at least a quarter of the total. In addition, a high proportion of those who were named as from other countries (the listing was by country of residence) were from the East: at least half of those from Germany, for example, were students from Russia, or men like David Wolff-sohn or Hermann Schapira who had settled in Germany as adults and whose deeper roots were in the East. Much the same was true of the groups from Austria and Bohemia, England, France, Switzerland, and the United States.

In the second place, the leading common attribute of the dele-gates—particularly of those who by virtue of their personal attain-ments and reputations effectively negated Herzl's half-serious expectation of an army of *schnorrers* gathered at Basel—was prior membership in Ḥibbat Ẓion. Moreover, it was eastern Ḥibbat Ẓion, the movement that had built up around, and been led by, Pinsker and his friends and successors of the Odessa committee, that was represented in greatest force in Basel. The veterans from Russia and Poland—Mandelstamm, Aḥad Ha-ʿAm, Sokolov, Ussishkin—were decidedly among the most powerful and interest-ing personalities present. And if few of the better-known Russians took an active part in the proceedings—out of caution, or initial scepticism, or simply because the Congress had been organized from Vienna—it was on arguments advanced by Motzkin, the leading figure among the younger Russian Zionists in Berlin, on whom the one real and significant debate turned. That, so far as the origins of its participants were concerned, the Congress was preponderantly an assembly of Hovevei Ẓion, some from the West, but mostly from the East, Herzl the westerner and the new-comer was quick to recognize.[14] And there was a measure of truth (along with some exaggeration) in the comment of the *Jewish Chronicle*'s correspondent that 'it seemed that Dr. Herzl had come to their Congress and not they to his.'[15]

[14] See his article 'The Zionist Congress' in the *Contemporary Review* (London), October 1897, especially pp. 594–5.
[15] *Jewish Chronicle*, 10 September 1897, p. 10.

iii

The views of the old school, their fears, and their reluctance to yield totally to Herzl were expressed in a variety of ways. The Russians did meet in caucus, as planned, to approve the only set speech to be made by one of their number (Bernstein-Cohen); and at several points in the debate asked for, and got, a suspension of the sitting to allow them to meet and formulate a common approach. However, it had been evident even before the beginning of the Congress that they themselves were divided between the old (peaceful settlement) school and the new (political) school and that it was the division of opinion between them, and the parallel division between such western Hovevei Zion as Bambus on the one hand and the Herzlians on the other, that would count for most. A Hovev Zion from the West, from Leipzig, protested the failure to mention 'the great deeds that Edmond de Rothschild had performed' in Erez-Israel and asked the Congress to pass a vote of thanks to the Baron. (Herzl's response was to point out that this would be asking the Congress to choose between ingratitude [to Rothschild] and renouncing a principle [opposition to 'infiltration' into Erez-Israel] which was due to be debated in any case—at which he was cheered and the proposal dropped.) A Russian Jew protested against the general use of German at the Congress, rather than Hebrew. There was pressure to include Birnbaum (whom Herzl loathed) on the executive of the new organization: 'Without Birnbaum there would be no Herzl, and no Zionist movement in Austria', an excited delegate from Lemberg called out amid cheers and counter-cheers. And these reminders of what had preceded Herzl's initiatives were the stronger for the audience on the floor being predominantly of the old school while the agenda of the Congress, its themes, and— broadly—its management and its direction had been set by the new men. For it was Herzl and Nordau who delivered the two key speeches—the one being a brief restatement of the rationale, purposes, and methods of political Zionism, and the other being an analysis of its sources in the contemporary social condition of the Jews; and it was unmistakably as Jews who had assimilated the West European languages and culture that the two men spoke.

'Our enemies', Herzl told the Congress, 'probably do not know how deeply they have wounded . . . those among us . . . who were modern, educated, and ghetto emancipated . . .' The effect of the revival of the old hatred for the Jews, however, was to restore to them that same sense of belonging [*das Gefühl der Zusammenge-hörigkeit*] of which they had been so sharply accused by the anti-Semites. Now, 'we have, so to speak, returned home'; and Zionism may be seen as our return to Jewry even before our return to the Land of the Jews. There, 'in the old home', we have been welcomed; and thus Zionism had 'achieved something remarkable which had formerly been regarded as impossible—the close union of the most modern elements in Jewry with the most conservative . . . without any unworthy concessions or intellectual sacrifice either on one side or on the other'. Nor did 'we [the moderns] have any intention of abandoning an iota of the culture we have acquired'. In any case, it was not the intellectual and spiritual life of the Jews that was now at issue. It was with their material needs and with the means whereby the Jewish national existence could be assured and protected that Zionism—and the Congress—were concerned.

Zionism, he went on, was a great popular movement and it wanted a free and public discussion of the problem. And what it urged in practice was self-help. 'A people can only help itself; if it cannot do that, it does not deserve to be helped [by others].' The Zionist movement must work openly and loyally, with the confidence of, and in agreement with, the states concerned. It was too early to say what form such agreement should take—except this, that its 'basis can only be one of legal rights, not sufferance. We have already had sufficient experience of toleration and *Schutz-judentum*.' Hibbat Zion, for all its virtues, could take us no further. For, quite simply, even if we assumed that the settlement movement as now constituted in Erez-Israel could handle as many as 10,000 Jews a year—an illusory figure for if it were ever approached the Turkish government would immediately reintroduce its prohibition on the immigration of Jews[16]—it would still take nine centuries to solve the Jewish Question! Moreover, the Turkish government would be right; for whoever thought the Jews could *smuggle* themselves into the land of their ancestors was deceiving himself, or others. 'Nowhere else is the arrival of Jews so quickly noticed as in the historic home of the people and that because it is their historic home.' What was needed was to put the entire question on a fresh, systematic, and public basis and to reach 'a proper

[16] Herzl was in error. The prohibition had never been lifted; but its enforcement had been slack.

agreement with the political factors concerned'. He and his friends had said all this many times. Yet it was worth saying so once more on this present,

solemn occasion when Jews from so many countries have met at one call, the old call of the nation . . . Must not a presentiment of great events come over us if we think that at this moment the hopes and expectations of many hundreds of thousands of our people rest on our assembly? . . . It will now be known everywhere that Zionism, which had been made out to be a chiliastic horror, is in reality a civilized, law-abiding, humane movement towards the ancient goal of our people. What we as individuals may have written or said can quite properly be passed over, but not what emanates from the Congress . . . In this Congress we are creating an organ for the Jewish people which it has not had before, but which it has urgently needed. Our cause is too great [to be subordinate to] the ambition and wilfulness of individuals. It must be lifted to the plane of the impersonal if it is to succeed . . . But however long it will take to complete our work let our Congress be serious and lofty, a blessing for the unfortunate, a threat to nobody, a source of honour to all Jews and worthy of a past, the glory of which is far off, but everlasting.[17]

'You all know, if only imprecisely,' Herzl had told the Congress at the beginning of his speech, 'that with a few exceptions, the condition [of the Jews] is not a happy one. We should scarcely have met here had it been otherwise.' But he himself did not go on to elaborate. Others, headed by Nordau, recounted and analysed the *Judennot*, the misery and Question of the Jews, country by country and topic by topic, some in such relentless detail that open (but unsuccessful) pleas for brevity began to be heard.

Nordau himself was not dull; he spoke extremely well and his theme was simple. The contemporary condition of the Jews could be depicted 'only in one colour'. Wherever they were settled in large numbers misery prevailed, but not the 'ordinary misery' which is probably the unalterable fate of mankind, but a peculiar misery which they suffer as Jews and from which they would be free if they were not Jews.

Jewish misery has two forms, the material and the moral. In Eastern Europe, North Africa and western Asia—in those very regions where the overwhelming majority, probably nine-tenths of all Jews, live—there the misery of the Jews is to be understood literally. It is a daily distress

---

[17] *Protokoll des I. Zionistenkongresses in Basel, vom 29 bis 31 August 1897*, [second edition] Prague, 1911, pp. 15-20.

of the body, anxiety for every day that follows, a tortured fight for bare existence. In Western Europe . . . the question of bread and shelter, and the question of security of life and limb concerns them less. There the misery is moral. It takes the form of perpetual injury to self-respect and honour and of a brutal suppression of the striving for spiritual satisfactions which no non-Jew is obliged to deny himself.

At the heart of Nordau's analysis was a paradox. In the East, at bottom, it was by action of government through the laws of the state, or else in hypocritical violation of the laws, that the reduction of the Jews to hopeless pauperism was taking place. Accordingly, many sensible people held the view that the lifting of these pressures and restrictions—i.e. the formal, legal emancipation of Jews— would necessarily lead to an improvement in their condition. And, indeed, just such an emancipation of the Jews in Western Europe had brought the Jewish qualities of industry, tenacity, sobriety, and thrift into play and made a great improvement in their material condition possible. There, at all events, the struggle for daily bread did not assume the terrible forms to be found in Russia, Romania, and Galicia. The western Jew had bread. And yet, said Nordau, he did not live by bread alone; the old forms of misery had been replaced by new ones. For the inner character and purpose of the Emancipation had been misunderstood by the Jews. It had not been instituted to remedy an ancient injustice, but only as a function of the logic of the men of the French Revolution and because, although popular sentiment rebelled against it, the philosophy of the Revolution decreed that principles must be placed above sentiment. The Jews had hastened, in a kind of intoxication, to burn their boats, to cut themselves off from the self-contained life of the ghetto. For a while all was well—until all at once, twenty years ago, after

a slumber of thirty to sixty years, anti-Semitism broke out once more from the innermost depth of the nations and his real situation was revealed to the mortified Jew . . . He has lost the home of the ghetto, but the land of his birth is denied to him as his home. He avoids his fellow Jew because anti-Semitism has made him hateful. His countrymen repel him when he wishes to associate with them. He has no ground under his feet and he has no community to which he belongs as a full member. He cannot reckon on his Christian countrymen viewing either his character or his intentions with justice, let alone with kindly feelings. With his Jewish countrymen he has lost touch. He feels that the world hates him and he sees no place where he can find warmth when he seeks it . . .

The emancipated Jew is insecure in his relations with his fellow beings, timid with strangers, even suspicious of the secret feelings of his friends. His best powers are exhausted in the suppression, or at least the difficult concealment, of his own real character. For he fears that this character might be recognized as Jewish, and he never has the satisfaction of showing himself as he is in all his thoughts and sentiments. He becomes an inner cripple.[18]

Nordau's oration was the high point of the Congress. He was the only speaker not to read from a written text. 'You should have seen the difference', he wrote to his wife. 'It was mad and touching. Old men cried like children. Herzl exaggerated, as was his wont, telling me, "Your speech was the Congress; it will be historic." Which terrifies me.'[19] 'He spoke wonderfully', Herzl duly noted in his diary. 'His speech is and will remain a monument of our age.'[20]

iv

The Congress sat for three days (from 29 to 31 August). Rather more than half the time was taken up by the opening addresses, reports on the condition of the Jews in various countries, no less than four separate reports on the settlement in Erez-Israel, a report on the revival of the Hebrew language, the reading of Rabbi Mohilever's long message to the Congress, and the announcement of other letters, telegrams, and 'petitions' (over 50,000 signatures to the latter alone). A number of minor proposals were made, among them one to establish a Jewish National Fund, another to set up a committee for Hebrew literature, and a third to collect reliable statistics on the Jews. Some of this was perfunctory and much of it was anticlimactic after the excitement of the opening and the initial appearance of Herzl and Nordau. But the discussion on the permanent institutions to be set up and the rules by which they were to be governed, though long, was livelier. The initial proposals (put forward by Bodenheimer) were not accepted, but referred to an *ad hoc* committee for further consideration. (This raised the question how such a committee was to be formed. Eventually, it was agreed that it would be on the basis of countries of origin—two from Russia, two from Germany, one from Bulgaria, and so on.)

[18] *Protokoll*, pp. 20–33.
[19] Shalom Schwartz, *Max Nordau be-igrotav*, Jerusalem, 1944, pp. 24–5.
[20] *Diaries*, ii, p. 584.

On the morning of the third day of the Congress the new proposals were debated, voted upon, and approved.

The Congress was to be the 'chief organ' of the movement; the right to participate in the election of delegates to the Congress could be easily acquired by payment of a small annual fee, to be known as the 'shekel' (amounting to 40 copecks in Russia, one mark in Germany, one franc in France, and so on); where the local Zionist society numbered over 100 members a second delegate would be elected; the business of the movement between Congresses was to be carried on by an 'Actions Committee' consisting of eighteen members elected on a country basis and a small group of five, all resident in Vienna and elected by the entire Congress as a body; the Vienna members were expected to serve as the working executive of the movement; and, finally, the local Zionist organizations in each country were guaranteed a high degree of autonomy under the terms of the last clause of the resolution on organization which laid down that all local activities were to conform to the laws of the country in question.

This simple institutional framework (to be maintained in its essentials for fifty years) thus comprised easy access to membership, an elected, representative, and, as it were, sovereign parliament, ample room for variation in the local, country organizations of Zionists, and an executive which was responsible to the Congress in the western parliamentary tradition and assured of a relatively free hand in the period intermediate between one Congress and another. The debate on organization was chiefly on matters of details and personalities; the plan to found the institutions of the movement on the principle of representative, parliamentary democracy was taken as a matter of course. It may even have gone unnoticed, as Herzl himself suspected. He himself attached the greatest importance to it, for it provided the basis of the claim that the Congress was in the nature of a national assembly. The debate on the programme of the movement (on 30 August) was very different: there issues of principle, not matters of detail and personality, dominated.

Delegates of the old school of thought had been pleasantly surprised to find that Herzl was a great deal more moderate on matters of doctrine than they had thought likely. 'The eyes of the nations of Europe and their governments are upon us', he had told them at the preparatory meeting; it was therefore important to try for unanimity, especially on the Zionist programme.[21] But it was clear to him that unanimity could only be attained by a measure of compromise on the definition of the central aim of Zionism, whether this was to be, as he had put it in his pamphlet, *the restoration of the Jewish State*—or not. In fact Herzl had realized long before the convening of the Congress that there could be no negotiation with the Turks on the basis of a plan to establish a Jewish *state* and had ceased to employ the term.

No serious statesman thinks of the partition of Turkey today [he had written in *Die Welt* on 9 July]. True, Turkey needs financial assistance more than ever she did in the past; and that she can only have from the Jews. But there is no question of taking a single province away from the Sultan, only of establishing a home [or homestead] secured by the law of nations [*eine völkerrechtlich gesicherte Heimstätte*] for those Jews who cannot survive elsewhere.

This was the formula which, with slight modifications, Bodenheimer put before the committee appointed to draft the programme. It was weaker than the one he and his colleagues from Cologne would have liked it to be,[22] but it was still too strong for the old school which wanted to avoid any term that could be taken to imply an independent state. After much discussion in the course of three sessions (there were no fewer than five lawyers on the committee), and at Nordau's urging, the phrase 'law of nations' with its implications of high politics and intervention by the Powers was altered to 'law'. The crucial preamble of the draft resolution now read: *Zionism aims at the creation of a home [heimstätte] for the Jewish people in Palestine to be secured by law.* But this was unacceptable precisely to those who had been drawn to Herzl—and to Basel— by hope of a bolder approach. Nordau's plea to accept the formula without discussion was ignored. 'Gentlemen!', cried Fabius Schach (of Cologne), 'What we want to express here are the basic ideas of

---

[21] *Ha-Magid*, 9 September 1897.

[22] The second of the three 'theses' formulated by the National Jewish Union which Bodenheimer and Wolffsohn had founded the year before read as follows: 'The civil emancipation of the Jews within other nations has not sufficed, as history shows, to secure the social and cultural future of the Jewish people; hence, the definitive solution of the Jewish problem depends upon the establishment of a Jewish state—for only it would be capable of representing the Jews as such under the Law of Nations and of accepting those Jews who either cannot remain in their native countries or do not wish to. The natural centre for such a state, to be established by legal means, is the historically consecrated land of Palestine.' Henriette Hannah Bodenheimer, *Toldot tokhnit Bazel*, Jerusalem, 1947, p. II.

Zionism and it is absolutely necessary that what we are striving for be stated clearly in the programme. A Jewish national home—that is what we aim at, not a refuge granted us by favour.' No national movement, said Schach, had ever attained anything by excessive and pedantic caution. The phrase 'by the law of nations' was of the greatest significance. Why should we not admit that we no longer wish to be tolerated, that what we want is autonomy on our own national soil? But without guarantees under international law the enduring existence of a small nation can never be assured. We must try to win the Sultan and the European states for our cause. We must prove to them that we are a peaceful and civilized element and that we shall be of help to ourselves and of use to all the world if we are helped to establish a safe, national homeland. But it must be under international law.[23]

Herzl, who was presiding, intervened to say that everyone knew what was needed in practice; and that no purpose would be served by making the task of the Zionist executive harder than it was in any case by insisting on precision—for in any event it went without saying that nothing that failed to meet the real needs of the Jews would be acceptable.

After some moments of confusion, when it was apparent that a full and angry debate could not be staved off, it was proposed that it be limited to two speakers, one for each side of the argument. The speaker for the radicals was Leo Motzkin.

The question is not one of a single word, but of our future strategy as a whole; the word is only its symbol. We believe it to be of the utmost importance that the Congress state its solution to the Jewish Question publicly. The world concerns itself with the Jewish Problem, while the Jews themselves adopt a position which only humiliates them. Our position, our protest are different when we state [openly]: we want a home of our own, a home for all the world to see. We do not want to be accused of concealing our aims . . .

It might well be, Motzkin went on, that our public utterances would create difficulties for the settlers in Erez-Israel. But what had been the results of fifteen years of settlement work? A few thousand farmers and no more than limited interest in them displayed by Jews elsewhere. The 'practical' approach had torn the movement out of the hearts of the people. 'At the beginning of the 1880s

[23] *Protokoll*, pp. 131-2.

Jewish students in Russia were jubilant about the Zionist ideas. But when the greatness in Zionism withered, the enthusiasm withered too.' Besides, what guarantee could there be that our strategy would not change yet again if we did not, at the very outset, agree on a firm programme saying precisely what it is we are after? Nothing was to be gained by concealment and a great deal was to be lost. If we did not speak frankly, we would not gain support among Jews; and we would only be deceiving ourselves if we thought that the Turkish government did not know that we wished to settle in Ereẓ-Israel and begin a political national life. Besides, it ought to know: it is with it that the great union of Zionists would have to treat.[24]

The argument for accepting the committee's draft was then put by one of its members (Mintz, a lawyer from Vienna) and Nordau pleaded once again for a quick and unanimous decision so as to stress the unity of the Congress and to minimize its divisions. Finally, Herzl intervened once more and proposed an amendment of his own: 'a home to be secured by *public* law' (*öffentlich-rechtlich* instead of *rechtlich*); and this, after some further commotion, was accepted by most of the radicals and carried by the Congress as a whole by acclamation.

The full Programme now read as follows:

Zionism aims at the creation of a home[25] for the Jewish people in Palestine to be secured by public law.

To that end, the Congress envisages the following:

1. The purposeful advancement of the settlement of Palestine with Jewish farmers, artisans, and tradesmen.

2. The organizing and unifying of all Jewry by means of appropriate local and general arrangements subject to the laws of each country.

3. The strengthening of Jewish national feeling and consciousness.

4. Preparatory moves towards obtaining such governmental consent as will be necessary to the achievement of the aims of Zionism.

Schach persisted in objecting to what he saw as a prevarication, but most people were satisfied. 'Public law' carried at least a hint of something broader than the ordinary, internal, or municipal law of a state and if the preamble was read in conjunction with the four operative clauses, and particularly with the last one, the *political* character, aims, and methods of the new school, it could be argued,

---

[24] *Protokoll*, pp. 133–5.
[25] In German: *Heimstätte*, of which the strict, but awkward, translation is 'homestead'.

were fully evident. The drafting committee, Nordau informed the Congress, could see no reason for the change, but since the addition of the term 'public' was meaningless to its collective legal mind it did not object. Motzkin and his friends had at least made their point and gained a concession. Herzl had not had his hands tied. And the old school's wariness of him had been considerably softened by his apparent moderation. 'The idea of a Jewish State has not been raised at all—and a very good thing too', the readers of *Ha-Magid* were promptly, if inaccurately, informed.[26]

Yet it was also the case that the issue under discussion had not been solely one of aims. The Congress had been considering, as Motzkin had correctly seen, an issue of tactics as well—whether or not it was *politic* to state the aims unambiguously. Motzkin thought that the risks of candour had to be taken. Nordau thought plain speaking likely to be fatal.[27] Herzl was no longer sure they could afford not to trim. It was not only a question of the probable Turkish reaction to a clear statement, nor one of his desire not to miss the opportunity to draw the old-school Zionists into the ranks of the new movement. There was his sense—made all the more acute by his experiences since the publication of *Der Judenstaat* eighteen months earlier—that the common judgement on the idea of a Jewish State was that it was an inherently implausible one, if not absurd. The famous entry in his diary for 3 September, after the Congress, reads: 'Were I to sum up the Basel Congress in a word— which I shall guard against pronouncing publicly—it would be this: At Basel I founded the Jewish State. If I said this out loud today, I would be answered by universal laughter.'[28]

There were thus too planes on which one was forced to operate— an outer, public one on which words were weighed and selected with the greatest caution and spoken for the most precise effect; and an inner private one on which one was free to speculate upon —and to desire—the improbable.

---

[26] *Ha-Magid*, 2 September 1897. In contrast, the Reuter report from Basel was a model of compression and accuracy: 'At the sitting of the Zionist Congress to-day the programme for the re-establishment of the Jews in Palestine with publicly recognized rights was unanimously adopted amid applause.' *The Times*, 31 August 1897.

[27] Cf. his retrospective (1920) comments in 'Ha-mandat shel Anglia ve-ha-zionut hamedinit', *Ketavim zioniim*, iv, Jerusalem, 1962, pp. 90–1.

[28] *Diaries*, ii, p. 581. The entry continues: 'Perhaps in five years, and certainly in fifty, everyone will know it . . . At Basel, then, I created this abstraction which, as such, is invisible to the vast majority of people. And with infinitesimal means, I gradually worked the people into the mood for a state and made them feel that they were its National Assembly.'

N

And thus the Congress was allowed to end on much the same note of high emotion as it had begun. A brief speech by Herzl: 'I believe that Zionism need not be ashamed of its first Congress. The Congress was moderate and at the same time determined.' A fervent speech of thanks to Herzl and Nordau by Mandelstamm. Cheering. Waving of handkerchiefs. And in some eyes—tears.

# Postscript

ZIONISM re-created the Jews as a political nation; and by so doing it revolutionized their collective and private lives. It did not do so immediately or completely or equally. For many Jews the effects of the Zionist Revolution have been subtle and even unsensed to this day. Unlike the classic national revolutions of the eighteenth, nineteenth, and twentieth centuries it involved no transfer of existing machinery of state from one set of hands to another. It was neither a precipitant nor a culmination of violent civil war. It is true that Zionism was preceded and to some extent induced (or, at any rate, made possible) by the most straightforward of the consequences of the Enlightenment for the Jews, as for other people—the onset of a steady draining away of the power of organized religion to uphold the traditional forms of social authority. It could be said, therefore, that what the Zionists proposed, in effect, was to step into the consequent semi-vacuum and seize such national leadership as the invertebrate structure of world Jewry permitted. But the conflict between Zionists and anti-(or non-)Zionists was almost wholly a non-violent one and a struggle for moral authority over the Jewish people, not for direct means of ruling them. Nor, of course, could it be otherwise, because in a strict sense no such means existed. On the contrary, in the last resort the conflict on which the Revolution turned was between, on the one hand, those who strove to create *ex nihilo* all the political, economic, and (ultimately) military machinery that independent nations commonly believe crucial to the furtherance of national policy and, on the other hand, those who wanted neither machinery, nor policy, nor even—in extreme, but important cases—a nation. The Zionists were the more daring for their being unquestionably a minority group within Jewry and for their own constituency long being one which they openly proposed, not only to lead but, in time, to govern.

In a strict sense, the Zionists have remained a minority within Jewry to this day; and as the citizens of the Jewish State number less than a quarter of the Jewish people a generation after its establishment, the political and moral authority of the Jewish government within and over Jewry remains heavily circumscribed. The historian of the Jews is therefore still comparatively free to choose between directing attention to the successes of the movement, great beyond the most shameless flights of fancy indulged in by its progenitors, or, alternatively, to its failures—failures to encompass the majority of the Jewish people, to put them on a firm footing of equality with other nations, even finally to remove that threat to life and security to which a high proportion of Jews have always been and are still subject. Nor is it easy—or proper—to look away from the much greater cloud that has hung over the movement, and over contemporary Jewry as a whole, since 1945: the fact that for a full third of all Jews the State of Israel came too late.

Yet it seems beyond question that this movement for revival and radical change in Jewry did attain results which may fairly be called revolutionary and, further, that its definitive form dates from 1897. For that reason alone the First Zionist Congress must now be judged one of the pivotal events in the modern history of the Jews. The Congress vividly confirmed that the movement was established and operating; and it was itself the first and, for long, the most important of the movement's institutions. It served to keep Zionism alive and the Zionist option—seen as a radical, alternative course for those who found the Jewish condition intolerable—open and buttressed with an accepted leader, with institutions which commanded a high degree of loyalty, and with a programme in terms of which specific lines of policy could be legitimated. In part, but only in part, this followed from what was accomplished in the course of the three days at Basel, and by whom, and to what purpose, and with what results; and in part because in the aftermath the participants overwhelmingly, fully, and willingly accepted the Congress as an occasion of great importance and of unique and symbolic character. The tension and the expectations of good or ill which had preceded the Congress, the unprecedented setting, the cathartic effect of the proceedings, and the participants' own retrospective judgement upon the Congress as a whole, as an event, and as the augury and instrument of the great departure in Jewish life it was intended to be—all these left an immensely powerful imprint on their minds which was rapidly communicated to all upon their return. Even Aḥad Ha-ʿAm, the sceptic, to whom the Congress had given little joy, who neither liked Herzl nor fully trusted him, and who had 'sat alone among my brothers like a mourner among the wedding guests', had been moved.

For three days, from morning to evening, some two hundred Jews from all countries and of all tendencies had debated in the open and before all the nations the matter of the foundation of a secure home for the Jewish people in the land of their fathers. Thus the *national* answer had burst the bounds of 'modesty' and been made public. It had been expounded to all the world aloud, in clear language, and with a straight back—something which had not occurred since Israel was exiled from its land.[1]

It was this public and, in the widest sense, political aspect of the assembly, the Congress as a living national manifesto and as a fair approximation to the 'glorious demonstration to the world of what Zionism is and of what it wants', that Herzl had aimed at that was decisive for the sequel.

However, the First Congress was crucial to the evolution of Zionism in a second respect. It established a precedent—and the principle—of unity, bringing together virtually all the diverse strains of which the movement was composed: romanticists and pragmatists, orthodox and secularists, socialists and bourgeois, easterners and westerners, men whose minds and language were barely influenced by the non-Jewish world and those who were largely products of it, and, above all, those whose primary concern was with the condition of the Jews as opposed to those, like Aḥad Ha-ʿAm, whose eyes were on the crisis of Judaism.

Zionism offered itself as the vehicle of, and recipe for, a solution to the Jewish Problem; but one great source of the peculiarly intricate and painful nature of the problem was the difficulty of disentangling the question What could be done for the Jews? from the question What should be done for them? For the simple notion that the solution to the Jewish Problem, however conceived, lay in the return of the Jews to Ereẓ-Israel and their re-entry into world society as a nation possessed of political autonomy implied the further notion that the time had come for a vastly long historical process to be brought to an end or, at the very least, sharply redirected. What would then replace the known patterns of Jewish life? What would be gained or lost in the course of change? Was the

---

[1] 'Ha-kongres ha-ẓioni ha-rishon', *Kol kitvei Aḥad Ha-ʿAm*, p. 275 (emphasis in original).

Jewish State intended to be an end in itself, a Utopia in which, and through which, life was to be transformed? Or was it to be primarily and more mundanely the means by which national political power, of the advantages of which the Jews had been deprived for twenty centuries, was to be restored? Or, again, was it, as Herzl himself dimly perceived, both—which is to say, both Utopia and the means to its own achievement? Alternatively, was a Jewish state no more than one possible solution to the problem of survival among others, perhaps more promising at first sight than any other and more attractive, but nevertheless legitimately to be discarded or tucked away out of sight and mind if it proved unworkable or unattainable or if something better was devised? But if there was to be no state, then were not the Jews destined to remain different from all, or almost all, other peoples? What then would have changed in their lives privately and collectively? For if there was to be no state there could be no end to the Exile in its deepest sense, not even—given the known conditions of minority existence in the Islamic lands, as elsewhere—in Erez-Israel itself.

All these were issues on which divisions necessarily ran so deep that an organized movement which proposed to bridge them could not be more than a coalition subject to periodic gains and losses of whole categories of supporters and militants and not infrequent conflicts on policy and principle within the main body of the membership. Unity, in a word, was difficult to come by. A well-knit, disciplined, like-minded force lending itself to manipulation by its own leader or leaders was out of the question. In a profound sense, many of the weaknesses of the Zionist movement were so many reflections of the internal weaknesses, the fissiparity and heterogeneity, of the Jewish people.

To these circumstances was added the fundamental—and almost fatal—handicap that for long it was not only materially impossible for the leaders of the movement to attain the stated goal, but that it was entirely reasonable to doubt whether it was attainable at all. Those who sought to sweep doubts away often tended—perhaps necessarily—to an obsessive, somewhat feverish, high-pitched style of thought and behaviour. Those whom these doubts did afflict tended to a modification and reduction of the aims and ambitions of Zionism, to a lowering of the sights, and to compromise, if not surrender. And since each of these broad tendencies, along with the positions intermediate between them, sought to justify itself in terms of a particular reading of the Jewish condition, no clear line could ever be drawn between what was possible in practice and what was desirable in principle.

What then did keep the Zionists together and their institutions intact and the painfully slow 'infiltration' into Erez-Israel in being until the great upheaval of the First World War unexpectedly made a break-through possible? The simple answer seems to be that the social reality was always stronger than the debates about it, that the Jews of the towns and villages of the Pale of Settlement, Galicia, and Romania could not wait for relief, and that for ever greater numbers of them the misery of their immediate condition out-weighed both the force of inertia and the force of religious teaching. The Zionists could not dissolve the predicament nor even do much to soften it. But the predicament was too deep and comprehensive ever to be put entirely out of mind. In the West too, the subtler indignities intrinsic to the condition of the emancipated Jew not only remained in being, but were, for the most part, subject to steady reinforcement as systematic political anti-Semitism gathered strength on the way to its ultimate triumph.

For the finer spirits passivity was therefore never tolerable for long. Nothing had worked convincingly, if at all. Neither legal emancipation where it had been granted, nor self-improvement, nor philanthropic self-help, nor migration, nor the spread of educa-tion and liberal principles in the population at large, nor formal minority rights, nor the slow spread of democratic government. But if nothing else offered hope, and if sheer stoicism and religious resignation were rejected, there was at least this, the Zionist mode of thinking and the Zionists' programme for action. 'And who knows?', wrote Lilienblum after Basel. 'We may succeed.'[2]

[2] Letter to 'Shefer', 11 November 1897. CZA, A 27/8/1.

# Select Bibliography

THE literature on Zionism is immense; but honourable (and ever more numerous) exceptions apart, a great deal of it is polemical and tendentious and of little use to the student except for clues to opinion for and against. This is not for lack of primary sources. The wealth of archival material is such that the effect on would-be historians of the movement has probably been daunting. Nor are there any serious problems of access to any of the collections, at any rate for the early period and until the years immediately prior to the outbreak of the triangular Jewish–Arab–British conflict in full force in 1946 (well beyond the scope of the present study). Language is a problem for some students. It is impossible to get to grips with the subject without a command of Hebrew, which is both the principal language of the sources themselves and, today, the language in which a very great deal of the scholarly work on the history of the Jews in the modern period in general, and on the Zionist movement in particular, is written and published. There is also a great deal of essential material in Russian and German for the early years and in English for the later years; there are both sources and important scholarly studies in Yiddish; and there is valuable material in French. For the study of certain, specialized issues, other languages are necessary: Turkish, Arabic, and the languages of the Balkan countries, for example. No one can cope with all this alone.

Still, the fundamental causes of the relative poverty of Zionist historiography, and, particularly, the dearth of studies which attempt a synoptic, interpretative view of the subject, probably lie deeper—perhaps in the fact that the serious historian wields a sharp knife, while the body of modern Jewry has been too deeply wounded and the wounds are still too painful for it to be easy to set to work on the subject in a sufficiently detached frame of mind. The subject does not yet belong to the past. The return of the Jews to Erez-Israel and the establishment there of a Third Commonwealth has thrown them into fresh conflicts which are immensely distant from resolution. And the great questions which relate to the character, ethos, and structure of the Jewish people as a whole— to which the Zionists have offered an explicit set of answers—remain difficult and, to some, painful. In the circumstances, it is not surprising that it is only in very recent years that the history of the modern national movement has begun to be tackled systematically.

GENERAL

Shlomo Shunami, *Bibliography of Jewish Bibliographies* (Jerusalem, 1969), is the basic guide for all topics in Jewish history. There are useful bibliographies for Zionism specifically by G. Kressel and I. Klausner in Y. Greenbaum, *Ha-tenuʿa ha-ẓionit be-hitpathuta* (Jerusalem, 1942–54). G. M. Portugalov *et al.*, *Ukazatel' Literatury o Sionizme* (St. Petersburg, 1903), is valuable as an index to the early periodical literature. A. Levinson and N. M. Gelber, *Bibliografia ẓionit* (Jerusalem, 1953), is a select bibliography, instructive for the range of topics covered.

The indispensable collection of documents is in the Central Zionist Archives in Jerusalem. The Schwadron Collection (Jerusalem), the collections of the YIVO Institute for Jewish Research (New York), and the Archives of Russian Zionism (Tel Aviv) all possess useful and sometimes important material. The Foreign Office files in the Public Record Office (London), which are essential for the later period, contain documents which throw additional light on some aspects of the subject of this book as well.

There is not much on the subject in general encyclopedias, but there is a great deal on the social and cultural background to Zionism to be elicited from three specialist series: *Evreiskaya Entsiklopedia* (St. Petersburg, 1906–13, 16 vols.), the still incomplete *Ha-enẓiklopedia ha-ʿivrit* (Jerusalem, 1949–  , 25 vols. to date), and *Encyclopaedia Judaica* (Jerusalem, 1971–2, 16 vols.) which contain valuable bibliographical information.

Of the two great single-handed attempts at a comprehensive history of the Jewish people, the first, Heinrich Graetz, *Geschichte der Juden von den ältesten Zeiten bis zur Gegenwart* (English edition: *History of the Jews* (Philadelphia, Pa., 1891–8, 6 vols.)), ends approximately at the time the modern Jewish national movement begins to emerge, but the second, Simon (Shimʿon) M. Dubnov, *Weltgeschichte des jüdischen Volkes* (third Hebrew edition: *Divrei yemei ʿam ʿolam* (Tel Aviv, 1939, 10 vols.)), does cover its beginnings and is an important if idiosyncratic document in its own right. In the much more recent co-operative history of the Jews, H. H. Ben-Sasson (ed.), *Toldot ʿam Israel* (Tel Aviv, 1969, 3 vols.), the third volume, S. Ettinger, *Toldot Israel ba-ʿet ha-hadasha*, is an excellent introduction to Jewish history from the seventeenth to the middle of the twentieth century. Salo W. Baron, *The Jewish Community* (Philadelphia, Pa., 1942, 3 vols.), is a sociological analysis of Jewry which touches on modern times. Louis Finkelstein (ed.), *The Jews: Their History* (New York, fourth edition, 1970), is one of the best of the many single-volume surveys. Raphael Mahler, *A History of Modern Jewry 1780–1815* (London, 1971), presents an analysis largely in class terms with a wealth of supporting detail and is a valuable corrective to that view of Jewish history which centres exclusively on issues of faith and religion on the one hand and relations between Jews and non-Jews on the other.

## THE EAST EUROPEAN BACKGROUND

S. M. Dubnov's pioneering works in the history of the Jews of Eastern Europe are still of great value and interest. The most accessible is *History of the Jews in Russia and Poland* (Philadelphia, Pa., 1916-20, 3 vols.). Many of his important articles and occasional papers are to be found in *Pis'ma o Starom i Novom Evreistvye, 1897-1907* (St. Petersburg, 1907) and in the quarterly he edited between 1909 and 1912, *Evreiskaya Starina*. A standard modern survey of the same subject is Louis Greenberg, *The Jews in Russia* (New Haven, Conn., 1944, 2 vols.). There is much illuminating material in Saul M. Ginsburg, *Historishe Verk* (New York, 1937, 2 vols.), and in E. Tcherikower, *Yehudim be-'itot mahpekha* (Tel Aviv, 1957). For an insight into some of the sources of Russian policy towards the Jews, see Hugh Seton-Watson, *The Decline of Imperial Russia* (New York, 1952), N. V. Riasanovsky, *Nicholas I and Official Nationality in Russia 1825-55* (Berkeley, Calif., 1967), Robert F. Byrnes, *Pobedonostev* (Bloomington, Ind., 1968), none of which is concerned specifically with the Jews of the Empire; and S. Ettinger, 'Ha-yesodot ve-ha-megamot be-'izuv mediniuto shel ha-shilton ha-rusi klapei ha-yehudim 'im halukot Polin', *He-'Avar*, xix, 1972, which is. Two well-known contemporary denunciations of that policy are Prince Demidoff San-Donato, *The Jewish Question in Russia* (London, 1884), and Lucien Wolf, *The Legal Sufferings of the Jews in Russia* (London, 1912). The Jewish press, which played a central role in the invertebrate communal life of Russian Jewry, is the subject of Yehuda Slutsky, *Ha-'itonut ha-yehudit-rusit ba-me'a ha-tesha'-'esre* (Jerusalem, 1970). On social unrest and Jewish workers' movements, see Hertz Burgin, *Di Geshikhte fun der Yiddisher Arbeiter Bavegung in Amerike, Rusland un England* (New York, 1915), which conveys the authentic period flavour and two modern academic studies: Ezra Mendelsohn, *Class Struggle in the Pale* (Cambridge, 1970), and Henry J. Tobias, *The Jewish Bund in Russia* (Stanford, Calif., 1972). A great deal of reliable contemporary reporting is to be found in the *Jewish Chronicle* (London) and in two regular publications of the Alliance Israélite Universelle (Paris), the bi-annual *Bulletin de l'Alliance Israélite Universelle* and the monthly *Bulletin Mensuel*. Much modern scholarship on nineteenth-century eastern Jewry must be sought, of course, in learned journals. Among the most important are, in this context, *Zion* (Jerusalem), *He-'Avar* (Tel Aviv), *Kazir* (Tel Aviv), *YIVO Bletter* (New York), *YIVO Annual of Jewish Social Science* (New York), and *Jewish Social Studies* (New York).

## THE WEST EUROPEAN BACKGROUND

In the absence of a comprehensive study of the predicament of emancipated West European Jewry in the face of modern anti-Semitism, the following, together, form an introduction to the subject: Léon Poliakov, *Histoire de l'antisémitisme* (Paris, 1968, 3 vols.); Edmund Silberner, *Ha-sozializm ha-ma'aravi u-she'elat ha-yehudim* (Jerusalem, 1955); Uriel Tal, *Yahadut ve-nazrut ba-Raikh ha-sheni, 1870–1914* (Jerusalem, 1959); Ismar Schorsch, *Jewish Reactions to German Anti-Semitism 1870–1914* (New York and Philadelphia, Pa., 1972); Nathaniel Katzburg, *Antishemiut be-Hungaria, 1867–1914* (Tel Aviv, 1969); and Michael R. Marrus, *The Politics of Assimilation* (Oxford, 1971). To these must be added a wealth of scholarship in successive volumes of the Leo Baeck Institute *Year Book* (London, 1956–72); and, on the other hand, such basic items of the overtly and covertly anti-Semitic literature of the latter half of the nineteenth century as Edouard Drumont, *La France juive* (Paris, 1886), Wilhelm Marr, *Der Sieg des Judenthums über das Germanenthum* (Berne, fourth edition, 1879), and on a higher, but to the Jews themselves more painful plane, Ernest Renan, *De la part des peuples sémitiques dans l'histoire de la civilisation* (Paris, fifth edition, 1862). The Jewish press in Eastern Europe is often an illuminating source for the subject—as in a series of articles in *Ha-Magid*, beginning in April 1881, on anti-Semitism in Germany and the confused reaction to it of the Jews of that country. No consideration of modern Western European Jewry is complete without mention of the role of the Rothschild family both in real events and in mythology, but they have been ill served by most writers—possibly because their private archives are not available. There is a massive history of their financial activities: Bertrand Gille, *Histoire de la maison Rothschild* (Geneva, 1965–7, 2 vols.). The best general account still seems to be Count Egon Corti, *The Rise of the House of Rothschild* and *The Reign of the House of Rothschild* (London, 1928).

## THE ZIONIST MOVEMENT

Out of the vast collections now preserved at the Central Zionist Archives in Jerusalem only one systematic, annotated series of documents, comprehensive for its period, has ever been prepared, A. Druyanov's pioneering and invaluable *Ketavim le-toldot Hibbat Zion ve-yishuv Erez-Israel* (Odessa, 1919, and Tel Aviv, 1925–32, 3 vols.) which contains most of the important correspondence and some other documents. These date from the beginning of Hibbat Zion to the grant of legal status by the Russian authorities in 1890. Two other useful collections are S. Yavne'eli (ed.), *Sefer ha-zionut: tekufat Hibbat Zion* (Jerusalem, 1961, 2 vols.);

and A. Druyanov (ed.), *Mi-yamim rishonim* (Tel Aviv, 1934-5, 2 vols.). Verbatim reports of all the Zionist Congresses were carefully kept and published, at first in German, later in Hebrew. Leib Jaffe (ed.), *Sefer ha-kongres* (Jerusalem, 1950), contains a great deal of subsidiary material on the First Zionist Congress.

Druyanov's series apart, the major printed sources for the history of early Zionism are the published writings and correspondence of its leading personalities, to which must be added some of the critical and biographical studies made of them. There is a substantial literature by and on Moses Hess, of which the most relevant to Hess the proto-Zionist are his own *Rome and Jerusalem* (English trans. M. Waxman, New York, 1918), a selection of his letters by T. Zlocisti and G. Kressel (eds.), *Moshe Hess u-venei doro* (Tel Aviv, 1947), and the best of the many introductions to his thinking, Isaiah Berlin, *The Life and Opinions of Moses Hess* (Cambridge, 1959).

There is no complete and definitive edition of Lilienblum's writings. However, much of his great output (mainly essays and articles) was collected soon after his death in *Kol kitvei M. L. Lilienblum* (Warsaw, 1910-13, 4 vols.). An annotated and more accessible collection of his autobiographical writings (with material not included in the above) is *Ketavim otobiografiim* (Jerusalem, 1970, 3 vols.), edited with a valuable introduction by S. Breiman. His correspondence with Y. L. Gordon, the poet, has been collected in S. Breiman (ed.), *Igrot M. L. Lilienblum le-Y. L. Gordon* (Jerusalem, 1968).

Much of what Pinsker wrote has remained unidentified; most of those of his letters which were written in connection with Ḥibbat Ẓion are to be found in Druyanov, *Ketavim*, etc. For a fuller picture of the man there is A. Druyanov, 'Pinsker u-zemano', *Ha-Tekufa*, xii (Tammuz–Ellul 5681 [1920/1]), 214-50; xiii (Tishrei–Kislev 5681 [1921/2]), 275-320; xvi (Tammuz–Ellul 5682 [1921/2]), 308-25; Yosef Klausner (ed.), *Sefer Pinsker* (Jerusalem, 1921); and M. Yo'eli (ed.), *Y. L. Pinsker* (Tel Aviv, 1960). There is an English edition of *Autoemancipation!* and some other writings: B. Netanyahu (ed.), *Road to Freedom* (New York, 1944).

The standard edition of Aḥad Ha-ʿAm's political, philosophical, and autobiographical writings is *Kol kitvei Aḥad Ha-ʿAm* (Jerusalem, 1947). His published letters, selected and annotated by himself, with some additions by his literary executors, are in *Igrot Aḥad Ha-ʿAm* (Tel Aviv, 1956-60, second edition, 6 vols.). The most thoroughgoing study of his life and thought is Arye [Leon] Simon and Yosef Eliahu Heller, *Aḥad Ha-ʿAm: ha-ish, poʿolo ve-torato* (Jerusalem, 1955). Several selections of his writings, edited, somewhat abridged, and translated into English by Leon Simon, have been published as *Selected Essays* (Philadelphia, Pa., 1912); *Ten Essays on Zionism and Judaism* (London, 1922); and

*Essays, Letters, Memoirs* (Oxford, 1946). On Aḥad Ha-ʿAm's circle, see S. Tchernovitz, *Benei Moshe u-tekufatam* (Warsaw, 1914).

The most important single source for the life and character of Theodor Herzl is his diary, begun in May 1895 and broken off in May 1904, less than two months before his death. The German original, somewhat abridged, was published as *Theodor Herzl's Tagebücher* (Berlin, 1922–3, 3 vols.). The unabridged published version is the English one: *The Complete Diaries of Theodor Herzl* (ed. Raphael Patai, trans. Harry Zohn, New York, 1960, 5 vols.). There is no definitive edition of all his literary and journalistic works, political speeches, and letters, although most important items and many unimportant ones have appeared under various auspices and in several languages. The annotated edition of his letters, *Igrot Herzl* (ed. Alex Bein *et al.*, Jerusalem, 1957–8), had not, by the seventieth year after Herzl's death, got beyond 1899. The most recent representative collection of writings is in Hebrew: *Kitvei Herzl* (Jerusalem, 1960–1, 10 vols.). It includes the standard biography by Alex Bein. This has been published in English in a slightly abridged version as *Theodore Herzl* (trans. Maurice Samuel, Philadelphia, Pa., 1940). Herzl's novel *Altneuland* (English trans. Paula Arnold, Haifa, 1960) should not be forgotten, nor the concise statement of his views recorded in the Minutes of Evidence (7 July 1902, pp. 211–21) in *Report of the Royal Commission on Alien Immigration* (Cmd. 1741–3, London, 1903, 4 vols.).

The literature on Herzl is of very uneven quality, and the collections of papers by and about him are comparatively numerous. One useful series is the *Herzl Year Book* (ed. Raphael Patai, New York, 1958–71, 7 vols.); but even there, scholarship and hagiography go side by side. Henriette Hannah Bodenheimer, *Im Anfang der zionistischen Bewegung* (Frankfurt a.M., 1965), contains the exchange of letters between Herzl and Bodenheimer, 1896–1904. Tulo Nussenblatt, *Theodor Herzl Jahrbuch* (Vienna, 1937), also contains some valuable material. Arthur Stern, 'The Genetic Tragedy of the Family of Theodor Herzl', *Israel Annals of Psychiatry and Related Disciplines*, vol. iii, fasc. 1, 1965, pp. 99–116, and Paula Arnold (the daughter of Leon Kellner, a close associate of Herzl), *Zikhronot be-ahava* (Jerusalem, 1968), are both very suggestive on Herzl's private life. Joseph Adler, *The Herzl Paradox* (New York, 1962), considers Herzl's social ideas, but tends to take him too seriously as a political thinker. These are a few out of many.

A selection of those of Max Nordau's voluminous writings which concern Jewry and Zionism was published as *Zionistische Schriften* (second edition, Berlin, 1923). The comprehensive edition of his Zionist writings and speeches, including his play *Doctor Kohn* (all in Hebrew translation), is B. Netanyahu (ed.), *Ketavim zioniim* (Jerusalem, 1954–62,

4 vols.). There is a small, over-edited selection of his letters: S. Schwartz, *Max Nordau be-igrotav* (Jerusalem, 1944). Meir Ben-Horin, *Max Nordau* (New York, 1956), stands out among the secondary works.

Other volumes of memoirs, letters, and other writings, in full, or in the form of selections and extracts appended to biographies, by figures of importance in their own right for the early period of the Zionist movement, or by minor contemporaries whose comments are of interest in themselves: Yehuda Appel, *Be-tokh reshit ha-teḥiya* (Tel Aviv, 1936); M. Bernstein-Cohen and Y. Korn (eds.), *Sefer Bernstein-Cohen* (Tel Aviv, 1946); Max Bodenheimer, *Darki le-Zion* (Jerusalem, 1952); Ephraim Deinard, *Se'u nes Ziona* (Pressburg, 1886); G. Kressel (ed.), *David Gordon* (Tel Aviv, n.d.); Mordekhai Ehrenpreis, *Bein mizraḥ le-ma'arav* (Tel Aviv, 1953); I. Klausner (ed.), *Ha-ketavim ha-zioniim shel ha-rav Kalischer* (Jerusalem, 1947); Bernard Lazare, *Job's Dungheap* (New York, 1948); Yehuda Leib Levin ('Yehalel'), *Zikhronot ve-hegyonot* (ed. Yehuda Slutsky, Jerusalem, 1968); Alex Bein (ed.), *Sefer Motzkin* (Jerusalem, 1939); *Igrot Shemaryahu Levin* (Tel Aviv, 1966); Y. L. Fishman (Maimon) (ed.), *Sefer Shemu'el [Mohilever]* (Jerusalem, 1923); Izḥak Nissenboim, *'Alei ḥeldi* (Warsaw, 1929); I. Shapira (ed.), *Igrot ha-rav Nissenboim* (Jerusalem, 1956); Yosef Meisel, *Rabbi Sha'ul Pinḥas Rabbinowitz* (*'Shefer'*) (Tel Aviv, 1943); Zevi Hermann Schapira, *Ketavim zioniim* (ed. B. Dinaburg (Dinur), Jerusalem, 1925); I. Klausner, *Karka' ve-ruaḥ: ḥayyav u-fo'olo shel Prof. Z. H. Schapira* (Jerusalem, 1966); A. I. Shahrai, *Rabbi 'Akiva Yosef Schlesinger* (Jerusalem, 1942); Perez Smolenskin, *Ma'amarim* (Jerusalem, 1925-6, 4 vols.); Florian Sokolov, *Avi, Nahum Sokolov* (Jerusalem, 1970); S. Rawidowicz (ed.), *Sefer Sokolov* (Jerusalem, 1943); *Kitvei Naḥman Syrkin* (introd. Berl Katznelson, Tel Aviv, 1939); S. Eisenstadt (ed.), *Yeḥiel Tchlenov* (Tel Aviv, 1937); *Sefer Ussishkin* (Jerusalem, 1934); S. Schwartz, *Ussishkin be-igrotav* (Jerusalem, 1950); Kelonymus Ze'ev Wissotzky, *Kevuzat mikhtavim* (Warsaw, 1898); Abraham Robinsohn, *David Wolffsohn* (Berlin, 1921); Maurice Wohlgelernter, *Israel Zangwill* (New York, 1964).

The first serious general study of the movement, still of considerable value, is Richard J. H. Gottheil, *Zionism* (Philadelphia, Pa., 1914). Naḥum Sokolov's enormous *History of Zionism, 1600-1918* (London, 1919, 2 vols.) is useful for some of the documents which it includes, but is too naïve to serve as more than a guide to Sokolov's own view of how the movement should be presented to the general public. Adolf Böhm, *Die Zionistische Bewegung* (second edition, Tel Aviv, 1935-7, 2 vols.), is strongest on the institutions of the movement. Arthur Hertzberg (ed.), *The Zionist Idea* (New York, 1959), is an anthology of Zionist writings with perceptive comments by the editor. The best modern survey of the subject is Ben Halpern, *The Idea of the Jewish State* (second edition, Cambridge, Mass., 1969). Walter Laqueur, *A History of Zionism* (London, 1972), is the only attempt, to date, at a narrative history which covers the full span from the 1880s to 1948 in reasonable detail. M. Medzini, *Ha-mediniut ha-zionit* (Jerusalem, 1934), deals chiefly with Zionist policy under Herzl.

Two scholarly series are of the greatest value for all periods and aspects of the movement. *Shivat Zion* (ed. B. Dinur *et al.*, Jerusalem, 1950–6, 4 vols.) has unfortunately been discontinued. *Ha-Zionut* (ed. D. Carpi, Tel Aviv) has come out regularly since 1970.

S. L. Zitron, *Toldot Hibbat Zion* (Odessa, 1914), and B. Dinaburg (Dinur), *Hibbat Zion* (Tel Aviv, 1932–4, 2 vols.), are both dated in approach and content, but are still the most useful general introductions to the Lilienblum–Pinsker period. They should be read in conjunction with modern essays of smaller compass and the many studies of the literary life of East European Jewry, among them Yeruham Lachower, *Bialik, hayyav v'izirato* (Tel Aviv, 1944–8, 3 vols.), David Patterson, *The Hebrew Novel in Czarist Russia* (Edinburgh, 1964), and Ruth Kartun-Blum (ed.), *Ha-shira ha-'ivrit bi-tekufat Hibbat Zion* (Jerusalem, 1969), to name only three.

Among the country studies, Israel Klausner's two books, *Mi-Katowiz 'ad Bazel* (Jerusalem, 1965, 2 vols.) and *Hibbat Zion be-Romania* (Jerusalem, 1958) on the early period in Russia and Romania respectively, and N. M. Gelber's *Toldot ha-tenu'a ha-zionit be-Galizia* (Jerusalem, 1958, 2 vols.) on Zionism in Austrian Poland (Galicia), all contain a great deal of detailed, but generally undigested information. Richard Lichtheim's *Die Geschichte des deutschen Zionismus* (Jerusalem, 1954) is a more elegant and perceptive work.

Arye Zenzipper (Rafaeli), *Pa'amei ha-ge'ula* (Tel Aviv, 1951), deserves special mention for its hundreds of rare photographs of the activists of the movement in Russia.

Izhak Ben-Zvi, *Erez-Israel ve-yishuva b'imei ha-shilton ha-'Otomani* (Jerusalem, 1955), is a general survey of the structure and history of the Jewish community in Erez-Israel under Turkish rule. N. J. Mandel, 'Turks, Arabs and Jewish Immigration into Palestine: 1882–1914' (unpublished D.Phil. thesis, Oxford, 1965), is a detailed account of the emerging Jewish–Arab conflict at the time of the First and Second 'Aliyot. Mordechai Eliav (ed.), *Ha-yishuv ha-yehudi be-Erez-Israel bi-re'i ha-mediniut ha-Germanit 1842–1914* (Tel Aviv, 1974, 2 vols.), is an illuminating collection of German diplomatic and consular correspondence on subjects relevant to the new *yishuv*.

The preparation of a detailed history of the new *yishuv* is under way under the auspices of the Israel National Academy of Sciences and

Humanities. Until it appears (at the end of the 1970s) the best modern studies should be sought in the form of scholarly articles in the journals and series already mentioned. Many settlements have celebrated their jubilees and other anniversaries by the publication of large volumes of early correspondence and other documents, many of which are extremely illuminating. Two which rate special mention are David Idelovitch, *Rishon le-Zion 1882-1941* (Rishon le-Zion, 1941), and Arye Samsonov, *Zikhron Ya‘akov* (Zikhron Ya‘akov, 1942), to which should be added Yosef Shapiro's account of the agricultural school established by the Alliance Israélite Universelle near Jaffa more than a decade before the First ‘*Aliya* began, *Me'a shana Mikve Israel* (Tel Aviv, 1970). For the origins of Bilu and other socialist strains in the *yishuv*, see Moshe Braslavsky, *Po‘alim ve-irguneihem ba-‘Aliya ha-rishona* (Tel Aviv, 1961); Israel Belkind, *Di Erste Shritt fun Yishuv Erez-Israel* (New York, 1917-18, 2 vols.); and Ḥayyim Ḥisin, *Mi-yoman aḥad ha-Biluim* (Petaḥ Tikva, 1967).

# Index

Russian-Jewish Scientific Society, 223-5
Russian Social-Democratic Workers' Party, 312

Sabbath, 169
Safed, 6-7, 16, 17, 93, 97
Salisbury, Lord, 94, 282-3, 324
Salz, Avraham, 339
Samarin, 93, 97, 99, 107, 216, 218 n. 29
Samsonov, Arye, 91 n. 17
Schach, Fabius, 366-8
Schapira, Zevi Hirsch (Hermann), 141-4, 358
Schechter, Solomon, 6 n. 2
Scheid, Elie, 216, 225
Schlesinger, Rabbi ʿAkiva, 8
Schnirer, Moshe, 222 n. 40, 348
secularism, 44, 46, 48, 89, 149, 200, 208, 222, 312-14
Sefarim, Mendele Mokher, 313
Sejera training farm, 183
*Selbstemanzipation*, 223
separatism, 221
Sephardi Jews, 18
Shaḥrai, A. I., 8 n. 5
Shalom Aleichem, 313
Shapira, Z. H., 199 n. 14
Shavei Zion, 225
*Shavuʾot*, 5
'Shefer', *see* Rabbinowitz, S. H.
*shtadlanim, shtadlanut*, 68-9, 90, 103 n. 33, 297-8
Simmel, Sigismund, 170-1
Simonyi, Ivan von, 268
Singer, Simeon, 257, 299-300, 321
Slutsky, Yehuda, 68
Smolenskin, Perez, 38, 46-8, 96, 136, 161, 164, 222, 313
socialism, 99, 161, 225, 240, 247 no. 6, 312-15 (*see also* Lilienblum)
'sociétés palestinophiles', 225
Society for the Colonization of Palestine, 12-15
Society for the Diffusion of Enlightenment, 45 n. 29
Society for the Promotion of Culture among the Jews, 123, 125-6
Society for the Support of Jewish Farmers and Artisans in Syria and Palestine, 175
Society of Jews, 263-5, 278, 300
Sokolov, Naḥum, 161, 274, 318-19, 341, 346, 357, 359
Sonnenscheim, Rosa, 357

Soskin, Selig, 225
South Africa, 32
Spain, Jewish exiles in, 5
Stand, Adolf, 324, 339
Steed, Henry Wickham, 235-6
Stiassny, Wilhelm, 351
Syrkin, Nachman, 225

Talmud, 5, 41, 111-12, 120 n. 12, 207
Tanzimat reforms, 17
Tcherikower, Eliahu, 39 n. 20, 42 n. 23, 52 n. 5, 55 n. 11
Tchlenov, Yehiel, 76 n. 6, 219, 276
'territorialism', 140
Theilhaber, F. A., 28 n. 5
Thon, Yehoshua, 334 n. 44
Tiberias, 7, 16, 97
'Tikvat ʿaniim', 150
*Times, The*, 236
Tiomkin, Zeʾev, 177
Tisza Eszlar affair, 205
Titus, 135
Tolstoy, Count D. A., 56
*Tora*, 47
traditionalism, 172-5
Treaty of Paris (1856), 18
Tschernichowsky, Shaʾul, 190, 313
Tsederbaum, Alexander, 191, 313
Tsetkin, Dr. Y., 146 n. 18
Turkey, 81, 94 (*see also* Ottoman Empire)
Turks, *see* Ottomans

United States, 32 n. 11, 61, 77-8, 84, 88, 90-1, 96, 101, 110, 119, 180-1, 195, 201, 225-6
Ussishkin, Menaḥem, 76 n. 6, 173 n. 60, 185, 276, 279, 339, 342-3, 346, 348, 350, 359
Uvarov, Count S. S., 41-2, 44

Vambéry, Arminius, 289
Veneziani, E. F., 60 n. 19, 107-8
Venturi, Franco, 45 n. 28
Vespasian, 135
'Viadrina', 221
Voronof, Serge, 225
*Voskhod*, 67-8, 141, 274-5

Warsaw Committee, *see* Ḥibbat Zion
Warsaw, pogrom in, 52
wealth as key to leadership, 35-7
Weizmann, Chaim, 202 n. 2, 225
*Welt, Die*, 337, 346, 354
Wessely, N. H., 44